Interviewed by Sergeant Gill Allen, Derek sketched the basics of the murder. "Why is Kevin God?"

"'Cause he's the one that planned and did everything," Derek explained.

"Did you see Kevin with the shotgun?"

"Yeah."

"Did you see him point it at Mr. Schwebes?"

"No, because I was running," Derek answered.

"Was he pointing the shotgun when you knocked?"

"Yeah."

"Was he waiting to ambush Mr. Schwebes?"

"Yes."

"Did he shoot Mr. Schwebes?" Allen asked.

"Yes."

"Anything else you want to tell me?"

"Can I have protection from Kevin?"

"I can't guarantee you anything. Not at this point." Off tape, Allen told Derek, "You're on your own." *Derek will get his protection from Kevin*, Allen thought. *Only the boy doesn't seem to understand in what form.* Derek's protection would be a Lee County Jail cell.

Advance praise for *Someone Has to Die Tonight*

"Meticulously reported and carefully crafted, a major debut."
—Greg Olsen, bestselling author of *Abandoned Prayers*

"Riveting and gut wrenching."
—Lt. Col. Dave Grossman, bestselling author of *On Killing*

"A searing look, by a true journalist, behind a sordid tale of murder and deception—a real page-turner."
—Investigate journalist M. Williams Phelps,
author of *Perfect Poison*, *Lethal Huardian*,
Every Move You Make, and *Sleep in Heavenly Peace*

SOMEONE HAS TO DIE TONIGHT

JIM GREENHILL

PINNACLE BOOKS
Kensington Publishing Corp.
http://www.kensingtonbooks.com

Some names have been changed to protect the privacy of individuals connected to this story.

PINNACLE BOOKS are published by

Kensington Publishing Corp.
850 Third Avenue
New York, NY 10022

All Kensington Titles, Imprints, and Distributed Lines are available at special quantity discounts for bulk purchases for sales promotions, premiums, fund-raising, educational or institutional use. Special book excerpts or customized printings can also be created to fit specific needs. For details, write or phone the office of the Kensington special sales manager: Kensington Publishing Corp., 850 Third Avenue, New York, NY 10022, attn: Special Sales Department, Phone: 1-800-221-2647.

Pinnacle and the P logo Reg. U.S. Pat. & TM Off.

First Printing: March 2006

10 9 8 7 6 5 4 3 2 1

Printed in the United States of America

For Annie and Papa,
who always believed.

Preface

The real names of the six boys charged with Lords of Chaos (LOC) crimes are used, as are those of family, police, attorneys and others directly involved. Chris Black is "Chris" and Chris Burnett is "Burnett." Other names are changed. Ranks are those at the time. Dialogue is reconstructed from firsthand recollections, as are thoughts, which are italicized. The level of detail results from voluminous investigative and court records and interviews. See also the Author's Note at the end of the book.

CONVERGENCE

CHAPTER 1

A Knock on the Door

Fort Myers, Florida; Tuesday, April 30, 1996

Band director Mark Schwebes (*Shh-we-beez*) left the Riverdale High School (RHS) band boosters' ice-cream social at 9:38 P.M. The thirty-two-year-old former marine had a military precision in his punctuality, reliability and dress. He never left school without checking for stragglers.

Mark steered his green Bronco II through campus, eyes sweeping the empty grounds, turning past the gymnasium, looking across the swimming pool and approaching the auditorium, where boys stood near the pay phone. *That phone doesn't work, vandalized.* He turned into the loop in front of the auditorium and stopped. One boy was tall and odd-looking; the other, short, fat and familiar. *I know him.* "What are y'all doing?"

"Makin' a phone call," the chubby kid said, with attitude.

A third boy peeked from behind a column, ten

feet away. Mark focused on the boys at the phone. "You're not calling; this phone doesn't work."

Hands behind backs, the boys fidgeted. "We're just waiting on a ride. We're waiting on a friend."

"Y'all need to wait somewhere else. You don't need to be hanging out here."

"This is where we told him to meet us."

The boy behind the column broke and ran across the road, disappearing into the woods. "Who was that?" Mark said.

"We don't know." The attitude dissolved into nervousness.

Mark got out. Staplers on the pay phone. A fire extinguisher and plastic grocery bag of canned goods at the boys' feet. "Well, gee, where did this come from?"

"We're just now seeing it."

Mark glimpsed the tall boy's hands. *Gloves.* "Hold out your hands. Why do you have gloves on?"

The boy looked terrified. The chubby one answered. "We like to wear gloves. Is it against the law?"

Auditorium windows had been repeatedly broken. *Gloves. Heavy cans.* "Give me that stuff."

The boys peeled off the gloves and put them in the grocery bag. The tall, silent kid loaded Mark's Bronco.

"Y'all need to find somewhere to go. If you can't, I'll take you up to Winn-Dixie."

"We know a guy across the street. We'll go to his house."

"Start walkin'. Use the phone over there." Mark got in the Bronco and pulled away. The tall kid trotted after him.

"What are you gonna do with the stuff? You're not gonna report this, are you?"

Mark stopped. "Don't be surprised if Deputy Montgomery calls you to his office in the morning." He turned to the chubby boy. "Don't I know you? Do you go here?"

"Nope. I don't know you from Adam."

Mark drove off. In the mirror, he saw the tall boy standing dejected, shoulders slumped as the fat boy stamped his feet, waving his arms. It came to him: *Keyboard class. He's in keyboard class.*

Shortly after 11:00 P.M., after a bite at Cracker Barrel with the band boosters' president, Mark pulled up to his duplex on Cypress Drive in Pine Manor, nicknamed Crime Manor. The once-secure middle-class neighborhood had deteriorated since Mark's parents bought the duplex. Retirement dreams faded as drug peddlers bicycled the streets. Deals gone bad erupted in drive-by shootings. Mark was repeatedly burgled. He couldn't wait to move to the new house being built south of town. It'd be comfortable when family visited. Big enough that his nephews could have their own room. Big enough for a piano. Mark hoped typical Southwest Florida afternoon thunderstorms hadn't pockmarked the concrete slab.

Padding around the living room in his socks, he was startled by a knock. *At this hour?* He listened. *Nothing.* Undid locks and dead bolts. "Who is it?" *A boy. Ball cap pulled down. Looking down.* "Yes, may I help you?"

The boy ducked his head farther. "Oh, shit." He turned and ran.

"Who's out there?" Mark said, stepping out. "Hello? . . . Who? . . ." *Another boy. Dark clothes. Tall. By the garbage can. Pointing.* Eye contact. A flash of adrenaline. Mark started to turn away, a reflex, his brain reacting before *Gun!* became a conscious thought.

11:34 p.m.

"Nine-one-one. What is your emergency?"

"I was sitting outside and heard shots. And a car went flying down the road."

"Okay. Where's your address at, ma'am?"

"Seventeen thirty-two Cypress Drive. It soun~~ded~~ like it was right up the street."

"How many shots?"

"Two."

"Can you give me a description of the vehicle?"

"I didn't see it—I ran inside. It scared me."

Emergency medical service (EMS) workers were on scene in two minutes, followed by firefighters and sheriff's homicide investigators. A man lay facedown on the doorstep, shotgun wound to his right buttock. The medics rolled him onto a backboard. Another shotgun wound to the side of his face. *Close range.* His chest rose and fell. The homicide investigators leaned close, hoping for a dying declaration. His chest rose and fell once more; then he was still. The medics declared him dead at 11:38 P.M. and covered him with a sheet.

By midnight, the duplex swarmed with Lee County sheriff's deputies, measuring, sketching, photographing, collecting and cataloging evidence. Busch beer bottles and a Marlboro Red packet in the yard. *Drinking with an acquaintance?* Shot pellets and two spent casings. *Why two? Why the backside? Wrong place for a coup de grâce. "Up yours?" Sexual revenge?* A school pass, cash and paycheck in the guy's pockets. *Teacher.* A green Bronco II. *Engine still warm.* A wallet containing $65 wedged between driver's seat and console. *Mark C. Schwebes, thirty-two . . . Doesn't look like robbery.* On the front passenger seat, a fire extinguisher, staplers and blue plastic Wal-Mart bag containing canned goods and inside-out latex gloves. *Doesn't make sense.*

Neighbors reported two shots . . . three? A guy with a little gun. . . . No, a big one. Short guy. . . . No, tall. Dark clothes. . . . No, a white . . . or blue short-sleeved shirt. Black guy. . . . No, white. Car idling in the driveway. . . . No, on a side street. The guy jumped in the passenger side, and it took off fast. Bad muffler. Gray . . . white . . . blue . . . a small, dark car. An '84 or '85. . . . An '82. Maybe a Ford Tempo. *Worthless. No one saw the same thing. Shit for evidence, too. No good prints, but there are records of fire extinguishers.* This one's serial number was CE587753. It came from Hallway C of Riverdale High School.

Built out in the country east of the Southwest Florida coastal sprawl, RHS cost $4.6 million and opened in 1972, a prisonlike campus at the intersection of State Road 80—also called Palm Beach Boulevard—and Buckingham Road.

The school was a product of forced busing for desegregation. Blacks from inner-city Fort Myers, whites from Lehigh Acres and surrounding rural areas. At first, an unhappy, violent mix, it settled into cliques: jocks, blacks, rednecks, Puerto Ricans, Mexicans, nerds, "trash" who smoked dope and crack and "freaks" who wore all black, had weird hairstyles, got piercings.

Students dubbed it "Reeferjail." Locals could cite a string of murderous felon alumni as easily as successful graduates. A pair kidnapped, carjacked and killed a German tourist; one made a contract hit for a thousand bucks; another one abducted three pubescent boys, groped and shot them.

CHAPTER 2

"Let's Do Something"

Friday, April 12, 1996

Eighteen evenings before Mark Schwebes was gunned down, Kevin Foster, Pete Magnotti and Chris Black met at Treasures Jewelry & Pawn, the Foster family store, before roller-blading through downtown Fort Myers, Florida. Kevin wore his black leather biker jacket, Colt Combat Commander stuffed in the front of his Wranglers, gold-nugget rings, ornate cross dangling from heavy gold neck chain.

Options were limited for seventeen and eighteen-year-old boys in Southwest Florida. No skateboard parks. No designated places for roller-blading or other popular teen activities. The boys couldn't buy alcohol. Teens were the subject of curfew debates. Marina 31, a redneck hangout Kevin favored, wasn't for Pete and Chris: testosterone, Jack Daniel's and cigarettes—they'd be picked on. That's where Kevin came in: "These guys are friends of mine." Nobody laughed when they were with him. Not to their faces.

In 1996, downtown Fort Myers was a hollow place. Dust devils in narrow streets between empty buildings with grimy, cracking facades picked up dry banyan leaves and twirled them in the air before they fell onto cracked sidewalks, collecting in corners nobody swept. It was an outdated Main Street downtown lined by empty stores; piles of trash and antiquated store fittings behind cracked plate glass. Most businesses died with Woolworth's and McCrory's. Survivors served the run-down federal courthouse, bank skyscrapers and the Lee County Justice Center, a looming pastel complex whose few windows were impenetrably tinted. A small downtown of awkward one-way streets running at angles into odd intersections, wide bridges over the Caloosahatchee (*Ka-loose-a-hat-chee*) funneling traffic onto inadequate roads. The place was nearly empty in the ill-lit night, a few patrons hurrying to the couple of bars that clung to downtown revival dreams. The boys roller-bladed on the broad federal courthouse steps, bouncing down shallow limestone stairs.

"Let's do something," Kevin said, an expression Pete and Chris recognized as a Kevin trademark. "Let's do something." Those words again—anything for entertainment, which meant vandalism, arson, criminal mischief.

Kevin yanked a wrench from a wall box, opened a hydrant. Roaming downtown streets, he swung the hydrant wrench as Pete and Chris trailed in his wake. He demolished a parking meter, took the timing mechanism, got no coins. Pete and Chris burned the cross in front of a nearby church.

Walking aimlessly, the boys saw county vehicles on a grass parking lot. Kevin moved his prized jacked-up Toyota pickup—the "Yota"—closer, easier to grab tools to break in, quicker to load with loot. Pete broke the hood ornament off a Dodge Ram. Kevin pried open a window, unlocked the door, took a coffee cup.

The boys broke windows and lights, snatched metal clipboards. Kevin twisted off the mounting brackets and stole two Motorola Spectra two-way radios. He tore down a sign, defecated on it and slapped it on a windshield. Kevin gave his followers sixty seconds to break windows. Not counting replacement costs—the radios were valued at more than $6,000—the boys caused $2,750 damage, leaving neither usable fingerprints nor witnesses.

They drove down Palm Beach Boulevard, passing a dozen yellow New York City taxicabs on a sales lot. Cocking an eyebrow, eyes sparkling mischievously, smile twitching, Kevin dared Pete and Chris to "do it for the rush," laughing as the boys smashed windows.

"Cut that out!" a man yelled. The boys cussed at him and fled in the Yota. At the Publix supermarket loading docks, sprayed with gang graffiti, they found a locked semitrailer. Kevin took a sledgehammer to the hasp. Disappointing sacks of flour and cornmeal.

Pete set an aerosol can of Snap gum remover, stolen from the Hardee's where he worked, on the sacks. Ripped up a paper bag. Lit it with his Zippo. The canister exploded, throwing the top twenty feet, lighting the sacks. Another $400 damage.

On to Buckingham Exceptional Student Center, where Pete's mother worked, near Riverdale High School. Failed to break a window. Opened another fire hydrant and drove to the high school. By now, it was after midnight, and Pete had blown his curfew by more than two hours. He and Chris sat in the Yota while Kevin threw the hydrant wrench through one of the auditorium's tinted windows.

Farther south, they pulled behind a church so close to Pete's house he could hear the bell from his bedroom. "I want the bell," Kevin said, climbing. Too big. He wanted to pull down the cross spotlighted in the churchyard. Embedded in concrete. He broke the spotlights and decided to take the flagpole. Backed the Yota, tied the halyard around his bumper, pulled the pole to the ground. Took the brass knob from the top. Threw it in the bed, a delinquent pack rat.

The Yota growled past shadowy palm trees, scrub pine and mature orange groves, past treeless pastures, the lights of scattered houses and retention ponds glimmering under the bright night sky, past the Hut Restaurant. Kevin stopped, improvising. The restaurant had a tropical Polynesian theme. Outdoors, a pit barbecue and benches. A chickee hut sheltering a birdcage occupied by two blue and gold macaws, Malicoo and Eurecka, a restaurant attraction for thirteen years. The chickees—open-sided structures with wood poles supporting a roof thatched with palm fronds—were a South Florida feature. A few Native Americans still built them, on the Seminole or Miccosukee reservations out in the Everglades, for places such as the Hut or for private homeowners desiring a backyard tropical conversation piece.

The boys scouted for something to steal or vandalize. Kevin thought he heard a monkey screeching in the chickee hut. *Dried palm fronds.* Kevin sprayed Snap on the fronds and lit them. He jumped in the Yota. "I think I lit a cage full of monkeys on fire." The animals—whatever they were—screamed.

The macaws couldn't escape the smoke, heat or pieces of burning palm that rained down. Replacing them would cost $3,000, fixing their cage another $1,000—but to restaurant regulars, the birds were priceless.

The boys took a back way, tires squealing, truck backfiring, loud enough in the rural peace to wake a neighbor boy, but not enough to prompt action. It wasn't unusual out there, squealing tires, gunshots, bottles thrown from passing trucks, kids flocking to the undeveloped fringes of Lehigh Acres, Timber Trails and the county's sprawling mosquito-control headquarters.

They drove back around to see if the fire department had arrived, testing their reaction time. The station was just down the road. It took fifteen minutes.

The boys spotted a construction site off Buckingham Road. Trusses and lumber were piled around a half-built garage. Kevin pushed over a Porta Potti with his truck. "Let's set this place on fire."

Like a maverick Boy Scout, Pete tried to ignite lumber using papers from the stolen clipboards, brush and dried grass. Wouldn't catch. Started some graffiti: "Free the Unabom—"

"Let's get some gas," Kevin said.

At a Circle K near his house, Kevin gassed the Yota. Put $5 worth in a milk jug, Pepsi bottle and gas can. Drove back to the construction site. Poured gas over the lumber.

"Make some torches," Kevin said, breaking a yardstick from the Yota. Pete and Chris tied old shirts around pieces of yardstick, dipped them in the pooling gas, lit and threw them. The lumber was quickly inflamed. At an abandoned grain silo, one of Kevin's favorite hangouts, Pete and Chris stayed in the truck; Kevin climbed, watching the fire.

Next morning, stacks of plywood and two-by-fours still burned. Deputies noticed four-by-four tire marks, though those could be a laborer's as easily as the perpetrators'. The fire destroyed $5,800 in building materials.

The boys stopped at Gunnery Road Baptist Church, parking out of sight behind a bus. Kevin cut down ornamental palm trees with a machete. He stole tools from a construction trailer. Pete tried to ignite the trailer's pink insulation with his Zippo. Flames flickered, then died.

The boys went back to the short white-painted school bus, GUNNERY ROAD BAPTIST CHURCH lettered on the sides. Kevin broke windows with his sledgehammer. Found a Bible inside, ripped it in half and threw pages around. "It's for kindling."

Pete put his Zippo to rotting cloth hanging from the

driver's seat. Kevin and Chris wiped the door, seats and steering wheel. *Ain't gonna be no prints.* The smoldering fire caused $1,000 in damage. The boys went to the Fosters' home on Lorraine Drive, where they rehashed the night. "Don't tell nobody," Kevin said. "We should do it again. It might be on the news; tell me if you catch anything."

They got ready for bed.

"We can be the LOC," Kevin said.

"What's the LOC?" Pete said.

"Lords of Chaos."

Only Kevin knew the name's origin: Lords of Chaos was a computer game, fantasy book, group of computer hackers and a twist on a phrase in a Dean Koontz novel. Kevin had toyed with other names, scrawling ideas in a notebook, trying to force acronyms. ARMY could be American Rebels Mercenaries Youths. SWIPER could incorporate his Texas Panhandle/Arizona childhood—South Western Insane Psycho Evil Rebels. Or maybe it should be SNIPER—except drunk as he was, he couldn't summon words to go with that. "Shooting myself," he scrawled, then drew his favorite symbol, (Ø). But now—now they had a name, and with it their loose association solidified.

The whole thing's gonna be a joke, Pete thought.

They slept in Kevin's room.

Saturday morning, April 13, 1996

At the trailer behind Publix, a sheriff's deputy lifted prints, took the lock and aerosol can, snapped pictures. An off-duty agent was called out. A lieutenant. A state fire marshal who'd investigated a burned church bus responded, too. A lot of officers for a small incident, but deputies surmised that—with the possible exception of the vandalized taxicabs—the string of overnight crimes might be related, and they ratcheted up the investigative pressure.

To Kevin, the night was fun yet frustrating. The boys failed to steal anything of great value or usefulness. Kevin got no cash from the parking meter; they'd been interrupted vandalizing the taxis; the semi-trailer yielded nothing valuable and wouldn't burn; Kevin couldn't steal the church bell, then failed to destroy the cross; Pete hadn't completed his construction site graffiti; neither the church trailer nor the bus burned worth a damn. Events had the odor of bad sex, of unsatisfying nervous teen groping. What had been fun at the time, in retrospect, was embarrassing. Seeking media coverage, the Lords of Chaos needed to up the ante. The paradox was Kevin couldn't be a successful criminal terrorist and gain recognition. It was fun to be an anarchist, a bummer to be anonymous. This conflict would undo the LOC.

CHAPTER 3

Scavenger Hunt

Tuesday, October 31, 1995

For Kevin Don Foster, known to classmates as "Psycho," recruitment of the boys who became the Lords of Chaos began five months earlier, on Halloween.

A fluorescent Bates Motel sign hung in Kevin's room on Lorraine Drive, where he typed a list: salt shaker, tray, fire extinguisher, mailbox (with numeral 6), floor mat, squeegee, pool accessory, hotel signs (tenth floor or higher), license plate, pumpkin, road sign, flag. Objective: get the most in two hours. The boys split into pairs.

Kevin's teammate, RHS senior Pete Magnotti, was thrilled to be with him after an involuntary eighteen-month separation. *Seems years.* Kevin was eighteen now, Pete a year younger and small at five feet nine inches, 110 pounds, though he'd filled out since their first acquaintance in middle school, when his shoulder blades poked against his shirt like budding wings. His straight black hair was long, though many RHS boys favored close-cropped. He had brown eyes and his Filipino mother's cappuccino skin. Sometimes, an awkward adolescent mustache. Parental restrictions couldn't break Pete's connection with Kevin. No matter Pete's father banned contact and Pete hadn't dropped by Lorraine Drive until his first car enabled sneak visits—Kevin was his best friend. Pete was enchanted with his real-life comic-book action-figure antihero, boasting about him during the separation to classmates Chris Black and Derek Shields. "Kevin torched a portable trailer, and the school never knew who did it." Pete couldn't be sure which boasts were true. *Did Kevin's ancestors own slaves? Is he part Comanche, part Cree? Did he kill a Texas uncle?* Kevin was the big brother he never had. "Kevin this . . ." and "Kevin that. . . ." "The little soldier." *My little soldier.* Parents, school, community and work bored Pete; Kevin enthralled him. Characters in Pete's sketches bore an uncanny resemblance. The name sneaked into school compositions. When he experimented with signatures, he tried variations of his own name and Kevin's—absorbed like a girl with a crush: Kevin Foster . . . Kevin Foster . . . Kevin Foster. He wanted to *be* Kevin. Wanted his closest friends to meet him, particularly Chris, whom he brought tonight.

Kevin. Spoiled redneck. Mischievous white boy. Lopsided face, out-of-kilter eyes, crooked grin, habitually cocked eyebrow. Photos didn't do him justice, couldn't capture a certain charisma, an impish charm. His restless motion erased his flaws. He'd grown to six feet three inches, 150 pounds, hazel eyes, close-cropped blond hair, freckled Irish skin that burned before tanning in the Florida sun. His mental self-image was more muscular than reality, but he fought the best of them. Smoked Marlboro Reds. Drank JD—Jack Daniel's. Eagerly drove the jacked-up Yota off-road. Kevin kept going when others quit, never balked at a dare, flouted limits. Had an arsenal of guns, a series of fathers and a mother who didn't enforce boundaries. Kevin's was the house where boys hung out; Ruby Foster was the mom who seemed like a friend. Kevin had filled out; Pete retained a child's physique. Kevin bragged about fucking; dating mystified Pete. Kevin was a young man; Pete was a boy-teen. Kevin was a carpenter and Pete a high schooler, but they had enough in common to bridge gaps: pyromania, fascination with violence and death, sick humor, indifference to animal suffering, iconoclasm. Even lazier than Pete, Kevin had the same sharp mind.

Pete drove Kevin into the city along Palm Beach Boulevard, a seven-lane swath of asphalt, an ill-lit chasm through a neighborhood, a speedway where a child leaving Dairy Queen was lost in shadows, unseen by drivers until too late.

The boys stole a fire extinguisher from a day laborers' motel where patrons paid by the hour. From one of the boulevard's car lots cluttered with vehicles rejected by big dealers (BUY HERE! PAY HERE! NO CREDIT? NO PROBLEM!), they stole a flag. Heading downtown, they passed loiterers, side-street hookers, crack addicts and pushers. . . . A glimpse of a hard, scarred face at a barred window before the curtain falls back. . . . Ratty fifthhand furniture for sale on the sidewalk. . . . Pawnshops. . . . Stanley's Army/Navy Store, which sold gloves, ski masks and smoke grenades. . . . Liquor stores. . . . Third-tier, off-brand, poorly stocked, grimy groceries.

Redneck Kevin and Amerasian Pete passed billboards peddling cheap, watery beer in Spanish, passed ethnic stores and eateries. They drove the seedy boulevard where even McDonald's and national auto-parts and grocery chains were small and old. They headed downtown, checking off Kevin's list.

* * *

Pete. Only child of Joseph and Rebecca Magnotti, born in Sylmar, California, on August 8, 1978. A World War II veteran of Okinawa, Joe earned a Purple Heart after a kamikaze attack. He met his Filipino third wife through correspondence. Joe retired when Pete was two, moved to Southwest Florida, picked Buckingham because it was a small community. *If Pete goes to the high school up the road, everything'll be fine.*

They lived near the Fosters on the dead end of Orange River Boulevard, just off Buckingham Road, behind a country store. Like most Southwest Florida homes, the Magnottis' was single-story. Mustard yellow paint with brown trim and decorative face-rock under a brown shingle roof. Grass more pasture than lawn. Dirt road. Basketball hoop beside concrete driveway. Joe ran a small-engine repair shop, Magnotti Motors, out of a detached garage. Rebecca was a teacher's aide at Buckingham Exceptional Student Center, just up the road near RHS.

In kindergarten, Pete's 158 genius IQ got him labeled gifted. But exceptional intelligence didn't guarantee exceptional performance. Pete's grades were all over the map. Bored even in the gifted program, he criticized peers and disrespected authority.

In Pete, Kevin saw an intellect to admire, a misfit to protect. They competed on the seventh-grade math team, part of a misfit corps—intense, genius Pete, with his girlish figure, and Kevin, nerdy in braces and glasses. At an Orlando meet, a Massachusetts Institute of Technology representative told the boys they'd win scholarships if they kept studying.

Pete was teased hard. Peers saw slight stature, femininity, darker skin and physical and emotional immaturity. Sang in choir, the lone male clarinet player at Lee Middle, an artist. He struggled to fit rural redneck culture. If Kevin hadn't repeated a grade, they might've passed in school corridors barely recognizing each other before Kevin dropped out. As it was, Kevin felt sorry for Pete. He took him under his wing, and the two hung out on weekends, Kevin teaching Pete to fight. Pete aspired to be "Billy Badass," the boy others feared. Kevin told him to act crazy to get classmates to leave him alone.

When he was thirteen, Pete shoplifted at a mall. Watched Kevin shoot out stoplights. They stole stop signs. Experimented with bombs Kevin made from black powder. Made fireworks and set them off in Kevin's yard or threw them from the car. Made silencers. Vandalized, stole, spray-painted, threw bottles, shoplifted sodas.

As Pete aged, his personality darkened. He had nothing good to say about his parents, little good to say about others. By his last year at Lee Middle, he was turning in twisted vocabulary assignments. A headless torso illustrated "partial."

During high school, Pete was computer-oriented, technologically sophisticated, artistic, a comedian. Yet, despite an affinity for "freaks" and an interest in one of their girls, he fit no clique. He craved acceptance, but was no athlete. His academic performance was average. Cut off, he withdrew. He fell into a pattern: came home, went to his room (where he listened to music, drew and used his computer), emerging only for dinner. His parents believed they knew him and his world, but there was a gulf between perception and reality.

"This is your world in which we grow, and we grow to hate you," Pete wrote over a carefully executed Marilyn Manson logo above a drawing of a gun-wielding man-boy saying, "Next Motherfucker's gonna get my metal!!"

A drooling, crazed, manic-smiling man, tongue hanging out between gleaming white teeth and eyes out of kilter, climbed cracked stairs, smoking handgun in each hand, another weapon stuffed in his pants, thinking, *KILL, KILL, KILL, KILL, KILL, KILL, KILL,*

KILL, KILL, KILL. A blood-spattered corpse lay on the bottom stair.

Pete liked comics so much he read magazines about comics. In a comic panel story he drew, a handgun-wielding man killed scientists raising a boy in a laboratory:

"We've gone too fucking far!" he says. "Noooo!" a woman screams. "Can't you see this is the only way?!" he says. "The boy . . . where the fuck's the boy?!" He hunts through the laboratory. Holds a gun to a man clutching a young child. "You're not taking him anywhere . . . hand it over, Dr. Travers. . . . Can't you see I'm doing this for the good of humanity? . . . To save the world, we all must die." The boy sits in a basket wired to electronics, hands to head, in pain. MEMORY WIPE INITIATED, a computer screen says. "Thank God it's over," the man says, head in hands, still holding a handgun. "I can't look as I kill the child. The mindwipe isn't 100% reliable . . . this is." He looks away as he shoots the boy. Soon he's standing silhouetted in the burning lab. "Next comes the lab and finally me," blowing his brains out with the handgun. Men in black descend on the wrecked lab. "Prep the baby for surgery and cremate the others," one says. "Yes sir," another replies, "we'll be back in operation by morning." The panels end with a label: "End of Prologue 1977"—the year before Pete was born.

"Contains material that may be offensive to parents, women, the elderly, children," Pete wrote on the cover of a journal—a school project, ten-line entries on assigned topics, graded by a teacher. "My best qualities are I can always think of something so disgustingly repulsive it'll make my best friend Kevin laugh into hysterics. I'm a sociopath-paranoid-pyromaniac. Kevin's my bad influence and the person who taught me all kinds of important things like how to load a Beretta and make bombs. I'm teaching others that stuff too."

Pete wrote of his love of comic books, Stephen King, music and "torturing small animals, cars, guns, bombs, fire. Something I'd like to do is KILL everybody on this stinking planet! End of story." He imagined shooting students from a roof on graduation, then diving to his death.

"If there's a problem, please see me," a teacher wrote. Pete scrawled through the teacher's comments and wrote "BITCH." He said happiness would be shooting someone, killing police, suicide and other violence, and the teacher wrote "1 day late" and put a check mark through the entry. He advocated more juvenile crime, less punishment, fewer rules and more anarchy and the teacher wrote, "You still have such a positive attitude."

"A lesson about life that I've learned," Pete concluded, "was that if you're a person of small stature, like me, you have to talk big, think big and nobody will say nothing (it also helps to have big friends), (big friends that own bigger guns) (big friends that own big guns that have a history of mental illness)."

After three years in math together, Kevin and Pete were separated. They still hung out occasionally, but Kevin's mom pulled him from school after a self-inflicted shooting, Pete's father declared Kevin a bad influence and banned contact, and the two drifted apart.

Pete's mother was kind to his friends, relaxed, let him go out. Joe was silent. Pete openly disrespected them, cursing to their faces. Yet they gave their only child whatever he wanted: music CDs, a guitar, computer games, Nintendo and Sega. Other boys' *parents* didn't have CDs yet; Pete had stacks. His dad tried to interest him in engines. Pete wasn't enthused.

Just before the scavenger hunt, Pete wheedled a car from his parents. Compared to many in the RHS lot, the 1991 Nissan Stanza was new, only seventy-four thousand miles. Pete was proud of the burgundy four-door with its tinted windows. He worked at Hardee's to come up with the $165 payments, but found little satisfaction in the effort. At school, he wrote about a time traveler with a computer chip in his brain on a killing spree ending at Hardee's, shooting the cashier. The mention of Hardee's ticked him off; he hated the place.

Pete drifted further from the mainstream. Other students admired his artwork (his senior class would vote him "most artistic"), but his father still thought of him as a baby. The girls who frequently phoned found "Petey" sweet, unthreatening and willing to give them rides, but they didn't consider him an eligible date.

Movie scenes, computer game scenarios, comic-book characters and novel dialogue fed a fertile fantasy world built on Pete's extraordinary intelligence, creative imagination and rejection. His drawings crossed from paper to computer-generated graphic art. In daily independent study, he created a college portfolio virtually unsupervised, a recognition of his talent. At grading time, art teachers were impressed. Some of Pete's macabre drawings escaped attention; teachers weren't therapists and chose not to judge.

Pete contemplated becoming a professional computer animator. In his senior yearbook ("It's Amazing How Things Change"), his goals included "to drive monster trucks . . . to animate . . . to live in a cabin in the woods . . . to build a wall." Genius mathematician Ted Kaczynski lived in a cabin in the woods. The Unabomber's essay "Industrial Society and Its Future" was published in Pete's final semester. Pete, likewise, felt alienated, outcast and critical of the social, economic and political order.

* * *

The scavenger hunt was Chris Black's first get-together with this Kevin he'd heard Pete talk about. Chris and Pete met as sophomores. Both gifted artists, Pete was more likely to create an original comic, Chris to color in sketches or copy characters. They shared an interest in Japanese anime, dreamed up bizarre Smurf characters that Pete drew, loved computer games and Stephen King, raved about Quentin Tarantino's *Pulp Fiction*. They started hanging out after school the summer of 1995, sometimes vandalizing or stealing signs.

At RHS, peers thought Chris childish—gentle, docile, passed out at the sight of his own blood. His front teeth were crooked and overcrowded. At 5 feet five inches, he weighed 210 pounds. "Pillsbury Doughboy," classmates mocked. "Cabbage Patch Kid." He tried different tactics to cope with being an outcast. Ingratiated himself. Volunteered. Joined. A community service organization. A blood bank, in spite of his phobia. Became a guidance counselor's aide. Showed new students around. Perhaps *they'd* be his friends.

Christopher Paul Black was born to high-school sweethearts David and Betty Black on April 17, 1978. Betty was twenty, David twenty-one. At Alva Elementary, Chris's 137 IQ indicated superior to outstandingly superior intellectual potential. A school psychologist impressed with the six-year-old put him in a gifted program. "Advanced verbal ability, creative, good sense of humor, retains information from stories read, outgoing and friendly, self-confident." The psychologist found him handsome, likable, mature and an enthusiastic learner.

Chris was no fan of Florida. In eighth grade and freshman year, the Blacks lived in Georgia, where there were cows and cotton and they had a house on three acres. Chris liked the community middle school of four hundred students, the majority black. At football games, he knew everyone—team, band, cheerleaders. He enjoyed biology and won awards in math. Art wasn't great, maybe because his talent exceeded the average. The place lacked the cliques he'd encounter at RHS.

In spite of lackluster study habits and inconsistent performance, Chris had some high-school classes for gifted learners. Sometimes he drew detention or internal suspension. "The same thing every day: he cannot keep his mouth shut. Moved him all over the room," one teacher wrote.

Although Chris had bad experiences at RHS, among the dross were smart kids he respected. As a senior, he liked knowing two dozen people since kindergarten, even if he wasn't always accepted and in spite of two years out of state. He enjoyed the gifted program's self-directed studies.

Some of his awkwardness came from innocence: He didn't smoke or use drugs. He tried alcohol, but like his parents, he didn't drink. He was a virgin. All these boys around him did all these adult things, and he was excluded. A bright, energetic boy possessing a striking, witty, hair-trigger—often childishly scatological—sense of humor that fired frequently, he took a childlike pleasure in life, retained a child's view of himself at the center of the universe, threw tantrums and maintained a fertile fantasy world.

When he was twelve, he stole a candy bar from Circle K, his first crime; though, like Pete, he avoided juvenile arrests. His worst transgression at home was procrastinating taking out the trash. Sometimes he baby-sat his little sister while his parents watched stock-car races in neighboring Charlotte County.

Judy Putnam, co-owner of the Hardee's franchise, was on maternity leave when Chris was hired in early 1995. The first time Putnam worked with him, she coached him through a large, complicated order. Chris was irritated: she thought he didn't know what he was doing. He mouthed off in front of the customer. His first evaluation included that incident, and Putnam noted he lacked initiative. Sometimes she counseled him: he wasn't cutting it. But she gave Chris a second chance, and he turned himself around. Putnam was impressed. She also felt sorry for him: he had a crush on a coworker who led him on, really liked that girl.

Chris drove his uniquely painted car to work. Coworkers laughed. "Leave it to Chris." His rusting primer-gray car, the "Love Machine," a 1978 Toyota Celica ("It's as old as me"), was a mobile artwork painted '60s style with graffiti, peace signs and, over the driver door, THE BOOTY MAN. At school, people spray-painted their names on it. Chris didn't seem to mind, even initiated it.

Chris clowned around at Hardee's, trying to fit in, and it worked. When he gave notice toward the end of summer, Putnam was sorry. He was honest, trained new recruits and helped her find the best high-school employee she'd hired: Pete Magnotti.

Senior year, Chris didn't fit in at school or at home. His parents tried as he grew up—coached his Little League, led his Webelos and Boy Scouts, handmade his Halloween costumes. But Chris wasn't like the country-boy father who loved stock-car racing, hunting and fishing. He shot his dad's twenty-gauge once; he didn't like the kick. Chris's unemployed father had been disabled at a furniture-moving company; his mother was a homemaker.

In the sanctuary of his room, Chris retreated into his fantasy world. Spent so much time there, the little sister who idolized him offered to clean, anything to get close. His favorite TV shows were *The Simpsons* and *Mega Man*. Comics were a passion. Masamune Shirow's *Ghost in the Shell* was challenging, and Chris read it repeatedly. Yukito Kishiro's two-thousand-page series *Battle Angel* was his favorite. Much taken with anime, he rented Masamune Shirow's *Appleseed* series.

Chris loved Dungeons & Dragons. He worked on toy models, building *Star Trek* spaceships, Transformers, sports cars and painstakingly painting a foot-tall Predator. He spent hours playing video games and could take apart a computer and fix it. He dreamed of college and a career creating bionic appendages, but neither filed college applications nor sought potential employers.

Though he saw little of him on the scavenger hunt, Chris immediately liked Kevin. A lot. *What's not to like?* he thought. *Kevin's charismatic. Older. This dude actually owns guns. He likes mayhem. He's an adult by physical age, but with the mind of a sixteen-year-old fascist. He buys alcohol and cigarettes. Kevin's an adrenaline junkie and, man, that's fun to be around.*

One kid was absent from the scavenger hunt. Derek Shields completed a trio at RHS: Pete, Chris, who thought of Pete as his brother, and Derek, who met Chris in elementary school. Larger and stronger, Derek stuck up for both. The three hung together, a misfit clique. Other students passed them in corridors without a word and flipped past their yearbook pictures without pause, yet they made an intimidating brain trust. Algebra students couldn't keep up. Derek was in Mu Alpha Theta, the national math club for honor students.

Derek and Kevin had crossed paths in class. Derek didn't impress Kevin, but in an American government class, Kevin struck Derek as the only competitive student. Somehow in contests between rows, Derek and Kevin always ended up together. Among the brightest, they got the best grades and highest final-exam scores. After that semester, the two lost contact—and Kevin shot himself and dropped out.

After two hours, Kevin and Pete's scavenger hunt had gone well. Downtown, they stole a pumpkin.

Raced above the tenth floor of the Sheraton Harbor Place—another Fort Myers failure, which was dirty and dusty, had peeling paint, torn and fading wallpaper, fingerprint-smudged glass and low occupancy rates—and stole signs. Snatched a salt shaker at Denny's near the city's abandoned historic Coca-Cola bottling plant. Unscrewed a license plate at the mall named for winter resident Thomas Edison. Threw these in the trunk of Pete's car with the Taco Bell tray, pool hose, gas station squeegee, mailbox from the gated community near Kevin's. Many of their scavenger souvenirs stayed there, theft and daring more the point than need or usefulness.

KIDS

CHAPTER 4

Mom

Christmas, 1991

Ruby Foster's camera traversed the display, microphone catching chirping crickets and frogs. Christmas Eve: low sixty-two, high seventy-eight, no rain, not half an inch this month, never snow, tomorrow identical. Some overcompensated, festooning homes and yards with lights and ornaments—150,000 bulbs on some homes—creating a Southwest Florida Whoville, imposing Christmas on the tropics. Debbie Dailey's bungalow was the most spectacular on Lorraine Drive, and Ruby lingered: Lights outlined the metal-framed jalousies, low-pitched roof and trio of Spanish arches in the front wall of the open-air entry courtyard. Dozens of lawn ornaments cast a multicolored glow. A seventeen-tree Christmas forest. A larger-than-life Santa Claus who'd wave and nod, except Dailey ran out of electric outlets. Ruby had a thing about Christmas. Never told her children there's no Santy Claus.

Into adulthood, they left him a gift. Dailey's display delighted her.

Ruby was an outsider in a region of outsiders. Born Ruby Catherine Albritton in Amarillo, Texas, on February 2, 1950, she was a twin in a family with two sets born nine months apart. The eight Albritton children had a strict Catholic upbringing. Most married and stayed around Amarillo. Not Ruby: Ruby Albritton . . . Ruby Newberry . . . Ruby Bates . . . Ruby Burns . . . Ruby Foster.

At 18, she wed Ron Newberry, conceived one daughter, Kelly, and divorced after eight years. Her father disowned her. "My father burned my house," she said. "Turned my family against me." For spite, she married Joe Bates, Kevin's father. Joe abandoned his tiny son and wife (she said), served federal prison time (she said), drugs (she said), snitched on the Mafia (she said). Brian Burns was next—quiet, steady . . . and seething. After Brian, divorced but not discarded, came John Foster, trucker with Vietnam stories Ruby wasn't sure she wanted the children to hear, claims of killing women and children with knives, slicing throats as an "adviser" before most Americans knew of Vietnam. "When I was your age, I was in the jungle killing people with a knife." Ruby clung to Brian and John. Years later, she maintained two driver's licenses, Ruby Burns and Ruby Foster. Kevin took his adoptive father's name.

Christmas morning, 1991, Ruby marshaled her men into the front room of her Lorraine Drive home, dominated by a decorated tree. Paul Gilbert, a disabled man in her guardianship, sat in his wheelchair. John Foster, husband number four, sat on one end of the sectional, clutching ashtray and coffee mug; Brian Burns, number three, in the corner, was reading the newspaper, shielding his face from her camera; Kevin on the other end, opposite the stepfathers; Kelly sitting apart on the other side of the tree. Someone turned music on loud, Michael Jackson's dance/rap out of sync with the tree's blinking lights.

Ruby lingered on her fourteen-year-old boy with his gold-framed glasses, mane of curly, dirty-blond hair swept behind his ears, heavy gold cross on a gold chain on his bare chest, Japanese martial-arts tunic with a red kanji emblazoned on the back.

Kevin unwrapped clothes, scrutinizing brands, setting them aside, tossing paper and boxes, bypassing some unopened. On to the next, bobbing his head to the music. He picked up a long, narrow box. Mom focused on him. Her son cut into the box with a folding knife. Pulled out one . . . two . . . three balls of paper, casting each aside to the beat of the music, smiling as his hand kept finding paper. A voice caught between childhood and adolescence, cracking, deepening: "You gave me a box full of wrapping"—his hand hit metal—"Ah." He broke into a gleeful rap in a white country boy's breaking voice: "Yeah, uh-huh, you saw my shotgun, uh-huh." Stabbed the corrugated cardboard with the knife, pulling off the box. Cradled the marine-edition twelve-gauge pump-action Mossberg 500A, with its stainless-steel barrel and synthetic black stock, between his legs, while stepfather John cautioned, "Since we'd like to have electricity the rest of the day, do not pick an insane target." Kevin grinned, indulging dad.

It wasn't uncommon for mom to give Kevin a Christmas gun. He had his eyes on this one more than a year. A man hawked it at the Fosters' pawnshop opposite Riverdale High, redeemed it, hawked it, redeemed it. If he couldn't get it out of hock, Kevin *wanted* that gun. A month after she gave her delighted son the Mossberg, mom voided the entry in Riverdale Gold, Gun & Pawn Shop's computer, typing "home" and her employee code, "RC," for Ruby Catherine. Out of inventory, the gun was Kevin's.

Ruby filmed as if she could preserve life, clinging like she clung to late adolescence—hair, clothes, posture frozen at her pinnacle, when she was most attractive, most desirable, still young. She photographed Kevin in intensive care at four days old. Kevin with Santa Claus. Kevin, cheeks puffed out, blowing out candles at a McDonald's birthday party. Kevin's first kiss, from a second cousin. Kevin in a tuxedo at a Texas cousin's wedding. Kevin and Kelly in cowboy costumes. Kelly taping the mouth of a baby alligator Kevin had caught with a hot dog. Kevin with twenty-seven girls—Kelly's Girl Scout troop—at a winery. Beside a vintage Chevy pickup in snow near Colorado Springs, Kevin's head just up to the hood. On the trampoline, with Kelly and Charlie, the family dog, a cocker spaniel named for Charles Manson. A safari-park lion at the car window. Space shuttle launch. Copper mine. Kevin at the Mexico border, camping in mountains, hiking in Palo Duro Canyon, singing chorus at a Texas museum, on a four-wheeler in Louisiana, learning to roller-skate in Santa Fe, visiting a Montana prison. Old Faithful. The St. Louis Arch. Alligator wrestling at Miccosukee Indian Village. Child Kevin naked in the shower, his first haircut, wearing Mickey Mouse ears, holding a pumpkin, in combat gear, doing homework with mom. An Easter-egg hunt. Amarillo parade. Slumber party. Kevin shooting, deep-sea fishing, riding, swimming at night. Sea World, Universal Studios, MGM, Epcot, Disney World. Weddings, parties, golfing, bowling, fishing, boating. Mesa Verde, Mount Rushmore, Versailles. "Mom, if I have to die, I've lived more of a life than people ten times my age, because you've showed the world to me."

A woman who clung to things, children and husbands, Ruby was drawn to flea markets, gimcracks, collectibles. Hoarding shiny things—jewelry, diamonds, gold—she kept every souvenir: a clipping when Kevin was elementary-school citizen of the week. Science fair ribbons. A pair of his shiny bikini underwear. "It's funny the things you keep," she said. And his trinkets—watch chain with bulls' heads, gold bullet earring, Mickey Mouse watch, gold nugget rings, monogrammed Zippo lighter with his initials, Pennsylvania KKK sword (hooded rider holding a cross, on a rearing horse), World War I German officer's sword (eagle atop an ivory hilt), World War II Japanese samurai sword.

Kelly Denise Newberry, Kevin's sister, was born March 16, 1973. Four years later came Kevin Don Bates. "My children were toxic to me," Ruby said. "I broke out. I couldn't deliver." Both were cesareans, Kevin's birth more traumatic than Kelly's. He was six weeks premature, skin yellow, lungs weak. Abandoned by his father (Ruby said) after one month. She demanded custody and support, and Joe signed away his rights. Later, on the rare occasions he mentioned Joe, Kevin told friends his real dad was mean, done them wrong, was never there for him.

Ruby's children were the center of her world, and she was determined their lives would outshine her own. Her parents were rigid, restrictive and critical. Her children would be disciplined but have approval and understanding. Better to be their friend. Ruby was close to both, but especially to Kevin, the beautiful, brilliant, exciting son who eclipsed her unsatisfactory husbands. Kevin had something—something shared with his mom—a heart, a light, an inner glow like no one else. "Have you noticed how Jesus Christ was a carpenter and my son's also a carpenter?" Ruby would later say. He was a leader, other boys drawn to his intensity. It was better for them to be with Kevin and be part of Ruby's extended family, and she informally adopted them, proud Kevin's friends gathered at her home—just like in the Kool-Aid ads. "The kids in the neighborhood would join at the house where the Kool-Aid was. My house is the Kool-Aid house. My house has always been the safe house for all the kids—Kevin's kids."

Lorraine Drive was a cool place to hang out or crash. Teens could use the phone and help themselves to food. Boys sat in cars outside and got high. Kevin wasn't even always there. "Have fun—I'm going out." And the Fosters respected teen privacy. A punching bag hung from a lone tree. A swinging rope extended from a pole above the swimming pool. There was a ramp from roof to pool that Kevin flew down on his bike. All those guns. Four-wheelers to explore trails through overgrown pasture behind the house. A small lake. A boat. A footbridge. Ditches to hide in, shooting rockets at each other in fireworks wars. Movies. Video games. Parties. Evening bonfires on the adjacent empty lot.

Ruby seemed wonderful to some teens. Bought gifts, made one a nugget ring, chaperoned trips to Epcot and Disney World. If a teen had trouble with parents, problems with girlfriends, needed advice or a condom, he knew where to go. "Everybody calls me 'Mom,'" she said.

CHAPTER 5

Seeds

After Kevin's birth on June 16, 1977, in Amarillo, Texas, Mom moved her brood to Arizona, Montana and then back to Amarillo, where Ruby replaced Brian Burns with husband number four, John Foster, who left another son and daughter in St. Louis. Moving to Cuba, Missouri, in the early 1980s, Kevin and Kelly met their stepsiblings, but never lived with them.

In the mid 1980s, the family moved to Fort Myers, Florida, living in Riverdale Estates, where Kevin met Drew Phillips, who'd be his best friend through his teens, the one Kevin bragged about to relatives, the one the Fosters took on a Texas road trip, a friendship based on being neighbors—same bus, same school— until they were like brothers.

The Fosters bought the Riverdale Estates house across from Riverdale High when Kevin was eight. The quiet subdivision of mature trees and well-kept yards was the nicest place they'd live. Within seven months, they defaulted on the mortgage and the bank foreclosed. The Fosters retreated to a mobile home in Canyon, Texas.

Kevin was all South and West, a childhood trek through five states and four fathers. The South of hardscrabble, pickups, Confederate flags, rebellion. The West of the outdoors, guns, individuality, authority questioned. Kevin was never a part *of*, he was apart *from*, an outsider from birth, toxic to Mom, abandoned by his dad, living in his fifth state with his third father by first grade. And now, back here in Texas, after the bank seized the Florida house, living in a trailer, with two fathers, neither his own.

The Fosters lived across a field from Brian Burns, who mowed their yard, raked leaves, watched the children. Kevin was back and forth between two trailers, two fathers, John and Brian. From John, Kevin developed an enthusiasm for guns, politics, and military history. From Brian, mechanics, hiking and the outdoors.

When John wasn't on the road, he took Kevin hunting. Doted on his son. Kelly was a girl, *she* had to be perfect. If Kevin didn't do as well in school, okay. When Kevin was twelve, John adopted him.

In Canyon, Ruby's children got to know their cousins. Relatives thought Kevin a real nice kid, who played real good with their own, sharing his Nintendo, still a novelty. Kevin and Kelly got to go out, but when Ruby said, "Be home," they were home. Mom didn't have to spank them much. Raised her voice, sent Kevin to his room, but they already had the close relationship they'd maintain for life.

Kevin and Kelly weren't as close as they once were, four years a gulf to children. At times, Kevin felt an only child. He bonded with a female cousin closer in age. Strong-willed and competitive, they played and explored. She stayed over, sometimes at John's trailer, sometimes Brian's. Kevin was still a boy who sailed boats in the bathtub in Mom's bedroom, but he was getting picky about clothes, and he was adventurous. He had

nosebleeds, anemia, allergy attacks and sensitive skin
that broke out under his watch, but he liked to be out
exploring, acquiring new wounds. He scarred his chin
on a countertop, his left eyebrow on a door, the back
of his head on a metal boot scraper, his face with a
hook that barely missed an eye and his foot on glass
shards.

The gem lay twelve miles east of Canyon. Twelve
miles of flat ranchland punctuated by windmills—and
then the canyon: Palo Duro Canyon State Park. There
were horseback rides and an RV park, but it wasn't
spoiled by tourist throngs. Here, Kevin found a plunging relief to the flat Texas Panhandle, an oasis in the
plains. Western legends came alive. Buffalo roaming
above the chasm. Native Americans—Kwahadi Comanches. The frontier. Billy the Kid. Frank and Jesse
James. Legends that Kevin felt strongly, believing he had
Comanche in his blood, gamblers in his ancestry. He
imagined Comanches rounded up in Palo Duro
Canyon, thousands of their cattle and horses killed
before the tribe was herded to Oklahoma. He'd later
say his Comanche grandfather taught him the language. *"Ish de nee to iello"*—or something that sounded
like that—was a phrase he often repeated. Perhaps he
said it right, perhaps he made it up—either way, the English was clear: "It's a good night to die."

Kevin's narrative included a maternal grandfather,
50 percent Comanche, 50 percent Mormon; a card-
sharp who operated on Mississippi gambling boats; a
paternal great-great-grandfather, a doctor, murdered
by a man angered that treatment didn't save his wife;
and another relative murdered, in a motel room over
an affair. He was told Quanah Parker was his ancestor.

Quanah, a half-breed, was the last Comanche war
chief—part of the Antelope band. Kevin claimed
Quanah's warrior spirit. He believed he was a Native
American warrior. An Old West outlaw. His destiny was
to lead others in hopeless causes, die violently or in

prison, see followers captive or dead. No reason life should be any different *this* time around.

As he aged, Kevin fixated on new antiheroes. Accused of a weapons violation, Randy Weaver holed up with his family in a cabin on a North Idaho ridge in the summer of 1992. A deputy U.S. marshal shot and killed a family dog; another fatally shot fourteen-year-old Sammy Weaver in the back; in the confusion, a U.S. marshal was killed; the shoot-out ended with a standoff, during which an FBI sniper shot and killed the family matriarch as she held her baby.

In the spring of 1993, four ATF officers were killed in a shoot-out at the Branch Davidian compound in Waco, Texas. On April 19, after a fifty-one-day standoff, cult leader David Koresh and eighty-six followers died in an inferno.

Timothy McVeigh visited Ruby Ridge and Waco. On the two-year anniversary of Waco, he destroyed the Oklahoma City federal building with a fertilizer bomb, killing 168 and catapulting militias into the public consciousness. Kevin had roots in the groups and places getting all this attention. He said his natural father was a member of the Aryan Nations (Joe, husband number two); his adoptive stepfather was a veteran with militia connections (John, husband number four); relatives included motorcycle gang members. His geographical roots lay in the West, where outlaws were his heroes. He identified with McVeigh, saw in him an adult version of himself, a tall, pale white boy with cropped hair and a wicked destructive streak. In Operation Desert Storm, McVeigh fulfilled military ambitions Kevin harbored. McVeigh's terrorism appealed to Kevin's grandiosity—such a huge explosion, such a searing scar of damage, such notoriety.

Kevin also followed the national soap opera that was

the O. J. Simpson murder trial. It was obvious Simpson killed his wife and her friend. The acquittal reinforced Kevin's conviction he could get away with anything. *You could murder and walk free.*

CHAPTER 6

Sunshine State

John, a know-it-all from "Up North," wasn't accepted in Texas. The family hadn't risen above trailer life. Who knew what other reasons Ruby had, but soon the Fosters returned to Florida. When they crested the Interstate 75 bridge across the Caloosahatchee and saw the Florida Power & Light chimney, stream of steam across clear blue sky . . . glimpsed the river, an aluminum johnboat glinting in the sun, the slow brown blur of a pelican lumbering low across the water . . . they knew they were home.

Sometimes mist steamed from the river, sometimes low dramatic cloud obscured it, sometimes dense fog swallowed the interstate, a void beyond the railing. Sunrises and sunsets flanked the bridge, filling the horizon. In summer storms, driving rain forced traffic to slow; in winter, distant plumes of smoke rose from Lehigh Acres brush fires.

The Fosters exited south of the bridge, turning under it on Palm Beach Boulevard at the city's edge, into the country along Orange River Boulevard to Lorraine Drive, last street before asphalt and con-

crete yielded to scrub pine, cow pastures, horse pad-
docks and orange groves. They moved into a tan
rancher with attached one-stall garage near the dead
end of Lorraine Drive. A chain-link fence divided the
backyard from a once-prosperous farm reverting to
jungle, an abandoned packing shed hidden in vegetation, graffiti on the walls, IV needles on the floor. Lorraine Drive was a step down from Riverdale Estates, a
step-up from Canyon. The Fosters swapped a trailer for
a house; after a heart attack, John would swap tractor-
trailers for a pawnshop; their roaming over, they
rooted on the edge of Florida.

Southwest Florida was three coastal and two inland
counties, a larger area than Connecticut or Delaware
or Rhode Island, one of the country's fastest-growing
regions. Lee County—named for the Confederate
general Robert E. Lee—was the Republican heart.
Highly segregated—economically and racially—gated
communities proliferating, new cities incorporating and
seizing local power, Lee grew 63 percent in the 1980s.
Unemployment was low. Development, tourism and
health care were major industries.

Before U.S. 41 became the region's main economic
artery, it was the Caloosahatchee, that river below
the interstate. "Hatchee" means river; "Caloosa" is for
the Native Americans, Calusas, now gone, leaving
only shell mounds. Even the river was altered: dredges
cut a new channel, straight and deep, so at the first
locks, twelve miles upstream from Fort Myers, the
Caloosahatchee resembled a canal, the Okeechobee
Waterway, a nearly straight line to Lake Okeechobee
at Southwest Florida's eastern border.

The lower Caloosahatchee separated Fort Myers
from North Fort Myers and Cape Coral, center of
population in a county that grew from less than fifty-
five thousand in 1960 to more than 335,000 in 1990.
Here the river was a mile wide en route to San Carlos
Bay and the Gulf of Mexico, a broad-shouldered

waterway lined by Centennial Park in downtown Fort Myers, Harborside Convention Hall and Sheraton Harbor Place.

Fort Myers—the South's most segregated city, one study said, and one of the nation's best places to live, according to another—was once site of Fort Harvie, a temporary post in the Second Seminole War (1835–42). Thomas Edison and Henry Ford wintered in Fort Myers, and their friends Harvey Firestone, Alexis Carrel and Charles Lindbergh visited. The Edison-Ford Winter Estates glimpsed between royal palms lining McGregor Boulevard were major tourist attractions in the "City of Palms." When the Fosters moved to Southwest Florida, the region had no university. Downtown Fort Myers languished.

The Edison Festival of Light Grand Parade capped the city's year. When February was warm, it was one of the nation's largest nighttime parades. Spectators staked out sidewalk viewing spots weeks in advance, a half-century tradition. Homemade floats, all fake grass and wide-eyed children, interspersed with elaborate professional floats and marching bands. A two-hour parade followed by fireworks.

In other states, you knew it was fall when leaves changed. In Southwest Florida, it was when out-of-state tags outnumbered local plates on U.S. 41, 150 miles through Southwest Florida's three coastal counties, the Tamiami Trail (a contraction of Tampa and Miami, which it connected). Winter was sunny, mild and dry, attracting seasonal visitors locals called snowbirds. Frosts, wind and low humidity dried vegetation, tinder for brush fires that burned hundreds of acres and sometimes homes. One of the hot spots was east of Lorraine Drive, Lehigh Acres, where light undergrowth fueled fast-running fires—and where Kevin would burn.

Summer was hot (ninety-plus degrees), humid (ninety-plus percent) and wet, the rainy season, when forty-two of the fifty-three annual inches fell, often in violent afternoon thunderstorms. No-see-ums, fleas, ticks, fire ants and mosquitoes flourished. Without the Lee County Mosquito Control District and its small air force, the place wouldn't be livable. Without insecticides, air-conditioning and canal-digging backhoes, Southwest Florida was swamp. In summer, it rained like it only rained here: dry, blue sky, then dark, downpour, stunning streaks of lightning in the world's lightning capital, headlights on, water across the road, trucks sending fountains six feet in the air. An hour later, it was a steaming, sunny ninety-six degrees. Occasionally, tornadoes or tropical storms hit. June through November was hurricane season. The Caloosahatchee was dredged partly for flood control, but the region hadn't had major hurricane damage in more than forty years.

Everything in Southwest Florida lacked permanence. Buildings perched on the sandy peninsula—houses without basements, people without roots—waiting to be blown away by progress or a hurricane. It was a southern frontier, almost everyone from someplace else. Blue-collar Midwestern retirees flooded Cape Coral—115 square miles, one hundred thousand people, more canals than Venice—where pickups were banned from driveways; the elephant's graveyard, whose residents retired here to die; the arthritic seeking warmth; second-home buyers seeking cheap land, even waterfront property, a better house than you could afford back North, a backyard orange tree, year-round gardening; leisure lovers seeking sunshine and water, year-round golf, boating, fishing, shelling, endless beach, calm breezes, warm sunsets; Republicans seeking low taxes (Florida had no income tax) and a low crime rate followed by young service workers who served early-bird specials, caddied, parked cars, maintained yards; and telemarketers and scam artists who preyed on the elderly. Traffic was a fatal mix of young and impatient versus old and infirm—enraged young people desperate to pass retirees peering over Cadillac or Lincoln Continental steering wheels, crawling along, turn signals uselessly flashing. WHEN I GET OLD, I'M GOING TO MOVE UP NORTH AND DRIVE SLOW, bumper stickers said.

Everywhere, an undercurrent of violence: Two teens bludgeoned an acquaintance for a joyride in his car. Three people were bound and left, throats slashed, in a Cracker Barrel freezer. A German labor attorney was shot and dumped on an isolated Lehigh Acres road, one of a string of internationally publicized tourist murders. A Hispanic man survived two Vietnam combat tours, drinking binges, an alligator attack and homelessness—to be killed by a Satan worshiper convinced he must make a blood sacrifice before Friday the Thirteenth. A fourteen-year-old girl stabbed a man to death in a convenience store argument over a fifty-cent box of cookies.

The region was a drug-trafficking conduit: 235 pounds of 80 percent pure cocaine arrived at a grocery store, tightly wrapped bricks nestled among premium bananas in boxes labeled PRODUCT OF COLOMBIA. Small planes dropped marijuana bales or cocaine bundles offshore to commercial fishermen, given $50 to bring "square grouper" in with the day's catch—or on remote, nameless roads on city fringes, asphalt breaking up into chunks, stop signs missing, remnants of unfulfilled Florida land scams. Drug cash piled up in storage units. A motorist found $4 million beside a county road. At a meeting of Cali cocaine cartel overlords, flyers promoted a Cape Coral real estate broker.

Geographically exotic, the region was also news-rich. Children drowned—in a canal, swimming pool, bucket of bleach. Lightning killed. A funeral director failed to bury or cremate, stashing bodies in a rented storage unit and his mortuary—keeping a mummified baby in a faded brown briefcase for fifteen years. Manatees—sea cows—faced extinction; T-shirts depicted them as FLORIDA SPEED BUMPS. County commissioners were imprisoned. A ValuJet DC-9 nose-dived into the Everglades: SWAMP SWALLOWS JET.

South Florida was like a chocolate egg: a developed coastal shell, a hollow center, more center than shell. Palm trees, sod, sugar, citrus, beef, vegetables, scrub and wetland filled the thinly populated flatland between coasts. Places for Kevin to explore, away from the parasitic hoards, alone and running wild. Woods, crickets, blue sky, a sudden breeze. A puddle teeming with tadpoles. Dense, lush vegetation. Cypresses, palms, palmettos, pines. Hawks, anhingas, blue herons, snowy egrets, cattle egrets following the lean beef herds.

Then, in the distance, the sound of a vehicle on some road not far enough away, a reminder natural Florida was all under pressure, so that even in his young life there were places he could no longer go because the trees were replaced with asphalt, a canal and rows of stuccoed concrete-block homes. Just as vegetation flourished in the perpetual summer, so did development, construction never interrupted by winter. Even in unspoiled areas, change: invasive Australian pine, Brazilian pepper and melaleuca—imported by man—choked native vegetation and sucked up precious water. Though surrounded by water, the region dodged drought less certainly with each year of growth. Even beaches survived only with intervention, pipes pumping sand from the Gulf of Mexico in multimillion-dollar renourishment projects.

The heart of Kevin's stomping grounds was Buckingham. In a remote, undeveloped area was a sand dune that local teens called "the Hill," a joke in a county where the highest point was the landfill. Buckingham bustled with soldiers in World War II, when aviators trained at Buckingham Army Airfield. After the war, the area reverted to a sparsely populated rural community. Kevin, with his interest in history and eye for detail, found pieces of the place. Evocative street names: Gunnery Road, Cadet Avenue, Ordnance Road. At the mosquito-control district's sprawling headquarters, some original runway; off Gunnery Road, concrete bunkers set low in the ground like those dotting Europe after World War II, except these never saw combat; at HRS's Gulf Coast Center, some barracks; running through woods, he stumbled over pilings that supported post buildings and now were swallowed by aggressive vegetation, concrete tree stumps. It was almost hopeful, how quickly development decayed.

Near the bunkers, a water tower and taller grain silo. Kevin knew they were old by their glazed brick, left from a farm now overgrown with scrub and patchy development. Holes in the silo's circular wall so a farmer or adventurous teen with a head for heights and a thirst for thrills could climb.

Or Kevin went four-wheeling in the undeveloped wasteland around Lehigh Acres, Lehigh to locals. Population twenty thousand, a hospital, Wal-Mart Supercenter, McDonald's, a *town* at center—surrounded by thousands of empty acres where asphalt was laid, canals dug, ground leveled and lots plotted for houses never built. The margins of Lehigh or Port Charlotte or North Port or Port La Belle or Golden Gate were the Florida land scams, the origin of, "If you believe *that*, I've got some Florida swampland to sell you." The book chronicling Cape Coral's history was called *Lies That Came True*, the city achieving critical mass in spite of the deception surrounding its birth, high-pressure fly-in sales to Midwestern workers ("$50 down, $50 a month!"), sight-unseen sales to Europeans promised paradise ("You from Southwest Florida, then?" from a Thames waterman. "I've got two lots in Lehigh."). Cape Coral was unusual—enough people came, it got built. In La Belle, the General Development Corp. bought thirty-five thousand acres, planned a huge community and sold lots for 36 percent over market value to northern retirees promised a monorail to Miami and a regional mall in the cane fields. A marina and inn were built, but little else. Golden Gate was such a scandal it was featured in a British TV documentary. The vast wastelands surrounding these communities made perfect teen stomping grounds. Timber Trails in the open woods of southern Lehigh was a popular redneck hangout, an open sand dune surrounding a mud pit, ribboned by miles of dirt trails ideal for four-by-four pickups and four-wheelers, not a place for a car, though Kevin got Kelly's Corsica stuck there. Sometimes one hundred kids were at the Trails on a Friday or Saturday night, and diehards staggered home after sunrise.

Boys tried to cross the mud pit—said to have swallowed trucks—and when they got stuck, they spent the night getting out. If they couldn't, then they slept in the truck, an abandoned pickup fair game to rob, vandalize or torch. A boy who went for help would return to find his truck stripped—bed liner, roll bar and favorite ball cap gone.

Sometimes the sylvan craziness turned surreal: There was a dude in a ball cap, LSD tabs he hoped to sell hidden under the rim. His profuse sweat absorbed the acid. He freaked. Shot at movement in the grass— which was a couple copulating. Hit the guy in the butt. Kevin was one of few capable of driving. A convoy of pickups headed into the night for Lehigh's East Pointe Hospital, shot dude howling, Kevin thinking it hysterical, a great adventure.

Sometimes the sylvan craziness turned deadly: a girl was murdered near the Trails; a boy fell to his death from a pickup.

Timber Trails was a party spot where kids guzzled beer or liquor or smoked pot, lives drifting off course like a slowly moving driverless car, futures fading into dirty trailers, backbreaking labor, unpaid bills and early pregnancies. A pickup in the shadows, Rebel flag in the rear window, cooler in the bed, cluster of redneck boys and girls in ball caps, cowboy hats, Wranglers—no shorts, regardless of the heat. Four-wheeling, drinking, fighting, sex, drugs. Nomadic boy partyers teetering between tame and wild. Older partyers who saw the cast around them change but never grew up themselves, briefly adulated by shifting groups of boys who rejected them when they saw their own futures in the prematurely lined faces of inadequate boy-men doomed to hacking Marlboro coughs, domestic violence raps and cirrhosis. A whites-only Southwest Florida *Lord of the Flies* set around a fire of packing crates and tires, sweeping truck lights circling the orange glow. Boys jumping through the fire, Kevin into it more than anyone, pushing things further, standing closer to the flames, standing *in* the fire, taking the heat. *See what I'm made of?*

CHAPTER 7

Stargazing

The street side of the Fosters' roof at Lorraine Drive faced city lights, amber glow of Fort Myers on western horizon. But back here on the pasture side, above porch and pool, you faced the rural east. Bright stars against a black sky above palm and scrub pine silhouettes.

Tonight, two boys lay on the roof, looking at stars. You stared at that sky long enough and it was like standing on the Texas plain: anything was possible. Two boys, best friends, one a little older and bigger, protector, big brother.

Kevin and Pete.

Entering Riverdale High, Kevin was physically transformed. He shot up to six feet two inches, facial chubbiness gone and freckles receding, voice deeper. He abandoned curly, long blond hair for a redneck buzz, shed glasses for contacts, donned $40 Hayloft Western shirts, sometimes a white cowboy hat—so transformed that a girl who knew him at Lee Middle didn't recognize him. "That's Kevin," she was told.

"No way!" *Kevin, all of a sudden, became a redneck, and he looked so fine.*

Kevin did exceptionally well at Lee Middle, repeating fifth grade. By third quarter, he made honor roll: "Not only does Kevin do well academically, he's also very well-behaved!" Fourth quarter, straight A's: "Kevin's such a mature and intelligent young man. I'll miss him."

But freshman year at RHS brought girls, a driver's license and a car. "How's my ass?" he asked Kelly on the way out, straining to check himself in the mirror, see how his Wranglers fit, convinced a cute butt was the redneck boy ambition, girl magnet. He gave girls gold from the pawnshop. Mom peeked through his bedroom door, where he lay with his girlfriend, teased him about his bikini underwear, snickered through his sex stories and shared her own. Yet, when he lost his virginity, she plunged into a psychodrama, claiming a baby was on the way, an emotional tirade Kevin never forgot.

But Ruby doted on Kevin. Lying in her bed, they chatted into the early hours. She giggled with him like a teen, more friend than mom. He teased her about the men she slept with. She blushed. He poked and pinched; she poked and pinched back. When he shot bottle rockets at the deputy's house and car across the street, she said, "Stop that!" even as she laughingly let loose her own. They scurried over and retrieved fireworks by flashlight, hushing each other and giggling.

Girls saw a sense of humor and sweetness in Kevin. "Hey sexy!" one scrawled in his freshman yearbook. "Thanks for letting me wear your gold. You've been really sweet and friendly. If you ever have to talk, come to me." Guys saw instability; they dubbed him Psycho from the Alfred Hitchcock movie, the coincidence of his birth name—Kevin Don Bates—and the Bates Motel. The movie centered on young Norman Bates, a sociopathic killer obsessed with his mom.

Both saw recklessness. "Please don't kill anyone this summer, because I hear it's pretty bad in prison," one boy wrote in his yearbook.

In high school, which failed to challenge, only a drafting and computer-design class interested Kevin, and in it he flourished, considering a career in architecture. His grade point average plunged from honor roll to F's.

Kevin printed (Ø) on Mr. Harris's freshman algebra honors exam. The correct answer was the empty set, which is ( ) or Ø but not both. Kevin's "double empty set"—double naught, double negative—became a class joke and a symbol that both Kevin and Pete would doodle and graffiti. In a drawing memorializing the day, Mr. Harris writes the symbol on the board as Kevin in shorts and T-shirt shoots him with one hand, holding a sword impaling a severed head with the other. A cigarette in his mouth, bloodshot eyes manic-large. "Bite me," he says.

Years later, Pete recalled Kevin's double empty set. "We got yelled at in ninth grade by our math teacher for that. We just thought it looked pretty neat, so we used that."

Kevin got yelled at in ninth grade by *Kevin's* math teacher for that. *Kevin* thought it looked pretty neat. *Kevin* put it as the wrong answer on the test, not Pete. But then, Pete signed Kevin's name on theme book covers, like pop idol Marilyn Manson, over and over.

Kevin had trouble writing a coherent sentence; Pete wrote eloquently. With straight edge and compass, Kevin could draw architectural plans; Pete could draw freehand anything in his head. Kevin had creative ideas; Pete put them into words and pictures. Most of Kevin's friends wouldn't cooperate with his wildest schemes—Pete would. Most had difficulty following instructions; Pete didn't have to be told twice. It was a sick, creative partnership.

* * *

"This year's been a blast, ragging on Harris and messing around on the roof" was Pete's meticulously printed entry in Kevin's yearbook. "And our little trip to Riverdale in the dead of night. I can't wait to see the shit you pull next year. F— it all and f— in no regrets." He signed his name, then added a postscript. "Short freshman."

On a whim they'd hoofed it from Lorraine Drive to Riverdale High School. By school bus, it took twelve minutes. It took the boys ten hours.

They'd left Lorraine Drive about 9:00 P.M., a chilly fog thickening the darkness. The road went on and on. It seemed to Kevin time stopped and life was nothing but picking up his feet and putting them down. He remembered a favorite Stephen King story, "The Long Walk." Nothing existed but the road and himself.

The boys stopped at a convenience store opposite RHS, Kevin craving a soda and a smoke. The sun was rising when they returned home. They'd walked thirteen miles.

Kevin sat at the computer writing about himself and Pete, pouring out thoughts in a stream of consciousness. The story portrayed the two as snipers "taking out bad guys," loved by police, feared by wrongdoers, anonymous to citizens whose lives their vigilante killings improved. Pete was "Death" and Kevin "Saint Nick," because he knew who'd been bad or good. "If bad, you DIE. But tonight they took out the wrong bad guy. Oh well."

Another story proved prophetic, Kevin typing as others threw out suggestions, cracking up as he caricatured friends partying with a Ouija board, drugs and booze. Inebriated partiers were consumed in a fire, the RHS football team drowned in a bus accident and Kevin chanced on his girlfriend sleeping with a paramedic. Enraged, Kevin got an AK-47 from the gun safe, killing his cheating lover and her man.

"The party ends in a jail cell, Kevin alone after snapping and killing everyone."

When Kevin's Texas relatives visited, Kevin, the doting stepuncle, held the baby, mimicked how she rolled her head, showed her off to Pete. Kevin, the polite nephew, showed an aunt around town. Kevin, the jovial guide, took his stepbrother golfing or fishing. Kevin, the dutiful stepson, ran out to get stepdad's fast-food lunch. Kevin, the happy kid, played with the family cats, demonstrated diving, showed off. Kevin, the well-mannered volunteer, helped neighbors.

But the house on Lorraine Drive was more *Married with Children* than *The Brady Bunch*.

Lorraine Drive had almost gone the way of Riverdale Estates. John's heart attack at the wheel of his truck ended his commercial driving; he filed for worker's compensation, skipping six months' mortgage payments. They faced new foreclosure, but stayed afloat with help from an insurance settlement. The foreclosure dismissed, they kept the house. John unilaterally bought a pawnshop while Ruby was in Europe.

Kevin helped out at the pawnshop, meeting clients, including militia members, who talked up meetings and left pamphlets. He solicited friends to go, hear about the looming Brady Bill, named for the Reagan aide critically injured in the assassination attempt, mandating a five-day waiting period for gun purchases.

Pawn was a murky business, full of cheating, manipulation and con games, and Ruby learned to play and know when she was being played. She was good—and proud to think the Fosters' Riverdale Gold, Guns, & Pawn Inc. ("AMMO! FAST CASH! BEEPERS!"), one of few with an honest reputation. The balance of power shifted with John's heart attack and Ruby's mastery of pawn. The balance also shifted with Kevin, who felt John judged him and found him inadequate. *He's thinking, "Ah, man, you're a fuckin' pussy. When I was your age, I was in the jungle killing people with a knife."* They bonded only at the pawnshop or working on engines.

Safe on the roof, Kevin could tell Pete about violence at home. A couple of times, Mom pummeled him, Kevin said. More often—and more as he grew older—he came between John and Ruby, telling his father not to treat Mom that way. Brian hit Kevin too, attacks excused as blackouts, never discussed again, and perhaps adults thought Kevin forgot. *They think you forget, but you don't.*

Kevin could tell Pete about the time Mom fired a shotgun into the pawnshop ceiling after weeks of John's pushing, yelling, threats and infidelity. She said she picked the weapon up intending to shoot John, but changed her mind and fired a warning shot. "He has many guns and thinks nothing of killing," Ruby wrote in a request for a restraining order. "He hates my daughter, and he will try to get my son to hurt me."

In the middle of one nasty verbal confrontation, the phone rang. Ruby's sister Mary was shot in Texas. Ruby screamed. John tried to comfort her, hold her. Hearing the scream, Brian came in and attacked John, thinking Ruby hurt. Brian and John fought. Ruby raged, "He killed her." Kelly called police. Kevin ran from his room, Beretta loaded, thinking someone hurt Mom. Felt like killing John, Brian, both, these men disrupting his home. He stormed out, up Lorraine Drive, up Orange River to the Cracker Barrel, clutching the handgun, consumed by violent impulses. Then . . . John's sports car coming toward him. *Fire on the car. Shoot John.* The car stopped. *Mom.* Intense relief.

Mom said Uncle Gary killed Aunt Mary. Kevin later said he gunned Uncle Gary down on his doorstep with a shotgun. Pete would wonder. For years, people wondered about dead Uncle Gary.

CHAPTER 8

A Self-Inflicted Wound

Ruby Foster broke the news to her children. "Shawn has leukemia. He'll need friends to help him through this. If you decide to be Shawn's friends, you'll be in it for the long haul. You can't be enthusiastic, then back out when he grows sicker."

So sixteen-year-old Kevin spent his summer introducing Shawn Jeffries to activities Kevin viewed as part of boyhood—driving, stealing, vandalizing. The boys turned Ruby's garage into a club room. A pool table. A Pepsi machine. Spray-painted graffiti—(Ø), a gun, a Rebel flag. The boys got into pool big-time—cheaper to practice in Kevin's garage than pay at the pool hall—and they weren't so closely watched.

Ruby liked to care for people. She hosted European exchange students. She was guardian of a disabled man, Paul Gilbert. After his wife died, she simultaneously held three corporate titles at his travel agency, and John was vice president. The business enabled her to take Kevin and Kelly to Europe and send Kelly to Japan. When Ruby chose, she sold the agency and involved herself in John's pawnshop. When she decided Kelly needed a place to live, she put her in Paul's house—and soon Kelly's boyfriend moved in, too. Kevin and other members of the family ran his errands, did his chores, gave him rides. They brought him to Lorraine Drive and sat him in the living room in his wheelchair while their family gatherings went on around him. Kevin helped take care of his house, got groceries and fixed food.

Saturday, March 5, 1994

Trish Edwards and Kevin on the phone. With a four-teen-year-old's exactness, Trish calculated the two had known each other eight months and dated three, on and off. Trish was in eighth grade when her best friend dated Drew, who introduced his best friend—Kevin. Trish thought Kevin's family the kindest, gentlest, most generous people she knew. Kevin was *perfect* with her father, one of the few people her dad allowed her to talk with or date. She agreed to go out with Drew once when they broke up, maddening Kevin. He was hurt she hadn't told him and furious his best friend betrayed him. "I have no reason to be here, because nobody cares," he said.

It was *so* sweet. "I care," she said, making up. It was difficult to tell when he was joking. Sometimes he talked about shooting himself. And there *were* all those guns.

Kevin had a growing gun collection, added to by John, encouraged by Mom. They had matching guns: Mom's black Beretta 9mm pistol and son's black Beretta 9mm pistol; Mom's 10/22 rifle and son's 10/22 rifle. They bonded through competitive target shooting. Mom fit hers with a scope worth more than the gun, as the two competed for closer target groupings. The pair sometimes went through a brick—one thousand rounds—or two at the range.

Kevin went to gun shows, where thousands packed

the hangarlike Lee Civic Center, trading weapons, showing off collector items, buying guns priced from a few hundred dollars to thousands, from the latest handguns to World War II collector pieces and other weapons from exotic crossbows to Klingon knives. Kevin roamed the aisles, looking at military identification cards, flags and medals. He bought military manuals: *Improvised Munitions Handbook . . . Explosives and Demolitions.*

He was surrounded by guns. Winchesters, Colts and Rugers. Berettas, Mossbergs and Savages. Rifles, pistols and revolvers. There were .45s, 9mms and .32s; .410s, twelve-gauges and sixteen-gauges; 10/22s, AR-15s and .300s. Kelly had one. John had six. By sixteen, Kevin had eight. Most were in safes, but Ruby kept a loaded revolver in her bedroom, and Kevin had a gun and bullets under his bed. Handled guns at the pawnshop and at home. Worked at the gun shows. Performed a nightly gun-cleaning ritual in his room. Always playing with guns. "If you keep on doin' that, one day you're gonna mess up and end up shootin' yourself," Trish would say.

"No, I won't."

Tonight, Mom was mad; although his license was suspended, she made Kevin drive John's blankets and pillows to the pawnshop so he could sleep there. "Come and see me," Trish said.

"I can't—my license is suspended." Kevin fell asleep on the phone.

Sunday, March, 6, 1994

Expecting some of Mom's Texas kin, the Fosters waged a cleanup and touch-up campaign on Lorraine Drive. Husbands number three (Brian) and four (John) pitched in. Kevin went target shooting at the state's Cecil M. Webb Shooting Range, off a dirt road in a sixty-six-thousand-acre wildlife-management area. Kevin loved the range, especially when deserted, found peace shooting alone. Back home, he was required to clean out the garage, help drain and clean the pool, shape up his room. About 8:35 P.M., Brian and John left. Kevin showered. Mom bathed. *Peaceful,* she thought. *Since John left, things have been calm. Him being here upset Kevin and Kelly to where they might've needed help.*

Kevin lay on his bed fiddling with the single-action .45 Mom had given him for Christmas, called Trish, twirling the gun like an Old West gunslinger. The revolver's six chambers were loaded. Since he was thirteen, Kevin had been reloading spent cartridge casings. Lately, he and John had experimented, varying the load. The number of grains of gunpowder poured into a cartridge affected a bullet's speed, trajectory and force of impact. The next round up had a light load.

Trish was turning down a date with Drew when her call waiting beeped. *Kevin, saying he thinks everybody's better than him, always downing himself.* "Where's your stepdad? Did he move out?"

"Yeah," Kevin said, pleased with the new development. "He got an apartment." Idly twirling the revolver.

Trish heard the distinctive clicking. "If you're messin' with a gun, you're gonna end up shooting yourself." Call waiting. *Drew.* After a minute, she was back to Kevin. "Drew wanted to call on three-way and talk to both of us. I said no, 'cause I want to talk to you."

"You're gonna call him back?" *Drew's being a jerk, trying to date Trish.* "I miss you. I'm sorry I didn't come see you Saturday."

Trish heard a loud bang. *Maybe he dropped something.*

Kevin dropped the phone. "I got—My gun went off."

Trish heard screams. *Kevin.* . . . She heard Ruby and Kelly. "Call 911!" . . . Paramedics: "Which gun was it?" . . . After a while, Trish just heard the TV.

On the other phone with John after her bath, Mom heard a loud pop. *A lightbulb exploding?* Kevin walked down the hall, holding his side. "Mom, I've shot myself." She dropped the phone. Screamed. "Lie down." She pressed a wet washcloth to the entrance wound on the side of her son's stomach. *Not much bleeding.*

"I was cleaning my gun, Mom," Kevin said. "Go in there and tell Trish I'm okay."

Near hysteria, thinking about dead sister Mary, Mom ignored Kevin's phone.

"Mom, calm down. I'm okay."

At 9:45 P.M., a sheriff's deputy responded to a shooting at Lorraine Drive. Kevin said he was getting ready to clean his weapon, picked up the handgun, forgetting the live round in the cylinder. The gun somehow fired, hitting him in the stomach, exiting his buttocks into his mattress. It was an accident. Paramedics took him to Lee Memorial Hospital.

At 10:00 P.M., Agent Gill Allen, of the sheriff's Major Crimes Unit, was called. He was born and raised in Lee County. Like Mom, he came up in the '60s. He felt he faced a choice between straight or on the hippie side; he understood the choice would stick, small as Lee County was. He picked straight arrow, pulled that way by his parents' friendship with Sheriff "Snag" Thompson and his own with the sheriff's son. Allen knew the influences facing boys like Kevin;

that was one of his strengths as a cop. Hunting and guns were features of Allen's adolescence, like school, dating, sports—not something he questioned. Neither he nor anyone he ran with contemplated pointing a gun at a person. Like Kevin, he had driven a pickup, an M16 carbine usually in it. Now, he had mixed feelings. Lee County was urban: what purpose did guns have on city streets?

Allen arrived at Lorraine Drive at 10:30 P.M. Found the revolver in Kevin's room . . . a rifle propped against a wall . . . a .22 pistol . . . a pellet gun . . . another long gun on the floor . . . cigar boxes of live rounds . . . empty .45 casings among dirty clothes. *Reloads.* A deerskin hung on the wall near the Bates Motel sign. Cups full of knickknacks. Scraps of paper. Contact lens solution. Acne medicine. Garfield and No Fear clothing brand stickers on the mirror. A Rebel flag hanging from the ceiling. No gun-cleaning tools.

John could explain the absence of cleaning materials: maybe Kevin was going to wipe the gun with an oily rag. John didn't think his adopted son suicidal, but the shooting perplexed him. "Unless he had his mind totally off what he was doing, I've a problem seeing it as an accident. He's too familiar with all types of handguns. Unfortunately, I wasn't here, but it raises some questions. Kevin knows well to check the gun to see if it's loaded."

John told Allen there were no problems between him and Kevin. None between him and Ruby. No trouble at school. No trouble with the law. No unusual punishments. Never treated for emotional problems. No drugs. No alcohol. No unusual behavior. Just the prospect of company and the work of the cleanup.

The hammer of a single-action revolver has to be fully cocked before the gun can fire. Allen examined the gun: fully loaded—one fired round, five live rounds. *That rules out Russian roulette.*

* * *

A surgeon told Mom her son would be all right, though Kevin wouldn't be allowed to make the two-hour trip to see Shawn, near death in a St. Petersburg hospital. The bullet hit the pelvic bone, threw bone fragments. They cleaned it, sewed up the exit wound, left the entry open. They'd keep him a week. If it didn't get infected, he'd be all right. "It could've been intentionally self-inflicted," the surgeon said. Kevin was seen by a psychiatrist.

Done at Lorraine Drive, Allen joined Ruby, Brian and Kelly in the hospital's second-floor quiet room. "Like I said, I was very upset," Mom told him. "A member of my family was shot last year and killed so—"

"Was that here locally?"

"No. Texas. My sister's husband shot and killed—"

"Killed your sister?"

"Yeah. Kevin knows what he's doing. There's a suspicion in my mind that . . . This gun's his Western cowboy, and he was doing a spinning job, twisting, do you know what I'm saying?"

Allen asked Kelly, "I know the doctor came out and talked to you and your mother and he said it appeared that it could've been intentional. What are your feelings on that?"

The stress of parental discord had pushed Kevin and Kelly closer. They shared fears, anger, pain. Kevin hated John. He'd demand Kevin be punished; Ruby would defend him, then ground him anyway, to make John shut up. But Kelly wasn't about to share any of this—just like Mom and John, who failed to mention Kevin had been skipping school since February. His license was suspended; he smoked pot, drank, lost a girlfriend. "I don't think so," she said. "My brother has a real bad habit of spinning the revolver and acting big and tough. He's stupid in that aspect, but I think—honestly—that he was sitting there, spinning it and didn't realize. . . ."

Friday, March 11, 1994

Five days later, Allen interviewed Kevin in the hospital. Kevin's narrative had changed since he talked with the deputy at the house: "I was sitting there spinning my revolver, and I cocked the hammer and I turned it around so I could de-cock it. I had my finger on the hammer and my other finger on the trigger, trying to let the hammer down slowly. The hammer slipped, my finger slipped off the hammer, and the gun went off."

Allen was skeptical. "I'm familiar with guns myself a little bit"—a typical understatement—"and I've de-cocked guns also—but never pointing it at my abdomen."

"It was pointed at the bed."

"*You* were between the bed and the gun."

"It was an accident."

"Who do you blame for this?"

"Myself."

One girlfriend marries someone else; the other's courted by his best friend. Allen closed the case "unfounded," evidence insufficient to support the intentional shooting he suspected. Seemed the whole thing might be a way of attracting attention—what with all eyes on the dying Shawn, the Fosters' marital difficulties, the impending relatives' visit, the suspended license, the tensions with Trish and Drew.

Mom told people she was annoyed Kevin didn't run outside and fire the weapon rather than try to uncock it. Knowing he could've died if the round was hotter, she clamped down on his access to guns. Had the simple Wal-Mart safe moved out of his room and bought a heavy-duty safe to which only she had the combination, for a while at least.

When Kevin was discharged, the hospital sent along a plastic bottle of saline solution to clean his wound, a souvenir Ruby kept for years.

Always insisting the shooting was accidental, Kevin was reticent about the incident and self-conscious around girls, keeping the scar covered.

The only person who'll ever know for damn sure is Kevin, his friend Abe Ellsworth thought.

Kevin met Abe offering him a ride home from RHS. The rides became daily, and the friendship spread beyond school. Kevin helped with a building project. They hunted. Stayed in the woods all night, washed the truck at sunrise, went home. They worked on Kevin's pickup, went to football games, traded licks, punching each other in the biceps, wrestled until Kevin wore out.

Kevin wanted to take Abe on a road trip to Texas, to a place he knew, a cool place, camp for a week. "We can always say we had fun that time back there in Texas."

At Palo Duro Canyon.

While Kevin was still in Lee Memorial, Shawn died. A couple of weeks later, Ruby, Kevin and Kelly joined Shawn's parents and friends and went out on a boat, under the Sanibel Causeway, around Lighthouse Beach at the southern tip of Sanibel Island, passing the lighthouse, following a chart to a freshwater spring in the open Gulf of Mexico, where Bud Jeffries emptied his son's ashes from a clear plastic bag. A single bird followed them home. "Turn the camera off, Mother," Kevin said, sullen.

The Fosters hosted a wake. Bud bounced on the trampoline with his son's friends. Shawn said good-bye in a hospital bed video, leaving his scuba gear to Kevin, a video camera to Kelly.

Ruby filmed kids on the trampoline and around the

pool. Kevin and Pete playing a video game, Kevin engrossed in shooting a target on the screen. Snatches of chatter. "Well, I ain't been to school since February twenty-eighth," Kevin said. He'd missed so much, RHS was going to hold him back.

Kevin spent much of the evening avoiding the camera aimed first by Mom, later by Pete. He climbed on the roof, but Ruby wouldn't let him jump into the pool. "You're spoiling my fun," he said.

Pete climbed on the roof, too. Though his clinginess irritated Kevin at times, he felt something close to fondness. There was more depth to his sense of Pete than of his own sister, who sometimes still called him "worm" and whose role from his point of view amounted to the stereotypical older sibling—annoying because she put a check on his behavior, someone to be taunted when bored. "The Great White One" in her bathing suit. Besides, Kelly didn't share the "heart" Kevin and Mom believed was in them.

Kevin was bigger now, filling out, moving with practiced teen nonchalance, cocky, monosyllabic, sometimes remembering to strut, much like Abe, who was even bigger and broader, more young man than teen. In the garage playing pool, Kevin and Abe were young men surrounded by boys. Kevin was silent, withdrawn. Pete buzzed around the bigger boys, talkative, giggly, girlie. Tried too hard for attention, pushing in front of the camera, insinuating himself into the video.

Kevin didn't get to jump from the roof at the wake, so he jumped from the State Road 31 drawbridge arching high above the Caloosahatchee, invincible, invulnerable to the staph infection he got in his wound.

Pete's father was even more opposed to Kevin's influence after the shooting. Kevin might annoy friends by hanging out too long with their parents, whom he impressed with maturity and respectfulness, but he hadn't seduced Joe Magnotti. Ruby ran interference, promising they'd keep the guns locked up, and not long after the wake, Pete visited again. "We're going to a movie," he told his father.

Plans changed and the boys stayed at Lorraine Drive playing video games. Joe expected his son to do what he said. Kevin was unreliable, accident-prone, had repeated car wrecks, shot himself. "That's it. No more." Joe banned Pete from seeing Kevin.

Ruby thought Pete was the problem. She remembered a fishing trip, Pete poking a live catfish with a fillet knife, drawing blood. *He's weird.* Kevin baited her, reinforcing the perception. "Mom, Pete told me he's evolved: he's now Satan."

Pete's Satanism was more calculated to bait authority than worship evil. He said he was an atheist. "Why would God let little kids die or be abused?" he argued. "Why would God tolerate unfairness?"

Ruby pulled Kevin from RHS. "Why repeat a year? Your sister will help you get your GED, and you can get your degree at Edison Community College." His RHS file noted he'd be home schooled—but he was done with schooling. He still wanted to be *educated*— but to educate himself, both formally (getting his General Equivalency Diploma, flirting with community college) and experientially (dreaming of rafting the Colorado River, skydiving, scuba diving). He neither rafted nor skydived and quit scuba lessons when an allergy attack thwarted a qualifying dive.

In his final RHS yearbook, a teacher wrote, "Thank you for being an outstanding drafting student. I know you'll be a success." The rest reflected Kevin's Jekyll and Hyde personae—"Man, you're one of my coolest friends. You'll always be my Marlboro buddy. Don't worry about how bad life sucks now 'cause life's what you make it and you still have a couple of years left.

Don't worry about Trish. Everything will work out."
... "I'm so proud of you! I wish you success as you
pursue your college career." ... "What's up, you
psycho crazed bitch. Don't shoot me or you and we
can chill forever." ... "How's it going, you psychotic
bitch? It was cool shooting yourself. Hope you do it
again this summer." ... "Kevin, Looking back at this
school year, at all the things we've done, all the experiences we've shared, I realize this year really sucked
ass. First of all, all my teachers were a pain, Shawn dies,
you ventilate yourself, we don't have any classes together (it's a conspiracy, you know) and then all my
friends are going to Lehigh next year. Pass me the gun.
Anyway I'll quit bitching, it must've been worse for
you. 'To all the happy memories . . .' click, pow,
thump. Well, I can't wait to see the shit we do in the
future, (with our mass assortment of weapons and our
complete disregard for life in general . . .). It's been
a bitch, Pete Magnotti."

Pulled out of school, Kevin decided the shooting
was a turning point, positive because it forced change.
He suggested friends drop out. "You should think about
it," he told Abe. "You might be able to get ahead like I
did and be into your job before anybody else." To the
surprise of friends, he quickly got his GED. Ran errands for Mom. Labored to keep the house and yard
clean. Said he wanted to open a business with Mom,
make jewelry like her, accumulate enough cash so they
could be partners, buy a house, use his carpentry skills
to fix it up, keep the family together. He spent more time
at the pawnshop, learning to make jewelry. Got his
computer-assisted drafting (CAD) certification from
Lee Vo-Tech and excelled at using the program. Worked,
including a short stint at Yoder Brothers, a wholesale
florist with a sprawling showcase farm in east Lee
County, acres of grow lamps decorating the rural dark
like a year-round Christmas.

Kevin enrolled at Edison Community College (ECC)

to study architecture. He scrawled "I am lost" in a notebook: College didn't work. He grasped abstract concepts, enjoyed debate, loved facts, especially historical ones, hoarded them like souvenirs. There was a moment when he saw the potential of college, when a black professor wearing a colorful robe and Kevin wearing ball cap and jeans discussed Kevin's cultural limitations and he stood up for himself, for one moment sensed the world beyond, the new horizons college offered, the potential growth, the challenges, exciting and scary. But he chose retreat, withdrawing from many classes.

Eventually, Shawn's father, Bud Jeffries, got Kevin on as an apprentice carpenter at Ken Bunting Carpentry, rough framing, roofing, hanging doors, fitting locks, trimming out. He was the gofer but a hard worker—an exceptional employee, the company manager said: peaceable, acted older than his chronological age, as though he'd been working for years. Considered a potential crew leader despite his youth, he was reliable, on time, rarely took sick days.

When he was assigned to work on RHS renovations and the construction of a new auditorium, teachers asked, "Shouldn't you be in class? Get back in class!" Girls scribbled phone numbers and stuffed them in his tool belt. "He loves Riverdale, even though he never finished," Ruby said.

Some coworkers noticed racism. After a brick fell on him, Kevin threw a claw hammer at a Mexican, hitting the man. When paired with Bud, he went to great lengths to hide his Marlboro habit, standing in the Porta Potti pulling on smokes. He feared Bud would snitch to Ruby about his smoking, which sometimes hit three packs a day. Ruby saw Marlboro Red packs in his truck, he smelled of smoke, yet she never caught him—knowing and not knowing.

Kevin hid other things from Mom, including the extent of his drug experimentation. He smoked so much pot, he wondered if it affected his short-term memory. He couldn't handle pot—might as well be taking heavy drugs. He binge drank Jack Daniel's. His experiment with LSD left him cowering under his pickup for hours. He didn't like where drugs took him, the feelings of futility, holding a gun, contemplating suicide. "People who smoke pot have nothing to do but get up in the morning and smoke pot," he told Abe. "And if they do get a job, it's at Wendy's or McDonald's, and they're making money for what? To smoke more pot. When I get home, I've made something."

Summer 1995

Kevin still had his core group of friends who shared normal teen fun and mischief. Mom ordered pizzas and sodas for a Fourth of July party. Drew, Abe, Pete and Kevin watched TV; then Kevin dug a fire pit and lit homemade firecrackers. When the pyrotechnics were over, the boys sat around a bonfire.

Abe knew the owner of undeveloped land off a dirt road just north of the county line. He, Kevin and a dozen other teens went target shooting, camping, bird hunting, mudding, tearing up the property with their trucks. Kevin detonated homemade explosives in a pond. Sometimes he set up targets on wooden poles out in Lehigh and took buddies shooting. He spent a week's pay on friends, bought food, paid for miniature golf. He fantasized about these boys, a close-knit rebel "crew," sharing the edgy, manic, no-limit craziness that bewitched Pete. They'd share good and bad times, get drunk together and wreak havoc on Southwest Florida.

Within months, all but Pete fell away.

CHAPTER 9

The Southwest Florida Fair

Kevin roamed the seventy-second annual Southwest Florida & Lee County Fair with Chris Burnett, a beer-drinking, pot-smoking redneck, and Burnett's buddy Tom Torrone, an impressionable sixteen-year-old wobbling between conformity and rebellion. Pete and Chris wouldn't fit this crowd—they were nerds; this was redneck. The persona fit Kevin like his favorite Wranglers, No Fear T-shirt and ball cap.

The nine-day fair at the one-hundred-acre Lee Civic Center was an annual high point, something to do other than Sunday Teen Night at Marina 31, off-roading in the sandy woods around Timber Trails or drag racing the straight hard roads near mosquito control, where hundreds of teens gathered at night, a miracle no car veered into the intoxicated crowd.

The fair had lawn mower races, 4-H exhibits, live country and bluegrass music—Kevin heard Alabama. But the classic midway was what made it—elephant ears and cotton candy, stomach-churning rides, target shooting for oversize stuffed toys—all neon and flashing lights and carnies. Friday Midnight Madness—a flat fee bought unlimited rides from midnight to 5:00 A.M.—was the best time to go, perfect for being stoned, drunk and just this side of the kind of rowdy that got you thrown out by moonlighting sheriff's deputies.

Kevin hung at Marina 31 every Sunday. The shabby marina named for the road was tucked away beside the Caloosahatchee in the shadows of the State Road 31 bridge Kevin jumped from, a secluded place to drink underage, scuffle, loaf in the parking lot. There were bars and a sprawling dance floor and a room where strippers gave lap dances between snorting lines of cocaine, and sometimes Kevin ran into John when his adoptive father was living there on a boat.

Marina 31 was a redneck oasis in rural east Lee County, away from blacks and Hispanics, away from the intimidating new ethnic wanna-be street gangs, street cliques worse than the school cliques. Marina 31, Timber Trails and mosquito control were safe even from nerds, such as Pete and Chris, who'd be scared off by the first challenge to fight.

It was at Marina 31 that Kevin cemented his friendship with Burnett. Both worked construction. Both liked mudding in pickups, doing wheelies on dirt bikes, working on engines. Both attended RHS and failed to graduate, Burnett dropping out after a series of disciplinary actions. Both had pickups—Burnett's a gray Isuzu P'up with a whip antenna. Both were country-music-listening rednecks, both liked Teen Night. Both had bouts of depression and low self-esteem. Both would even obsess over the same girl.

Burnett and Tom had a long-standing competitive friendship, trying to prove who was "badder." Now they hung out with Kevin so much, the three got on each other's nerves, tension underlying camaraderie. "Shut the hell up," Tom would say.

Born in Staten Island, New York, Tom Torrone played junior-varsity football freshman year at RHS, where he was occasionally tardy and disruptive, nothing major, no arrests. A goofy, directionless kid, he was the youngest of eight. Though some considered him dumb, an easily influenced wanna-be, Tom was popular, with friends across cliques, including Puerto Ricans and blacks, from whom he picked up mannerisms and slang. "What's up, dog?" and "Sucks to be you" were his catchphrases. His distinctive laugh, repertoire of facial expressions and habitual grunt—like Beavis in MTV's *Beavis and Butt-Head*—tickled peers. Outside school, he cruised with buddies, slept over, partied, played pickup basketball, bowled and fished.

Burnett and Kevin hung out and shot pool at Burnett's house and worked on trucks at Kevin's. They wrestled. Shot at the gun range. Kevin boasted he'd been stealing and burning cars for a couple of years. Soon Burnett was boasting he helped Kevin steal.

Burnett pulled up beside an acquaintance at a red light. "Where's your truck?" Knowing the Toyota extended cab four-by-four pickup was backed up into a bunch of junk behind the Burnetts' barn, on blocks, spray-painted black, no motor, parts stripped and thrown in the bed, tires and wheels gone.

The acquaintance had parked his truck Saturday night after taking his girlfriend home. When the family got up for church on Sunday, the pickup was gone.

"I blew the motor on my truck and need a new one," Kevin explained when he drove the pickup to Burnett's. They lifted the motor out with a cherry picker, lowered it into the bed of the P'up, then drove it to Kevin's, where Tom helped install it in Kevin's truck. The stolen motor turned out to be no good.

Kevin and Burnett's friendship was strained by competition over an RHS girl. A transfer from another school, Cindi Schmidt was popular at Marina 31, deliberately last to show, fashionably late, her arrival an event. ("Sheee's *here!*" the DJ would announce.) She went every weekend night, won dance contests, dancing her favorite hobby. "I want you to meet somebody," her fourteen-year-old brother said. "This is Kevin."

"Hi, how are you?" she said, breaking the silence. *Kevin's cute in his own way.* He and Burnett kept to the side, nursing drinks, smoking, people-watching, and she pulled them out on the dance floor. Outside school in the first few months of 1996, Cindi, Kevin and Burnett were best friends. Kevin bought a pool cue and—at Burnett's, where there was a pool table— taught Cindi to play. Promised to teach her to shoot. The three went to the mall.

It cost Cindi a bit of her precious "rep," hanging with Kevin and them so much. Kevin and Burnett were labeled at RHS—losers, didn't dress well, somehow dirty. After Burnett dropped out, Cindi's friends worried those boys might lead her to mess up, too.

Cindi was impressed by how hard Kevin worked and how varied his skills were. *Kevin's real smart. So much general knowledge. Works math problems so fast in his head.* Whenever they passed RHS, he'd say, "I helped build that." *He can fix anything. Does more work than I've ever seen a real man do.*

Kevin and Burnett called daily. Kevin bought her a teddy bear, Burnett a stuffed pony. Two chains and a Florida State University (FSU) charm from Kevin, a chain from Burnett. "Y'all are driving me crazy," Cindi said. "I don't want anything from you except to be friends."

They'd stop by the Subway where she was assistant manager. Walk around on the tables or jump from table to table, chasing each other. "You got to go," she'd say, throwing them out. Kevin once put down a $50 bill. "That's your tip." Once, they came in and said, "Somebody hit your truck." Outside, she was speechless: it was Valentine's Day, and the boys had tied balloons to her truck and left dozens of roses in the bed.

They hung out at her house, sometimes at Lorraine Drive, dinners at the kitchen table, a real family home, glamour shots all over. *Kevin could have a lot in life.* One hot Southwest Florida night, the boys were up in Kevin's favorite spot on the roof, both fully dressed. "I'm going swimming," Kevin said. They jumped into the pool. You had to make a high, wide jump to clear the pool deck. "Y'all are so *dumb*," Cindi said.

Kevin and Cindi competed with their pickups—which looked best, was lifted highest, had the biggest tires. Both drove crazy. Both liked gold jewelry. He got a big grin whenever he saw her, even avoided cussing around her, not wanting to mess up his chances. Told her he wanted to marry her, told her he'd make sacrifices for her, trusted when he trusted almost no one, wrote poems. ("What the hell is *that?*" she'd said when she saw his handwriting.) After he ran over a kitten, he cried and was quiet the rest of the day. It was so sweet. *He's emotional. The type of person you can talk to. Warm, cute, attractive. Thinks about things a lot. That boy's so in love with me. He has a pretty smile.* "What do I have?" Burnett would say whenever Cindi complimented the Kevin grin.

"You got attitude." Cindi never seriously considered dating Burnett, but when she found out he smoked pot, she was even less interested: "You dropped out of school. You're on dope. You're turning into a big L—loser."

Kevin enjoyed it. "You can have her," he told Burnett.

"But first you have to get her." He cracked up, immensely amused by himself.

Once, when Cindi told Burnett she didn't want to see him anymore, he took one of Kevin's guns, went out by the pool behind Lorraine Drive, barrel in his mouth. "I don't have nothing to live for."

"Go ahead. If you're dumb enough to do that, go right ahead," somebody said, munching French fries.

A show, Cindi thought. *Just a depressed kid. Always wants what he can't have.*

"You know, acting stupid can do your life over," Kevin said. "You don't even know if there's a bullet in there." The same Kevin who—when picking on a scapegoat spiraled and someone suggested scaring him with a gun—had said, "You better go over there yourself, you dumb motherfucker. First of all, it's trespassing. Second of all, it's assault. And third, if the gun goes off, it's your ass."

That's what Cindi meant by responsible. *Kevin's so smart.*

But she'd seen Kevin's low self-esteem, too. At Circuit City, he tried to get credit for her to buy a phone. Declined. "I'm sorry, Cindi. I bet you think I'm a loser now." A theme, especially when he got in trouble with Mom. After one fight, he broke down crying in Cindi's front yard. Fretted he was a loser. "Are you stupid?" Cindi said. "Look at what you have in this world."

Kevin drove the Yota along Orange River Boulevard, an ATV up in the bed, heading to Lehigh to ride the dirt trails with Cindi, following a truck towing a steel box trailer. The trailer lights weren't working; the truck stopped. Kevin rear-ended it, damaging his front bumper. For once, he was under the speed limit. He apologized and offered restitution without contacting insurance companies. By the time he got to the Lehigh woods, he was inconsolable. He'd get blamed, though it wasn't his fault. The driver would take him to court. Mom would kick his ass, take the Yota away. "I'm gonna run my truck off the edge."

"You're out of your mind," Cindi said.

Kevin fishtailed the Yota, wheels close to the edge in slippery sand. Didn't seem scared. Cindi was, however. *Oh, my God.* "What's the matter with you?"

"I'm just playing around. I'm just trying to work out my anger. Do you think I'd do that? I put too much money into it."

"I'm not hanging out with y'all anymore. Y'all are crazy."

She was seeing Kevin and Burnett too much. They saw her as their girl, she saw them as friends. Burnett got mad when she hung out with Kevin and vice versa. Phone conversations were a paranoid three-way nightmare. "Which is it gonna be?" they'd say.

"Neither one." It was all too dramatic. Maybe she wasn't helping by even talking to them. "I'm gonna stop hanging out with y'all till y'all calm down."

Years later, still smarting from rejection, Kevin would say if she'd gone out with him, none of the rest would have happened.

Cindi wasn't alone backing away from Kevin. Abe, friend through the self-inflicted gunshot wound and Shawn's death, stopped hanging with him. Kevin's unreliability rankled. When they did do something, Kevin was given to crazy boasting about shooting people. He was a liability, got hyper, talked too much, uncomfortable with silence.

They took the Yota out in the swamp, got it muddy, Kevin didn't notice. Ruby did. "Abe took it out and beat it up." Ruby yelled at Abe, "Why did you take his truck out in the mud?" It was the last straw. "If you're gonna blame stuff on me that you did, it's not right." Abe was through. Kevin tried to patch up the damage, but gifts and apologies weren't going to work. Abe was sick of Kevin's mercurial nature.

Other longtime friends weren't spending as much time around Kevin. Drew would say he was around less because of senior year basketball and track commitments and Marina 31 Teen Nights lost their appeal and he was in with a different crowd and he wasn't into country music.

Some felt Kevin pushed *them* away. Acted weird, was short-tempered, whined about work, seemed racist, often fantasizing about destruction and violence. It wasn't conscious—friends just stopped showing up to play Sega or eat dinner or watch the big-screen TV.

Kevin viewed a true friend as someone who was down with anything he wanted to do and someone who'd look out for his interests as their own. But Kevin's long-term friends *weren't* down with anything he wanted to do. If he was going to fulfill his crew fantasy, it'd have to be drawn from newcomers, from a crowd Kevin's best buddies knew slightly, if at all—a crowd of nerds and losers they couldn't imagine him casting his lot with.

CHAPTER 10

Tipping Point

Sunday, March 24, 1996

A sheriff's sergeant patrolling those miles of Lehigh asphalt wasteland found the charred remains. Two twisted Grand Cherokee hulks abandoned on five blackened acres. *Only an accelerant produces such intense burning.* Total losses: no salvage value, no tags. One Jeep so warped it was hard to find a vehicle identification number (VIN), and when a dispatcher ran a VIN from the other, "No record found." *Straight off a dealer's lot, never registered. Who sells Jeeps?* A deputy checked Galeana Chrysler-Plymouth-Jeep-Eagle, and the service manager realized two Grand Cherokee Sports valued at $60,000 were missing.

"I'm glad I ain't getting caught," Kevin said, cackling atop the grain silo the boys climbed to watch the Jeeps burn. March was always jinxed. The bank took the Riverdale Estates house in March; he shot himself in March; Shawn died in March. This March was no better—old friends drifting away; the tedious carpentry job; work missed for nebulous sicknesses explained as allergy attacks; the failure to capture Cindi, who declined his bid to accompany her to the RHS prom; Mom gone to a Montana grandmother's funeral, leaving him alone at Lorraine Drive; his inability to accumulate money; thwarted college ambitions. John was gone, the failing Riverdale pawnshop sold. Mom leased a building closer to town for Treasures Jewelry & Pawn Inc. She was absorbed in moving and renovations and expected his help, cutting into his free time. Kevin fantasized about hedonism, would rather live five years a hedonist and die than grow old. ("Suicide by cop," he told friends.)

Burnett and Tom joined Kevin and some of his longtime friends for the Jeep caper. Diverting police from the car dealership with a bomb threat was Kevin's idea. He filled a soda can with brake powder—resembling gunpowder—attached wires, wrapped it in duct tape and left it on a Wal-Mart Supercenter pharmacy department shelf.

First call: "There's a bomb in the store."

"Yeah, right." *Click.*

Second call: "Y'all need to evacuate."

"Fuck off." *Click.*

Third call: "There's a *fucking device* in the store. It's on a shelf in aisle three-B."

"You need to stop calling, or I'll call the police."

"That's what I want you to do: Call the police. I'm not kidding. There's a bomb."

"Fuck you." *Click.*

Unbelievable, Kevin thought, *just fucking unbelievable.* A stock clerk eventually found the device, one hundred people were evacuated and the store closed four hours while bomb disposal technicians removed Kevin's diversion.

They got the teal Jeep on Friday night. Sped around Kevin's neighborhood, tore up yards, hit signs, bickered about damage to the SUV as though they owned it. The next night, Kevin drove a white Grand Cherokee off the Galeana lot. The boys took turns doing doughnuts, running down stop signs, blowing tires. Kevin rolled the Jeep in a pool hall parking lot. He was afraid he'd have to wipe off fingerprints right there and run, but it landed upright and he kept going.

On to Timber Trails, where they played bumper cars, rammed trees, got stuck in mud, high centered, blew a motor. "They're my parents' cars," Kevin told intoxicated onlookers. He tore off a front cowling for a souvenir, dumped smokeless gunpowder and alcohol over the interiors, pulled his Zippo: *click. . . . whoosh . . . boom.*

Though unaware who he was, the Lee County Sheriff's Office had sought Kevin since March 3, when a stolen pickup marked the start of a spree.

While Mom was in Montana, he drove Kelly's Corsica in defiance of orders, hit a dog and dented a fender. Called around for parts, getting quotes he couldn't afford. Struck out at scrap yards. Less than twenty-four hours before Mom's return, he broke into a parking garage and—surveillance camera filming—removed the fender from a marked police Corsica. At home, he peeled off the blue letters and numbers. The fender wasn't a perfect fit, but close enough.

The eve of Mom's return found him in a stranger's garage slamming a hammer against a Toyota 4Runner window, a buddy lying guard across the hood, clutch-

ing a revolver. Kevin shattered the glass, started the
SUV, and they fled. Awakened by the engine at 5:30
A.M., the owner made it outside in time to see his
truck disappear around a corner. Later, Kevin, Burnett and Tom put the motor in the Yota. As Mom arrived home, Kevin was in the woods pouring oil over
the 4Runner. Lobbed in his trademark road flares and
burned several more acres.

Dancing his nocturnal dance of meaningless delinquency, Kevin had grander plans rooted in popular
culture and mass-media news entertainment. His current enthusiasm was Michael Mann's *Heat*, playing in
Fort Myers at a discount movie theater. In the movie,
Robert De Niro leads a criminal crew. Members are
intelligent, loyal, disciplined. They plan crimes, clock
emergency personnel response times and shoot
anyone who gets in their way.

Even as Kevin encouraged friends to go see *Heat* for
$1.50 at the Edison Park 8, more current events fired his
imagination: The day after deputies found the burned-
out Jeeps, the Freemen of Montana—who repudiated
federal, state and local government—refused to leave the
"sovereign territory" of their 960-acre ranch, the start of
the longest federal siege in modern U.S. history, another
in the series of events that began at Ruby Ridge. Kevin
rooted for the Freemen. Then, on April 3, federal agents
arrested hermit Theodore Kaczynski at his Montana
mountain cabin and unmasked him as the Unabomber,
who'd perpetrated sometimes fatal bombings since
1978 with impunity and blackmailed newspapers into
publishing his thirty-five-thousand-word manifesto, "Industrial Society and Its Future." Its opening line, "The
Industrial Revolution and its consequences have been
a disaster for the human race" resonated with Kevin's
angst. The Unabomber hated the things that Kevin said

alienated him—materialism, capitalism, the rape of the environment.

Sometimes Pete and Chris showed up at Lorraine Drive asking, "What are we gonna do tonight?" Kevin would tell them, "Nothing, I'm too tired." They didn't belong partying at Timber Trails, drag-racing at mosquito control, fistfighting at Marina 31, stealing cars, drinking, chasing girls. But Kevin still wanted his crew, and it wasn't going to be formed with his longtime friends: Drew wasn't into it, and Kevin dismissed him as a punk coward; Abe—mystifyingly outgrowing delinquency— wasn't talking to him, earning the sobriquet of bitch; debilitating drug abuse ruled out another old friend; still another was an unreliable coward who blabbed; none were bright like Pete and Chris, whose intelligence compensated for their geekiness. Both had boundless imaginations and not only accepted but reveled in his violent antisocial fantasy life, a world where he believed he couldn't welcome even Mom, where he'd seen contemporaries flinch, recoiling like he was dangerously infectious. It was a strain, trying to master impulses and hide where his mind was. With Pete and Chris, he didn't need to.

The front cowling ripped from one of the Jeeps became a fetish to illustrate Kevin's delinquent tale, which he repeatedly told Burnett and Tom (though they'd been there) and Pete and Chris. He showed off the stolen pickup behind Burnett's barn and the place he'd burned the Jeeps. He glamorized auto theft—the joyrides, thrill of rolling a Jeep, arson, acres burned. He boasted of crimes to come. Maybe they could form a crew.

With the scavenger hunt resumption of their friendship, Pete had deteriorated. His report card never made it home, though the envelope did, and Joe found it: the Marilyn Manson logo . . . "Kill every thing" . . . "Hate" . . . "666" . . . "I love evil." Joe called the school requesting the grades. Physics, F. . . . Pre-calculus (honors), D. "He stopped doing his *homework* this quarter." . . . Economics, F. "Eight daily assignments never handed in." . . . "He's a virtual 'do nothing' with a very sarcastic attitude."

As Pete reentered Kevin's sphere, he pulled Chris with him. Before long, Kevin had Pete, Chris, Burnett and Tom working on the new pawnshop Mom and Kevin said they co-owned.

Thursday, April 11, 1996

Ruby wanted a rented steam cleaner returned. Glad for an excuse, Kevin assembled Pete, Burnett and Tom. "Let's do something." The four piled into Burnett's truck, Kevin and Pete riding in the bed, lobbing bricks and pieces of wood.

"Pull in there," Kevin said, pointing to a church. Kevin and Pete shattered the windows of a Lincoln Town Car. Then on to the Winn-Dixie across Buckingham Road from RHS, where Kevin smashed an electric meter and opened a fire hydrant. The boys broke out more car windows. They returned the steam cleaner. As they rode to Tom's—he had horses to feed—Kevin threw things at road signs.

Meanwhile, Chris Black rode to a Fort Myers Beach party in Derek Shields's '88 Chevy Cavalier. The Cavalier had 167,005 miles, a broken turn signal, a loud muffler and a habit of stalling. Faded, blotchy, peeling, its red paint had been baked by the Florida sun.

It was spring break, local high schoolers mingling on the beach with out-of-state college students. Though he hadn't touched booze since a cousin got him drunk when he was eight, didn't use drugs and didn't even like taking aspirin, Derek got trashed.

Kevin's old-guard and new-guard friends crossed paths at the party. Abe stopped by, figured it wasn't much fun and split. Drew regaled Derek with stories of Kevin's criminal mischief.

Derek had grown into a big kid. At five-feet-eleven inches, he weighed 220 pounds. In a few years—when it wouldn't matter anymore—he'd look like a young Christopher Reeve. Replace Reeve's sparkling eyes with a vacant sadness, and that's Derek. He was square-jawed, and his face had the pleasing symmetry and wide-set eyes sought in male models, but the all-American face was marred by acne.

After the party, Derek drank glass upon glass of water, trying to sober up and passing the time playing chess on a stolen laptop someone had borrowed from Kevin. On the brink of graduation, he wondered if his life would turn out any better than his brother's. Fred's nineteen years were summed up in a paid obituary and a death certificate: born in Mount Kisco, New York . . . moved to Alva in 1986 . . . attended RHS . . . graduated Valdosta Technical Institute . . . construction mason . . . never married.

Born two months premature, on August 19, 1977, in New York, Derek faced a litany of health problems. He'd be troubled by one ailment or another until he was seven—and then he'd be shot.

Derek's father moved in with his wife's newly divorced best friend when Derek was two. He didn't love Derek's mother anymore, and the three preschoolers were a nuisance. He didn't contest allegations of cruel and inhumane treatment when Virginia filed for divorce; a court found his conduct endangered her physical and mental well-being.

Virginia made time for her kids and attended parent-teacher conferences, even while working three jobs. They had clothes and food, but sometimes no electricity. A paycheck went to buy Fred's Nike Air Jordans and then another because Virginia saw how badly Derek wanted them.

When Derek was five, his grandfather died, and suddenly his father wasn't around anymore, either—he just vanished.

Derek idolized his three-years-older brother. Nothing separated them. Christmas 1985, Fred got a BB gun. Playing outside, he fell on ice. The gun hit the ground. A BB ricocheted off a door and, by a one-in-a-billion chance, fulfilled every mothers' you-could-shoot-someone's-eye-out nightmare, hitting eight-year-old Derek in the pupil of his left eye. He never forgot the pain and fear, the beginning of a lifelong dislike of guns. By the time Derek got an implant lens, he'd been blind in that eye five years and was amazed what it was like to see out of both.

Derek was nine when his grandmother retired to Southwest Florida. Virginia suggested they follow. They arrived on September 6, 1986. Derek hated the place from the get-go. School wasn't up to New York standards—far less advanced and challenging. There was some discussion of promoting Derek, but his social development was considered inadequate. He was shy—stemming from early hearing and speech problems—and teased.

Derek's mother remarried. The family lived in Alva, a rural crossroads community on the Caloosahatchee near the Hendry County line. Derek's stepfather started a trucking business, and Derek spent a month with his parents on a trucking run through Chicago, Albany, the Smokies, the Carolinas, Tennessee, Kentucky. He longed to see every corner of the country and was delighted every time they passed a baseball stadium. *We love baseball, Fred and me.*

Virginia told her son about God and the Bible and sometimes took him to church. Derek was drawn to faith, but he would come to hate God.

On April 6, 1993, Fred returned from Georgia intent

on reform. He'd had a wild streak—burglaries, car thefts, expelled from RHS. In Valdosta, he'd gotten his GED. He won a two-year scholarship, but he didn't take it. Time to grow up, settle down. He wasn't sure what he'd do. He loved sports, though it'd be a long shot he'd use his baseball talents. Whatever happened, it was good to be home, to see his mother and the kid brother who'd grown so much.

Derek had been counting the days. He loved Fred's humor and their common ground. Both could be lazy. Both got into mischief—they were caught breaking into a school as boys. Now, both vowed to go straight. Before Fred went to Georgia, they wrestled daily. Fred always won, laughing as Derek struggled. But today, fifteen-year-old Derek won. As Fred was leaving, Derek called, "I never gave up."

Fred smiled from the doorway. "That's what I was trying to teach you."

They never wrestled again.

Fred had gotten Derek into country music. After he died, Derek kept hearing a lyric about "brotherly love." It was more than he could stand.

Years later, the wound still raw, Derek didn't connect easily, and his job kept him from his closest friends. He tried to entertain himself, then started dropping in on Pete and Chris. *They're home: they don't have lives.* He'd been good friends with Chris a decade, known Pete through high school. The trio sat together at the back of classes. Emotionally more mature, Derek was the best student, the one with the $20,000 scholarship to the Florida Institute of Technology (FIT), yet not as bright or creative.

Derek didn't like Pete's music, considered Marilyn Manson satanic, favored rhythm and blues, inoffensive rap and soft rock—Mariah Carey his favorite.

Pete and Chris savored the violence of *Pulp Fiction, Reservoir Dogs, Natural Born Killers*. Derek watched

Top Gun repeatedly, feeding his ambition to join the air force and segue into space science at NASA; *Field of Dreams* nurtured his baseball enthusiasm and belief in Hollywood endings; in *Red Dawn,* he saw himself among small-town teens heroically resisting Communist invaders.

Pete was either pushy or so intensely brooding he attracted attention even in silence; Chris was always wisecracking; Derek faded into the background.

Pete and Chris weren't into after-school activities; Derek was in jazz band and RHS band director Mark Schwebes was a friend.

Pete and Chris weren't athletes. Derek was a decent recreational basketball and baseball player, avidly followed the New York Mets, wanted to play pro baseball. Just like Fred.

Their parents weren't rich, but Pete and Chris got most of what they wanted. Neither *had* to work. Derek had known poverty, and when he traded the $200 Mustang for the $500 Cavalier, he knew he appreciated it more than Pete appreciated his $6,500 Nissan.

"You're a good influence," Joe Magnotti told Derek. "Pete should hang around with you more, not Kevin."

Derek worked thirty to fifty hours—in addition to school—at the Alva Country Diner, pulling weekend double shifts, three months without a day off. Though proud to contribute money to his family, he believed students shouldn't work that many hours and thought his boss a slave driver. Emory Lewis, the family's landlord, hired him as a dishwasher. In less than a year, Lewis—impressed by the sixteen-year-old—trained him as a cook. *Never a minute's problem.* Couldn't say as much for his family, always three or four months behind on rent. *Disgusting.* He suspected Derek's mother drank too much. She'd call the restaurant asking for Derek's help disciplining his younger sisters. Eventually, Derek quit, believing Lewis insulted his mother. The same day he applied at Hardee's, referred by Pete, as Pete was referred by Chris. Starting as a back-line cook at minimum wage—a 43 percent pay cut—he'd bring home perhaps $80 working three or four days each week, but he could be more of a kid at the end of senior year.

RHS seemed wild during freshman year, with a disproportionate number of troublemakers kicked out of other schools. Derek skipped assigned reading, did no homework and little class work, yet pulled A's and B's. "You're not setting a good example," a teacher said, frustrated he was skating to an A average.

"You're not challenging me," Derek said.

He felt he'd overcome his shyness by high school and got along better with other kids. He accumulated nicknames: "D," "Big D," "New York." With his Italian roots and New York accent, people teased him about mob connections. Sometimes at lunch as many as fifteen people from three different cliques were at his table, and he was the only boy with a foot in each. But he struck most as quiet and painfully shy, notable for how little he said beyond the occasional cynical crack.

At his center was a void. Had been since Fred's death, perhaps even before. A stunned empty place, a shutdown vacuum. Things looked okay on the surface to others and even to Derek, but they weren't. RHS didn't engage him. The cliques either weren't appealing or weren't interested—he didn't want to be a redneck or a gangbanger, enter a trade or be a small-time felon. He didn't like hanging out with drunks on Teen Night at Marina 31. There wasn't much for a cash-strapped teen to do.

Flickers of hope had been dashed. He'd made great progress chasing his air force goal—high enough test scores to qualify for any job in any military branch, signed papers, picked a specialty. It seemed the easiest route to NASA. Derek had mentioned the implant lens and been reassured he'd get in. Two days after Christmas, 1995, he learned he'd been rejected. Crushed, he retreated to his bedroom and cried. His mother tried to comfort him, but the partial scholarship mightn't be enough to see him through college. He saw a yawning abyss of days working at some place like Hardee's—a relentless routine of showing on time, working, clocking out, maybe some TV, maybe a movie, what else?

By the second week of April, the six boys were on a collision course with their community and each other: Kevin . . . Pete . . . Chris . . . Derek . . . Burnett . . . and Tom shared a need to belong so strong it'd overcome their differences, brought them together, given them— perhaps for the first time—a sense of community. Kevin and Pete were friends; Pete and Chris were friends. Chris and Derek were as well. Derek's friendship with Chris pulled him into Pete's orbit; Chris's friendship with Pete pulled him into Kevin's; so Derek's friendship with Chris pulled him into Kevin's orbit, too. Burnett and Tom were different, unconnected with Pete, Chris or Derek, pulled in by their own affinity with Kevin, Marina 31, pot and country music.

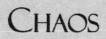

CHAOS

CHAPTER 11

The Lords of Chaos

Tuesday, April 16, 1996

So, on April 12, Kevin Foster, Pete Magnotti and Chris Black went on their delinquent spree through downtown Fort Myers and out into the rural east, leaving vandalized vehicles, burned macaws and a smoldering construction site in their wake. As they fell asleep, Kevin schemed to transform a group of kids into a teen militia—yet he knew the night had been one of mindless pettiness.

Which was how the community viewed it, too.

The first publicity came in the *East Lee Tribune*, a small-circulation community newspaper that appeared Tuesdays under a masthead proclaiming, KNOW THE TRUTH AND THE TRUTH SHALL SET YOU FREE. The newspaper mixed ads from small merchants with minor news and reports reading like editorials. The anonymous writer didn't know of the Lords of Chaos, but he recognized an aberration in his semi-rural community. Friday's vandalism was beyond normal teen spirit, sufficiently out of kilter to be noticed by the tiny paper. Able to say whatever he wanted, not operating under the constraints imposed on reporters at larger papers, the writer dismissed the LOC's actions, unwittingly pushing almost every button that could goad Kevin and his cohorts. The writer had the intuition to connect a series of apparently unrelated acts. Kevin was involved in every incident cited. Headlined HELL RAISING IN BUCKINGHAM, the piece cited the Hut fire, church arson, vandalism at RHS and elsewhere and a shooting at a nocturnal party in the Buckingham woods. The reporter opined that the perpetrators were "obviously pea-brained vandals" and "person(s) of less than average intelligence and a cretin's personality.

"Some of this area's young adults aren't nearly as *adult* as they'd have us believe," the writer concluded.

Kevin was offended. Nothing, he later said, is more irritating for a teen who wants to be taken seriously than to be dismissed as childish. He aspired to be a great anarchist leader. He talked up militias. He had pamphlets. A library of military explosives manuals. Military patches (SWIFT-SILENT-DEADLY 1ST RECON BN . . . U.S. ARMY: MESS WITH THE BEST, DIE LIKE THE REST). With the help of his new recruits, Kevin was starting to plan, moving from disorganized, spontaneous delinquency to more organized crime. April 19—anniversary of Waco and Oklahoma City—approached.

The Lords of Chaos could prove they were better than the newspaper portrait if they marked the anniversary with a bombing. Kevin wanted Pete to write a document claiming responsibility and justifying the arson and vandalism.

Pete also resented being judged juvenile and stupid. Like the others, he wanted serious recognition. He started a draft document.

* * *

Derek saw Kevin at RHS's senior-class picnic off State Road 80 at the Florida Power & Light facility, a sprawling set of chimneys, exposed battleship-gray generator machinery and thickets of wiring surrounded by Cyclone fencing. In three days, Kevin would lead Derek into a crime that'd put an FBI reward on his head. In five days, Derek would come to fear and dislike Kevin. In fourteen days, his acquaintance with Kevin would destroy him. He'd already bought his cap and gown; he wouldn't use them. Derek didn't need to be in school—he'd completed the required credits. If he could augment the partial college scholarship with work and financial aid, he could complete college, majoring in space sciences. So far as he knew, he'd be the first in his family to get a degree, surpassing Fred.

Fred . . . Fred . . . Fred. Everywhere, he carried Fred—memories of Fred, anger at Fred's death, suspicion about how Fred died. . . . Virginia woke him, told him Fred was in a coma, not expected to live. For two days, Derek wouldn't go into Fred's hospital room. Finally, on the third day, he went in to see Fred, saw a tear roll from his left eye, knew his brother was aware of him. They'd said good-bye. Derek blamed God. He still believed, but they were no longer on speaking terms. God took his brother. Derek wanted nothing to do with Him.

Pete and Chris left the picnic and met up with Kevin. The boys stood between their cars. Chris kicked up dust. Kevin pulled on a Marlboro. Pete fidgeted, moving around the others in jittery, overexcited circles. Kevin said he'd decided to bomb the Coca-Cola bottling plant in Fort Myers. He wanted to contradict the media coverage of the first Terror Night. He had another reason, but he wasn't sharing: he liked layers of secrets.

* * *

Derek left the picnic alone. Went over to Chris's. "He isn't home; he should be in school," Betty Black said. Derek explained they got out early for the picnic and Chris left with Pete. "Probably still driving around," she said.

Derek dropped by RHS, gave his sister and buddies rides. Went back to the Blacks' at 6:00 P.M. Still no Chris. Pete would be in night school. Chris's parents were worried. "I'll go look," Derek said.

Back at the school, a teacher wouldn't let Derek ask Pete where Chris was. He'd just have to tell Chris's parents he couldn't find their son. He headed back to the Blacks' yet again, falling easily into the familiar role: He helped his mother with his younger sisters, helped older people with their cars. He was a good boy, a solid influence on other boys, liked by parents.

The jacked-up blue Toyota pickup was in the Blacks' driveway. Kevin and Chris walked out of the house. Chris introduced Kevin. It was all casual. Chris didn't invite Derek over to meet Kevin. Didn't encourage him to join the LOC. Neither did Kevin or Pete. It just happened. Derek slid into it.

For all their differences, Kevin and Derek had much in common: Both were born premature; both abandoned by natural fathers who had problems with the law. Both lacked strong, stable male role models; both had relatives who died violently. Both had Vietnam veteran stepfathers; both had unfulfilled military ambitions. Both saw themselves as protectors of more vulnerable kids.

The three went to RHS and sat in the parking lot waiting for Pete to get out of night school. Kevin pulled up his T-shirt, displaying his scar. "It was an accident." He said he was twirling his gun. *Dumb blond,* Derek thought.

Burnett pulled up in his old gray Isuzu P'up. Derek and Chris met him for the first time. Pete got out of class. "We're gonna break some windows up at the auditorium," Kevin told Derek. Handed him a rusty railroad spike, a sweater to wipe off fingerprints, then a sandwich wrapper to hold the metal, avoiding new prints. Derek threw the spike at a window. It bounced off the glass. Yielding to peer pressure, Derek was scared. He felt no thrill. How could he? He was a good boy. He was only along for the ride. The boys kept at it, breaking some of the plate glass windows. Chris took a sledgehammer to a pay phone—which would backfire, denying him an alibi when he needed one, leading him to murder.

"Let's go over to Tom's."

The boys lived within a short distance of each other: go west out Kevin's front door and you're in the working-class, racially mixed Tice community; keep going on Palm Beach Boulevard and you're in downtown Fort Myers. The areas had different names, and lines on the map showed them inside "incorporated Fort Myers" or in "unincorporated Lee County," but the reality was one big concrete and asphalt strip mall sprawl from North Fort Myers, south on U.S. 41, to San Carlos Park and from western Cape Coral east to Riverdale, an urban mass: east coast Florida with neither youth culture nor money. Head east from Kevin's back door and you're in the old Flint farm . . . then Buckingham Rural Preserve . . . sporadically developed Lehigh Acres . . . past the tiny road-and-river crossroads communities of Alva and Olga . . . and finally to the Hendry County line.

Orange River Boulevard runs dead east from Lorraine Drive; the Circle K near the intersection was a frequent meeting place for the boys. Keep going east, and you pass Tom's house. A left turn where the boulevard ends at Buckingham Road takes you north past Pete's house to the high school and Chris's house.

Turn right instead, and you go south past the road to Burnett's.

Only Derek didn't live within that tiny area. His family was farther east in Alva; but even so, with the scant rural traffic, it wasn't far.

When the Lords of Chaos struck, they confined themselves to places they knew, lashing out at the familiar.

Burnett went in to get Tom, and they walked out to the church lot next door, where the Yota, Derek's Cavalier and Pete's Nissan were parked.

Once Kevin started recruiting, things escalated fast. The first night. it was Kevin and Pete. The second night, the group grew to three with Chris. Now—with Derek, Burnett and Tom—there were six. It started with boisterous bragging, boasting and rowdy one-up-manship. Kevin described breaking windows. Chris pantomimed destroying the pay phone. Souvenirs were produced—metal clipboards from the county vehicles. Kevin and Pete kept a sort of LOC diary in one of the clipboards.

"We thought the animals were monkeys," Pete said, boasting about what he called the first "Terror Night."

"Remember where we chased the pigs?" Kevin said, referring to the construction site behind Burnett's house. "It's not there anymore." Pete threw in details.

Kevin showed Burnett two Motorola Spectra radios in the back of the Yota. "Could you hook those up in my truck?"

Just bullshitin', Derek thought. Didn't take it too seriously. He hadn't seen much. Breaking school windows was no big deal: simple vandalism. As for arson, Derek doubted Kevin. Nothing in the newspaper.

The recruitment was classic Kevin. Bragging, grandiosity, inclusion, working the boys up, playing on their loneliness, resentment and need for acceptance and belonging. "This town's boring. . . . We're gonna raise havoc . . . make headlines. . . . An anarchy group . . . not messin' anymore . . . a force to be reckoned with."

Kevin outlined his vision. Wanted no part of the Hollywood image of the Bloods and Crips, the hand signs, colors. More of a militia. A crew at his beck and call. He'd be the leader. "Us against the world." Somebody to call on if you needed somebody. They'd go on missions of criminal destruction—Terror Nights. It wouldn't be about money but the rush. Ultimately they'd end the world—starting with chaos and mayhem in Lee County. "I'll head the world," Kevin said. "I hate everyone equally." Eyes glinting, he ground out a cigarette with the toe of his boot and lit another.

Chris could appreciate Kevin's desire for recognition. *Wants to read about himself.*

Kevin knows how to do everything, Pete thought. *He's the oldest and a natural leader. He's got a numerous amount of information packed in that head of his. He's like a little soldier, a little terrorist.*

Clearly, Kevin's leader, Derek thought. *And Pete's his right-hand man, his second in command, his best friend.*

Kevin felt more for Pete, Burnett and Tom than for either Chris or Derek, whom he viewed as children, only included because they were Pete's friends. "Now we got a group, we need a name," he said.

"LOC," said Chris, recalling the acronym Kevin mentioned the night in his bedroom.

"Yeah, that's L-O-C," Kevin said. "Lords of Chaos."

A clique with a name, Tom thought.

Kevin wanted each member to have a simple, easily remembered nickname he could yell out during missions. "Pick one-syllable names that don't pertain to yourself," he said. At first, he wanted to call himself "Death," the nickname he'd given Pete in the "Snipers" story. Rejected it, but couldn't settle on a substitute.

"Well, you're the leader, so why don't you just call yourself 'God'?" Derek said.

Kevin's whole face brightened. "Yuh! Thank you," stretching out his hand and shaking Derek's.

Chris was easy. "'Slim,'" Pete suggested.

Derek drew a blank. "You're from New York," Pete said. "Call yourself 'Mob.'"

Pete was "Fried." He worked at a fast-food restaurant. Liked fire.

"Who you want to be called?" Kevin asked Burnett and Tom.

They'd share a name. They debated Red Neck and the beer brand Red Dog. Burnett would be Red and Tom would be Dog.

That fits, Chris thought—*Burnett's a redneck, and Tom follows people around like a puppy.*

Tom felt he was only there because he was tight with Burnett. Kevin, Pete, Chris and Derek saw them as screwups. Burnett's reputation was partly based on alcohol and drug use; Tom's derived from his puppy-like, goofy personality. He wasn't, in the eyes of the others, the sharpest tool in the shed.

Sitting on the hood of his car, Derek contemplated the pair. He couldn't stand either one. Although Burnett went to RHS, Derek had never met him; now he took an instant dislike. Saw him as a pure redneck, slimy, someone Derek wouldn't buy anything from. As for Tom, Derek thought him an idiot. Had a phys ed class with him. Had a bad vibe the moment they met.

Pete drew the double empty set, now an LOC symbol, on Kevin's arm.

Burnett thought Pete was the brains of the outfit. He drew cool pictures and maps. Said he could make a bomb.

Pete's closer to Kevin than anybody, Tom thought. *They grew up together.*

The LOC had rules. From the start, Kevin was emphatic members wouldn't boast. That was real clear in Tom's mind. Anyone who disclosed the LOC's existence would die. So would their families—a threat Burnett took to heart. He would come to consider himself a member under duress. "If you run your mouth, you die," Kevin said. The group was all-important and would be defended by whatever means necessary. Any outsider who threatened them would be killed. Kevin logged names, nicknames and phone numbers. "You're gonna get pagers. My mom will get you a good deal from the pawnshop. Everyone get a pair of gloves." There'd be no dues, but they'd pool funds for food or gas, or to help a member low on cash. Tuesdays and Thursdays, the nights everyone was free, they'd hold meetings to plan missions. Anyone who broke the lesser rules would be verbally reprimanded by Kevin or another member, and they'd forfeit their share of any loot.

Loot sounded good. *If I was the leader, it'd be about nothing but money,* Derek thought—*no hurting people, no thrill-seeking, no torturing animals. I could always use more money.* So could Chris; he was unemployed.

Actually, Derek's motivation was a little more complicated. He didn't really feel a part of the Lords of Chaos—he was mostly there because of Chris—but if he was, it was because he liked the idea of retribution against Emory Lewis for the way he dissed Derek's mother. Perhaps the LOC would help him avenge Fred. Over time, he came to believe he knew the names of some of those involved in Fred's death. There were rumors of drugs, rumors about a gang, rumors Fred had been to Fort Myers Beach that night, where there was a gang-related fight, where he was beaten with a baseball bat and driven into town before being pushed from a speeding car. Too, he remembered Fred coming into the house that last time saying he'd been followed by sheriff's deputies, two of whose cars Derek recalled seeing. This memory and that no one was held accountable for Fred's death left him angry and vengeful.

Pete didn't care about money. He was a genius. Should've been admired, but no. He'd been screwed by a society he had little respect for. Denied the attention he deserved, he'd get some now. Kevin was smart, all right, knew guns and bombs and all kinds of weapons. And he was brave. But he, Pete, was more sophisticated. There was some rivalry, an intellectual contest, that carried over into the LOC, where Pete wanted planning: ordered chaos. He was less focused on physical violence than Kevin, more on property destruction. He'd go along with this game if it meant he could meet his own goals. The LOC would be fun.

Chris was tired of being picked on and teased. He craved power, wanted to be in some mystical, magical, comic-book-style group of avengers, everybody scared of them, nobody knowing who they were.

Chris seems above all to want to be accepted, Burnett thought. *Maybe it makes him feel like he has somebody, 'cause he has no friends.*

Chris thinks Kevin can do anything, Tom thought. It seemed to Tom it was Kevin and Chris who wanted to create havoc.

Burnett and Tom didn't inject many ideas. Burnett had faith in Pete's intelligence. *He'll straighten out Kevin's plans, get the flaws out. Those four are the baddest.* Burnett and Tom knew they were the kids of the group, the gutless ones. They were told so often enough. "I'm glad that's what they thought of me," Tom said much, much later, "'cause they were pretty much right: I didn't have guts."

Still pissed about the *East Lee Tribune* piece, Kevin had plans for the following Friday. "Let's do something else." Something more destructive and more intelligent.

Vandalism and arson were foreplay. With the formal creation of the group in the church lot, such juvenile delinquency was done with. The other boys had no idea how quickly they'd accelerate to bombing, armed robbery—and murder.

CHAPTER 12

A Well-Organized Militia

Wednesday, April 17, 1996

Pete, Chris and Derek skipped school on Chris's eighteenth birthday. Readying themselves for Friday night, Pete bought black leather driving gloves, Derek bought black gloves for himself and—as a birthday present—for Chris, perpetually broke.

Bragging about the previous Friday's crimes, Pete showed off the document Kevin ordered, handwritten on a yellow pad: "Declaration of War—Formal Introduction of Lords of Chaos."

Won't write for English, but when he comes up with these crazy ideas, he writes forever, Derek thought. He said, "You're nuts, but you have a way with words."

They'd type it up and send it to the Lee County Clerk/Traffic Violations Bureau. Pete sat at his word processor. Peering over his shoulder, Chris checked spelling and grammar and suggested they not mention breaking the taxi windows because they were seen.

Pete's declaration was "a claim to criminal acts

committed against society by the militant, anarchist group LOC (Lords of Chaos)." It began with an obsessively detailed account of the LOC's vandalism that corrected minor media errors, expressed particular delight in arson and promised future and more destructive Terror Nights.

"WE ARE NOT PLAYING ANYMORE!" Pete warned, saying the boys were developing a well-organized militia. "Lee County is dealing with a formidable foe, with high caliber intelligence, balls of titanium alloy, and a wicked destructive streak. . . . Be prepared for destruction of biblical proportions, for this is the coming of a NEW GOD, whose fiery hand shall lay waste to the populous.

"THE GAMES HAVE JUST BEGUN, AND TERROR SHALL ENSUE. . . ."

Pete signed the Declaration of War with Kevin's double empty set. He devised a second symbol, a geometric design based on the acronym, two partial triangles on each side of a circle, the first representing an *L*, the second a *C*.

Wearing gloves to avoid fingerprints, Pete and Chris fumbled to put the document in a green envelope from one of the stolen clipboards. They sealed it in a Ziploc bag and later gave it to Kevin to mail. The envelope was proof the authors vandalized the trucks— and the addressee an appropriate recipient for a message from Kevin, with his string of traffic tickets. His driver's license had just been suspended again.

Friday, April 19, 1996

Pete ran errands for his parents, while his passenger Kevin—favorite Combat Commander stuffed in his Wranglers—scouted for a getaway vehicle. At a Big Lots discount store, Kevin bought leather work gloves for himself, Burnett and Tom. At Galeana, they failed to steal another Cherokee. Errands completed, Pete drove through Taco Bell. The boys sat in the car in an empty lot across Edison Avenue, eating and surveilling the Coca-Cola plant, recon for an LOC mission: borrowing an idea from a military manual, Kevin wanted to steal propane tanks and blow up the building. *It's deserted, unguarded, an easy target. But it's a historic landmark, it'll make the newspaper.* Kevin showed Pete an ignition device he called a flash bomb made—with intentional irony—from a Pepsi can packed with gunpowder and wrapped in duct tape. He'd cut a hole in the can, stick a twenty-five-foot firework fuse in it, and hang the fuse out the window and light it, setting off the stolen propane tanks.

Time was when schoolchildren trooped through the Fort Myers Coca-Cola Bottling Company on field trips. One of the oldest bottlers, the company was among the last independent holdouts, granted an envied perpetual franchise. The Fort Myers plant was almost as old as the classic curvaceous Coke bottle created in 1916. When B. B. Hawkins first bottled Coke in Fort Myers, workers hauled buckets of Caloosahatchee river water, mixing it with the sweet sticky syrup shipped from Punta Gorda by sailboat and delivered in mule-drawn wagons. The sixty-seven-year-old landmark sat on 2½-acres beside the region's busiest highway, just up the street from the biggest mall, across from the major hospital, a few blocks from the heart of downtown. The 12,300-square-foot two-story brick bottling plant was heavy on timber—floors, wall frames, ceiling joists, roof supports—a wooden building with a sandy-brick surround. The charm was in the details: shiny inset mosaic tiles, architectural flourishes paying homage to America's best-selling soft drink, the company's classic signature carved in stone high above the front door. Children used to peer through the windows at women inspecting the contoured bottles coming off the assembly line, light catching them in a way that made them sparkle. But in the five years since it was abandoned in favor of a modern plant just off the interstate, termites damaged the building, the flat roof leaked, it became a vagrant hangout. Inspired by Beale Street, the Memphis blues Mecca, a prospective buyer pondered restoration, offering $485,000 and making a video to attract investors.

Firebombing run-down historic landmarks wasn't what Pete hoped the Lords of Chaos would do. He gave Kevin a school notebook containing a plan to rob Hardee's. Chris and Derek had contributed ideas, but Pete wrote and sketched it.

They met up with Chris and Tom at Burnett's. Burnett worked on his mother to let him spend the night at Lorraine Drive. The boys piled into Burnett's pickup. Avoiding driving on the suspended license because of his propensity for traffic stops, Kevin directed Burnett behind a car lot, pointing out a red Toyota 4Runner. Dusk. "Cut the fence," he told Tom and Chris. To Burnett: "When I flash the flashlight, that's your signal to start your truck."

Stoned, paranoid, edgy, Burnett waited . . . cranked the ignition. Kevin came running. "Stupid idiot. I'll kill you for that." The boys hopped in the bed, headed away from town. Kevin pointed at a U-Save supermarket. "Pull over. I want to make a phone call."

"Fort Myers Police Department."

"My wife's been shot." *Distract 'em!*

Back at the car lot, the 4Runner wouldn't start. The boys went back to Lorraine Drive.

Pete was now an arsonist, vandal, burglar and thief contemplating bombing and armed robbery. His parents required him to be home with his car by a 10:00 P.M. curfew. He drove home and pretended to turn in for the night.

Burnett's mother called Ruby. "They're in? They're not going anywhere else?"

"They're helping me hang pictures."

Saturday, April 20, 1996

As Derek got off work, Burnett pulled up with Kevin, Chris and Tom. *Burnett seems all dopey*, Derek thought. *Just out of it. Bloodshot eyes.* All but Burnett were dressed in black T-shirts, military camouflage pants and black army boots. *They look stupid dressed that way.* Especially Chris: short, fat, in camo, like some child dressing up. Kevin and Chris jumped in Derek's car, and as they rode to Lorraine Drive, the boys tried to explain where the Coke building was. Derek didn't get it. He'd gone to school, then worked until 1:00 A.M., three hours later than planned because a coworker called in sick. Awake nineteen hours, he was tired and reluctant, but feeling pressured. He changed out of his Hardee's uniform. Pulled on black jeans. Tied his white Reeboks. Kevin didn't like the sneakers. *Too bright. Not covert enough.*

Kevin and Tom went back to the car lot, this time with Derek, and tried a third time for the 4Runner. Gave up when Derek saw someone who seemed to be watching. Tom was hungry.

"The night's shot," Kevin said, disgusted. "Let's go to Taco Bell and get something to eat."

Under the bright lights in the fast-food restaurant, traffic whizzing past plate glass windows, the boys inhaled their food from the paper wrappers, reenergizing, rehashing the plan, working each other up, Kevin's frustration lifting as his vision of bricks flying across U.S. 41 returned.

Clutching his leather gloves, Pete walked to the Buckingham store, where Burnett and Chris picked him up. They took a dirt road into the woods. Kevin, Derek and Tom showed. Tom realized his gloves were missing. An unsettled feeling in his stomach, Tom kept quiet, hoping the others wouldn't notice.

Kevin wanted to use the Yota, but he didn't want to wake Mom. At Lorraine Drive, the boys pushed the Yota into the street. The six piled in, Pete squeezed between Kevin and Burnett, the others sprawled in the bed. Kevin cranked the ignition. They'd show what they were capable of. *Less than average intelligence? A cretin's personality? Pea-brained? Ha!*

CHAPTER 13

The Real Thing

Kevin pulled up to a pay phone on the Starvin Marvin gas station forecourt. "Get out." He told Burnett to act like he was on the phone and watch Buckingham Road. Kevin popped the locks off a rack of propane tanks with a crowbar. "Everyone, grab at least one." He and Chris sauntered up to the glass door and peered into the closed, dimly lit store.

What the hell am I doing, Tom thought, walking empty-handed back to the pickup, where Burnett stood, shaking, looking down. "No," he was saying to Kevin. High, nervous and paranoid, he was having second thoughts. Kevin pulled the Combat Commander and held it to Burnett's head: "You're coming with us."

Tom hopped in the pickup bed. The others handed him tanks.

Derek glanced toward Winn-Dixie. A man was watching, pointing toward the boys, picking up a pay phone. *He might be calling the cops.* "Okay," Kevin said. "Hurry up."

The boys jumped in the Yota. "We have to get more tanks," Kevin said.

* * *

Inside the deserted Starvin Marvin convenience store, a surveillance camera hung from the ceiling, pointing at the glass door, filming.

At 2:20 A.M., Jeff Roberts walked outside the Winn-Dixie to call his wife. Crickets and frogs chirped from the shadows. A slight breeze in the clear night. How many years was it since Roberts needed a coat? Chatting, he stared into the night, across the box store's football-field-size parking lot, toward the highway. Four or five guys scurrying like caffeinated ants, lugging white objects, throwing them into a pickup. "Now listen up,"somebody hollered in the background. "I think the Starvin Marvin's being robbed," Roberts told his wife.

The pickup backed up, going the wrong way through a one-way loop, pulling onto Buckingham. At the Palm Beach Boulevard light, it turned toward the city. Roberts went inside, got his boss. The two walked across the dark, empty Winn-Dixie lot, which seemed unnecessarily big. Walked along one side of the Starvin Marvin. Peered in. *Nothing tore up.* Walked around the other side. Propane canisters scattered. "We better call the sheriff," Roberts said.

"They won't even bother coming," the manager said. "Just get back to work."

He's probably right, Roberts thought. *That substation's just across the street, but you make several calls, and if they come at all, they're real slow.*

Parker-French Ace Hardware was almost catty-corner to the Starvin Marvin. Some of the boys were reluctant to steal from a store right beside the road, well lit, close to the sheriff's substation. "Now listen up," Kevin said. "Y'all know too much as it is. If y'all help me, you ain't gonna squeal on yourself, right? Y'all might as well start participating, 'cause if you don't, I'll kill you."

Kevin popped the lock off the propane tank cage. Each boy grabbed what he could carry, piled them in the pickup bed. Six boys and ten propane tanks crammed into a compact pickup, leaving their territory, heading west, following Palm Beach Boulevard away from home. On a suspended license, Kevin drove his Lords of Chaos into the city, the too-wide boulevard virtually empty, stoplights on overhead wires swinging slightly in the wind, a speeding sheriff's car, bars on the windows of unlit stores, prostitutes in the shadows, crack dealers clustered at a pay phone.

Kevin parked in a vacant lot north of the plant. "Walk around the building. Scout it out. Try to find a way in. Make sure no one's inside, no bums." He, Pete and Derek went one way, Chris, Burnett and Tom another. Vagrants had made it easy to get in—a hole in the Cyclone fence, a crate pushed against the wall below a broken-out window. A light inside. Kevin and Pete climbed in. Derek's broad shoulders wouldn't fit. Kevin opened the front door.

Rhonda Glover stopped her northward drive up U.S. 41 at the Edison Avenue red light. More traffic than she expected at 4:00 A.M. Newspaper, bread and mail trucks. She glanced toward the vacant lot with the white perimeter chain. *A pickup. The kind you see driving through mud on the commercials. Lights off. Two white men standing shoulder to shoulder by the passenger side. Up to something.* The men glanced toward traffic. Fidgeting. Taking a step or two. Idly kicking at the asphalt. Watching to see if anybody was watching.

As Derek headed back to the truck, where Chris and Burnett were keeping watch, he saw a white car circle, then stop on the north side. The driver got out and peered through the fence. Kevin, Pete and Tom came back. They'd seen the car. Almost ran into the guy when they came out. The layout was perfect. They just needed to get the north-side door open to carry tanks in, unseen. They piled into the pickup, and Kevin drove across U.S. 41. The white car circled again. Kevin considered forgetting it, going home. They waited until the car was gone.

"Ready?" Kevin brandished the flash bomb. "It's a Pepsi can." He didn't want the others to miss the irony. To Chris, the only other boy good with a stick shift: "You'll be drivin'. Pull back over here after we unload." Kevin drove back across the street. All except Chris got out. Kevin grabbed tools, went in by himself, took the doorknob and deadbolt off and opened the north-side door. Tom wondered how.

"Carpenters know these things." Kevin told everyone to grab two tanks. Put them in pairs in upstairs rooms. Burnett would've preferred to be the getaway driver, but Kevin didn't trust him; he seemed intoxicated. He *always* seemed high, whether he'd smoked or drunk anything. "No. Let Chris do it. He's fat and can't run. Let's do this."

They waited until traffic cleared. Walked the tanks across Edison, Kevin barking orders, Pete struggling to carry even one, Burnett dropping another. Derek was first in, Kevin right behind. Pete, Burnett and Tom passed tanks in to Kevin, who handed them to Derek. Ten tanks. Tom kicked out a window. "You're acting like an idiot," Kevin said.

The boys carried the tanks upstairs and placed them in pairs in the musty vacant offices. Kevin pulled the flash bomb from his No Fear jacket. "I'm gonna smash a window, drop the fuse, and on the count of three, you open the tanks and run." Kevin set the Pepsi can on a sill.

Scared and having a hard time paying attention, Tom misunderstood. Thought Kevin meant to turn on the tanks. Turned his on and ran back to the others.

Kevin smelled gas. "Turn the things off," he yelled. Tom went back, dashed into the room holding his breath. "You just can't make stupid mistakes like that no more," Kevin said. "I oughta kill you—punch you out and leave you here."

Chris sat in the Yota awaiting a signal. A police car drove by. The officer looked at Chris, who waved. The officer waved back.

Derek poked his head out the door. "Is he gone? . . . Go ahead across forty-one," waving Chris away. He went back upstairs.

"When I count three, turn your tanks on and run downstairs. Get out of the building." Kevin called for a group hug. The five interlocked arms like a football huddle. The boys took position by their tanks.

"Ready?" Kevin broke a window. Unrolled the fuse. Counted three. The boys opened the tanks. Heavier than air, propane poured out, dropping to the floor. Everyone fled. Tom jostled people going down the stairs. Stepped on Burnett. The boys met on the sidewalk.

From across the street, it seemed to Chris everybody in the neighborhood could hear the hissing gas.

Burnett stopped at the corner for traffic. Saw Kevin running toward the end of the fuse dangling from the broken window. The other boys ran across U.S. 41. Almost got hit, dashing across the street, cars swerving, honking. Kevin caught up and crossed. Everyone jumped in the Yota.

"Get in back," Kevin said to Chris. He drove over to the Lions Park next to the hospital. The boys sat on a picnic table in a public park by the region's main road in sight of traffic waiting for the explosion. To Derek, the hissing gas sounded like brother Fred on the respirator.

"Ready to see an explosion?" Kevin said. "Expect a little boom, and then watch the building go up. It'll take about twelve-and-a-half minutes for the fuse to burn down." He based his estimate on the fuse length.

Kevin was so close that Chris assumed he used a
timer. A small pop. In seconds, the propane ig-
nited, blowing out the upstairs windows, shooting
flames. Glass shattered. Debris flew. A sound like
thunder across the city, shaking houses a block
away. Smoke billowed across the highway, drifting
through neighborhoods around McGregor Boulevard, across the Caloosahatchee. Glass shards rained
across the seven lanes of U.S. 41. The upper floor
engulfed. It exceeded the boys' wildest expecta-
tions. Kevin bounced up and down. This was a highlight of his life, a thrill akin to the touchdowns he
hadn't made, because he wasn't a jock; the graduation march he couldn't take, because Mom pulled
him from school; the military career he dreamed of,
but never undertook. He'd emulated Tim McVeigh
like a Riverdale Raider emulating Joe Montana.
Flames shot twenty feet into the night sky, and
Kevin saw fire blazing through the Waco compound.
Glass scattered across the highway, and Kevin saw the
Oklahoma City federal building crumble. The
others were yelling, screaming, celebrating. *Majes-
tic,* Chris thought. *We wanted everyone to know we
weren't playing,* Pete thought. Derek had been
halfway asleep, it was so late. He was stunned. A car
stopped, then drove on. The boys heard sirens. Decided to get the hell out of there.

With the boys crammed in the Yota, Kevin drove
past the front of the plant, all but Derek cheering.
These guys are nuts. If it wasn't for revenge against
Emory Lewis, he'd back off. As it was, he'd hang in,
see what Kevin could do.

"LOC," Chris yelled.

"LOC!" . . . "Yeah!" . . . "Yeah!" . . . "Yeah, burn, baby,
burn!" the boys screamed.

4:19 A.M.: "Nine-one-one, what is your emergency?"

"I'm at Denny's and— the building right next to me,
the whole front of it, just blew. It's on fire."

Another call came in to the Lee County Sheriff's

Office and was transferred to Lee Control, which dispatched fire trucks and ambulances while deputies called the Fort Myers Police Department, because the bombing was in the city's jurisdiction. Police notified Lee County Emergency Medical Services, which already had overheard calls. The airwaves were filled with interagency radio transmissions long into the night.

A fire truck returning from a medical call was first on scene. From blocks away, its crew saw the orange glow and shooting flames. They parked sideways across the lanes, blocking traffic, the rescue truck too small to be any use fighting this inferno. People poured from their houses, drawn by the explosion. Within thirty seconds, other firefighters started arriving . . . Engine 11 . . . Engine 31 . . . Rescue 11 . . . Ladder 31 . . . Chief 4. Firefighters circled the building, looking for the easiest access. The front door was open, and downstairs lights still burned. A previously dead-bolted north-side door stood open. *Someone broke in. Vagrants?*
"A few weeks ago, this door was locked," the incident commander said.
The open door led right to the stairway.

A bombing in Fort Myers was so unlikely, it wasn't on the radar screen—there must be another explanation for reports of an explosion. "All the windows blew out," one officer radioed. "That's probably what the explosion was." But neighbors gathering on sidewalks were certain a detonation woke them. If it was a bombing, it was huge for the Fort Myers area, where there'd been only one in modern history—when a young Fort Myers Beach cocaine dealer blew up the U.S. Drug Enforcement Administration (DEA) building.
At first, firefighters and police had more pressing concerns. Finding the closest hydrants. Calling Florida Power & Light to cut power. Shutting down U.S. 41 because smoke was covering the roadway and

passersby would get in the way of emergency crews. Getting oxygen tanks and calling in an air trailer to recharge breathing cylinders.

Firefighters tackled the fire, initially confined to the second floor, from inside. Flames rose, hit the ceiling and spread, came out the windows. Burning debris fell from the ceiling and rained down the elevator shaft. A firefighter squatting on the floor realized he was next to two propane tanks. *Why am I here?* Men on tall ladders shooting water through second-story windows could see more propane tanks. A firefighter on a first-floor roof also saw tanks through a window and radioed a warning to others coming up the stairwell. The magnitude of the fire, the explosion, the propane tanks, clearly indicated arson. The ceiling sagged—roof collapse was imminent. The floor might go. Searing flame and pitch-black smoke. Decreasing visibility. The exposed steel columns could fail without warning. The interior attack was abandoned. Firefighters were ordered out.

Another department was asked to cover Fort Myers as additional units and numerous chiefs, including the city's top fire chief, were called in. A second aerial truck arrived. A pumper drew water from a hydrant, aimed its deck gun through a second-floor window and started laying lines for arriving trucks.

Kevin stopped at the end of Lorraine Drive for an after-action critique. "Everyone did a good job, but it could've been faster. Some things were sloppy." He yelled at Tom for kicking out the window, being loud, opening his tanks too soon, losing his gloves. "Get your act straight." Because of Tom's carelessness, Kevin was the only boy not wearing gloves. He wouldn't include Tom in everything anymore. Kevin also reprimanded Burnett for his paranoia, insobriety, dropping the tank. He added another LOC rule: "You have to be sober during anything we do."

* * *

Ruby woke at 4:45 A.M. to the chirping of Kevin punching in the burglar-alarm code. She found him unlatching the front door. "What's up?"

"Derek's at my window. I have to see what they need."

Kevin opened the door. "It's the boys, Mom. They need a place to crash. Can they spend the night?"

"Keep it quiet. Don't wake me."

At 5:00 A.M., Alice Henson arrived for work at Starvin Marvin and found empty propane tanks scattered. *Three missing.* She called the manager, then the sheriff, then her husband, a retired Fort Myers firefighter. He immediately saw the possible connection to the fire in progress downtown. *Propane tanks have serial numbers.* He called the department. Henson removed the surveillance tape. "Stolen propane tanks," she wrote on the label, and tossed it in the safe.

The fire burned fiercely, getting into hidden voids, unreachable places, gaps where new ceilings had been put over old. The roof and interior walls buckled; the second floor collapsed into the first, leaving a hole to the sky. Vented, the fire roared, flames shooting, spectacular for spectators and easier for firefighters, who sprayed a thousand gallons of water a minute into the building from an aerial truck.

Knocked down within forty minutes, the fire wasn't controlled until long after dawn. Unable to get the multilayer collapsed roof extinguished, they soaked it and let it burn itself out. Meanwhile, deputies volunteered to help firefighters hustling to find barricades; call in a media coordinator; bring in a backhoe; order a wrecker in case vehicles needed to be pulled back from the intense heat; close side streets; reassign officers from a thin early-Saturday shift to relieve those at the fire; check a suspicious vehicle; rustle up a Polaroid from the sergeants' office back at the station; partly reopen U.S. 41; corral pedestrians, bicy-

clists and sightseers; release an ambulance standing
by; move a chief's car parked in the way.

A Coke representative arrived.

"Was your building empty?" the fire chief asked.

"It was vacated two years ago, and we cleaned everything out."

"Were there propane tanks in the building?"

"No."

"There's propane tanks in there now."

Leaving for work with Kelly at 7:00 A.M., Ruby found
the boys asleep in her front room, Kevin passed out on
the floor with his feet crossed. *Strange.* Food and sodas
in the fridge, and no one took anything. Normally,
she'd have found an empty pizza box. Normally, someone would've played a computer game or turned the
TV up too loud, and she'd have called out for more
quiet: "People are sleeping." Normally, Kevin got them
blankets and pillows. None of that. What was up with
Kevin's friends, the ones he let in, in the middle of the
night?

He didn't tell the other boys, but Kevin specifically
wanted to bomb something April 19—the date his hero
Tim McVeigh blew up the Alfred P. Murrah Federal
Building in Oklahoma City, and the date the FBI in-
vaded the Branch Davidian compound at Waco. The fact
he didn't succeed until the early-morning hours of
April 20 led people to speculate he was celebrating
Hitler's birthday. They missed that Waco led to Oklahoma City, and Oklahoma City—at least in Kevin's
mind—to Fort Myers.

Kevin had talked up McVeigh and militias, and the
boys liked the idea of being part of something anti-
establishment, antigovernment. Kevin was disillusioned with the local militia, all talk and no action. So
he wanted the bombing to be April 19. But since
Derek was to be in his audience, the time Derek left

work thwarted commemorating the exact anniversary. *Close enough.*

The two-alarm fire drew twenty-four firefighters, four engines, a ladder company and five other fire vehicles—not including ambulances, police cars and sheriff's cruisers. It closed U.S. 41 and lit up the night over Fort Myers. The smoke drifted for blocks, hanging over the Edison Estate and palm-lined McGregor Boulevard like B-movie fog. Three hours after the explosion, at 7:11 A.M., the fire was finally declared under control, and it'd be 3:00 P.M. before the last firefighter left.

Though the earlier acts were individually petty, Kevin had already inflicted more than $100,000 of damage, not counting the cost in time and manpower to police, other agencies and insurance companies. Official estimates tended to be conservative, rarely approximating replacement costs. The fire department pegged the damage to the Coca-Cola building at another $100,000, a figure the state fire marshal's office later doubled, meaning Kevin's economic toll on Lee County now exceeded $300,000.

With the Coke bombing, Kevin hit the heart of Lee County. He dominated the front page of the newspaper and led every TV newscast. A success in his twin goals for the Lords of Chaos: wreaking havoc, making headlines.

CHAPTER 14

"Not Playing Anymore"

About 1:30 P.M., Saturday, a state fire marshal's investigator met a Fort Myers police detective and started work in the gutted Coke building. The fire marshal found four pairs of twenty-gallon propane tanks with open valves. *Arson.*

The fire drew the attention of at least six law enforcement agencies. The old bottling plant was in the city, in police jurisdiction. The fire was deliberate, prompting a fire department investigation and triggering the involvement of the state fire marshal. A bomb was used, bringing in the feds, in the form of the Bureau of Alcohol, Tobacco and Firearms (ATF). Deputies were investigating the propane tank thefts, because they occurred in unincorporated Lee County. The use of liquid propane (LP) gas brought in yet another agency, the state's little-known Bureau of LP Gas Inspection.

Coca-Cola was the coming of age of the Lords of Chaos. The bombing gave the group credibility—to its members and to the increasing number of outsiders hearing rumors.

Kevin saw his followers as children who didn't believe

they could do the things they saw on TV—armed robberies, arson, bombings. He'd proved otherwise. Pete
took the lesson to heart, his fantasy world emerging into
reality through the absurdly detailed Hardee's plan.

Hardee's

Pete's robbery plan was closer to the elaborate, thorough preparations he felt the LOC should make. If
Kevin wanted to do an armed robbery, Pete would
apply his meticulous mind to planning and encourage
other members of the group to do the same. He'd
impose order on the LOC. After hundreds of sketches
and dozens of penmanship exercises, Pete found a
way to bring his dreamworld to life. The LOC was a
bridge across which his dark visions could come, born
as arson, animal cruelty, robbery, bombing and—
finally—murder.

In a school notebook, Pete drew up an objective and
step-by-step instructions for the Hardee's robbery. He
sketched the building layout, including camera posi-
tions. "The minute gun is exposed the agents have the
danger of being on camera." He wrote paragraph
profiles of each employee, predicting robbery reactions. Estimated the take at up to $1,000, to be split
equally between Pete and Kevin, with $50 thrown to
Derek for "climate control." The plan called for "Oscar
caliber acting and cast iron testicles." Pete would work
the drive-in window. Dressed in black, skin covered,
Kevin would pull up and "rob" him at gunpoint, while
Derek, back-line cook, distracted other employees.
Pete would feign shock, "hysterically screaming."

One pregnant employee "will crack when weapon
is exposed." One employee ("dimwitted spick")
shouldn't resist—but "if confronted don't hesitate
to kill." Another employee sympathized with the LOC

and could be counted on for pretending panic as a distraction.

Saturday afternoon, April 20, 1996, Disney World

Another plan was born in Kevin's bedroom. RHS seniors would join thousands of kids bused in for Grad Nite at Walt Disney World in Orlando. Kevin was *supposed* to be a senior. He'd get a ticket somehow. Since he probably couldn't get away with riding a school bus, he'd find his own way. At first, the boys planned to get drunk. Kevin would sneak in liquor. It'd be funny to steal Disney character costumes, Burnett suggested. Run around, kick little kids in the butt, give people wedgies.

"How would you get 'em?" Kevin said.

"Hell, just hold 'em up at gunpoint in the bathroom and take their stuff," Burnett said.

It escalated: "If you got guns, why not run around shootin' people?"

At first, everybody thought that a big joke. But soon Kevin was talking about knocking out a Disney character, wearing the costume, putting a silencer on the gun.

"Imagine one of the Rescue Rangers coming out shooting people," Chris said. He imitated gunshots. Talked like one of the animated chipmunks.

Tom was struck by Chris's enthusiasm. *My God, that boy's crazy.* Pete just sat there, saying little.

Kevin started talking about blowing things up with dynamite. He could escape by going down in the tunnels under the park and acting crazy, telling people he was digging for gold. There was talk about *parachuting* into Disney World.

"I can do it," Derek said when Kevin later asked him to arrange a Grad Nite ticket. Derek didn't know

Kevin's plan for the theme park. He had his own ideas, and they didn't include the Lords of Chaos. He was going to party. He wasn't scheduled to be on the same bus as the others. If they found him anyway, he'd lose them in the crowd. Pete and Chris were no asset when it came to attracting girls.

Saturday, April 20, 1996, 6:00 P.M.

Kevin watched the local news, ecstatic, the bombing of the Coke plant leading the day's stories. The mission had been a complete success and a huge rush, an adrenaline surge better than any drug. The subject brought a glow of pride. *Six hours. It burned six hours.*

He called Mom at the pawnshop, impatient. "I want to drive over to Burnett's." His suspended license was infuriating.

"Have Burnett or someone pick you up."

"I can't get them to."

Ruby was busy with a customer. "I can't talk." She hung up. Kevin called back a couple of times, to no avail: MOM GROUNDS TERRORIST BOMBER. He took the Yota anyway, picking up Chris, then stopping by Tom's.

"We going to Burnett's?" Tom said as they pulled out of the driveway.

"There's something I gotta take care of first." Kevin had turned toward Burnett's to mislead Tom's parents. Now, taking the Orange River loop, he backtracked to Palm Beach Boulevard, where he'd spotted a black Toyota he wanted.

At Hardee's, Pete brought Derek up to speed. The fast-food restaurant would be robbed tonight. "Kevin's supposed to be coming to the drive-through in a stolen vehicle. When I open the window, he'll hold a gun and act like he's robbing me. Make sure you keep the other employees distracted in the back."

Kevin didn't attempt the black Toyota—too many people around. On the way to Burnett's, he swerved out of his lane. A Fort Myers police officer pulled him over at 11:00 P.M.

A Motorola radio mount was thrown in the pickup bed near a piece from a steering column. In the Yota's cab, the loaded Mossberg lay on the floor. A dent puller. Miscellaneous ammunition—including armor-piercing .223 rounds—on the floor and in the glove box. A black Zippo. The No Fear jacket and a No Fear T-shirt (NO SCARS, NO PROOF). A piece of black cloth with eyeholes cut in it. Gum remover. A knife. Car theft souvenirs. A miniature flashlight Kevin used when stealing vehicles. The Yota was a virtual roaming crime scene. It was only when the officer seemed about to notice a green leafy substance in a cup wedged near Kevin's seat that he felt a twinge of apprehension. So he deliberately drew the officer's attention to the dent puller, volunteering an explanation for a tool associated with car theft in hopes he'd fixate on that. Kevin understood the damning evidence of theft, vandalism, arson and robbery meant nothing to the officer, who likely wouldn't even notice most of it unless Kevin gave him reason to search the cab. Only a failure to summon the appropriate nonchalance would trigger the cop's antennae.

There was nothing, though, that Kevin could do about his driver's license. A routine radio check showed it suspended. He was arrested. Under the circumstances, it was best to yield to the charge without a fuss. No need for the cops to look closely at the Yota. No need for them to see the engine, frame and cab VINs didn't match. No need for them to look at the VIN on the bed, which would show it was manufactured six years after the truck's registration. No need for some expert to notice missing VIN plates and missing seat-belt decals and start wondering what year, exactly, this supposed 1980 truck was made. No need for them to wonder how there could be only 25,244 miles on the odometer of a sixteen-year-old truck. No need for them to look closely at the lock on the driver's door or the telltale marks around the ignition or the stolen tires.

Chris and Tom took the Yota to Lorraine Drive. "Kevin's been arrested. The officer's holding him at McDonald's until you get there."

At McDonald's, the officer told Ruby and Kelly he had to book Kevin into jail. At the Lee County Jail, Ruby learned bond would be $500 cash. She and Kelly got it from the pawnshop.

Sunday, April 21, 1996

It was 4:30 A.M. by the time a furious Ruby bailed her son out of the jail. If he was *ever* arrested again, there was no point calling or writing: She wouldn't help— a threat Kevin would remember. He was furious about the arrest and irritated by the inconvenience to Mom. It was a horrible comedown after the bombing, but it strengthened his resolve to plunge into what he wanted to do, to get it on: "I have plans for the Lee County Justice Center and Lee Memorial Hospital."

Kevin developed an elaborate scheme for the justice center. A towering, nearly windowless fortress dominating downtown—in 1996 one of only a few buildings that gave Fort Myers a skyline—the justice center housed the courts and the jail. Inspired by the opening scene of *Heat,* where De Niro and crew use a stolen ambulance in a crime, Kevin dreamed of hijacking an ambulance or one of the vans that carried inmates along Dr. Martin Luther King Jr. Boulevard to the stockade. Filling the vehicle with propane tanks, he would drive it—lights flashing—to the jail sally port, wait for the door to open, light a fuse and walk away. He also wanted revenge against the officer who arrested him. He wondered how he might use a stolen laptop to hack into the cop's files.

LANDMARK BUILDING LOST, the headline blared from the front page of the Sunday *News-Press* above a picture of the inferno visible in newspaper-vending machines across a five-county area. "Fire guts former Coca-Cola plant. . . . Memories go up in flames." . . . "It looks like structurally it'll be ruined," a city council member pronounced. TV news reports were satisfying, but newspapers were souvenirs, portable reminders that Kevin could tuck in corners of the Yota and stash on his bedroom dresser. He started avidly following the paper, clipping stories, yearning for more front-page attention.

About 11:00 A.M., Burnett's phone rang. "Did you see the newspaper?" Kevin said. "I told you it'd make headlines. It's great. I jacked off all over it."

Alva

Kevin, Chris and Derek hung out at Lorraine Drive. "We got to think of more things to do," Kevin said.

Derek brought up the Alva Country Diner, rehashed his falling out with Emory Lewis. Lewis had struck a nerve. Insulting his family was a cardinal sin.

He'd been in PE with Pete and Chris. Called out of class, he was given a pass to take a call. His mother was crying: Lewis had called her, impatient about rent. "My husband's out on a truck run," she'd said. "When he returns, we'll try to pay some of the back rent."

"Look," Lewis had said, according to Virginia, "I've been hearing this for a year or two now, and I definitely want you to get paid up or I'm gonna kick you out, you bitch. You're poor white trash."

Derek went back to class steaming. "I can't work at that job anymore. I can't be around this guy, because I don't know what I might do."

"That's as mad as I've ever seen him," Chris said.

When he got home, Derek called Lewis, who repeated the expletive and further opined that Derek's stepdad was lazy.

"You were too harsh on my mother. I'm gonna quit."

"Derek, you know why I was harsh on your mother is because they're always three or four months behind. It's time for them to catch up."

"I had enough. I'm sorry. I quit."

"Well—since you quit—you and your family gotta find a new place to live."

"I'm gonna get ya back," Derek said, missing the backhanded compliment, his work being what justified his family's continued stay in the house. He'd thought about not quitting to save his family eviction. Decided he had to go through with it. "He screwed my family over."

"We can pay him back," Kevin said. "We can rob his diner."

"We could get a whole lot of money," Derek said. "The guy walks out with a bag full of money."

"Yeah. That sounds easy. You think it up. You and Chris do all the maps and stuff. You have four days."

Kevin gave the pair military manuals from the gun shows. Derek's was *Explosives and Demolitions*. "Read it through and trade it with Chris." It would've suited Derek just fine not to have the darn book, but it was easier to accept than refuse. Threw it in his car. Never read it. Wasn't interested. While wary in the way he'd be wary of a rattlesnake, he was also drawn to Kevin, fascinated. *Kevin's something different, the things he does something different to do.* If Derek didn't like some of them, perhaps he could intervene, though he'd formulated no way to communicate his reservations.

Derek, with the Stars and Stripes on his own bedroom wall, was offended by seeing the Stars and Bars, the Confederate flag—Rebel flag to him—hanging from Kevin's ceiling. He suggested Kevin burn it, initiating a heated argument about racism.

An uneasy silence. Chris sat on Kevin's bed, Derek in a chair, leafing through Kevin's yearbooks. Kevin started fiddling with something. *Loading a handgun.* He cocked it and put it to Derek's forehead, full of malicious triumph, grinning, threatening. "Now what are you gonna do?" He chuckled.

Derek was silent. *What the fuck's he doing now? He's crazy, just plain-out crazy. You'd have to be crazy to shoot yourself.* Derek's view of Kevin shifted. He *was* a psycho. Derek wanted to back away, and yet he kept coming back. Years later, with all the time in the world to ponder all that happened, he still couldn't say why. Derek saw Kevin as smart and more mature than the others. He also saw him as evil. He saw Kevin's hatred of minorities, his lust to hurt, his nonchalance toward life. Kevin misused his smarts. Derek was ambivalent about Kevin, but the reverse wasn't true. To Kevin, Derek was furniture.

Monday, April 22, 1996

Now the newspaper reported the prospective buyer said the Coke plant could be salvaged. "We'll have to go back and finish the job," Kevin said.

At Chris's, Derek profiled diner employees, told what vehicles they drove, where Lewis parked, when the diner had the most money, when it closed, what day would be best for the robbery. Sketched a map. Chris took notes.

The diner generally closed at 8:30 P.M. Lewis left with the day's take—a couple of grand. The robbery would be something only the core four would execute. Kevin would hold up Lewis, Pete would be backup, Chris would be getaway driver, Derek would provide the inside intelligence to make the robbery a success.

"When are you working?" Chris said.

"Friday." Derek had a motive; if they struck Friday, he'd have an alibi.

Chris made another map, threw out Derek's, gave the plans to Kevin. "Just make it like a forceful robbery."

Kevin dismissed most of the plan. He just needed the map. Had his own plan: shoot Lewis in the head, drag him inside the Yota, decapitate him with a machete, put his severed head in a bucket of concrete and dump it in a river.

Also Monday, a Starvin Marvin manager played a surveillance videotape for a fire marshal. People on the forecourt were within camera range, though distorted. For a few seconds, two came up to the glass door and peered in. "I'll have to take the tape," the fire marshal said. He stopped by the Coke plant and put up an arson reward sign. Then he waited while a sheriff's specialist enhanced the surveillance video. Grainy, but you could see people. He planned to send stills to the FBI for further enhancement.

The fire marshal's office was so far ahead of the curve it might've bothered Kevin. A witness had described a blue four-by-four pickup with a chrome roll bar. Fire marshals theorized the bombing was related to the incident at the Hut restaurant and a string of other arsons. A Fort Myers police detective instinctively felt they were looking for teens. They should work with high-school resource officers, perhaps at a school east of Fort Myers, which meant RHS.

Seeking recruits, Pete, Chris and Derek boasted to selected school friends about the Coke bombing, LOC, Kevin and the planned diner robbery. And Tom started telling RHS students he was involved with some kind of militia. If anybody wanted to join, he'd introduce him to the leader. Word spread. Two kids came up to Derek at Hardee's. "Why are you in this thing?" . . . "Is it any good?" . . . "Can we get in?"

"I've no idea what you're talking about," Derek said. "I think you need to leave."

Kevin didn't like Tom running his mouth. "When we're out in the woods mudding, maybe Tom will get into a little accident," he told Burnett.

Tom wouldn't be the first boy to fall from a moving vehicle. It was tough for investigators to pin down whether such incidents were accidents or more sinister. Police faced that question in the death of Derek's brother.

Fred hit the asphalt at the intersection of Colonial Boulevard and Winkler Avenue in Fort Myers at 3:22 A.M. Paramedics found him in the road unresponsive, snoring. His chest barely rose and fell with labored, shallow breaths. His skin was ashen. The paramedics felt a deformity on the back of his skull. An ambulance took Fred to Southwest Florida Regional Medical Center.

A friend said Fred was asleep on the backseat. The car was going thirty to forty miles per hour when a door somehow swung open and he fell out, striking his head.

A Fort Myers police officer estimated the car was going sixty miles per hour. He thought Fred fell while *trying* to get out, perhaps trying to climb up on the roof and back in the other side in a stunt known as car surfing, popularized by *Teen Wolf* with Michael J. Fox. Officers found a bottle of pills, raising suspicion that drugs were a factor, and gave them to the Florida Department of Law Enforcement (FDLE) for analysis. It took about a week to identify them as ephedrine—speed.

Another possibility: Fred was pushed.

CHAPTER 15

The Alva Country Diner

"You got to meet my friends," Burnett was saying.

Brad Young had hired on as a Mabry Brothers Electric trainee. Burnett sometimes gave him rides, shared a joint, had him over to eat. Brad had the new job and a new apartment; he could use new friends. "I just moved back from California," he said. "I've got one friend." He meant best friend Craig Lesh.

"We're a crazy bunch." Burnett said. "Have you heard of the Coke building? Do you know who did it?"

"Let me guess: you?"

"Me and my boys." Burnett considered Brad a potential LOC recruit. "Don't tell nobody, but that was us—the LOC."

"What does that mean?"

"Lords of Chaos."

"Whatever," Brad said. *Like he's king of destruction or something. I oughta tell the cops.*

Brad dropped out of RHS on his birthday, with just two credits to go, and got a job as a mechanic. Seventeen and hotheaded, he thought he didn't need to go to school. A mistake, he quickly realized. Moved to California. He had a muscular build and blondish brown hair, worn in a ponytail in California, where he was into the surfing scene. Returning to Southwest Florida, Brad cut his hair short and usually wore a ball cap to fit in with the East Fort Myers crowd.

Brad smoked pot, but not obsessively, and he was considering quitting. He'd already quit drinking. He went to night school at RHS to make up those credits and graduate. Burnett also was trying to earn his GED in night school.

Brad had just moved into a second-floor apartment. Exterior stairs led to a metal door above Palm Beach Depot, a used-car dealership off the boulevard. Eye-catching because of its bright pink paint, it was next door to a railroad caboose turned restaurant. Sometimes Brad worked at the dealership detailing cars with Craig. He was the one Craig talked to when, as frequently happened, his life took a nasty turn. They'd known each other three years. On his own, Brad was sometimes so short of cash he missed meals. He'd go over to Craig's to eat. The boys talked to each other over CBs. "Little Yota" was Craig's handle. He loved Toyotas. Brad was "Little Hippie."

Born and raised in Lee County, Craig lived all his life on Chattanooga Drive, between the boulevard and the river. At RHS, he was in the pass program, with easier credit work, in one classroom all day except for phys ed, driver's ed and shop. Craig liked working with his hands. Like many East Lee County boys, he had a passion for four-by-fours and planned to open a customizing shop. Going four-wheeling and detailing cars at Palm Beach Depot didn't leave much time for study. He dropped out of RHS after sophomore year and enrolled in an alternative learning center that offered school credits for his job. He quit even that last-ditch effort, but now he, too, was taking RHS night classes.

Craig also smoked pot. The real trouble started when a neighbor introduced him to crack. It got bad enough to be the subject of neighborhood gossip in a city once featured in a TV documentary as "Crack Town USA." He stole his mother's jewelry and was jailed on a grand-theft charge. She later had the charge dropped. He even sold the treasured Toyota truck his father—who left the family when Craig was twelve—bought him. He'd over-come the habit in Georgia, where he'd gone to get away.

The light in Craig's life was on-again, off-again girl-friend Julie Schuchard (*shoe-shard*). They'd known each other for the seven years since the Schuchard family set-tled on Chattanooga Drive. Almost the girl next door, she lived on the same side of the same street. They'd dated on and off since seventh grade. Julie had a daugh-ter. Craig loved that little girl. *She should've been mine.* The only thing he cared about as much as Julie and her daughter was another Toyota four-by-four, which he worked on at her house. Julie's father bought it for Craig, who was paying him back. It wasn't leaving the house until he'd done so. In a pinch, Craig would choose Julie over the pickup.

Tuesday, April 23, 1996

Fort Myers looked to seasonal visitors even for its heroes and found them in Thomas Edison, Henry Ford and Harvey Firestone, famous friends who wintered there. The three were memorialized in a larger-than-life, ill-proportioned statue called "Uncommon Friends," in downtown Centennial Park on the south bank of the Caloosahatchee. Giants of modern industry, they're incongruously portrayed in a Disney-like setting loung-ing around a campfire on an island ringed by sculpted ducks, frogs and water lilies.

Present-day uncommon friends Kevin, Pete, Chris, Derek, Burnett and Tom met at the park, which ran beside the river from a gracefully rotting abandoned commercial fishing pier a half-mile east to the Exhibition Hall, which would've been more at home among the World War II Quonset huts of Buckingham Field than as a downtown riverside landmark. The park was mostly well-kept grass. A small children's play area was dotted with structures made from wood and brightly colored plastic. A concrete pier, where couples watched spectacular sunsets, ran out between the mangroves. Picnickers sheltered beneath an open pavilion typical of Florida, where walls were optional, but a roof for shelter from the midday sun or late-afternoon thunderstorms was mandatory. A wide concrete walkway wound along the river. Periodically, the city or its businesses arranged a festival, boat show or concert, usually by some waning star. Junior League of Fort Myers "Taste of the Town." . . . Edison Festival of Light "Crafts on the River." . . . "River and Blues." Crowds gathered on the grass, and bands played under the pavilion. Arching high above was the Caloosahatchee Bridge, which bisected the park, carrying U.S. 41 over the river to North Fort Myers, the city's down-at-heel unincorporated sister. The constant thrum of tires on concrete and clicking of wheels crossing expansion joints buzzed overhead. Sitting on the grass, the boys had the park almost to themselves. Kevin pulled out the newspaper. "I'm glad it made the front page." He gestured at a photograph of the burned-out building. "What's wrong with this picture?" He pointed at the Coca-Cola sign above the entrance. "This needs to be destroyed. I want to go back and finish the job." He'd envisioned bricks blowing everywhere, the cast-concrete sign crashing from the facade.

Kevin talked up an idea for a series of bank robberies: split into teams, three teams of two. Create a series of distractions. Blow up the propane tanks behind Lee Memorial Hospital and by the police substation. Occupy police and firefighters. Take the focus off the robberies. Each team robs a different bank. Everything synchronized, just like *Heat*. With the

Coke bombing, the LOC had tied up several agencies, illustrating how effectively they could divert law enforcement and public safety.

Wednesday, April 24, 1996

"No connection found between suspicious fires." Kevin read a report about a blast at New Life Fitness World, an exercise center a block south of the Coke building. A trash-area fire heated a carbon dioxide cylinder, causing an explosion heard two miles away that blew metal chunks into the street. Kevin laughed. "Somebody's trying to beat us. We're gonna have to do something."

Thursday, April 25, 1996

At Lorraine Drive, Kevin told Chris and Derek they'd steal a getaway car for the Alva Country Diner robbery. When Burnett and Tom arrived, the boys piled into Derek's car, the beat-up old Chevy Cavalier almost bursting with Kevin, Derek and Tom crammed in the back and Chris and Burnett up front.

Chris pulled up beside a Dumpster one hundred feet from Palm Beach Interstate Motors. Kevin and Derek got out, wearing gloves. Kevin liked stealing late-1980s Toyotas. They took him less than a minute. The back window of a black Toyota four-by-four pickup was already smashed. Kevin reached in and unlocked the doors.

A Fort Myers police car drove by. Derek jumped in the pickup's passenger seat. Kevin yanked out the ignition, stuck a screwdriver in and got the truck going. He met up with the other boys at a dirt lot next to a store off Buckingham Road. "Follow me. I want to stash the truck in some woods out toward Lehigh," he told Chris.

Kevin ran over some stop signs and got the Toyota

stuck on palmetto bushes. The four-wheel drive didn't work. The boys decided to retrieve it the next morning.

Kevin gave Derek $70 and told him to buy him a Grad Nite ticket for the senior trip to Disney World. "Find someone. Get the ticket."

Kevin had called an RHS senior who was advertising a Grad Nite ticket for sale. Since he wasn't in school, he couldn't buy the ticket directly. It was Derek who procured it for him. When a teacher said it couldn't be bought on Kevin's behalf, Derek got another student to pose as the buyer. For $70, he secured the ticket.

Friday, April 26, 1996

Pete, Chris and Derek skipped school. They gave Kevin a ride to the Lee County Justice Center to pay the ticket he got the night he was arrested.

At Jerry's Diner, they discussed the upcoming robbery. Derek couldn't do it—he needed his alibi. Chris couldn't do it—he was short, fat, easily described. It fell on Kevin and Pete, who was apprehensive. Still, he felt a thrill, which spurred him on. He anticipated a $2,000 to $3,000 take, from what Derek said.

"Make sure no one's hurt," Derek told Kevin, wishing he could threaten or scare Kevin into not hurting anyone. *Not much I can do.*

The boys stopped at a hardware store—where Kevin bought PVC pipe, copper tubing and black paint—then returned to Lorraine Drive. In the garage, Kevin put a Ruger 10/22 magazine-fed semiautomatic rifle up against the washing machine and fashioned a homemade silencer, spray-painting it black to match the gun.

He and Pete went to the backyard. Kevin put a piece of garbage bag around the ejector to catch the shells. Fired twice into the ground. Pete fired a shot. Maybe muffled enough that bystanders wouldn't immediately recognize gunshots. Much later, an ATF report would characterize Kevin's silencer as "crude and amateurish" and tests of the rifle with and without the device would find a negligible effect on noise.

To Chris, the robbery was about money. To Derek, it was revenge. Pete was in it for the thrill. As ever, Kevin's real motives were obscure. Whatever the others believed, he wasn't going to all this effort for no reason: he intended to kill Lewis. Making the silencer was a step closer to realizing his killing fantasies.

Kevin and the others went to retrieve the stolen pickup, jerking it with the Yota and Pete's car. No good. They were running behind schedule. Pete locked his keys in the car. Knowing the dangers facing unattended cars in the Lehigh woods, Chris stayed behind to guard it while Kevin drove Pete home to get his spare keys. The pair came back, opened up the car; they went to Lorraine Drive, gathered guns and camouflage clothing.

Pete drove. Chris sat up front loading .22 rounds into a banana clip. *We still don't know whether he's gonna do this guy or not,* he thought. *Hard to tell with him.* Kevin had picked the .22 in case he decided to shoot Lewis, believing professional killers favor the caliber. Kevin sat behind Pete loading the Combat Commander. Chris would have the Mossberg.

The boys stopped at a Handy convenience store. Pete filled a gas can. If Kevin had to cap this guy, he'd take his vehicle out in the woods and burn it. They drove to a volunteer fire department lot and pulled on their camouflage clothes and hats. A little after 8:30 P.M., Chris drove up behind the diner, turned out the lights, drove up closer, dropped Kevin and Pete off, backed up and waited near a semi. Kevin and Pete hid. Lewis came out. They pulled the masks over their faces.

* * *

Lewis was setting up his start-out pouch for the following day. He needed fives. The seventy-one-year-old diner owner took a $100 bill from the cash register and went out to get change from a pouch in his vehicle. Normally at this time, he carried the day's receipts. This night, he had only $100.

The Alva Country Diner was vulnerable right on State Road 80. Anyone could pull off the cross-state highway, rob and be gone. But Lewis never had been robbed and still kept cash in his vehicle. The red Chevrolet Blazer was parked under a carport out back. When he opened the door, two masked men walked up, the first with a pistol, the second with a rifle. It was dark, and Lewis couldn't see much.

Kevin was caught off guard. He planned to climb a ladder leaning against a copper freezer under the carport to take a good shot. *Whack his fuck-ass.* "Hey man, come here," Kevin said to Pete. "Switch guns with me." Pete held out the silenced rifle, but now here was Lewis coming around the side of his truck. "Fuck," Kevin said. He wasn't in position and had the wrong weapon. The Combat Commander would alert the whole community. What was Lewis going to do? *Is he fixing to get in and haul ass?* If he did, they'd fail completely. Kevin had to act. He jumped out from behind the truck. Pointed the Combat Commander. Pete stood back, pointing the 10/22 with the homemade silencer. He noticed Lewis wasn't carrying a money bag. They'd blown it.

Kevin did the talking. "Give me the money."

Lewis handed over the $100 bill.

The plan shot, Kevin improvised: a carjacking. "The car keys. Give me your keys."

Lewis dropped two rings, a dozen keys. *What are they going to do with me?*

"Pick 'em up and show me the ignition key," Kevin said, hesitating, stumbling around with his words, shaky, agitated, in part because it was his first armed robbery, in part because he was so angry they blew the big hit.

"Just take it easy," Lewis said.

"Give me your wallet."

Lewis handed it over. Walked around the front of the truck back toward the building, eyes fixed on the two robbers.

"Jump in the car, Pete." Kevin backed onto Packinghouse Road and spun out in the direction of State Road 80, heading east.

A wall blocked Chris's view. It was dark, unlit, tree-shadowed. After a minute or two, he saw a Blazer peel out in reverse. Taking that as his signal, he headed to an abandoned Alva construction site, where they'd arranged to meet.

Driving the Blazer on back roads in parts of Lehigh that Pete didn't know, Kevin flew along the heat-warped asphalt, hitting bumps fast, sparks flying from the undercarriage, infuriated. "I know he had like three grand," he said.

They ended up at Cemetery Road, near Burnett's. Kevin and Pete had gotten $121 off Lewis. "Fuck," Kevin said. They went through the truck. In a bag, the pair found another $518.50 in small bills and change. Pete suggested they not tell Chris and Derek: they'd split the $121 between the four of them and the rest between themselves. Kevin and Pete shared a "good work" postrobbery hug.

The pair parked at the end of Burnett's road. Kevin hid the guns, masks and gloves in the forks of a live oak.

Smoking, the two walked to Burnett's. Kevin liked to have one of something after he pulled off a particularly satisfying stunt. One cigarette. One shot of whiskey. *A celebratory thing, like the hugging,* Pete thought. He was nervous: Kevin called him "Pete" during the robbery. He kind of liked smoking, felt it took the edge off his neuroses. *Cigarettes seem to calm me down a little bit.*

"We were out driving around, and my car run out of gas at the end of Cemetery," Kevin told Burnett's mother. "We need to go get gas."

Tom was over, watching TV. In the hallway, the boys told Burnett about the robbery. "It was great," Pete said. "It went well."

"We stole his truck but we only got one hundred twenty-one dollars," Kevin was saying. They had to find Chris. Would Burnett drive them? They'd look in the familiar hangouts. Didn't want to run the stolen Blazer around. They all piled into the Burnetts' Cadillac. They drove past the diner, finally to the pre-arranged meeting spot. No Chris. Drove by Hardee's.

Pete came running into the back of Hardee's, where Derek was working. "Kevin's pissed. The robbery didn't go as planned. We only got one-twenty. We had to steal Lewis's vehicle, because we couldn't get the Toyota unstuck. Kevin's really pissed. Make sure you go to his house afterward." *I'm getting blamed because* they *screwed up,* Derek thought. He watched out the back door as Pete left. Kevin pointed at him from the car. "When you're through, go over to my house. You better be at my house." Kevin sure looked pissed.

Chris took off his disguise. Unemployed, he was looking forward to his share of the loot. He sat for an hour. Worried, he started driving around, back past the diner. Saw two sheriff's cars—deputies talking with Lewis. Scared now, he kept looking. *Kevin and Pete will get picked up. I met 'em in the wrong place. Or they dipped out on me. Kevin's gonna be mad.* He drove to Burnett's. "Have they been here?"

"Yes," Burnett's mother said. They were out with her son getting the car. Always wavering in a no-man's-land between childhood, adolescence and adulthood, the Lords of Chaos just now were in slapstick kid mode, Chris on a wild-goose chase pursuing a lie told a parent. He went over to Cemetery. Kevin and Pete weren't there.

Meanwhile, not finding Chris, the boys stopped at Taco Bell.

Chris went back to Burnett's. "They weren't there."
"I'll page him," Burnett's mother said.

At Taco Bell, Burnett's pager went off. "Chris is at the house," Burnett's mother said, handing Chris the phone.

"Put Kevin on," Chris said.

"Where the hell have you been?" Kevin said. "What took you so long? Meet me at the end of my road."

Kevin *was* pissed. "We only got one-twenty."

We went through all that shit—carjacking, armed robbery, evading cops, all kinds of stress and pressure—for $30 apiece? Chris thought. *Bullshit.*

"I shoulda killed the old man," Kevin said.

Chris told his own story: "I got chased. Some rednecks followed me. I had to shake 'em off. Had to pull my gun." Kevin was tickled.

"We need to go back and get the guns. I hid 'em up in a tree, where I ditched the Blazer."

* * *

Burnett didn't boast about the robbery. He was afraid of Kevin and, to a lesser extent, the others. "You know too much," Kevin repeatedly told Burnett, who sometimes ate dinner at the Fosters and slept over. Thought spending time there would reassure Kevin he wasn't blabbing.

Sheriff's agents interviewed Lewis: Two people masked, gloved and dressed in camouflage—Boys? Men? White? Black?—robbed him in the dark. They took a $190 GTE cell phone, a $250 box of mechanic's tools, a white jacket, company checkbook, wallet, keys to his business, keys to his home, keys to his wife's Camaro, keys to his vehicle, a money bag and more than $500. And the vehicle. "Full tank of gas," said Lewis. "I just filled the damn thing up. They can go a long way."

"Anything else you can think of?"

"No . . . uh"—managing a laugh—"my first experience." Nothing about the robbers was familiar. Nothing reminiscent of anyone who'd ever been in his restaurant. It wasn't a promising start to a robbery investigation.

Derek's mother called him at Hardee's. He'd already arranged with her to spend the night at Lorraine Drive. She told him the diner had been robbed. All the money was taken. Derek went to Kevin's with a knife stuck in his waistband. Frightened by Kevin's threats, he focused on defending himself instead of thinking too hard about the discrepancy between the small amount of money Kevin said he got and what Lewis told his mother, although he asked about it.

"Lewis reported *all* the money stolen," Derek said, confused.

"We ought to go check the vehicle again and see if

we can find the bag he kept the money in," Kevin said. Pete went home to make curfew.

Kevin, Chris and Derek searched the Blazer for the presumed missing money bag. Derek following in his car, Kevin and Chris drove the Blazer back behind mosquito control, where teens met for the drag races.

Kevin wanted to flip the Blazer, but Chris dissuaded him. Kevin drove hard, doing doughnuts. A stolen vehicle was his own personal Disney ride, as much as a source of pirated parts or fodder for his chop shop friends. Kevin fired a round into the radio. They parked in the middle of an open field. Kevin worked on Derek to join in the vandalism. "Lewis talked bad about your mother. Lewis evicted your family."

Derek attacked the truck with a fishing club and a hammer. The boys beat the Blazer with sticks and stones. Kevin rammed it into rocks. Redlined the engine—pushing the revs beyond a safe level—until it blew. The Blazer was a mess—windows, radio, dials, steering wheel, seats, tires—everything trashed.

For the first time since he drifted into the LOC, Derek enjoyed himself. He liked bashing the truck, for the sheer destructiveness and because he was getting revenge, the one LOC activity he'd enjoy without reservation.

As the boys left, Kevin turned and fired the Combat Commander at the radiator. Derek was walking to the car. He jumped at the report. It was the same handgun Kevin had pointed at him. He told Kevin how he felt after Pete stopped by Hardee's. "I thought you were gonna kill me."

Sitting behind him in the car, Kevin kept messing with Derek, holding the gun to the back of his head, talking into Lewis's cell phone, making it sound as though he were instructing guys waiting in ambush to kill Derek. "We're coming up on you guys now. Make sure you get the guy in the driver's seat." Derek slammed on the brakes. Almost slid into a deep ditch on a curve on Buckingham Road.

It was easy to play these games with Derek. Fred was always there, reminding him a boy might die violently, mysteriously in the night. To Kevin, it was funny; to Derek, haunted by a ghost, it was deadly serious. "I was just playing around," Kevin said, though he was starting to contemplate killing Derek. "Get back to the house."

At Lorraine Drive, Chris and Derek stayed the night.

After Fred died, Virginia wrote the district medical examiner asking for a copy of the autopsy report. "If one teenager stops doing stupid, crazy nonsense and doesn't mix drinking, drugs and reckless stupidity after the loss of my child, maybe the pain I'm feeling will be justified," she wrote. She'd later learn drinking and drugs aren't necessary—reckless stupidity alone could inflict pain not unlike what she experienced when her oldest son died.

The medical examiner's office sent the report, which stated the cause of death was head trauma. Tests on blood drawn at the hospital before Fred died detected no drugs. He had a 0.04 blood-alcohol content, well below Florida's then 0.10 legal limit for drivers and equivalent to about two beers. He had blunt injuries to his head and neck, and scrapes and bruises all over his body, all explainable by a fall onto a hard surface from a rapidly moving vehicle and not consistent with a blow to the head. "Rear seat passenger; attempted to exit auto at high speed," the report concluded. The manner of death was certified accidental. Derek never accepted that verdict: Fred was murdered.

It was reasonable speculation. The conclusions of police and the medical examiner didn't mean Fred *wasn't* murdered. They meant neither police nor the medical examiner had any *evidence* of murder. Based on the information available, accident was a reasonable conclusion. Two things reinforced Derek's belief: the discovery Fred was neither drunk nor—despite the speed—on drugs, and a troubling discovery in the car. The boys Fred was with had driven to the hospital, then to Derek's, where they left the car. Derek and his mother searched it and found a bloody blanket and a bloodied metal baseball bat. The family didn't submit the blanket and bat to a law enforcement agency. They assumed the blood was Fred's. They hadn't done anything about it, but they couldn't shake it off.

Kevin lay awake. With the vandalism, bombing and robbery, he was on a near-constant adrenaline high. Hell, it was an addiction better than any drug. Between LOC activities by night and work by day, he was getting minimal sleep. He pushed himself to exhaustion and beyond, and loved it. He often sat or lay awake hours plotting. Wanted a better plan for the Hardee's robbery. Pete's written plan—pulling up to the drive-through window, holding a gun to Pete, faking an armed robbery, taking the cash drawer—was simple, but it wasn't good enough. They wouldn't get that much money from the drive-through cash register. Derek would be working. Kevin had *two* soldiers inside the restaurant, not one. And Chris had worked there. He was familiar with the place. If they went *into* the restaurant, they could get *all* the money. The higher risk was offset by having friends on the inside. Not that he was opposed to risk.

CHAPTER 16

Going to Disney World

Saturday, April 27, 1996

In the morning, Kevin broke Lewis's $100 bill, giving Chris and Derek $30 each.

Was it worth it for $30? Chris and Derek wondered. *Why didn't Kevin and Pete get more money? How did they screw up that bad? Are they holding out?*

Chris and Derek headed home along State Road 80. An elderly couple had pulled their Lincoln Continental over near Parker-French Ace Hardware. They had a flat. *They don't know nothing about changing tires,* Chris thought. *Mightn't be strong enough to jack up the car.* An opportunity to be a Boy Scout again. The boys stopped. Jacked up the car. Changed the tire. The couple said three sheriff's cars drove by, and they tried to flag them down, but they wouldn't stop. They'd been waiting an hour. As thanks, the couple gave them $5 for sodas. Derek dropped off Chris and headed home.

Despite his enjoyment of the vandalism and retribution, a typically conflicted Derek was irked Lewis had been carjacked. He was only supposed to be threatened.

Derek had helped Kevin steal the Toyota specifically for
the robbery. The boys then went out screwing around
when he was working and got it stuck in the woods.
Made a halfhearted effort to retrieve it, too. He felt antipa-
thy toward Kevin from the start, an ambivalence that
made his relationship with the leader different from
that of Pete or Chris. He was growing more uncomfortable about being threatened, Kevin's lack of limits,
the questions over the money.

After the boys were gone, Kevin stopped at Burnett's. Tom was watching Burnett feed his animals.
Kevin flashed a wad of cash.

"That looks like more than just the hundred twenty-
one you were talking about," Tom said.

Kevin put his finger to his lips: "Shhhh." Kevin could
be conspiratorial even with people he didn't especially like. He wanted people to know he had secrets—
especially humorous secrets about manipulating others.
What was the point in screwing Chris and Derek out
of their share without an audience?

Sheriff's deputies found Lewis's mangled Blazer
where the boys left it off Sunniland Boulevard behind
mosquito control, wallet and credit cards scattered on
the ground. The company checkbook was in the truck.
Nothing else was recovered. It was towed to the Alva
Garage in lamentable condition, a hole shot in the
hood, every window shattered, extensive body damage.
The Blazer was valued at $11,500 when stolen, $2,000
when recovered. Lewis was reimbursed by his insurance
company; he never recovered the stolen cash.

Brad wasn't home when Burnett brought Kevin by
at 11:00 P.M. to meet him. Craig was using the apart-

ment. They hung. Listened to music. Went out to mosquito control. Joined the hundreds who gathered for drag racing. Downing Budweiser as he did every Saturday night, Craig spent the evening with Kevin. Craig and Kevin discovered some things in common, such as similar Toyota trucks. "I could help you out with some brakes," Kevin said.

Later, after Craig was drunk, he and Kevin rode along Orange River Boulevard, lying in the bed of Burnett's pickup. Dropped Kevin home about 1:30 A.M.

It was the last near-normal teenage weekend night Kevin would have, a night of no crime, a reprise of just being a wild kid, meeting new people like Craig, lying in the pickup bed, flying along the boulevard under the stars, a little chilly, trees rushing by.

Sunday, April 28, 1996

As it got dark, Kevin and Burnett told Craig about the plan to go to Disney World. A murderous Mickey Mouse, Kevin would go hunting in the park. "The gun's really silent," he said. "Nobody will be hearing anything. People will just be dropping dead all over." The rest of the boys would go around and tear shit up, create a distraction, cause chaos while Kevin killed. "Just shoot every nigger we see."

Aspects of the LOC appealed to Craig. He liked the rejection of colors, bandannas, even the word "gang." It seemed if they had any flag, it was the Rebel flag. He had nothing against a little marijuana, breaking some windows, rolling a car. Of particular appeal was that the LOC seemed above consequences. But the escalating crimes troubled him.

Craig wasn't one of Kevin's favorites, but he was a perfect candidate to expand the Lords of Chaos. Unfettered by many emotional or material ties. A bored high-school dropout disillusioned with his minimum-wage job. An addictive streak proved by the tussle with crack cocaine. A criminal streak proved by stealing his mother's jewelry to buy crack. A failed romance. Perfect fodder for Kevin's forceful sense of purpose.

Kevin shifted his shape depending on who he was with, easier in twos or threes than in larger groups. It was easy to play to Craig in front of Burnett. Kevin could be racist Rebel redneck, white country boy, criminal mischief-maker. Others, like Derek, were a little harder to play to, especially in groups. The effort was frustrating and tiring. Kevin hadn't emphasized shooting *blacks* to Chris or Tom. It wouldn't play with them. There were interracial marriages on both sides of Chris's family. His few friends included blacks who'd stayed at his house, and a black boy had been his best friend in Georgia. Tom also had black friends and teammates.

Monday, April 29, 1996

Word was spreading about the Lords of Chaos. A dark vortex, swirling, expanding, threatening to engulf others, pull them down—the unwary, like Derek, the naive, like Chris, the bored, like Pete—anyone who lacked a moral center. Other kids at RHS were being approached to join. Pete boasted in third-period physics: "We robbed the diner owner and took his Blazer. We had guns." Some boys were getting used to this: Pete, Chris and Derek had been talking about doing "something big" all month.

"We burned the Coke plant," Derek had told two buddies as he drove them home from school. "There's a thousand-dollar reward out. The FBI's looking for me. If you tell anybody, we'll have you killed. Kevin will do it. He killed before, and he won't hesitate to kill again. This is just the beginning. We just started."

* * *

Jesse Mitchell, an RHS senior who considered Chris a best friend, spent hours playing video games with him and sometimes stayed over, sat on Chris's mother's car watching Chris pace, riled up like a preacher. "This is deep stuff," he was saying. "I don't know if I should let you in on this." Said he had a $50,000 reward on his head. Jesse heard about the scavenger hunt. A version of the diner story that included only Chris and Kevin. And about the Coke building. Chris was across the street: Boom. . . . Flames. . . . Some guy was walking by, fell down, said, "Whoa, what the heck was that?" wiped himself off, kept walking. In Chris's retelling, the destruction took on a dark, comic quality, his invention of the falling guy a touch of Gothic slapstick. Chris also outlined a new plan for Hardee's in which Kevin would take Derek hostage with a knife to his throat. The money they got would pay for Grad Nite. Jesse laughed at Chris's code name, Slim.

Much later, Jesse said he didn't drift into the LOC because he had a girlfriend. He'd look back with a nagging sense he might've done something to intervene. He'd feel Chris was conflicted, sometimes wanting to do something with him as an excuse to stay away from the rest of the Lords of Chaos. "What the heck, let's go to the movies," Chris had said one night, and Jesse sensed he was avoiding some LOC activity. *These aren't Chris's actions,* he thought, sensing some chemistry, something to do with power and the group, bigger than Chris, a composite thing that acted differently than any one of its individual members would alone.

"It's crazy," Jesse said. "Someday you're gonna get caught."

"You can't turn me in," Chris said. "Don't even think about it, 'cause we have connections." He sat on Jesse's truck, with a piece of ice, drawing a symbol on the hood of the beat-up eleven-year-old rusty brown Chevy Blazer.

Jesse figured Chris's group of friends—and that's what he saw it as, hearing neither the word "gang" nor the name "Lords of Chaos"—didn't know Chris was telling him this stuff. He'd known Chris four years and thought he detected something different when he boasted, a bad-boy attitude. It was weird. And this Kevin, whom Jesse had never met, this Kevin had a gun, and it seemed if Chris and the others in the group needed help, they could call Kevin. "If anyone's messing with you, just tell us. We'll take care of it."

Not a lot of people bother me, Jesse thought. *He's offering for them to be almost a bodyguard. This can't be serious.* "You're joking, aren't you?"

"Yeah, I'm joking, I'm joking."

Jesse couldn't believe it. None of it fit the lightness of their friendship, the endless jokes, the teasing and poking fun. No, Chris couldn't be serious. This had to be just another new if darker twist to the humorous banter of their high-school years. "Oh," Jesse said, momentarily convinced it was all a sidesplitting joke, "that's a great movie, if you're gonna make it a movie."

Faintly uneasy, a little scared for Chris, Jesse felt, *Chris is with me, out of danger this moment, safe. We're having a good time.* It was the last time the boys had such simple fun. Jesse's company on silly drives, hanging outside Circle K and at his house, would come to look a lot to Chris like the Texas Panhandle came to look to Kevin—it wasn't much at the time, but, boy, could it make a person wistful looking back on it.

CHAPTER 17

Tantrum

Tuesday, April 30, 1996

License suspended, Kevin copped a ride with other carpenters back up Interstate 75 from the day's work. "I'm not gonna be working Wednesday," he said. "I'll be at my lawyer's trying to get my driver's license back."

Northbound traffic slowed, stopped, crawled forward again, drivers rubbernecking an incident across the median. Flashing lights on the southbound lanes. A sheet covering something on the hard shoulder. A tall, thin man in jeans and a T-shirt scribbling in a notebook as a state trooper talked.

Kevin strained to see past the buddy driving him home, catch a glimpse of whatever had happened across the interstate. Dragged on a Marlboro Red, thinking about the evening ahead, how to pull off a robbery. The previous evening, he, Chris and Derek walked around Edison Mall. At Dillard's, they were given Grad Nite pins. If they were spotted wearing the pins ("Dillard's is your Walt Disney World Grad Nite '96 Fashion Headquarters") at Disney

World on Saturday, they could win prizes. Today, they'd return to the mall and pick out Grad Nite clothes. Which, Kevin thought, with enough people to create a distraction, there was no reason to pay for.

About 4:30 P.M., Kevin called Mom at the pawnshop, as was his habit. Called Cindi, suggested shooting cans. "What are you doing? You want to hang out?"

"I'm going to Moore Haven. If you want to come, you're more than welcome."

It was her birthday, though Kevin had forgotten. She was going sixty miles to the small inland town on Lake Okeechobee for a party.

"No, that's all right," he said, feeling rejected.

Burnett drove Brad home after work. "Why don't you come meet my friends?" he said. Hoping Kevin might think Brad a good recruit, Burnett continued working on him. "Did you hear what happened out in Alva?" he said, a reprise of their Coke conversation. "We hijacked a car. Just don't tell Kevin I said anything."

Kevin was eighteen, out of school, a working man. Yet here he was, living with Mom, leeching rides to work, failing community college, chronically short of money, frustrated in love. He needed a fix. Pete, Chris, Derek and a couple of their friends had descended on Lorraine Drive. "We got this many people, why don't we just *steal* some clothes?"

The six LOC members were joined by three potential recruits, including Brad.

"Hey, how's it going?" Brad remembered Kevin, who worked with his stepfather at Ken Bunting Carpentry, from Timber Trails, but this was the first time they'd really talked. Kevin encouraged him to stay paired up with Burnett, stick with night school, complete his GED, start at Edison Community College in the fall. "We're fixing to go rip off Dillard's," he said. "You wanna go?"

Brad didn't, but he was stuck with Kevin now. Burnett was his ride and didn't seem to have any intention of taking him home.

The first idea was the boys would pile up clothes, distract a Dillard's clerk, run out. Typically, Kevin worked up a more elaborate plan, with a smoke grenade he'd set off as a distraction. He showed off some grenades under the bathroom sink off Ruby's bedroom. "They're live." But what if the serial numbers could be traced? He'd buy one from Stanley's Army/Navy. "Go pick up Tom," he told Burnett. "Get some fishing line."

The boys stared at the olive drab canister in Stanley's Army/Navy. "Is it live?" Kevin said.

"Yeah."

Grimacing, Kevin counted out $35. Cash seemed to slip through his fingers as fast as he got it.

Chris bought a black ski mask with a couple of borrowed dollars. Still unemployed, he also was perpetually short of cash. Pete bought a switchblade with diner money. *Neat trinket.*

It was raining. Burnett, Tom and Brad showed up without the requested fishing line. "We got to go get some," Kevin said, annoyed his cohorts failed. "Let's go to K mart."

Pete pulled a Wite-Out pen from his backpack. "Smile," he wrote on the grenade. "Go fuck yourself," Kevin wrote.

At K mart, Kevin reeled off a couple of feet of fishing line, pocketed it and walked out. His plan: tie the lever down with the fishing line, pull the pin, insert a lit cigarette under the line to burn through it, releasing the lever and setting it off. He rigged it up in the parking lot. The boys caravanned to Edison Mall and congregated outside Dillard's.

"We're gonna need another license plate so nobody recognizes the car," Kevin said.

"If you need tools, here are my tools," Brad said. *That's as far as I'm willing to go.* Kevin fished out a cordless drill and told Burnett and Tom to get a tag. He'd put it on Derek's car for the crew's getaway. As usual, Chris would drive.

Burnett and Tom picked a tag on a dark blue pickup: KFC 20D in red letters. Reminded Chris of Kentucky Fried Chicken. *Neat.* Kevin took the tag off Derek's car. The ploy was a risk. It'd defeat witnesses—they'd get a bad tag number, and it likely would be gone by the time police started looking. But any officer who happened to call it in—one behind the car in traffic, for example—would have probable cause for a stop if the tag didn't match.

Derek pulled a jacket out of his car and put it on. "You got an inside pocket?" Kevin said. He slipped the grenade into Derek's pocket.

Burnett and Tom walked through Dillard's and wandered over to Camelot Music, where Tom bought a Smoking Armadillos CD. The others went looking for them.

"Come on, it's time."

Kevin was sitting on a bench, smoking a cigarette. "Get the cars ready. It's raining. I don't want the clothes to get wet."

Brad slipped away and walked around the mall. Went out and sat in Burnett's truck. His tools were getting wet. He wanted to leave.

"Look around for clothes you want and stand next to 'em," Kevin said. "I'll tell you after I got the grenade set up. Then grab what you want, walk around till it goes off."

A couple of clerks came over. "Can I help you?"

"We're looking for some clothes for Grad Nite," Derek said, brushing them off with the truth.

"Let's go ahead and do it," Kevin said. "Derek, open

your jacket." Kevin pulled out the grenade. Knelt. "Get ready, guys." Set the grenade on a shelf among stacks of men's jeans. "I'm lighting it now." The boys spread out. Kevin pulled the pin. The spoon flew off. The line wasn't correctly tied. No explosion. No fire. No smoke. Nothing. "Let's go," he said, angry. "It's a dud."

Kevin fumed. No one got any clothes. He paid $35 for a piece of metal. Robbed. "He's supposed to be a friend of the family and he sold me a dud." Pissed as he was, Kevin was secretly relieved. *It would've burned the skin off my arms,* he thought.

The boys went to Taco Bell.

"I spent thirty-five dollars on a piece of shit," Kevin said. "If it would've went off, it would've went off in my hand. I'm about ready to kill somebody. We can't go out like this, we've gotta destroy something. Let's go to Riverdale."

They headed out to their vehicles. "I still haven't been home," Brad said. To Burnett: "I want to go home." To everyone: "You can come over and see my place." The boys followed Burnett, sun setting in their rearview mirrors as the convoy headed to Palm Beach Boulevard.

About the time the boys left Taco Bell, Craig got off work. Went upstairs to Brad's. Nobody there. Walked home. He went to dinner at Sonny's, on account it was his mother's boyfriend's mother's birthday.

And an honor society induction was under way in the RHS auditorium. Plywood covered a broken window. After watching his son's induction, Jeremy Arnold, a self-employed chain-link fence contractor who was president of the band booster association, joined an ice-cream social in progress in the band room, about 8:30 P.M. His son was in band. His daughter was a mascot. Director Mark Schwebes, most of his band and a couple of incoming freshmen were there. Arnold stayed to help Mark clean up. When Mark was new, he'd called Arnold for advice about the band. The two hit it off pretty well, frequently shared dinner.

Craig was having a nightmare evening. He'd done the dinner to celebrate the mother's boyfriend's mother's birthday. Now they were driving past Brad's to go to the boyfriend's to eat cake, and, lo and behold, there was Burnett's truck and two other cars. He wanted to stop and talk with Burnett about truck parts, but his mother wouldn't let him on account of this whole boyfriend's mother's birthday deal. It sucked.

It also might have saved Craig's life.

Chris thought Brad was cool as fuck: the only person he knew with his own place. The boys listened to the radio, looked at car and porn magazines and—despite the LOC's secrecy rule—rehashed the Coke bombing. "I want to finish it off," Kevin said, still fixating on the incomplete destruction.

"Did you hear about Alva?" Kevin asked Brad.

"No," Brad said, not wanting to rat on Burnett.

Kevin recounted the story. He dropped a cigarette butt in a soda can and lit another smoke. "You got to make up your mind whether or not you want in," he told Brad. Though he remained ambivalent, Brad was given a new LOC name, "Haze."

They discussed the Hardee's robbery. Kevin explained how he'd changed Pete's plan. His wakeful scheming had produced something more complicated, but potentially more lucrative. They'd execute the robbery with a minimum of customers, right after the dinner rush, around 9:30 P.M., when registers would be at their peak. Chris would drop them off. Kevin would go in through the back, pretending to hold Derek hostage. The other LOC members who didn't work at Hardee's would rush in behind him.

They'd get everyone on the floor, including Derek. Pete would open all the registers—not just the drive-through one—and grab cash while Kevin cleaned out the safe. They'd steal an employee's car for their get-away. It had Quentin Tarantino potential now, something from *Pulp Fiction* or *Reservoir Dogs*. If anything went wrong, if anyone pushed an alarm or something, Kevin said he'd shoot.

Pete didn't like the idea. *That's a real pain-in-the-ass kind of thing to do: I don't want to go to the trouble.* But, still, he drew a map.

The manager could be a man or a woman. "The woman's pregnant, don't shoot her," Pete said.

"I don't care. Shoot them all."

Scary, Derek thought. Still, he went along. The boys were low on cash.

"I want to be a part of it," Burnett said. "Are there any niggers I could shoot?"

"I want to be a part of it, too," Tom said.

"No," Kevin said. Tom always did something to piss Kevin off: this time, he wouldn't get the chance.

"I want to make up for not getting anything at Dillard's," Kevin said, a spur-of-the-moment suggestion. "Let's go to Riverdale." It'd be a rerun of the first spree, vandalizing the auditorium. "Yeah," let's go out there," everybody said. "Let's go take care of Riverdale."

When Craig passed Brad's apartment on the way home, all the vehicles were gone. *No point stopping now.*

At RHS, Brad, Burnett and Tom made a cursory effort to find the others, then started mudding behind the school—churning up the mud with four-wheel-drive trucks like they did at Timber Trails.

* * *

Kevin, Chris and Derek parked near Pete's Nissan, southwest of the RHS auditorium. Derek stayed in the car. Kevin, Chris and Pete walked off around the track, climbed the bleachers, sat. Something going on. People hanging out. Cars parked. Night school? By 9:30 P.M., night school would be ending. The boys waited for everyone to clear out. "Let's vandalize the auditorium again," Kevin said. "Find something to break the windows."

Burnett's mud-plastered pickup spun, gripped, broke free, whipped around. They saw Derek and Pete's cars in the parking lot. Heard yelling in the bleachers. Parked and went up there.

"I want something to eat," Mark Schwebes said, tired of ice cream.

Jeremy Arnold looked at his watch: 9:35. "This late hour, we're probably gonna have to go down to Cracker Barrel. We need to hurry before they close."

The two locked up. Mark pulled out in his Bronco II. Arnold and his family followed a couple of minutes later.

"Let's go up to the school," Kevin said. "Who wants to go with me?" Pete, Chris and Tom stepped forward.

Not interested in breaking windows again, Derek stayed in the car. Bored and restless, he fiddled with the screws on the stolen tag. He unscrewed them, took the tag off, wiped it down, tossed it, put his own back on.

The boys went into the English department through an open door near the auditorium. Pete tore a soap dispenser off a bathroom wall. Kevin took a fire extinguisher and two staplers.

Kevin noticed Tom sidling toward a door. Motioned him into a classroom. "Come in here. . . . What are you doin'?"

"I'm fixin' to leave. I don't want to do this."

Kevin pulled the Combat Commander. "I'm sick of all of y'all punks backin' down and tryin' to get out of this, expecting me to do everything by myself, so it's always gonna come back on me."

"Stop," Tom said. He looked around. A bag of canned peaches incongruously sitting on a desk. "Here ya go, I got this." *I'm not gonna make it. He's gonna kill me. He thinks I'm the weak link, the one running my mouth around school.* "When you say something, you die," he said.

They returned to Pete's car, where Kevin wiped everything down with a rag. Pete handed out latex gloves he'd stolen from RHS.

Boards still covered the broken windows. Now they'd finish what they started. Kevin assigned Chris and Tom to carry stuff to the pay phone and wait. They started across the street.

"We ought to burn it, you know, since we didn't get nothin' at Dillard's," Kevin said, spontaneous again.

"I got gas in the back of my truck," Burnett said. He kept an old white plastic Clorox bottle full in case the Isuzu ran out.

"I need a rag," Kevin said. Burnett found him one, and Kevin stuffed it in the top of the bottle, like a Molotov cocktail. He'd light the rag and throw it through a window.

"Wait," Burnett said. "They know that's my truck. I'll go across the street."

Brad, who didn't want any part of any vandalism,

stayed with Burnett, the only one he really knew. Pete and Derek followed, moving their cars across the street into Riverdale Estates, where the Fosters once lived.

Kevin headed to the auditorium. Chris and Tom were standing by the pay phone.

Mark followed the long driveway through campus, turning past the gymnasium, looking across at the swimming pool, coming up to the auditorium, where he saw kids at the pay phone, an obvious place to go after band functions, meeting point for those waiting on rides. He turned into the loop in front of the auditorium, circled around, stopped next to the boys.

Brad got out of Burnett's pickup and started back across the street, tripping in a ditch, the other boys close behind. Saw Chris and Tom standing at the pay phone, staplers on top of the phone, fire extinguisher on the ground, Tom pulling on his gloves. Saw a Bronco II approaching. Kevin was nowhere to be seen.

"I know who that is," Derek said. "That's my band teacher, Mr. Schwebes. That's his Bronco."

Brad turned around. Didn't want to be seen. He'd been in Mr. Schwebes's class. Pete had no idea *who* the school's band director was, just saw a guy alone in a Bronco. The truck stopped, blocking his view of Chris and Tom. The boys decided to walk up to the basketball courts and back across the street so the teacher wouldn't see them.

Arnold was used to Mark's ritual. Sure enough, Mark was stopped beside a couple of boys. *Not band kids. RHS kids? A little short, fat kid, next to one a foot taller.*

* * *

Kevin was about to say "Let's go!" when he saw the Bronco. He ducked behind a concrete pillar. Peeked to see if it was going to stop. It did. Lean and tall, he ran fast across the street, right in front of a car, into the woods.

When the boy ran in front of his car, forcing him to choose between slowing or hitting him, and disappeared into the woods, Arnold paid more attention. That made three boys Mark had been dealing with, one of whom had run. Arnold tried to see where the boy went. The other kids were standing with their hands in their back pockets. Four more were at the basketball courts. The lights were on, but these boys weren't playing ball. They were huddled in a corner, apparently talking. He thought about getting out. *Well, they aren't band kids.* His family was getting hungry. Looked at his watch: 9:40. "Looks like he's got it under control. Let's go down to Cracker Barrel and get a table before they close."

Chris and Tom stood at the phone. Saw the other boys walking toward them from Riverdale Estates. As Mr. Schwebes went by, he glanced at them. They thought he'd drive on. He circled through the loop in front of the auditorium. Stopped beside them. Rolled down his window. "What are y'all doing?"

"Makin' a phone call," Chris said, with attitude.

"You're not calling; this phone doesn't work."

They knew that: they were the ones who had vandalized it. "We're just waiting on a ride." Chris fidgeted, trying to work the gloves off his hands behind his back. "We're waiting on a friend."

"Y'all need to wait somewhere else. You don't need to be hanging out here."

"This is where we told him to meet us."

Mr. Schwebes glimpsed someone running from behind a column. "Who was that?"

"We don't know." *He knows we're lying,* Chris thought.

Mr. Schwebes got out of the Bronco. Staplers on the pay phone. He looked down, saw the fire extinguisher. "Well, gee, where did this come from?"

"Oh, I don't know. We didn't see it."

"Why do you have your hands behind your backs?"

"Just standing here."

Mr. Schwebes saw the bag of cans. "What's that?"

"It was there when we got here. We're just now seeing it."

Mr. Schwebes glimpsed Tom's gloves. "Hold out your hands." Tom did. "Why do you have gloves on?"

Chris answered for him. "We like to wear gloves. Is it against the law?"

"Give me that stuff."

The boys peeled the gloves off and put them in the bag with the cans. Tom helped load the Bronco.

"Y'all need to find somewhere to go. If you can't, I'll take you up to Winn-Dixie."

"We know a guy across the street," Chris said, wanting to get the hell out of there. "We'll go to his house."

"Start walkin'. Use the phone over there."

The boys started across to the cars. The teacher started pulling away.

"What are you gonna do with the stuff?" Tom called after him. "You're not gonna report this, are you? Are you gonna turn us in?"

"Don't be surprised if Officer Montgomery calls you to his office in the morning." Looking at Chris. "Don't I know you? Do you go here?"

"Nope, I don't know you from Adam," hoping he wouldn't make the connection.

Mr. Schwebes drove off. Chris threw a temper tantrum. It startled Tom, Chris acting like a three-year-old.

* * *

The Bronco pulled away, with Chris and Tom running behind. The boys who'd been watching walked back to their vehicles. Kevin jumped out from behind a Riverdale Estates sign, furious. *Thwarted again.*

Chris knew he was in trouble. The thought infuriated him. Tom, too, was angry—and worried. The boys gathered at the vehicles.

"What the hell was going on?" Kevin said. "I want some answers right now."

Chris summarized the exchange with Schwebes. "We're probably gonna have to go down and answer some questions, Tom and I, 'cause he's gonna find out who we are. All he has to do is go through the records and look at the pictures. He really screwed up our night."

Kevin threw the gas bottle in the back of Burnett's truck. "Maybe we should do something about that," he said, eyes glinting.

Tom was scared. "I can't go in there and answer questions. I might slip and say something."

The kid's even afraid of himself *telling on somebody,* Chris thought. Yelled at him for acting like a little baby. Kevin yelled at him. Tom yelled at everybody. Everybody yelled at one another, trying to figure out what to do.

"Hey, we got to kill this guy. We got to get him out of the picture. He's gonna turn us in, and that's gonna open up this whole can of worms," Chris said. "He's got to die tonight."

Chris is joking around, Burnett thought.

"He needs to die. He knows too much," Chris said, again.

Chris is really boiling, Pete thought.

Chris is joking, Brad thought. *He's just trying to show off in front of Kevin.*

"Something has to be done," Chris said. "This has to be fixed tonight, because tomorrow's a school day. So. He's gotta die tonight."

"All right," Kevin said. He tugged at his crotch. "We can do that."

Burnett was stunned. *Kevin seems serious. . . . Nah, I don't believe it.* Now he wanted to see what Kevin would do.

Kevin's excited, Pete thought.

"We ought to go follow him," Chris said. "Let's go follow him."

"No. We can't," Kevin said. "I ain't got my gun, and he's too far ahead." Besides, he had a better plan.

Burnett had assumed Kevin was carrying the Combat Commander. He *always* carried the .45. Tom had just seen it in the classroom. But Kevin was thinking of a different gun: the Mossberg. "We got to find out where he lives," Kevin said. "And get him."

"Yeah, yeah," Chris said.

"We got to find him." . . . "We should've followed him." . . . This was all Derek heard. "He's my teacher," he said, to Kevin.

Derek was making an A in third-period jazz ensemble, taught by Mark Schwebes, who tried to persuade him to be active in band again. "I need a bass player." Derek saw Mr. Schwebes every school day, liked him. Sometimes Derek and Chris practiced keyboard in the band room, and Mr. Schwebes popped in and taught the pair a little, even though it wasn't a formal class.

"He's gay," someone said.

The boys rambled on about how sick they were of fags.

"I don't think he's gay," Brad said. *Chris is showing off. This ain't gonna happen.* At worst, the boys would harass Mr. Schwebes. Brad was ready to go home, get some sleep. Had to work the next morning.

"Maybe we should get Derek to lie, give us an alibi," Chris said. Something about the boys being at the movies. They could get some ticket stubs.

Kevin didn't like it. "No. It'd be his word against yours, and y'all might get arrested. Tom might say something. You might slip and say something. The police might be investigating. They might follow you. Man, they're gonna tap your phone, gonna find out if you did it or not, 'cause they're gonna try to bill you for the windows. They're gonna throw you in jail. Gonna put Tom in juvi."

Kevin's paranoid, Chris thought. "All right, this motherfucker's got to die," he said. "He's got to die tonight. We're not going to jail." His anger peaked. He was fucking *hot.* He waited for an argument *against* Mr. Schwebes being killed. Hearing none, he assumed everyone agreed. He'd expected an argument from Derek, at least. Or Brad. But nobody argued. Everybody just said, "Yeah."

Derek didn't believe Mr. Schwebes would be killed; a suggestion he should be the shooter was ridiculous.

Kevin didn't know Mr. Schwebes at all. "What does everybody know?"

"I know him from class," Derek said.

"I don't know his first name," Chris said.

Derek couldn't think of it.

"Mark," Brad said.

"Yeah, that's it," Derek said.

"We'll find out where he lives. Do you know the part of town or anything?" Kevin asked Derek.

"No."

Kevin asked Brad. No. Asked everyone. No.

"We can look him up in the phone book and get the address," Chris said.

"Good idea," Kevin said. "Let's go to Winn-Dixie."

They piled in the cars again. Burnett was disturbed by the turn of events—but not enough to leave. What was Kevin going to do? Would the other boys follow through? He doubted it. Tom went to Winn-Dixie because Burnett was his ride: he had no choice.

Mark *had* seen Kevin. It would've been hard to miss him. He kept peeking from behind the column to see if the teacher would stop, then ran. Mark knew full well the boys were up to no good. The auditorium and pay phone had been vandalized, and he suspected it was about to happen again. *Maybe breaking more windows . . . probably using the cans.* He drove to Cracker Barrel, passing the Winn-Dixie, where boys more sinister than he suspected, boys who called themselves the Lords of Chaos, would soon plot the adult crime of murder—his.

Vicki Enders, an RHS junior, worked a cash register at Winn-Dixie in the Riverdale Shopping Plaza, across from the school. She called her mother from the pay phone outside. "I'm gonna be home a little late. I don't have a ride." She'd wait for someone to get off work and drop her home, maybe by 10:30 P.M. She wanted a ride sooner—and now here were these boys driving up in front of the Family Dollar, including Peter, who, she knew, found her attractive.

"Go get the phone book," Kevin told Chris, pointing to the pay phone between Winn-Dixie and Eckerd. Only ten days earlier, an employee of this same Winn-Dixie had stood at the same pay phone, looked across the oversize parking lot and saw the same boys stealing propane tanks.

Chris ripped the phone book off the rack. Brought it back to Kevin, who flipped through the pages. No "Schwebes." Ticked off, he ripped the book and threw it down. *The fuck if he'll get away that easy.*

Mark walked into Cracker Barrel in his green pants, maroon belt and gray button-down shirt, clothes that gave the ex-marine a preppy look. Arnold and his family were waiting at a table behind the hostess stand. "What happened? Who were the kids?"

Although vandalism was annoying, Mark was struck by the humor—the tall, goofy boy and the familiar short, fat one, the odd couple with their bizarre tools, lame excuses and awkward efforts to hide their gloves, failing miserably at attempted nonchalance, trying to act tough but clearly scared. He laughed. "You wouldn't believe what they were doing. The one kid turned around and pulled his hands out, and he had gloves on. So, I knew they were up to no good."

Mark ordered soup, a BLT and hot tea. While they were waiting for their food, he played checkers with Arnold's daughter. Things were going his way. He'd achieved his ambition to be a high-school band director in Southwest Florida. Riverdale wasn't his first choice, but it was close enough. Things were proceeding nicely with Paula Dodd, too, the striking blond colleague he occasionally dated. *Too bad she couldn't make it tonight.*

Smiling, Vicki strolled toward the boys. *Pete likes me.* "Can you give me a ride?" She threw her stuff in Pete's car. He drove her the ten minutes home. A chance to spend some time together. At school, he saw her in hallways—no classes together. They went to the mall once, and she borrowed his car twice. There was always a chance.

"I got to take my buddy home, 'cause he has a ten P.M. curfew," Derek told Kevin. "And I need to be getting home myself."

"No, you're not. You're gonna be coming back. You take him home, but you come back. You better come back, or you'll pay for it."

"Okay." Yielding to Kevin once more, Derek drove

his friend home. Had a 10:30 P.M. curfew himself, but didn't feel obliged to stick to it.

Mark was still telling his story. "I recognized one boy: he's in Mr. Stewart's keyboard class. Tomorrow I'll look in the book and see if I can put a name with the face." The conversation moved on. They discussed summer band camp. Contractors had broken ground for the home Mark was building in San Carlos Park. The concrete slab had been poured earlier in the day. *Hope that rain didn't pockmark it.* Mark was also irritated: he'd asked for an electrical outlet in the center of the floor and had been quoted $250. *Seems way too much.* But it'd be a relief to get out of Crime Manor.

Vicki realized she'd left a bottle of wine and her work uniform in Pete's car. She repeatedly paged him.

Derek's home was on the way back to Winn-Dixie. He pulled into the turn at the top of the driveway. Sat ten minutes. He didn't think they'd kill Mr. Schwebes. Hoped they wouldn't. Thought about Kevin's threats, the boasts about killing his Texas uncle. *Kevin and them won't let it go. They'll come back, tell me I got to go. Besides, maybe I can talk them out of it.* He pulled out onto State Road 80 and drove toward Winn-Dixie. He could dissuade them. He could stop it. By going back, he'd keep Kevin away from his family.

"Call the operator," Kevin told Chris.

Chris dropped a quarter in the phone. Asked for Mark Schwebes's number.

"What city?"

"I don't know. Fort Myers."

Chris hung up. Keeping the number in his head, he repeated it to Kevin, who wrote it on his hand. "What about the address?"

"I didn't get the address."

"Get your ass back on the phone and get the address."

Chris dialed 411 again. Gave Mark Schwebes's name and phone number and asked for the address.

CHAPTER 18

To Prove a Point

Chris gave the Cypress Drive address to Kevin, who wrote that down on his hand, too.

"Go back and call the house."

Tom kept following Chris back and forth to the phone. "Is he there? Is he there?"

Chris was considering talking with Mr. Schwebes if he answered. Got a machine. The moment was gone. "It *sounded* like his voice. I guess we got the right place."

"If I told you to do this, do you think you could?" Kevin said.

Chris visualized walking up to the guy with a gun and shooting him at point-blank range. "Naw. Not even if you told me. I'm just not sick like you."

Kevin laughed. Asked Burnett.

"Hell, yeah. I'd do it. You just give me a gun." They'd been hanging out all day and Chris hadn't seen Burnett drink a damn thing, yet he seemed drunk. Burnett's beeper went off every three or four minutes. "My mom wants me home. It's getting late. I have to leave."

"Wait with me until everybody gets back," Kevin said.

* * *

"I got this page. It's just a number, right? I don't know it," Pete was saying to Chris.

"Well, call it."

Vicki. "I'm back at Winn-Dixie, 'cause I left my friends here," Pete told her.

"I left some stuff in your car."

"I've got to go to her house again," he told Kevin.

"Either meet me back here or at my house," Kevin said. To Brad: "Do you want to go with us?"

"No." He wanted home. "I'm gonna go with *you*," he said, getting into Pete's car. "I'm not doing this. I have to work at six."

Kevin was no obstacle to Brad's departure. "That's cool. If you want to go ahead and go home, go home— it's gonna be pretty late."

Derek pulled up and rolled his window down. "Where did Brad go?"

Tom shook his hand through the open window. "Hey, good luck."

"What are you talking about?"

"My mom will kill me if I don't get home," Burnett told Kevin. "Take care of this and let us know how it turns out." *I don't know if he's going to go through with it or not. I don't believe him.* He took Tom home and headed home himself, answering his mother's insistent paging. Like Brad, he had to work early.

Right before he left Winn-Dixie, obsessing about her birthday even as he planned murder, Kevin made another call to Cindi. No answer.

* * *

They don't have the address, Derek thought. Chris and Kevin jumped in his car. "Let's go to my house," Kevin said. On the way, Derek learned Chris *had* gotten Mr. Schwebes's address from 411. He didn't think you *could* get the address like that. They were actually going to try to kill Mr. Schwebes.

"You still have that stolen tag?" Kevin said.

"No. I threw it in the Riverdale parking lot."

"Let's go get it."

Arnold tried to pay for dinner. "Leave a tip, I'll get it," Mark said.

"It's late," Arnold's son said. "It's ten thirty-eight. It's a school night."

"I'm going home to bed," Mark said. "I've had a long day." He pulled out of the Cracker Barrel parking lot, Arnold right behind. At Palm Beach Boulevard, they waited for the light. Mark turned left. Arnold turned right. He never saw Mark again.

Back at Lorraine Drive, Derek and Chris sat on couches and talked while Kevin gathered a gun, ski mask, map. Derek made an effort to do what he'd resolved. "We don't have to go do any murder. I can say you were with me at the movies. Schwebes didn't see *you* at the school, it was someone else. They'll probably believe me." Derek didn't like to lie, didn't think himself a liar. His primary concern was Chris, not the LOC. He'd lie to get Chris out of trouble.

"Yeah." Chris was calmer, no longer enraged. *Kevin's house is filthy.* "That should work."

Heat was playing. Maybe Derek would go see it. He knew employees at the Edison Park 8. They could say he was there. Kevin had been urging him to see the movie anyway.

Kevin was focused, mumbling, hyper, thinking out loud, making a mental checklist, fixated on murder. Dropped the Mossberg out his bedroom window. Carrying a phone, he disappeared into Mom's bedroom.

Chris paged Pete, adding a 666 so he'd know who it was.

Kevin came back into the room. Derek thought he'd convinced Chris not to be involved in any murder, but now Kevin was back, Chris started talking about how to do the killing. *Kevin's decided he's gonna kill this guy,* Chris thought. *He's psyching himself up. Isn't even hearing us anymore, hasn't been since Winn-Dixie. He was always planning on doing* somebody. If Chris had been on the fence with Derek, talking with Kevin solidified his decision: He was helping plan murder. "How are we gonna get in?" . . . "Through his window?" . . . "What are we gonna do?" . . . "Are you gonna take a weapon?" . . . "Are you gonna kill him?" . . . "Are you gonna tie him up?" . . . "Are you gonna tell him to keep his mouth shut?"

"I don't know. I haven't decided," Kevin said. "Why don't we just waste him. Just blow his shit away."

"Why don't you make it look like a robbery?" Chris said. "'Cause if you just leave this guy just stranded on his doorstep like that, it's gonna seem odd. It's gonna look like a gang hit."

"I'm using a shotgun here," Kevin said. "It's kind of gonna draw some fucking attention."

"Why *don't* we make it look like a robbery?" Chris said. "We take his TV, VCR. All his shit. Any kind of jewelry he has. Watches. Wallet. Electronics. Everything. Make it look like a robbery. Tell him to keep his mouth shut about the auditorium."

"No, that'll take too long," Kevin said.

"Why don't we just take his car? I know he's gonna leave the shit in his car, 'cause any normal person isn't

gonna take all that crap in the house. Take it to
school the next day. It's a Bronco. I know you can take
it. All you gotta do is, like, peel the column. It looks
like an older model."

"I ain't never stole a Bronco. It'd be easier to have
somebody knock on the door." Kevin shoots Mr.
Schwebes when he answers. They take off in Derek's car.

Derek neither agreed nor openly rejected the plan—
just sat and listened. Inside, he churned; outside, he
was blank to his companions. He expected them to
know his feelings; they saw none.

Kevin knew he could kill the teacher. Nothing could
stop him. You could do anything if you had the testic-
ular fortitude. A boy could go and kill a man and drive
away, on to the next diversion. It wasn't Tom; it wasn't
Chris; it wasn't the risk of exposure; it wasn't being
thwarted yet again—it was to prove a point. *To prove a
point to these—these children who don't believe this can be done.
To show them it* can *be done.* "Go get the shotgun and put
it in your car," he told Derek.

Derek walked out, saw the shotgun outside Kevin's
window. Didn't touch it. Chris looked at it. Didn't
touch it. Kevin grabbed the Mossberg. "Open your
trunk." Threw the shotgun in. Derek and Chris followed him back inside. He paged Pete, wanting his
lieutenant with him.

On the way to Vicki's, Pete and Brad discussed
music, bands, CDs, computers. This was Pete's second
opportunity not to join the killing party. Pete was a
little scared when he thought about it. *Something'll make
us nix the plan. Schwebes won't be home. We won't find his
house. We'll see a cop.* Calling the police wasn't an
option. He didn't want to get caught for what the boys
had already done. And then there was something
else: he'd always wanted to see a man die.

Pete and Brad spent about a half hour drinking

punch at Vicki's. "Are we gonna go to the prom?" she asked Pete. A friend who worked at Hardee's suggested it. Vicki wasn't attracted to him, just friends. The prom didn't have to be a big deal.

They discussed Hardee's. "I'm trying to find a job that pays a little bit better." Mostly, Pete was quiet, though, and Vicki found herself talking more with Brad. Pete lit a cigarette. It might help him relax. Talking to girls was tough under the best of circumstances. With Brad there, it was impossible.

Pete's always real quiet, Vicki thought. Perhaps they'd go to the beach Saturday. He'd be working Saturday morning. She'd be off at 3:00 P.M. and could stop by.

"It's a bit late," her mother said. "It's a school night."

Vicki walked the boys to Pete's car. "Could I borrow one of your CDs?" Pete let her borrow Nine Inch Nails' *Rusty Nails.* She'd never return the CD; she wouldn't see him again.

Pete had left his pager in the car. It had a new message: 693-7626-666. Kevin's personal line and Chris's code, the sign of Satan.

Pete swung by Winn-Dixie. The lot was deserted. On the way to Brad's, his pager went off again. "It's the guys," he said.

"We're almost to my house," Brad said. "Can you drop me off?"

Brad didn't believe the boys would kill Mr. Schwebes, and Pete didn't say anything to make him think otherwise. After all, guys often said, "I'm gonna kill him" or "I'm gonna kill you," talking tough. It meant at worst there'd be a confrontation, maybe somebody's property would get vandalized, maybe there'd be a fight. It'd never occurred to Brad it was meant literally. He went in, thinking Pete wouldn't go.

* * *

Craig's phone rang. "Come over here quick, man. I've gotta talk to you about something," Brad said. "I don't want to talk about it on the phone."

"What's wrong?" *Brad doesn't have a phone. He had to go out to call. He knows I crash early when I'm working. This must be important.*

"Nothing. You just need to come over here."

Something serious *is up.* Craig pulled on some clothes and set out for the fifteen-minute walk.

Tom slammed the door of Burnett's Isuzu and sauntered into his house before 10:00 P.M. Ringing phone. Burnett. *He hardly had time to get home.* Kevin wouldn't do it, Burnett said. Tom wasn't sure. *A lot of people* act *mad, but then Kevin's talked about other stuff he's done, like murderin' his uncle. It might happen, it might not.* Tom was completely conflicted. Weird, how he felt. He didn't like it. Something in his stomach.

Brad told Craig the whole story, starting at the mall. "They're out to his house, gonna do something. They said they were gonna take care of him. Something serious is gonna happen." Like Burnett and Tom, Brad was conflicted. Murder seemed unlikely. *They'll scare him. Blow up his mailbox? Maybe. . . . Murder him? No. . . . Dudes say, "I'm gonna kill you" all the time. Most that means is fight. It's not literal.*

"Yeah, right. This is all gonna be bullshit," Craig drawled. "It's just one of those threats, you know? To make him look big."

Craig went home; Brad went to sleep.

Pete walked into Kevin's frustrated he didn't get to talk to Vicki more, irritated Brad was there. Kevin, Chris and Derek were crowded around a coffee table, hunched over a map. It was down to the core four. *No Ruby. No Kelly. Perhaps they're sleeping.* The boys looked at the map, trying to find Cypress Drive. Lee County had two, miles apart. No one was sure which was Mr. Schwebes's. Going by the 547 phone prefix, they guessed it was the Pine Manor one, not the other in Lehigh Acres.

The plan: go to Pine Manor, the closer Cypress Drive; if Mr. Schwebes's car is in the driveway, someone knocks on the door, baits him out; Kevin waits in the bushes with the shotgun; Derek identifies Mr. Schwebes; Kevin shoots; Chris drives; Pete observes.

"I don't particularly like this," Pete said. "Too simple. Just going up there and shooting him and leaving him on his doorstep would get the cops on us really quick." *Sloppy.*

"I like my plan," Kevin said, in no mood to hash out something better. "It'll work. We're definitely going over there tonight, so we might as well get ready"—gesturing to the map—"Take that with us." He changed into his favorite black Wranglers and an off-white No Fear T-shirt. Changed the Nike boots he habitually wore for army boots. Carried a black ski mask, black gloves and an oversize army jacket he'd once given Shawn.

Pete and Chris tried to come up with a last-ditch excuse. A test they needed to study for: "We need to go home. You and Derek handle this."

"Y'all ain't going nowhere," Kevin said.

"Why can't we just go? You and Derek can take care of this."

"I need somebody to drive. I'm gonna need somebody to knock on the door. I want Pete to go along, 'cause I want him to see and remember what happened today." *I'm gonna prove a point.*

Chris didn't know what the hell Kevin meant. Perhaps Pete would log it in a journal? Kevin was like a little kid: "Watch me! Watch me!"

The plan was determined, Pete realized. Everyone had

their role. He'd sit in the car. "You know, I really don't need to go," he said, peevish. "I mean, there's nothing I'm gonna do. So, I don't really need to be here."

"I *want* you there."

That made Pete feel good. *Kevin just wants to show off. Show us he can do all this stuff without feeling bad.*

Around 11:00 P.M., Cindi's answering machine recorded another message. "Happy birthday," Kevin said. It was the type of machine that logs the time, and much later that'd come to seem of paramount importance to Cindi.

CHAPTER 19

Murder

Derek drove the red Chevy Cavalier away from Kevin's about 11:00 P.M. It sat low to the ground—not fashionably modified, just old and worn. The muffler hung loose, growling. Kevin sat up front, Chris behind Kevin, Pete behind Derek. Gloved, Kevin fiddled with a pair of shells. The Mossberg was in the trunk.

They stopped at the Circle K on Orange River Boulevard. Kevin sent Chris to the pay phone again. "See if he's home yet," giving him the number and a quarter. Chris got the machine.

"Maybe he's just not answering, or maybe he's on his way," Kevin said. "Either way, we're still gonna go check, see if we can find his vehicle or at least the address." He sent Chris back to the phone to wipe it down. The call might be traced, the phone dusted for prints.

They headed toward Pine Manor, Kevin giving directions. The boys took Interstate 75 south.

Pete was aware of Chris next to him, snickering, trying to tell jokes. Kevin sat up front, sullen, brooding. *Psyching himself up for the kill*, Pete thought. Derek was quiet as ever. *Nervous,* Pete thought. The way Pete looked at it, they were just along for the ride.

"Shut up," Kevin said, annoyed at Chris's efforts to lighten the mood.

"I don't think I'll be able to do it," Derek said. "I don't *want* to."

"Fine." Kevin turned to Pete. "You do it."

"I don't want to," Pete said.

Kevin reached back, looked at Chris, handed him two 3-inch dark green shells. "Here."

Like I'm supposed to know what he means, Chris thought. *And I do know.* Chris handled the shells. Visualized what they'd do to the guy's head or stomach or wherever he got shot. Handed them back. "No, I can't do that shit."

"Pussy," Kevin said.

"Pussy for trying to put it on somebody else."

The two traded expletives.

"Fuck it, I'll do it myself," Kevin said, putting the shells in his pocket. Derek pulled off I-75 onto Colonial Boulevard.

Chris and Derek again discussed an alibi. Mr. Schwebes knew Chris by sight. *He mightn't remember my name, but he might still be able to identify me,* Chris thought.

Derek explained to Chris they didn't have to do this killing. He was really hoping Kevin would hear, typically reluctant to be direct. Kevin didn't react. He just sat, going over in his mind how to do the murder. "I can just say Chris was with me and they'd believe me, you know?" Derek said.

Chris was agreeing. Kevin turned around. "Shut up. I don't want to hear it no more. We're gonna kill him, and if I don't, I'm gonna kill you guys, 'cause someone has to die tonight."

Derek drove on in silence, not really thinking at all. He lost track of time.

The boys passed a RaceTrac gas station. A stoplight. McGregor Baptist Church. Kevin started singing a twisted version of "Santa Claus is Coming to Town":

> *He sees you when you're sleeping,*
> *He knows when you're awake.*
> *He knows if you've been bad or good,*
> *So be good for goodness' sake!*
> *O! You better watch out!*
> *You better not cry,*
> *Better shut up*
> *And prepare to die.*
> *Kevin Foster's coming to your house.*

The boys thought it funny, particularly Chris. He and Kevin enjoyed the coincidence of Santa's anagram: Satan.

Pete remembered Kevin's story about the two of them, "Snipers." *Santa Claus was in that, too—or was it St. Nick? Both. It was both. Kevin has a thing about Christmas.* Kevin got his favorite guns for Christmas.

Clever but sick, Derek thought. Hidden meanings escaped him. He got to U.S. 41 and turned south.

Derek drove a short way along Cypress Drive, into Pine Manor. The boys cruised apartment complexes for the Bronco II. Didn't find it. They got to a T intersection, where the road seemed to end. Perhaps this wasn't the right place. *We'll just go back to Kevin's,* Derek thought, relieved. Also relieved, Chris said, "We'll have to go to our little fallback plan and make up a little alibi and just lie our little asses off and try to get away with it."

Derek drove back to U.S. 41 and pulled into a Site gas station and convenience store. "Park under the light," Kevin said. Pulled out the map. Derek hoped he wouldn't find any other Cypress Drives. "I found it," Kevin said, happy. He folded the map. "It goes around the bend. It *has* to be there. Let's go back down there."

When they saw it, Derek started shaking.

Kevin slapped the dashboard. "Right there. That's his car."

Mark's plain white stuccoed concrete-block duplex with gray trim faced Cypress Drive. A side street, Eighth Avenue, ran beside his half of the duplex.

Kevin told Derek to circle the block. "Go by the house real slow. . . . Okay, when we do it, we're gonna park here." He gestured to the side of Eighth Avenue. "Let's go back up to forty-one and get everything straightened out."

Now Derek was so nervous he couldn't drive straight. Kevin pointed to a parking lot by a Havertys furniture store. "Pull in."

Kevin, Derek and Chris got out. "Open the trunk," Kevin told Derek. Got the Mossberg out. "Somebody's gonna knock on the door, and I'll shoot Schwebes. Derek, you can knock."

"No, I'm not. Why the hell I got to knock?" His first "no" to Kevin.

"Okay, fine." Kevin turned around. "Chris, you're knocking."

"No, I'm not, either. He isn't gonna open the door for me, because he just saw me this evening."

"Fine. You'll knock," Kevin said to Pete, who also refused.

Kevin turned back to Derek, who shook his head. "What about Pete? Why can't Pete knock?"

"I don't want to," Pete said.

"He doesn't know Pete," Kevin said. "He won't open it."

"Why don't you just do it your damn self?" Derek said.

"No. I'm dressed in black. What if he looks out, sees me holding a shotgun? I don't think he's gonna open the door. He'll open the door for you. He *might* open it for Chris, but I doubt it. 'Cause he just seen him about to commit a crime. You know the guy, you have band with him every day. He sees you out there, he'll think you're in trouble. He'll open the door. He'll come out and ask what's going on. Might even invite you in to use the phone or something, who knows? So, Derek, you're gonna go up to the door and Chris'll drive, 'cause Pete can't drive worth a damn."

Derek was trembling. *Kevin said if any of us ever got caught and snitched, he'd kill him.*

"Maybe this is a bad idea," Pete said. "Maybe we should just let things be, leave well enough alone."

Kevin isn't even hearing that, Chris thought. "How are you gonna make us do this shit?"

Kevin racked the shotgun. "That's it. Derek, you're knocking on the door. Chris, you're driving. Someone has to die tonight. If it's not Schwebes, it's gonna be you guys."

Kevin took the stolen tag out of the trunk and put it back on. Slammed the trunk. "Everyone, get in the car." He pulled on Shawn's army jacket and got in the backseat. Propped the Mossberg haphazardly against the driver's headrest. "Drive."

Derek, facing the miserable task of luring Mr. Schwebes out because he knew him—but afraid to refuse—heard Kevin rack a round into the shotgun. Kevin told Chris to drive around the block for one final scope of the area. "Pass Schwebes's house slow."

Chris came to this murder because he wanted to. He knew it wasn't smart, and he didn't care. *Accessory,* he thought. *At worst, I'll get accessory. Maybe five years. Nothing's gonna happen to me.* The crimes were experiences, and they'd all been different: The boys experienced animal cruelty, breaking and entering, arson, car theft, armed robbery, bombing. Now they'd experience murder. It was obvious Derek didn't want to be there, but Chris liked to finish what was started: he started this; he'd finish it, too.

"Go around the block a couple of times," Kevin said. The neighborhood was poorly lit—just a couple of streetlights. Chris settled into his customary role—in the car, lookout and getaway driver.

As Kevin pulled on a black ski mask, Derek schemed. His best judgment deserted him, obscured by his racing heart. A rising, jittery panic. Somehow he couldn't grab onto his thoughts, couldn't focus long enough to act. He'd wait until Mr. Schwebes answered, then yell, "Run," or "Get out of the way!" _By the time that clicks, he'll be shot. I could_ push _him out of the way._

Walking home, Virgil Phipps passed right by Mark Schwebes's duplex and right by the Eighth Avenue intersection and saw nothing unusual. Mark's two vehicles, just like always. Virgil's neighbor was quiet. Didn't come out of his house much. Virgil went inside, tipped food in the dog bowl, turned on the end of the NBC local TV news. Walked to his bedroom. Pulled on slippers. Sat on the bed.

Chris pulled up at the stop sign on Eighth Avenue alongside Mark's duplex. "Stop right here," Kevin said. "Derek, go up, knock, try to get him outside or get the door open as far as you can and get out of the way." To Pete and Chris: "When you hear gunshots, y'all make sure the car doors are open."

Kevin came out behind Derek, crouched. "Oh, fuck," Derek said as he walked away.

Pete watched the two walk through bushes toward the front of the house—Kevin carrying the Mossberg, in ski mask and gloves, Derek in his New York Mets baseball cap, walking toward a murder. Then they rounded a corner of the duplex, and he couldn't see them anymore.

* * *

Kevin walked behind Derek. He spoke. Derek stopped and turned. Kevin held the shotgun angled up, pointed right at him. It occurred to Derek that Kevin might shoot him.

"Knock on the door and run for the car," in a low tone. "You jump in the front and I'll take the back."

Leaving Kevin standing back near a trash can, out of sight, Derek walked up to the door, thinking again of getting Mr. Schwebes out of the way, trying to summon the will. He thought again about telling the teacher to run or pushing Mr. Schwebes out of the way. That might get *him* killed.

Pete and Chris sat in the Cavalier, engine clunking. *It's very, very dark,* Chris thought.

Pete was amazed and excited and scared. *I don't want to do it,* he thought, uselessly. "You think he's really gonna do it?"

"Yup, probably," Chris said. "He's got a loaded shotgun there and a pissed-off temper—and he's probably gonna do it."

"Crap, crap, crap," Pete said to himself. They'd seen no cop. Nothing else had prompted them to abandon their plan. Up until this second, Pete hadn't believed it. It didn't seem real.

Dick Ellis, who once had a lawn service and now lived on a VA check, considered getting out of bed, going out there, saying, "Hey, move the car!" It'd been sitting on Eighth Avenue at the Cypress Drive stop sign at least seven minutes. Maybe longer. It was hard to tell, seeing he'd been trying to sleep after watching the fights on the USA Network. The bouts were disappointing. He stayed up waiting for the main event. Didn't look too good. Now he was lying with the windows open in the Southwest Florida spring, the last weeks before the heat, and this car was idling away right there. It'd been parked so long, engine running rough . . . *clunk, clunk, clunk* . . . like it might be a diesel—that or it had an engine or muffler problem. An old car. Didn't sound smooth like a new one. *I'm gonna get up and tell them, move, man. Either arrest him or get him out of here.*

Truth about Pine Manor was, it was the kind of place where Dick just assumed that's why a car was sitting so long, engine running, at the stop sign outside his window—because the police had it pulled over.

Derek knocked. No answer. Stepped back, turned to walk away, looked back at Kevin. God stood with the Mossberg raised, still near the garbage can, shotgun pointing at the doorway and also kind of at Derek. *He's gonna shoot me.*

Later, Derek regretted turning to look at Kevin. *Had I not turned and looked, I could've saved him.*

God lining up the shot. Adrenaline. A jolting white flash in Derek's mind. Everything slowed. It got real cold. He shook. Locks clicked. Sounded real loud. He turned back around. Froze. The door opened. Derek yanked his Mets cap down and looked down, trying to hide his identity. He couldn't face Mr. Schwebes or what he knew was about to happen. Legs and feet, a glimpse of green slacks and white socks. "Who is it? Yes, may I help you? Who's out there? Hello?"

"Oh, shit," Derek said. He turned and ran. "Who? . . . " Mr. Schwebes yelled. Derek kept running, down the driveway, avoiding God before he turned and ran back behind Schwebes's vehicles toward the waiting car. As he passed Kevin, he heard a single shot.

Derek didn't turn around and look, didn't see Kevin shoot, didn't see the flash from the barrel, didn't see

Mr. Schwebes fall, didn't see his teacher curled up in his own doorway. Derek could only be certain it was Mr. Schwebes from his voice, hadn't seen his face. Though he was there to make sure Kevin shot the right man, he realized it didn't matter by the time the door opened—Kevin would've shot whoever answered. What mattered was this moment when Kevin got to kill, with an audience, releasing a load from the gun like he released a load when he jerked off, just so many shotgun pellets spilled for the thrill. It mightn't have been Mark Schwebes. They might've been at the wrong half of the duplex. It might've been Tom, in an accident in the woods—like Derek's brother falling from a moving car. It might've been Derek, on the way back from trashing Lewis's Blazer. The .45 always in his hand or in his waistband, the Mossberg in the truck, Kevin itching to kill *someone.*

Kevin fired.

"Faggot motherfucker," he said, aloud. "You like it up the ass?" He shot Mark a second time, in the buttocks.

He turned and ran for the waiting car, the silence after the second shot broken by the sound of his laughter.

CHAPTER 20

Aftermath

Right side of his face riddled, pellets striking a glancing frontal blow, Mark Schwebes flipped, landed facedown in the doorway and curled in a fetal position. Blood spattered the door, the frame, the floor.

Standing in her yard talking with her boyfriend, Lucia Carillo heard voices. Melaleuca and slash pine obscured her view. Two loud reports half a football field away. A man with a gun. Seeing dark clothes, she mistook the shooter's race. *Black man. Extended his hands, firing two shots. Looking around, pointing the gun. Running to a dark car . . . on Eighth Avenue. No one else in the car. No one else running.* She ran to her house, boyfriend running beside her. *Don't look back. Don't look at the car.* Got to the door. *A short-sleeved . . . white? blue? . . . shirt and long blue pants. Skinny. Maybe five feet five inches. Carrying a little gun. Loud car. Something wrong with the muffler. Never seen the man. Never seen the car. Windows tinted?*

* * *

Chris looked at the Cavalier's instrument panel. The engine idled. A shot. Looked up, toward the house. Derek running full tilt, disappearing behind the Bronco II. A second shot. *Why would he need two? He was only like six feet from the guy. Shot Derek?*

Sitting on his bed, Virgil Phipps heard a double backfiring sound. Watched the sports another five minutes. Heard a ratty-sounding car, maybe a struggling four-cylinder with a bad or missing muffler.

From the end of the driveway, Derek heard another shot, seconds after the first. *A second shot? Shooting at me?* Ran to the car. Doors opened. He flew into the front passenger seat, hitting Chris. Closed the door. Curled into a ball, head between knees, eyes closed. Shocked. Scared. Shaking.

"Where's Kevin?" Chris said.

"Who cares?" Derek wanted to get away as fast as possible. "Let's go. Let's leave. Forget him." Derek started mumbling.

Holding the Mossberg, Kevin slammed into the backseat, shaking the car, threw the shotgun down. "Go! Go! Go! Haul ass!"

To Derek, it seemed Chris took off slow. He was caught behind a car on the way to U.S. 41. To Pete, it seemed fast.

"Speed it up. Get us out of here!" Kevin said.

Pete saw the difference: Derek shaking, nervous, apparently sick—Kevin laughing. "Is he dead?" Pete said.

Kevin chuckled. "He sure the hell ain't alive."

"I heard two shots," Chris said. The bad muffler growled. "Why two?"

Kevin chuckled. "I shot him in the face. He fell over in a fetal position. I shot him in the butt."

Derek stayed curled in a ball. If anyone talked anymore, he blocked it out.

Returning from World Gym about 11:30 P.M., Julia Knight noticed the parked car as she pulled into her Eighth Avenue driveway. Carried her groceries to the door. Heard two shots. Paused. Went into the triplex. Heard the departing car, loud muffler receding up Cypress toward 41. *Something wrong with the exhaust.* Went over to see what happened. A body half in, half out the doorway, facedown. Still. *Dead.* Blood on the doorway. "Call nine-one-one!" she yelled.

Two shots . . . *three?* . . . woke Carlos Sanchez. TV on. Had a couple of beers; didn't stay up working in the garage as late as sometimes. To his wife: "What happened?"

"Somebody shoot somebody," Rita Sanchez said.

"Where?" He looked out a window. *A gray or white '84 or '85 Ford Tempo parked about 250 feet away . . . Eighth at Cypress.* A mechanic, he *heard* the car as much as saw it. It took off fast, east on Cypress. *Lacks power . . . four-cylinder . . . broken muffler.*

What Carlos knew of his neighbor: few visitors, taught music, played saxophone, had a blonde in a red convertible over Sunday . . . or was it Monday? Broken into around Christmas, lost a stereo. Occasionally confronted the guys who rode through the neighborhood on bicycles, challenging them: "Hey! What are you doing here?" Couldn't remember the music teacher's name.

Della and Ken Crowley stood outside their duplex diagonally across the street from Mark. *Neighborhood quiet tonight.* They went in. *Baywatch* on TV. Della cooked, gave her husband the plate, sat in the living room. A loud car. Looked out the window and saw it parked in Mark's driveway, facing the house. *Baywatch's* first commercials came on. The car backed out the driveway fast, parked at the stop sign on Eighth. She heard the car running about five minutes. *Bad neighborhood. Always racing up and down the streets.*

Bang!

Some people know cars by the engine sound; Ken knew guns by the report. This was a twelve-gauge. *Close.* Poked his head out. No one. Opened the door wider and went out. A second or two.

Bang!

Ken got to his fence, looked up the street. Someone maybe fifty yards away running from Mark's house and jumping in the front passenger seat. *Taller than the car.* It was so sudden and fast it didn't register what he was seeing, so he didn't look for a gun or note more than that the clothes were dark and maybe it was a male, his absorption of details hindered by a nagging concern not to be seen. Race didn't register. It was dark and difficult to see anyway. Maybe three more seconds and the car sped up the street. *Loud exhaust or no muffler. White '82 to '84 Ford Tempo. Running real bad. Rear end sagging. Two occupants?* Tried to read the Florida tag. *Too far away.* Taillights disappeared around the curve in Cypress.

Della heard two loud gunshots, ran out behind her husband, didn't make it to the fence, saw a small, old, loud *white? . . . light blue?* car going up the road fast. *Sounds like it doesn't have a muffler.* She walked up to the duplex. Somebody prone in the doorway.

Julia came around the corner. "He's just laying there," she said.

"Where?" Ken said. He went over and saw Mark had been shot in the face. Della was right behind him, wanting to help. "Don't come up. You don't want to see it."

"I seen the guy jumping in his car," Ken told his wife.

"In the passenger side. Two white guys. Somebody standing in front of the house. They ran through these bushes . . . the car was there . . . and these bushes here . . . and they ran in between and jumped in the car."

Must be at least two, Della thought. *He jumped in on the passenger side and the car left right away.*

Ken rarely saw anyone over at the duplex. Rarely home, Mark bothered no one. Figured him for a truck driver or traveling salesman. No more contact than a hello or a wave.

A white Cadillac pulled up, black lady driving, white lady passenger. "Is he dead?" Ken brushed them off, more interested in the scene. The women talked with someone else in the gathering crowd. They turned around in Mark's driveway, then left.

Elsie Shoemaker woke to a bang. *A shot.* She didn't own a firearm, but she knew a gunshot when she heard one. A long, loud noise that surely must be from a big gun. Elsie's bedroom faced the street. She went to the window. *Just another shooting. Hear a lot of it around here lately.* Looking out, she saw a car coming fast out of Eighth Avenue right across from her. Going up Cypress toward 41. Tires squealing. *Burning rubber. Hope he doesn't hit my mailbox.* Without her glasses, she thought it was a small dark car. *Two-door?* She turned on the outside light.

Elsie knew Mark better than her neighbors. Mark's mother visited him, walked the dog, stopped at the driveway to chat. She talked with Mark when he worked in the yard.

Other lights came on. She pulled on clothes and went out.

As it turned out, Elsie saw more than any of her neighbors, and that wasn't much. More than a year later, now living in Connecticut because of all the shooting in the deteriorating community that'd been her retirement dream, the eighty-three-year-old widow recalled every detail, right on the money.

Eddie Liu lived in the other half of Mark's duplex. A noise woke him. *A car backfiring*. He went back to sleep.

Liu's neighbor was friendly, a good guy, quiet, no loud parties. The extent of their contact was Mark's passing "Hi!" when he walked down his driveway. Thought he taught computers and couldn't recall his first or last name. Eddie also remembered the girl in the red convertible.

Lucia Carillo reached the door to her house as the small car sped by. The car ran loud, and she could hear it a long way away. She was afraid those guys might come back and get her. She didn't call 911.

Lucia saw Mark drive by in his green Bronco II every day. They never talked. She knew nothing of who he was.

Dick Ellis heard the *pow, pow;* tires squealed; car peeling out. *Well, that settles that, no need to get up now. Just kids throwing firecrackers. No point calling 911, happens all the time.* After a few more minutes, Dick's sleep was again disturbed, this time by lights flashing everywhere, the whole world lit up out there.

What he knew of Mark: cut the grass, kept up the yard, worked at RHS. Books arrived for him and he was never home. Real quiet. Mark had an avocado tree. Dick had intended to go over, introduce himself, maybe get some avocados.

Virgil Phipps got up to go out. Heard a firetruck and an ambulance. In a month in Pine Manor, Virgil talked with Mark only once. He was a quiet man who didn't have parties or people over—except for the blonde in the red convertible yesterday.

Pete eyed Kevin next to him in the backseat. Kevin spoke quietly, gesturing, not wanting to disturb Derek, balled up and shaking. Brought the side of his hand to the middle of his face and swept it to the right: "Gone."

"Nine-one-one. What is your emergency?"
"I was sitting outside and heard shots. And a car went flying down the road."
"Okay. Where's your address at, ma'am?"
"Cypress Drive. It sounded like it was right up the street."
"How many shots?"
"Two."
"Can you give me a description of the vehicle?"
"I didn't see it—I ran inside. It scared me."

Rose Watson had just moved across Pine Manor, from Oak to Cypress—wasn't even completely settled in her new home. About 11:30 P.M., just home from Night Owls bingo, she was in her bedroom on the phone with her sister when she heard the bang. Thinking maybe something broke, she hollered at her son.
"I didn't break nothing! It was a gunshot."
Bang!
A second one. A drive-by. She went to the living room. *Maybe they're arguing next door.* Ran to the window, opened the blind. A car taking off. A small car's taillights. Loud muffler. The car struggling to pick up speed. Rose heard Julia yell, "Call nine-one-one!"
"Is anyone hurt?" the dispatcher asked.
"I don't know. I just heard the gunshots."
"Well, go out and find out if anybody is hurt!"

She went outside, saw two neighbors at Mark Schwebes's house. "Is anybody hurt?"

"Oh, my God!" a neighbor lady hollered. "He's dead!"

"He's dead! He's laying there!" someone else hollered.

At 11:36 P.M., Deputy John Glowacki's routine night on patrol around Pine Manor ended: he was dispatched to the reported shooting.

Chris turned south onto U.S. 41.

"If anybody seen us back there," Kevin was saying, "they're gonna report this car with this tag. I want it off."

Chris took a left behind the upscale Bell Tower Shops. Two blocks east of U.S. 41, hotels, restaurants and parking lots gave way to poorly lit, undeveloped woods. Chris took another left, through an oasis of scrubby trees. Kevin removed the stolen tag, wiped it, tossed it into the woods, replaced the original.

Derek was aware the car stopped. Someone got out and changed the tag. After that, back on U.S. 41, he just heard voices.

Kevin passed around a hard pack of Marlboro Reds like a proud father passing out cigars. "Shooting somebody in the face, like point-blank, is a lot different than snipering somebody through a telescopic sight. I shot my uncle the same way in Texas."

"Does your mom know about that?" Pete said.

"She doesn't care."

She knows, Pete thought. "You're cold," he told Kevin, who took it as a compliment.

Derek took a couple of drags from his cigarette and flicked it out the window. The thought Kevin had

killed before scared him even more. He hyperventi-
lated, balled up again, blanked out.

In whispers and hand gestures, Kevin re-created the
murder for Pete, who figured the second shot was a
coup de grâce. Kevin had quickly recovered his sick
sense of humor: "I was gonna take his wallet, but it was
full of holes."

As Kevin boasted, Pete watched Derek. "Shit, shit,
shit," he was saying. "We killed him; we killed him."
Derek unballed, glanced up, saw the gas gauge on *E*.
Pointed. "Gas," he managed.

Chris pulled into a RaceTrac gas station. Kevin
pumped. Pete went up to the drawer in front, slid in
$5, bought a Dr Pepper.

"Can I use the bathroom?" Derek asked.

"It's locked." The boys all went to the side of the
building and took a leak.

"Man, Derek, you're white," Pete said. "You look like
a ghost."

"Leave him alone," Kevin said. "He knew the guy."

Derek stared at Kevin.

They pulled out of the RaceTrac. "This one's for
Chris and Tom," Kevin said. "This is what happens
when you try to fuck with the LOC."

To Chris, who felt he'd played no active role, the
words seemed a warning—Kevin was implicating him.
Derek curled back into a ball and tried to block everything out again. The boys headed back to Lorraine
Drive.

The EMS workers beat Deputy Glowacki to the
duplex. Their station close, they were on scene in
two minutes. A crowd was gathering. Emergency medical technician (EMT) John Magin and paramedic
Cory Younger pulled up to Cypress and Eighth in
Medic 34 at 11:37 P.M., looking around, uncertain of
the exact address because the 911 callers were uncer-

tain. An EMT provides basic life support; more highly trained, a paramedic can provide advanced life support. Mark got the best in a county where the ambulance service was highly respected, where people had come from Europe to observe paramedics, and he got it about as fast as possible, and still nothing could save him. Two people in the road waved the ambulance toward the duplex. "Right there."

Younger saw a man facedown in the open doorway, motionless, upper body in the house, legs out on the step. *Gunshot wounds in the buttocks, upper thigh.* Took vital signs. Called for an airway bag. Firefighters got oxygen and a heart monitor from the ambulance. The medics pulled Mark out of the doorway and turned him over onto a blue fiberglass backboard in case they decided to transport him.

Rolling the man over with his partner, shining his penlight, Younger saw massive facial injuries . . . *pellet wounds . . . shotgun.* Magin saw brain tissue on the floor. *Right eye missing. No pulse.*

Two sheriff's agents—homicide investigators—happened to be close by, Charles Ferrante and Gary Kamp. Ferrante saw the missing eye and the spray of shotgun pellets across the face. *Pellet wounds to his backside.* The guy's chest rose and fell. Kamp listened. *He might say something.* The chest rose and fell once more, then was still. The man said nothing. The agents had years of experience, but they could be forgiven for believing he might be alive, for thinking they watched him die. The apparent breathing was convincing. The mind wanted to interpret it as life.

The medics explained they were sympathetic breaths. Magin had seen it, too, but he recognized the slow, agonal respiratory attempts for what they were—a brain stem reflex. There was no real breathing. *Blood in the right ear, mouth and nose. No pulse. Dead.* The medics—who in Lee County often carried lifesaving efforts so far that some investigators griped they packed obviously dead bodies into ambulances—ceased trying to save Mark. Younger formally declared him dead at 11:38 P.M. The partners covered Mark with a sheet and turned the scene and body over to the Lee County Sheriff's Office.

The medics noted two spent Magnum buckshot shells just outside the doorway. Engine idling, lights still sending a message of useless urgency, radio squawking, the ambulance stood by thirty minutes or so; then the partners left.

Glowacki snapped two photos of the victim, asked witnesses to stay around and started suspending yellow crime-scene tape.

At 11:45 P.M.—nine minutes after the first deputy was dispatched to check out the possible drive-by shooting and less than fifiteen minutes after the shots were fired—a phone woke sheriff's agent Dean Taber, who got up, dressed with customary fastidiousness and headed for Pine Manor.

The boys got to Kevin's around midnight. Kevin took the shotgun out of Derek's car. He wanted a group hug in the driveway. Then he hugged each individually. Derek took it as a celebration. Chris took it as congratulatory, a sick display of camaraderie. Pete had come to think of them as the "good work" hugs. Chris leaned against an open flatbed trailer, the steel-mesh kind that could haul a lawn mower or ATV. Kevin and Pete sat on it, smoking. Neither Chris nor Derek liked Kevin's Marlboros, and both gave up after a drag. It made Chris nauseous.

"Y'all did a good job," Kevin said. "No major fuck-ups. Congratulations. We're the core four. Only people like us could do it. I don't think anybody saw us. Nobody followed us."

Kevin hadn't picked up the shell casings. "Don't worry about the shells," he said, his nonchalance angering Chris. "They're not able to trace the shells to the gun." The boys took it at face value: Kevin knows. *It won't matter unless we're caught, and that doesn't seem likely,* Chris thought.

"Chalk one up for Chris; he gets credit for this one," Kevin said. "It was his mission."

It was *kind of Chris's fault,* Pete thought. *Kevin had to do it to get Chris off the hook. If Schwebes would've went to the cops, the only people he could've got was Chris and maybe Tom. He didn't know Kevin. Didn't see Derek or me or any of the others. I could've lived without him being killed. Chris would've gotten nothing really big. Just had to throw it out of proportion.*

"Don't tell anybody else in the group," Kevin was saying. "If anybody's gonna tell them, let it be me."

"Make sure you don't tell anyone about this." . . . "Don't talk about this." . . . "We've got to keep a hush on it." Derek wasn't even sure who was talking. "We'll have to lay low for a while," he said.

Pete thought it mutual they weren't going to do anything for a while—they'd get too much heat. They'd joked about running off to Mexico. *Be a neat, fun trip.* Pete got in his car and drove home.

Kevin cared only that he'd proved his point. He stashed the Mossberg in the backseat of a derelict black Duster on the Foster lot and covered the weapon.

Chris needed a ride, but Derek wasn't up to driving, so Chris drove. Tried to make conversation. Derek was quiet, nothing sinking in. Chris got out at his house. Derek drove home slowly.

Derek pulled into his driveway. Sat in his car, crying. He felt dazed, like he was in a dream. Numb. He wouldn't shake the disoriented, stressed feeling for months. *What's going on? What's going on?* he wanted to ask. But who to ask? Terrified of Kevin, paralyzed with fear he was going to be caught, he knew he was in way

over his head. He stayed out there nearly two hours. Finally he went in and went to bed. Nothing else to do.
The next day, he was back in school.

"I used a shotgun 'cause there ain't no ballistics traces and the gun can't be identified," Kevin would later tell Pete. Kevin knew the Mossberg had a smooth bore with no rifling. Rifling—grooves inside rifle, revolver and pistol barrels—imparts spin, like Joe Montana hurling a football, stabilizing the bullet in flight. These grooves—unique to each weapon—leave fine scratches on passing projectiles. They're as different as fingerprints. All bullets fired from the same gun bear the same unique pattern. Given a bullet recovered from a crime scene and a suspect's gun, a firearms examiner can make comparisons that can damn or free the accused. The examiner fires a second bullet through the suspect weapon. He compares this bullet with the one recovered at the scene. With a specialized microscope, he can view both simultaneously, superimpose their images, rotate them and compare patterns. Photographs taken through the microscope are so compelling that a match is easily demonstrated and obvious even to a novice observer—such as a juror. Because the Mossberg—like most shotguns—had no rifling, Kevin thought there'd be no marks on the shells that could be matched to the gun. He was overlooking other unique patterns, such as firing-pin imprints on the base of shells or marks along the side made by chambering and ejection mechanisms. Any irregularity inside a supposedly smooth barrel—from modification or just wear—can make unique, reproducible and identifiable marks on any projectile fired through that weapon. For example, a sight screwed onto the barrel could be overtightened, creating a projection inside that could score passing projectiles.

* * *

Pete drove home alone. *Schwebes was getting too close,* he thought. *We didn't want to get caught.* Though he didn't agree with the plan, it'd been a well-executed, calculated mission. They'd done it and no one got sick, no one really freaked out. No one was drunk or using drugs. Pete hadn't even seen the front of the duplex, just the view from the side road. He didn't so much as get out to change the tag. He *still* hadn't seen a man die. He went, as best he figured it, to keep the group complete. Heck, Kevin *wanted* him there. They were the brightest, smartest, most reliable. They were the ones that could do it. And that was weird. Burnett, Tom, Brad—all those others seemed bigger, tougher, meaner; yet he, Pete, was among those who could actually do it when it came down to it. *That* was a twist.

The Moore Haven party hadn't gone well. Fistfights. Drinking. A guy slashed his own arm with a knife and bled all over Cindi's new truck. Patsy Miller had been at the party, and Cindi ended up going back to Patsy's house in Fort Myers. It was her birthday, and it sucked. Bitching stupid people out, then coming home to find her stupid answering machine cluttered with stupid messages, including from stupid Burnett and stupid Kevin. Around midnight, her phone rang once more.

"Happy birthday," Kevin said, again. "Did you have fun?"

"Yeah. Whatever. Thanks, Kevin, I gotta go. Call me tomorrow. Dude, I don't want to brush you off, but I'm tired. I'm going to bed."

Burnett's phone rang.

"It's done," Kevin said. "I can't talk about it right

now. I'll talk to you about it tomorrow. There ain't nothing to worry about. You should've been there."

After Kevin hung up, Mom talked with him about the meeting with the attorney to fix his suspended license, planned for the next morning. "Mr. Fuller needs us to be there twenty minutes early so we can fill out the paperwork." She set her alarm for 7:00 A.M. and went to sleep.

The phone rang in Tom's bedroom. He fumbled for the receiver, grabbed his clock instead: 12:32 A.M. Picked up the phone.

"We've done him," Kevin said. "It's done. You have nothin' to worry about no more. See me tomorrow."

Tom hung up. *Nah, he didn't do that. I don't think he did that. I'm hopin' he didn't do that. I'm hopin' he's lying to me.*

Kevin jerked off. But shooting the teacher didn't give him the same rush as blowing up the Coke building. *That* was the high point. The windows blowing out, the flames shooting forty feet into the night sky, the sheer power. Kevin's greatest moment. Firing the Mossberg at Schwebes was second; murder a little disappointing. He kept seeing Schwebes's face. He masturbated again, to get to sleep. Made himself bleed.

CHAPTER 21

"We Done That"

Deputies weren't sleeping. Homicide and major-crimes officers descended on the duplex and stayed the night. Canvassing neighbors. Measuring the position of Mark's body. Sketching. Videotaping. Maintaining a perimeter around the house and curtilage. Lifting fingerprints. Keeping a contamination list of anyone entering the crime scene, including Major David Bonsall, in charge of the sheriff's special operations division, firefighters, paramedics, the two neighbor women, the medical examiner's investigator, the body transport people, crime scene technicians and deputies, command officers and assorted agents—twenty-seven people. Now—less than four hours after the shooting—the LOC had a lot of attention. The street crawled with senior sheriff's staff . . . Lieutenant Randy Collmer . . . the road watch commander . . . three agents from the robbery/auto theft unit . . . and then Sergeant Gill Allen—who'd investigated Kevin's self-inflicted shooting—and his partner, Agent Dean Taber, the pair who'd lead the homicide investigation.

* * *

Joe Magnotti was asleep, but Rebecca stayed up, angry: Pete had blown his 10:00 P.M. curfew by two hours. He was supposed to come right home from Hardee's. They didn't discuss it. He went straight to bed. Rebecca would come to wish he hadn't come home at all, because if he hadn't, there might be another explanation. If he hadn't, then maybe he didn't kill. But she'd remember it too clearly, sitting up waiting, worried and angry, and she wasn't a woman inclined to lie.

Chris tried to go to bed. Couldn't sleep. Watched television.

Arriving in Pine Manor, Taber was told he'd be lead agent. Allen walked him through the scene. Taber talked with Deputy Glowacki, gathered neighbors' names and recollections. He'd generate a six-inch-thick investigative report. His work would take him down a blind alley and then into the bizarre world of a would-be teen militia and a crime spree that continued beyond murder.

It was 1:00 A.M. when Specialist Rick Joslin arrived at the duplex to lead the sheriff's forensic investigation and begin laboriously cataloging evidence, dotting the yard with yellow markers. Joslin would still be working more than sixteen hours later. On the ground near the front of Mark's collectible Mercury Cougar, the two spent shell casings Kevin uncharacteristically failed to retrieve. No usable prints.

Open floor plans were typical of Florida houses—no walls separating a living room from a kitchen on one side, a dining area on another. Mark's front door opened directly into the living room. One of his teeth lay on a plaid shirt on a love seat. Seven teeth were scattered across the floor. Shotshell wadding near a potted plant. Blood on the concrete walk, the door frame, Mark's welcome mat. The rug was blood-stained, though less than might be imagined from such severe wounds, since active bleeding stops at death. Some cash was in Mark's pants pocket: this didn't look like a robbery.

Shot pellets spread when ejected from their shell, so not all of them hit Mark, even at fairly close range. A pellet lay on top of a coffee table. The back wall of the duplex—the wall Mark stood in front of when he opened the door to his student—had seventeen pro-jectile holes. Joslin's team removed a fifty-six-by-thirty-two-inch chunk of drywall. Found three pellets between the studs. When it was all done, between the crime scene and Mark's body, deputies accounted for forty-seven of the forty-eight pellets from the two shells Kevin fired.

Not knowing what might be important, investigators meticulously gathered evidence. Busch beer bottles and a Marlboro Red packet from the yard. The mur-derer might've been drinking; they often were. Or the bottles might be litter tossed by passersby. Investigators turned to Mark's Bronco. A bumper sticker: MUSIC MAKES A DIFFERENCE IN LEE COUNTY SCHOOLS—LET'S KEEP IT ALIVE! A wallet wedged between driver's seat and con-sole, $65 in it. A maroon briefcase containing personal papers. If the teacher was a robbery victim, it hadn't been an efficient crime. On the front passenger seat, an eight-pound Mini-10 ABC fire extinguisher, sta-plers, a blue plastic Wal-Mart bag containing canned goods and latex gloves—objects that didn't immedi-ately make sense.

Joslin documented the scene—took photos out-side and inside, collected evidence, took laborious measurements to triangulate each piece of evidence in relation to every other piece.

The evidence included: a fire extinguisher, a maroon briefcase, a wallet with $65, a blue plastic Wal-Mart bag with cans and latex gloves from the Bronco; a blue and white disposable EMS blanket from the ground near the body; two spent No. 1 Buck twelve-gauge casings from the yard; a tooth from the love seat; teeth, shotshell wadding and blood samples from the floor; a shotgun pellet from a coffee table; a piece of drywall; three pellets from behind the drywall; blood samples from the walkway and door frame; a yellow spiral-bound notepad on the floor next to the front door. The notepad might've fallen from a shirt pocket. A shopping list . . . so many gallons of ice cream . . . toppings . . . ingredients for an ice-cream party.

In Lee County, law enforcement summoned a medical examiner's investigator to violent deaths. So, Keith Von Qualen, the forensic investigator who handled the 1993 death of Fred Shields Jr., made his way to Mark Schwebes's house. Von Qualen arrived at 12:26 A.M., less than an hour after the shots were fired. Got a summary of what happened, documented the scene, photographing the body, the setting of the duplex at the intersection, details pointed out by deputies, such as the shell casing lying in a roll of garden hose. Pulled the blue EMS sheet off the body. Noted the backboard underneath the body and that the body had been moved. Two independent contractors, whose job was transporting the dead, took Mark's body the short distance from Cypress Drive to the District 21 Medical Examiner's Office, arriving at 3:02 A.M. The office numbered the dead with a simple count, beginning January 1 each year. Mark C. Schwebes became medical examiner's case number 247-96.

* * *

At 5:15 A.M., Taber took a second statement from Della Crowley, who recalled her neighbor coming out Sunday like he'd been watching for the lady in the red convertible with the top down. The blonde had been nicely dressed in a shorts outfit, her neighbor carrying bags of groceries into his house. Della had watched from her living room, the first time she ever saw her neighbor have a visitor. On the rare occasions he was there, she waved. Mark always waved back, friendly; exchanges that amounted to "Hello." . . . "Hi." . . . "How're you doing?"

Wednesday morning, May 1, 1996

The blonde in the red convertible was Paula Dodd, and she was a colleague of Mark's at RHS. She also was a cheerleader coordinator, seeing Mark at functions that brought band and cheerleaders together. An attractive blonde, vivacious, with a crowd of friends, she was several years older than he, but she'd kept her looks and young attitude. Mark was interested, though careful to keep this from other female teachers and the kids.

Paula got out of the shower. The phone rang.

"Are you sitting down?" She sat on the bed. "Mark's been murdered." She was speechless. Caught something about a drive-by.

She hadn't gone to the ice-cream social. Wanted to meet an ex-boyfriend, hash some things out. She'd called Mark at RHS and left a message. It'd bothered her, backing out without talking to him. She'd called his home and left a second message, saying how sorry she was. Had he even got that? An evening of crying and discussing the ex's debts and resolving to be friends. An evening she could've spent with Mark.

Maybe if she'd gone to the social, all this wouldn't have happened.

They met at the beginning of the school year. Mark had a one-track mind: band, making the program better, plunging into the new job with enthusiasm—which left little time for dating. He joined a pool league, but mostly kept to himself. He put his personal life on hold for the kids. Not until half the year was done, not until marching season was over, did he start dating. Colleagues were pleased. He deserved it. Once in a while, he stopped with other teachers after school for happy hour at R.J. Gator's or Fat Tuesday's or Shooters Water Front Cafe USA.

When she got to Mark's house on Sunday, he was on the phone with his father. They bought ice cream at Sam's Club for the social . . . carrying grocery sacks . . . juggling freezer contents. He grilled on the back porch and described his new house in San Carlos Park. Talked about Pine Manor, his concern over his collectible car: the waterproof cover was stolen. In the couple of years he lived in Pine Manor, Mark found himself calling the cops to report attempted burglary and neighborhood disturbances. The duplex had been broken into twice. In 1994, he'd discovered a burglary on Christmas Day. They broke in through the patio in back, hidden by trees and a fence. Took his stereo, jazz CD collection, stripped the duplex of small electrical appliances, metronome, cash, even his beloved trumpet, mouthpieces and mutes. Things to pawn, cash for crack. It seemed he couldn't leave for two days without worrying he'd return to a ransacked house. "Wow, I bet you're really glad to get out of here," she'd said.

"Yeah. I felt like it'd never get built." The two planned to take the band and cheerleaders to Orlando next month for the annual trip. Party. Poolside barbecue. Play at a water park. Stay in a hotel. Visit Universal Studios.

* * *

Chris knocked on his parents' bedroom door. "I'm sick. I can't go to school." Later his mother wondered if this meant her boy at least had a conscience.

Allen and Taber were still at it at 6:42 A.M., going on tape with Paula. "There's a reason Mark's dead," Allen said.

"I don't know what it is," Paula said. Neither did they. But Paula's relationship with Mark seemed a lead, especially when it turned out she broke up with the boyfriend right before Mark's murder. How did her ex's car run? Was he driving it last night? . . . Did he own guns? No. *She* owned a .357 revolver, and it was under her bed. . . . Did her ex hunt? No. . . . Had he ever been violent with her? No. . . . The sheriff's investigators were intrigued by the coincidence of the intense conversation between Paula and the ex that very night, that the ex had drunk alcohol, the coincidences that he apparently left Paula's minutes before the murder and Paula's was close to Mark's—within ten minutes. Pressed, she wasn't certain when he left, just that it was sometime after 11:00 P.M. That was *so* close to when Mark was gunned down. The detectives wanted to know about the ex's roommate and *his* car and whether the ex had any other cars or drove another for work. Paula said the ex never threatened Mark. He was six feet three inches and weighed two hundred pounds: that didn't match witness descriptions, and neither did his clothes, but witnesses were notoriously unreliable.

"Any jealousy? Problems with any students? He lose anybody from the band, have to let someone go?" Mark had no major problems with teachers, parents or students. He didn't drink much. Her ex didn't even know Mark's last name. He didn't know where he

lived. Not the kind to follow her. She drove a red
Mazda Miata convertible.

"Oh, my God," she said, not hearing a question, the
direction the detectives were taking sinking in.

About forty-five minutes into school, the principal
called the band members together and told them
about the murder. Students moped around the band
room. Cried in the RHS parking lot. Skipped classes.
Band brought kids closer together, and now they sat
and grieved together, consoled each other: "We don't
know why, but it'll be okay." Or, "Whoever did it, we
hope they get caught, get what they deserve."

Among them was Derek, who'd barely slept, hugging
everybody, carrying on and on, repeating like an echo:
"Don't worry, I'll make sure the murderer gets found one
day." . . . "Don't worry, they'll catch who did it." He was
thinking about going to the police. He hadn't been able
to right Fred's murder, but he could right this one. He
was scared Kevin would retaliate against him or his family.
He was spacey the entire day, crying repeatedly.

Before Mark was even autopsied, Jeremy Arnold was
being interviewed by Agent Ron Curtis, following
the homicide detective's axiom to find the last people
to see the deceased. The two went over the last hours
of Mark's life after the ice-cream social. Arnold mentioned the dinner conversation about the boys at the
auditorium. Curtis listened, letting him get the story
out—and on tape—before he asked questions. Once
Arnold was through, the agent asked about Mark's
girlfriends instead of focusing on the story about the
encounter at the auditorium. The interview covered
a range of conflicts in Mark's life and the lives of
those around him. Arnold said a couple of women
were attracted to Mark: Paula . . . Donna. Could

Donna be jealous of Paula? . . . What about Donna's ex-husband? He was a sheriff's deputy, so that didn't seem likely, though he'd be familiar with guns. . . . What about Paula's ex, the one she threw out? Would he be mortally jealous? . . . What about Paula's adult son? Might he resent Mark? Had the son ever been in trouble with the police? . . . Why was Mark jumping around between schools? . . . Did Mark keep a lot of cash around?

"This question might make you mad, but I've got to ask anyhow: has there been any incidents where he's been caught messing with any of the kids?"

"No."

"Any talk of it among the kids?"

"No."

"You have any idea who may've killed him?"

"No. I don't."

One of the rules of a good homicide detective is to keep an open mind. That said, it seemed reasonable to look into Mark's dating life, the possibility of a classic love triangle gone awry. Nobody thought a bunch of teens would kill over a few confiscated cans of fruit.

Kevin kept his 8:00 A.M. appointment with criminal defense lawyer Richard Fuller, arriving to complete paperwork before Fuller got there. Later, Kevin's attorney remembered his client as calm and cool. Because he'd missed work, Kevin took a rare nap after he got home. It was a treat, being able to sleep, given his usual schedule.

After the detectives were done, Paula called ex-boyfriend Bob Mann.

"Does he live in a bad neighborhood?" Bob said.

"Yeah, kind of. It's off Summerlin—Pine Manor." Paula gave him the number, and Bob called deputies.

* * *

The District 21 Medical Examiner's Office was an anonymous squat concrete building across U.S. 41, not far from Mark's home. Dr. Wallace Graves Jr. autopsied the teacher at 11:05 A.M. with his assistant, Sal Medina, classical music playing softly.

Graves, the district's first medical examiner, led Southwest Florida from autopsies in a shed with neither running water nor air-conditioning—sometimes open-air autopsies at crime scenes—to examinations in a modern, well-equipped facility. "Florida never seemed like home," the New England native often said. He'd retire to Massachusetts at the end of the month, ending a thirty-year Fort Myers career. "The whole time, I thought it was temporary."

His primary task was to determine the cause and manner of death. A death by gunshot could be accident, suicide or homicide. In Mark's case, Graves would certify the cause: shotgun wounds to the head and pelvis. The manner: homicide.

When Graves married in Cincinnati, Medina drove the 1,042 miles to be best man. One of Medina's five marriages was held poolside at Graves's home. The assistant was a tactile man given to hugging and patting. His eyes seemed ever merry. To women of all ages, he was a magnet. They were drawn to his Latin chivalry. He was expecting his ninth child by his fifth wife; his oldest son was forty-six. A Cuban émigré who lost everything to Castro, he was part of South Florida's community of exiles. Short, wiry, with a grizzled beard, he bought shirts and trousers in boys' departments and, he bragged, women's shoes. He had a keen mind, an irreverent razor wit that ignored political correctness, a probing intellect and a voracious reading habit. A lover of people and life, he didn't at all fit the somber stereotype of those in the business of death.

Medina set up and labeled containers for specimens

to determine if Mark drank or used drugs before he was shot: he did neither.

Medina undressed Mark. In the left pocket of his gray button-down shirt, a school pass. In the left pocket of his green pants, $24 in bills, eighty-nine cents in loose change and an uncashed paycheck. On his left wrist, a gold watch. Joslin, who'd now been up twenty-nine hours and counting, observed and collected evidence: he took these things and also fingernail clippings and scrapings and hair samples. A Polylite illuminated trace evidence, and Joslin collected fibers. He even kept the white sheet that wrapped Mark for his ride to the morgue.

Using a gently flowing hose and soft yellow sponge, Medina washed Mark, scrubbing dried blood from around his wounds. Graves took photographs. Reactions to these would be quite varied. Ruby said Mark appeared to have been beaten. She was surprised how good he looked. To Derek, the pictures would be so appalling he'd be unable to view more than two, and seeing them would change the course of his life. To an objective observer who knew what Mark looked like **before** he was shot, one word described him after Kevin was through: unrecognizable. He didn't look simply bruised—he didn't look like Mark Schwebes. Making sure the body on the table was Mark was easy: employment fingerprints.

It'd be one of Graves's last autopsies—and Mark's last and best physical. With a scalpel, Medina made the classic Y incision across Mark's chest and down his torso. Because active bleeding ceases at death, this was a bloodless cut. The incision allowed Graves to open the body— using tree loppers to remove the ribs—and remove organs, which were washed, weighed and examined. A sample was drawn from the heart as a standard to differentiate Mark's blood from any other. Medina stood at a chalkboard as Graves called out organ weights and observations: the teacher was five feet eleven inches and

179 pounds; ate red meat with corn, onions and green peppers for his last meal, recently enough it was recognizable; aside from the wounds, nothing appeared wrong with any of his organs; no reason he shouldn't have lived a long and healthy life.

Medina parted Mark's hair and made a careful cut across the top of his head from ear to ear, rolling his scalp forward and opening his skull using a saw and a T-shaped metal skull key, allowing Graves to document trauma to Mark's brain.

Graves removed five pea-size shotgun pellets and two fragments from Mark's pelvis and three pellets from his head. Evidence, which Joslin took. Medina's X rays showed additional pellets, which weren't removed. The pellets entered the right side of Mark's face and his buttocks across areas three inches in diameter, with stippling—small red marks from the impact of unburned powder fragments, tiny metal shavings or shell packing discharged from a firearm—to five inches. The stippling and the diameter of the shot pattern—directly proportional to the distance between shooter and victim—betrayed the close range from which Mark's killer fired.

It was likely either wound would've been fatal. The pelvic wound could've killed, since it severed the vein from one of Mark's kidneys and an artery, the iliac, that'd cause a quick death from internal bleeding. Even without the head wound, he mightn't have been saved, even by immediate transfer to a hospital. As it was, he wouldn't have been aware he was shot twice: the head wound killed instantly.

After Medina returned organs to the cavity, closed and sewed the Y incision, replaced the top of the skull, pulled the scalp back, sewed that incision and again washed Mark's body, it'd be possible to have an open-casket funeral without evidence of the intrusive procedure.

Medina wheeled the body on a gurney back to the

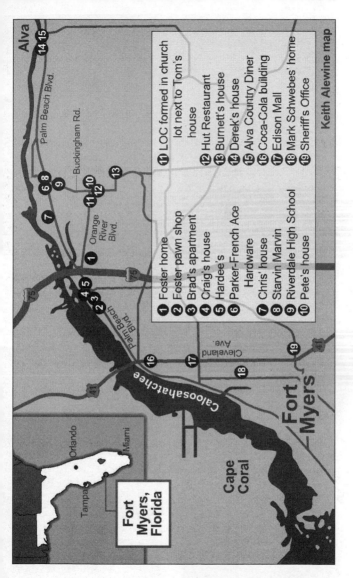

1 Foster home
2 Foster pawn shop
3 Brad's apartment
4 Craig's house
5 Hardee's
6 Parker-French Ace Hardware
7 Chris' house
8 Starvin Marvin
9 Riverdale High School
10 Pete's house
11 LOC formed in church lot next to Tom's house
12 Hut Restaurant
13 Burnett's house
14 Derek's house
15 Alva Country Diner
16 Coca-Cola building
17 Edison Mall
18 Mark Schwebes' home
19 Sheriff's Office

Keith Alewine map

Southwest Florida was the playground of the Lords of Chaos.
(Map courtesy of Keith Alewine)

Young Mark Schwebes grew up to become a marine—but Mark's real passion was music. At Riverdale High School, he quickly became highly regarded as band director.
(Band photo courtesy of Pat Schwebes Dunbar)

Mark Schwebes planned to move out of his parents' duplex on Cypress Drive in Pine Manor, nicknamed Crime Manor.
(Photo courtesy of the Lee County Sheriff's Office)

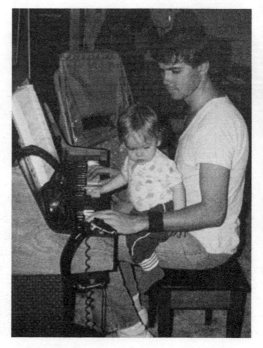

Mark's new house was going to be decorated with musical instruments and have enough room for his nephews to stay— but he wouldn't live to see it.
(Photo courtesy of Pat Schwebes Dunbar)

Kevin Foster dreamed of enlisting in the army, but his leadership of the Lords of Chaos landed him in jail. *(Photo courtesy of the Lee County Sheriff's Office)*

From the Buckingham silo, Foster watched the fires his Lords of Chaos set. *(Author photo)*

Foster was born Kevin Bates, but his nickname was Psycho, for the Hitchcock movie set at the Bates Motel. Deputies found this sign in his bedroom. *(Photo courtesy of the Lee County Sheriff's Office)*

The Foster home on Lorraine Drive. *(Author photo)*

Kevin Foster nicknamed his Toyota pickup, a virtual roving crime scene, "the Yota."
(Photo courtesy of the Lee County Sheriff's Office)

Before he turned to crime, Kevin Foster's thrills included jumping from the State Road 31 bridge east of Fort Myers. *(Author photo)*

Pete Magnotti had a genius-level IQ, but he retreated into a fantasy world when classmates rejected him. (*Yearbook photo*)

Chris Black's flawed teeth and overweight physique attracted classmates' derision; they called him the Pillsbury Doughboy. (*Yearbook photo*)

Derek Shields dreamed of studying space sciences and joining NASA, but following Kevin Foster earned him life in prison. (*Yearbook photo*)

Southwest Florida's broad waterways, flat landscapes, and proliferating communities were the Lords of Chaos' turf.
(Samuel Johnson/PBS Photography Studio photo)

The Lords of Chaos set fire to a cage at The Hut Restaurant during an early "Terror Night," killing macaws Malicoo and Eurecka.
(Author photos)

The Lords of Chaos got the attention they sought when the gang blew up the historic Coca-Cola Bottling Co. building in Fort Myers, Florida. *(Photo courtesy of the Lee County Sheriff's Office)*

After the bombing, the Lords of Chaos met near the Uncommon Friends statue on the Caloosahatchee in downtown Fort Myers, where Kevin Foster planned more crimes. *(Author photo)*

Derek Shields wanted revenge, so the Lords of Chaos robbed the owner of the Alva Country Diner at gunpoint; Kevin Foster meant to kill him. *(Author photo)*

A Palm Beach Boulevard army surplus store sold the smoke grenade Kevin Foster needed to create a diversion at the mall while the Lords of Chaos robbed a department store. *(Author photo)*

After Kevin Foster's plan to steal clothes at Edison Mall for Grad Nite '96 was thwarted, the boys headed to their school to burn down the auditorium. *(Author photo)*

When RHS band director Mark Schwebes interrupted the boys' plan to burn down the school auditorium, an infuriated Chris Black said his teacher must die. *(Author photo)*

After calling from their favorite pay phone to see if Mark Schwebes was home *(author photo)* the Lords of Chaos headed to Pine Manor, where Kevin Foster gunned down the band director. *(Photo courtesy of the Lee County Sheriff's Office)*

At Brad Young's apartment above the Palm Beach Depot, Kevin Foster boasted about the murder even as he planned more crimes. *(Author photo)*

Craig Lesh *(courtesy of the Lee County Sheriff's Office)* took Julie Schuchard to a Caloosahatchee pier to test her loyalty by telling her he saw the murder. *(Author photo)*

When sheriff's deputies heard that the Lords of Chaos intended to rob the Hardee's where some of the gang worked, they staked the restaurant out for hours. *(Author photo)*

Gill Allen had investigated Kevin Foster's self-inflicted gunshot wound before Schwebes's murder put him back on Foster's trail. *(Photo courtesy of the Lee County Sheriff's Office)*

Dean Taber was fastidious in the details of the investigation that brought the Lords of Chaos to justice. *(Photo courtesy of the Lee County Sheriff's Office)*

Sheriff John J. McDougall said that Kevin Foster led the Lords of Chaos into "a vortex of blood lust and arson." *(Photo courtesy of the Lee County Sheriff's Office)*

Derek Shields *(above)*, *(courtesy of the Lee County Sheriff's Office)* knocked on his band teacher's door, luring Mark Schwebes *(left)* to his death. *(Photo courtesy Pat Schwebes Dunbar)*

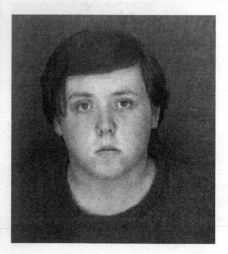

Chris Black said Mark Schwebes had to die. *(Photo courtesy of the Lee County Sheriff's Office)*

Pete Magnotti defied his father's ban on seeing Kevin Foster; the price was a thirty-two-year prison sentence. *(Photo courtesy of the Lee County Sheriff's Office)*

One of Kevin Foster's best friends, Chris Burnett, made a deal with prosecutors that helped bring down the Lords of Chaos. *(Photo courtesy of the Lee County Sheriff's Office)*

Mark Schwebes was murdered in part to protect Tom Torrone—but none of the members of the Lords of Chaos even knew Tom's last name. *(Photo courtesy of the Lee County Sheriff's Office)*

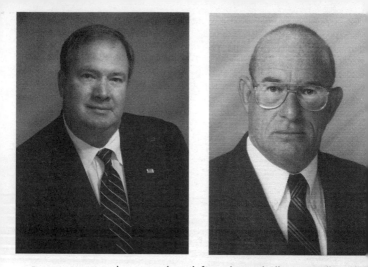

Prosecutors Randy McGruther *(left)* and Marshall King Hall *(right)* were determined to see Kevin Foster and his Lords of Chaos brought to justice for the crime spree that ended in murder. *(Photos courtesy of the Office of the State Attorney)*

Public Defender Bob Jacobs pleaded with jurors and Judge Isaac Anderson, Jr. to spare Kevin Foster's life. *(Photo courtesy of the Office of the Public Defender)*

room-size walk-in fridge across the hall. He cleaned the autopsy room and called the funeral home to tell them Mark was ready. He'd done this thousands of times in more than thirty years, including a stint in Cook County, Illinois, then one of the most violent places in the United States. Perhaps this was why he cracked jokes in the lunchroom, engaged every visitor, probed strangers far beyond customary superficial greetings, insisted on living to the fullest, in the moment, with whomever he was with, because Medina was always aware of something: life is short.

Tom was sailing close to the wind, confirming Kevin's worst fears. "There's something they just did that was big," he boasted to a buddy on the way to lunch.

"Who? What happened?"

Tom wouldn't tell. "LOC," he said.

"What's that?"

"Lords of Chaos."

Tom started talking about the Alva Country Diner. "Pete, Chris, Derek, me and Burnett are in the gang." The boys walked into the lunchroom.

Pete, Chris, Derek and some other boys were having lunch. Pete and Chris seemed sad, out of it, spacey. Derek cried the entire meal, didn't eat.

"It had to be done," Pete said. "Don't get too upset. Derek, don't worry about it, we had to do it." Chris nodded.

"It had to be done," Tom echoed. *Schwebes ain't gonna say nothing now,* he thought, bitterly.

Derek looked at Tom. "We saved you and Chris from going to jail by killing Mr. Schwebes," he said, crying.

"Yeah," Pete said.

Tom just looked at Derek and the others, watched their solemn faces. Other students were crying. It

hit Tom: *He's a human being. He had no reason to be killed.*
Tom was silent the rest of lunch.

It got worse as the day went on and Tom saw how close
the band members were to Mr. Schwebes. With all that
emotion in the classrooms and corridors, Mark Schwebes
seemed a person. His death started to matter. It was too
late. The reminders of Tom's knowledge, intimations of
his complicity, were everywhere. This wasn't how it was
in the movies, the computer games or music—this was
something entirely different, unsettling, raw.

With more and more boys hearing what happened,
the LOC was on the verge of expanding like a cancer-
ous tumor—it might grow to include boys still in
school and boys already gone. As students learned what
had happened, they talked among themselves: They
didn't tell their parents; they didn't talk with teachers;
they didn't go to guidance counselors; they didn't
call deputies. At best, they sat on what they knew. At
worst, they contemplated joining in. Classmates weren't
expelling the cancer among them—they were circling it, fascinated.

A bullet is a single projectile. A shotshell contains multiple projectiles that spread farther apart the farther they
go. Each shell Kevin fired contained two dozen pellets:
some killed Mark; some fell to the floor; some embedded in wall studs. A murderer is like a shotshell, not a
bullet. His action doesn't carry only one consequence,
the death of his victim. It carries multiple consequences
that spread for years. With each pull of the trigger,
Kevin unleashed a dozen consequences beyond Mark's
death—for himself, for his cohorts, for Mark's family and
friends, for his own family and for people he'd never
even know. Bob Mann, ex-boyfriend of Paula Dodd, was
one of Kevin's victims.

By noon, Allen and Taber were interviewing Bob,
who said he met Paula at Shooters, a riverfront bar

and restaurant, and the two dated a little more than a year. He moved in with her after his lease expired. They lived together seven months. Had a lot of fun until it dissolved in Bob's unemployment and subsequent financial problems that meant he no longer could pay Paula's mother rent. The two drifted apart, and he moved out.

Where did Bob go after he talked with Paula the night of the murder? Taber wondered.

"Home."

"You live by yourself?"

"Ah . . . no, actually I'm staying with my . . . ah . . . my wife and my two kids. We've been separated for almost two years."

"Where were you staying before that?"

"At Paula's."

"Okay. No place in between there?"

"No, no. She thinks I was staying at a friend of mine's house."

"Why would she think that?"

"Because that's what I told her. I didn't want her to think that I was going back to my ex-wife—"

"Are you?" Allen interrupted.

"Uhm . . . kind of and kind of not. Kind of working things out. We have two kids . . . a fifteen— . . . ah . . . sixteen-year-old and a ten-year-old."

"What's your wife's—ex-wife's—name?" Allen said.

"Ah . . . Myra. *M-Y-R-A.*"

"Does she know where you were at?" Taber said.

"No, no. Those two don't know each other."

"So you just told her you were staying at Jack's," Taber concluded.

Allen picked up the theme. "Your wife didn't know you were living with . . . ah—this lady for a year?"

"No."

Included in the price Bob paid for Kevin's crimes were the loss of his privacy, revelation of an extramarital affair, stress of repeated interviews by sheriff's agents and, later, depositions by a half-dozen lawyers, interviews of his wife and children, hours of lost work enduring hours of questioning. It wasn't just the invasion of privacy—it was the stress. The price he paid for Kevin included the brief suspicion he might be a killer and the lingering strange taste that left in his life and the lives of those around him long after the questions were satisfactorily answered.

Bob put his departure from Paula's a whole hour earlier than she did, but that didn't allay suspicion. They asked if he'd fired any guns in the last forty-eight hours, whether his buddy had a gun, what car he drove, what color it was, the kind and color of his buddy's vehicle, what kind of car his wife had, what color and—after he said gray—what year. They were especially interested when Bob said his wife's gray '80s car had an intermittent engine tap. They wanted to know about Paula's nearly adult son, *his* car, its color, the son's best friend, whether he'd been arrested, how he got along with his mother, whether he had a drug or alcohol problem, where he was in school, whether he'd met Mark, whether he had guns, whether Paula had guns, how long it took to get from Paula's to Bob's wife's.

"This area that he lives in is a very . . . ," Allen said, "ah . . . I don't know how to explain it. It's not one of the better neighborhoods, but the people there, lack of a better word, they're nosy. So they kind of watch all the movements and stuff that goes on. They have a real good community crime watch." Allen hammered his point home. "Any reason why anybody, you know, later on will tell us that they'd seen your car—or you in that neighborhood?"

"No, no, not at all."

The officers concluded by asking Bob to undergo a test to see if he'd fired a gun recently. He didn't resist. No reason to.

* * *

"Kevin shot Mr. Schwebes in the face," Pete boasted to a friend later that day at school. "He shot him in the ass." Four boys took part—Kevin, Derek, Chris and Pete. Another five boys knew it might happen and did nothing to stop it—including Burnett, Tom, Brad and Craig. Now there was a new category: boys who heard about the murder afterward and didn't report it.

Derek went to work at 3:00 P.M., Pete a little later.
"It was wrong," Derek said. "It was all messed up. The guy didn't need to die."
Pete agreed.
"I want out, and I'm gonna be getting out," Derek said. "I'm gonna quit this whole shit."
"No, you can't," Pete said. "We need you—me and Chris need you. You can't leave." Derek walked away. He didn't want to talk with anyone about the murder again.

Judy Putnam, the Hardee's co-owner, let Pete have Friday night off. He was going to take it easy. The following night was Grad Nite, and he wanted an evening to prepare for the big party at Disney. "I absolutely need it off," he said. Peter had never been like this before, always worked his shifts. Still, if any of the high-school employees had earned the right, it was Peter. From the perspective of management, he was the most trusted and liked high-school employee Hardee's had.

Burnett picked Tom up after work, and the pair went to Lorraine Drive. Kevin stood in the front doorway. "It was cool. Derek knocked on the door. Schwebes opened the door. I stepped out from around the corner and blasted the whole side of his head off. Brains went everywhere. He fell in the fetal position, and then I shot him in the ass. 'Ha, ha, how do you like *that* in your ass?' It was great. You should've been there. Yuh! And then when I went home, I laid down on my bed and I closed my eyes. I seen his face. All I did was rolled over and jacked off and went to sleep. It was the best sleep I ever had."

Meanwhile, deputies still were at Mark's duplex. They photographed it from a helicopter and from the ground. They searched the Bronco and the Mercury for usable fingerprints, finding none. They searched the front door and doorbell for fingerprints. No use. Finally, at 5:35 P.M., they called it a day, sealing the windows and doors with tape.

Burnett got home about 6:00 P.M. Kevin called from the pawnshop. "Watch the news. Tell me what they say."

Reporters interviewed people at school . . . a teacher . . . the principal. Neighbors told of gunshots and a loud car. In a film clip, deputies fingerprinted a truck. Burnett couldn't believe it. Now he *knew* Kevin killed the teacher. This wasn't one of his boasts that could be brushed aside—this was leading the evening news. He didn't call Kevin back.

Brad got home from work. Went out to a pay phone. Paged Burnett. "Well, did anything happen?"

"Yeah, it's all over the news. Watch the news."

"Oh, shit." Brad ran upstairs, but the news was over. He threw up. *He was one of my old teachers.*

Craig came up after work. They sat around. Looked at magazines. Talked. Craig went home, worked on his truck. Frustrated, he punched a piece of Styrofoam. Reopened a cut on his finger. Blood dropped on his shoes.

* * *

At 7:00 P.M., a Dillard's associate made a discovery in the men's denim department. Colleen Whitaker was putting some jeans away. She heard two metal objects clank together. Saw a cylinder. Left it there. A couple of times, she went back and picked it up, concerned a customer might see it. She didn't know what it was. Perhaps it was supposed to be there. She wondered if it might be some kind of display piece. That didn't fit with the expletive written on it. The fourth or fifth time she looked at it, she saw the clip and realized it was a grenade. *I probably shouldn't touch it anymore.* She called over a man from the shoe department who also worked at the sheriff's office at "Six Mile Cypress." He summoned Fort Myers police detective Mark Chitwood, who happened to be moonlighting, working his weekly uniform detail.

The olive-drab cylinder lay on a bottom shelf between two stacks of jeans, the spoon next to it, some powder residue around it. "Fuck you," Chitwood read on the grenade in bold white letters. "Smile." He recognized it as the kind of canister they used on the SWAT team. *Oh, why does this happen on my shift?* He evacuated the sales area. Investigators who descended on the store determined the grenade was inert, photographed it and took it. There had been no bomb threats. No video camera filmed that area of the store. It was logged as a hoax destructive device and sent to the FDLE.

At 8:00 P.M., Kevin called Burnett again, this time from his house. "Come over." Burnett drove Kevin and Tom to Chris's; he was asleep. His dad woke him; he came out and sat in the back of Burnett's truck. "It was awesome," Chris said.

"It was great," Kevin said. "I need to do this more often. You and Tom should've been there. Blood went everywhere." Later he'd explain it was Chris's idea—Chris was the one who said Schwebes had to die—but it wasn't Chris who shot him. "He didn't have the guts, and even if he did, I didn't know if he could do it right and run fast enough." All four boys went back to Kevin's, where Derek and Pete showed up on break from work.

In the front yard, Kevin acted it all out again. "Derek ran out of the way. I was like this. He was right there, and I looked him in the face and he looked at me for a minute, and he, like, went to move or went to turn or something, and he only moved just a little bit, and that's when I pulled the trigger. I was looking at him in his right eye, and when I pulled the trigger, his eye was gone; it was just like a red cloud all around his head. He flew up in the air, curled up and landed in a fetal position with his ass in the air. I chambered the second one, and I just pointed down and shot him in the ass." Kevin laughed. "I was gonna take his wallet, but it was probably full of holes. I was running back to the car, and I was laughing on the way back to the car, and I jumped in. It was kind of like when I shot my uncle. And that was different from snipering people. It takes a real coldhearted bastard to do that, and you *know* that's what I am. Couldn't get that guy's face out of my mind, and I had to go home and jack off and go to sleep. I did it twice, made myself bleed. Why don't you take a look? Why don't you look at my dick?"

The boys declined.

Kevin had done most of the talking, with Pete sometimes interjecting, "Yeah, that's right; yeah, it was cool." Pete seemed to be taking it okay, nothing bothering him. "It was great," he'd said, whereas "It was all right" was the most Derek offered. Chris thought Derek was feeling better already, a read not shared by Burnett: *Only Derek seems to have any remorse*, he thought. He saw Derek was smoking. *That must be nerves. It's hard for Derek. He looks in bad, bad shape. He isn't taking things real well.* Himself, Burnett felt overwhelmed. Didn't know how to take it. "Why did you guys *do* that?" he said.

"He knew too much," Chris said.

"It's just another person," Kevin said. "Pretty soon they'll all be wiped out."

"Keep your mouth shut," the boys told Burnett. "If you tell anybody, you die."

Burnett played with Kevin's Combat Commander. Kevin loaded and unloaded the gun; Burnett loaded and unloaded the gun. Kevin held the .45 to Burnett's head, threatening him as he had since the beginning, but now specifically about the murder. He racked the pistol's slide. "If you ever let anybody know anything, I'll kill you and your family." Threatened Chris the same way. "If you tell about the murder or the crimes, I'll kill you, too."

"I don't know how I'm gonna like having a gun held to my head at Hardee's," Derek said.

"Oh, I just might load it and accidentally get a shaky finger," Kevin said, grinning.

Burnett felt sick to his stomach. He didn't eat dinner. Didn't sleep.

As the reality sank in for Tom, he was getting more and more uncomfortable. "It wasn't right," he told Kevin. "That's fucked up. I'll tell you straight up, that's fucked up." Tom felt the warmth drain away, felt Kevin turn to stone. He never felt warmth from Kevin again.

Kevin, Chris, Burnett and Tom gathered at Brad's to watch the news. Burnett invited Craig over to introduce him to the group. "He's okay," Burnett said. "He really wants to be in."

"This is Slim," Kevin said, introducing Chris. "You want to be part of the LOC?" His eagerness to recruit outweighed his dislike of Craig. "Yota," Kevin nicknamed Craig, because he liked Toyotas, something they had in common.

At 10:00 P.M., the Fox local news came on. When they showed Mark's feet out on the doorstep, the image opened Kevin's verbal floodgates. "Yuh! That was me, I did that," excited as a child. "We done that."

Craig looked at him. "You should've seen the hole," Kevin said, standing up and reenacting the whole thing in detail, how he was standing, where he shot him, what it looked like, gesturing. Kevin made the hand gesture that started at his nose and went to the right of his face: "All of a sudden, half of his face was flyin'." Pantomiming holding a shotgun. A macabre show-and-tell in which Kevin showed and told how he shot and killed. Hooting, hollering, bragging. "You got what you deserved!" Kevin was saying to the TV. "And we're not gonna get caught. I shot him in the ass. Since he was a fag, I figured he liked it like that." Kevin had chambered the second round and shot him in the butt: "You like that, huh?" Kevin was laughing as he ran back to the waiting car.

"I heard you laugh," Chris said.

"If anyone talks to the police, I'll dig a grave," Kevin told Brad. He looked at Craig. "Two graves."

The cops were looking for three Hispanic males. *Hilarious,* Kevin thought. The news report mentioned the loud muffler. "Oh, shit," Kevin said. "Jesus Christ, we've got to get that muffler fixed."

When the report ended, Kevin said, "I went home and jacked off and went to bed. I didn't lose any sleep."

Kevin's crazy, Brad thought.

Chris was angry Kevin was running his mouth in front of Craig. *I've known this guy about ten minutes. He's sitting here telling him about this shit. He's just telling this to a total stranger.* He kept his thoughts to himself and, in spite of misgivings, followed Kevin's example, boasting he brought up the idea to kill Mr. Schwebes. The boys told Brad about breaking windows, ripping off cars, tearing them up. Kevin asked Brad if he knew about the diner robbery. Burnett had told him, but also asked Brad not to say anything, so he acted dumb. Now Kevin told the story.

"Yeah, we were yelling, 'LOC! LOC!'" Tom said about the Coke bombing. Tom seemed a liability, a loudmouthed braggart. *Another nut, but not one to fear.* Brad also thought Kevin might shoot Tom or get rid of him somehow, because Tom was going to give everything away. "Yeah, we burned that place, and whenever we go by, I take my hat off and salute," Tom said.

"Does he know about Friday night?" Kevin said, looking at Brad.

"No," Burnett said.

So the boys told Brad about the plan for Hardee's, how easy it'd be with Pete and Derek working there. They wanted Brad, a starter electrician, to strip out the alarm system. "Can you disable the alarm?" Kevin asked him.

"Yeah." *Why did I say that? It's not true. I don't want any part of this.*

Kevin wanted to get a couple of cars from inside the gates at Interstate Motors on Palm Beach Boulevard, too. "That's not a wise idea," Brad said. "They got dogs, and they've got a watchman there every night." *They're not all that bright,* he thought. *No matter how sure he is of himself, Kevin's gonna get caught.*

Craig also was coming to see Kevin as crazy. He'd lost any respect he had for Kevin from the night at mosquito control. He knew about the Coke plant, Dillard's, Disney. Kevin had taken to talking up the scheme among the group, asking the others, "You're going to Disney World, right?" Craig wasn't interested in crime, figured he'd bypass the gang part, just join to have friends, hang out. Seeing the TV news scared Craig, though—for Brad, for himself, made him think he'd rather sit at home, stay away from these guys.

Working Saturday would give him an excuse to avoid Disney.

"I'm telling you, you say anything, I can dig two graves," Kevin said, looking at Brad and Craig.

If he shot a teacher to keep from getting in trouble, what's he gonna do to me? Brad thought. In Kevin, Brad saw a kid who'd do anything to escape boredom. Kevin wanted to be known, be top dog, be followed. Which suited the others around him just fine, because they wanted someone to follow. *He says jump, they ask how high. If they please him, that makes them feel good.* Brad was sick to his stomach about the murder. When he thought about it, he wanted no part of the Hardee's robbery. *Okay, this kid, if I tell him no . . . he's whacked-out. . . . He just killed a guy for stopping his buddies from burning down a school.*

Kevin and Cindi talked a couple of times between the night Mark died and Friday. Kevin asked if she'd come hang out or go to the pawnshop, neither of which she did. In retrospect, what struck her was Kevin mentioned nothing about any LOC crimes. "I'm going to Orlando," Kevin said. "You should come. It's gonna be a blast. We're gonna have a blast."

Cindi later would wonder what Kevin meant by that.

Deputies were coming to know Mark after death. *Danced at the Riverdale Raiders' band ice-cream social . . . in high spirits. . . . Former marine. . . . No criminal record. . . . Spotless school district personnel file . . . above-average evaluations glowing about his infectious enthusiasm. . . . Born October 7, 1963, in Patchogue, New York. . . . Raised here . . . . Bachelor. . . . Briefly married in college . . . divorced . . . no children . . . but look at what he did for children. . . .*

And it was clear the RHS community felt fortunate, because here was a former marine who knew how to keep discipline, and a young man who liked to work with kids and was a musician. Mark was hired just in time for August band camp.

Answered his door to . . . someone . . . about 11:30 P.M. . . . He'd kicked off his shoes . . . padding around in his socks. . . . And maybe he was thinking about that concrete pad . . . and maybe he was thinking about Paula . . . and maybe he was just thinking what a long day he had . . . when . . . someone knocked. . . . Not a great neighborhood . . . . But he's young . . . thirty-two . . . and he's an ex-marine . . . and he's altruistic . . . and he's the kind of man who opens doors to people, believing he might be of help.

Bang!

However immune you think you've become, all this emotion gets to you. For investigators, often it hit as an overwhelming tiredness. *It's the cumulative effect. All these people. Contagious emotion.* Investigators didn't even know Mark, but despite their best efforts felt it anyway. A weakness, some felt, but difficult to avoid. Mark's father was so shocked, he was unable to articulate much of anything.

Bang!

Then there was Arnold. "He went left, I went right. Then I got a call early this morning." That's how it was: Sudden. Violent. Emotionally traumatizing.

The longer you stare at it, the uglier it gets.

Deputies weren't contemplating a gang. They focused on the apparent love triangle. People rarely were gunned down by strangers in Lee County in 1996: random killings were rare—maybe one or two in a decade. Alcoholic hazes and domestic fights, easy money trading drugs or sex on shadowy street corners, forays into the seamier side of the night: homicides mostly resulted from bad choices—lifestyle murders. If you weren't drunk, using illegal drugs, a prostitute, a player in the drug trade, someone caught up in an increasingly abusive relationship, your chances of being murdered in Lee County were slight. In the '90s, 45 percent of victims had been drinking, and on average, they were legally drunk; one in three had been using marijuana, cocaine or both. Detectives called crack cocaine a serial killer. Mark was one of twenty murder victims in the county that year: for every homicide, three died on the roads. So it made sense for sheriff's investigators to inquire whether Mark might've been killed by someone close to him. Mark's encounter at the auditorium didn't seem important. It'd been a story at his last dinner. No one linked it to murder.

Sobered, Burnett started to see things differently. Some of the stuff they were talking about was crazy. Disney, for example. In the version that stuck in Burnett's mind, Kevin would meet up with Pete, Chris and Derek at Disney. Breaking the sobriety rule, they'd get drunk. Kevin would shoot some of the costumed characters—maybe some of the others would join him. Kevin and perhaps the others would put on the costumes. Kevin would shoot everybody. "I hate everyone equally," Kevin had said. "I'm just gonna kill everybody."

The weapons, he said, would have homemade silencers.

"It'll be cool," the others had said. "It'll be awesome."

If Kevin thought he couldn't get out of Disney World, he'd go to the tunnels, try to hide; if discovered, he'd tell everyone he was digging for gold, act crazy to escape responsibility. Or maybe he'd blow something up. They were gonna have a mine shaft explosion, he'd said with a hint of manic craziness.

But Kevin isn't crazy, Burnett thought. *Kev's actually very smart.*

* * *

Kevin lay awake thinking. He had no regrets about killing the teacher. *It really ain't shit. It ain't shit: it's like stepping on a cockroach.* The way he saw it, the only possible regret would be getting caught, and that just didn't seem likely. There was nothing they could do with the shotshells without a gun. Even if they got the Mossberg, the shells would be useless. The noisy muffler would be fixed. There was nothing else to connect him to the scene. No fingerprints. Nothing he dropped. Nothing he left with. No blood. Nothing—except words. The only thing that could hurt would be the blabbing of the other boys, and they were so tied up in the crimes, they weren't going to rat on themselves.

Derek's behavior was particularly puzzling. Why weep? Why lose sleep? Why not just sit back and laugh at all the trouble they caused? *It's a weakness.*

He languidly wished he'd killed the other boys that night. The problem was, everyone knew who they hung with. Plus, they were his crew, who would help him with further schemes.

CHAPTER 22

Craig + Julie

Julie Schuchard lived with her parents, siblings and ten-month-old daughter, Katie, on Chattanooga Drive a few doors from sometime-boyfriend Craig. They dated . . . broke up . . . dated . . . broke up . . . four or five times. Her own soap opera. She would've been graduating with the Class of '96 but dropped out in sophomore year. Whatever else was going on, Craig was there. She came to love him like a brother—which from Craig's perspective was the problem.

The year 1995 was a rough one in the Craig and Julie saga. Julie didn't see much of Craig, who spent part of the year in Georgia getting over his crack habit. He moved back to Chattanooga Drive in December, done with crack. Stuck to alcohol and only beer at that—Budweiser.

Craig's best friend Brad was in Julie's sophomore class at Fort Myers High. She thought him good-looking. He was stocky; Craig was skinny with short reddish brown hair and lots of freckles—always dressed in T-shirts, jeans, cowboy boots and his favorite Dixie ball cap. Julie had never seen Brad in trouble. He was always trying to talk Craig out of bad decisions. In contrast, Craig was quite capable of saying things that made trouble for Brad.

Craig had a split personality, Julie thought. He loved her and was always trying to get back with her, but he could be careless and mean. The only time she saw him with a gun, he accidentally shot her sister with a BB. He often voiced racism. When a mixed-race neighbor moved in, he told Julie they should burn a cross in the front yard. Julie's truck was repeatedly egged. Someone locked the four-by-four hubs, which could've messed up the bearings if she hadn't noticed it. She suspected Craig and Brad.

One moment, Craig would help with Katie—changing her, making a bottle, rocking her to sleep. The next moment, he wouldn't let Julie leave the room, saying, "How long do I have to wait for you?" Pushing her around when she rebuffed him. For a while, Julie watched Katie real close, because Craig would come to the house, walk in, say nothing, sit staring at the baby, not talking to her, not playing with her, off in his own world. "She should've been mine," he said.

When Craig came back from Georgia, they resumed dating. Then there was one of those dramatic evenings—fighting, screaming, tears, accusations—and they broke up. He went home and swallowed a bottle of aspirin, then called 911. Ended up in Charter Glade for depression. The next morning, Julie's mother was hollering, "It's all your fault. . . . You broke up with him."

They didn't date after Craig got out of Charter Glade.

Thursday, May 2, 1996

The front page of the *News-Press* was enough to make Kevin want to puke. *Fuck, makes him into a fuck-*

ing saint. HIS MUSIC FALLS SILENT, the headline said, below a flattering portrait of the smiling band director and above a photo of band members and boosters hugging or wiping tears. "A man who brought merriment into the lives of many students," the story raved, "former U.S. Marine . . . above-average evaluations glowed about his infectious enthusiasm." *Schwebes was a fag who deserved what he got.* The content was annoying, the attention wonderful—and it was nice to see reporters and cops nowhere near the truth. He kept the paper and later tossed it in Pete's trunk, another souvenir among scavenger hunt loot.

At 2:15 P.M., Gill Allen and Dean Taber were still aggressively pursuing the love triangle, calling Bob Mann again. The detectives covered a lot of the same ground they went over yesterday, looking for inconsistencies, locking Bob into his story. How many times had Bob seen Mark? Any hostile words? Four times they crossed paths: twice in after-school gatherings at bars, once distributing pamphlets—and then there was Paula's Thanksgiving dinner back in November. She had a dozen people over, who otherwise would be alone for an "orphan" Thanksgiving. Mark was first to arrive. Bob was helping cook and set up. They talked a few minutes, Mark drawn to the computer sitting in a corner. "Help yourself," Bob said. "We got stuff to do."

Around Bob, Mark was withdrawn. Drank too many cocktails. Smoked, dropping ash and butts on the lanai tile floor. "I wonder if he does this at his house?" Bob said, cleaning up. He wondered aloud, not for the last time, if Mark was gay. "I never seen him with a girl," Paula said. But Mark told her he wasn't homosexual.

"He's either gay or he's a mama's boy," Bob said. It was Mark's mannerisms, an aura. *Gay mannerisms,* Bob thought.

It was clear Bob hadn't liked Mark. Was it a murderous dislike? Allen showed Bob a photo of Mark, gauging his reaction. Why was the relationship with Paula falling apart? They asked about Bob's tattoos. His childhood in a New Jersey resort town. Whether guys he ran with up there got into trouble. His parents' divorce. His relationship with them. Allen became as much psychiatrist as cop, exploring whether Bob was possessive or jealous, how he felt when he wanted to go out with Paula and she'd no longer go. She went with other people, but suggested staying home if it was Bob—almost like she didn't want to be seen in public with him. "You and I need to be a little bit more up front with each other as far as the relationship between you and Paula and Mark," Allen said. "We've all been through relationships. We all had things ripped apart. There's always an obvious reason. Even though maybe we don't want to admit to them in open public. Even to a couple of cops, right off the bat. But we need to get more information out about your relationship with Paula and Mark. The relationship with your wife. Mark's relationships. Ah . . . what happened in January? Mark come into the picture?"

"From what I understand, they've been working together for longer. He was with the band, and she was a cheerleader. And they were working on plays together and things like that."

Allen owned a fish house in Pine Island Sound. The stilt houses were surrounded by shallow water, almost within sight of Boca Grande Pass, one of the world's prime tarpon spots. A fisherman would fight a tarpon for hours. Reel the great fish in. Let it swim. Let it tire. Reel it in. Give it room to run, tire some more. Reel it in. The battle continued until the fish was exhausted and the angler landed it. Which was how the interview went. Two conversations were going on between Bob and the detectives, primarily Allen. Moments such as the discussion about Paula and Mark were the battles, when Allen reeled Mann in. Then he let him swim on some slack. And so it was now. They drifted off into lighter subjects. What he did with his son. How much he drank. What brand of beer (it wasn't Busch). About the TV movie he started watching at Paula's, then returned home to. Reeled him in again. The time discrepancy. Why Bob and Paula drifted apart. Why he and his wife separated. How his wife would react to the affair. How the kids felt. Then Taber, too, reeled Bob in: "When you and Paula would go out with the whole group and Mark was there, how did you feel? How did you feel if they were out and you came up and Mark was there? Did it bother you?"

"If it was just her and Mark?"

"Or if even Mark was there every, *every, everywhere* you went. I mean, you went and there they were together or they were not *together,* but they were there. Did it bother you?"

"Ah . . . no, not—"

"It didn't upset you that everywhere you went, there's Mark?"

"It wasn't like that. He wasn't everywhere I went."

"Do you think that . . . ah . . . relationship between Paula and Mark was—"

"I know *now* it was, yes. Paula broke down and told me about it. She told me that . . . ah . . . first she told me she went to bed with him once, and then later on she told me she's slept with him three times."

"Do you know when the first time was?"

"She said . . . ah . . . before spring break, after I moved out. Somewheres around that area."

"You ask her if she slept with him or what?"

"What brought it up was we were talking about the situation with me coming back here. I said, 'You know, this doesn't look good as far as, you know, you . . . Mark . . . and, you know.' I said, 'If there's anything you got to tell me—'"

"And she told you she slept with him how many times?"

"Three times. Twice before Easter, their Easter break . . . and then Sunday night."

"Last time was Sunday night?"

"Yeah."

"Did you ever suspect?" Allen said. "Be honest now."

"Well, have I *ever* suspected Paula?"

"Paula and Mark."

"Paula's a very . . . well . . . Not just Paula and Mark, but Paula and anybody, really, I mean—"

"So Paula's—"

"She's a very vibrant . . . She's a very . . . ah . . . she's very . . . ah . . . ah . . . What am I trying to say?"

"Vivacious."

"Vivacious . . . ah . . . she's—"

"Okay, so Paula—"

"—she's not shy."

He had his suspicions; he'd asked about Mark. Allen got him to concede he wondered for at least two months. Allen pushed to see if he might've spied on Paula or followed her, which he denied. He pushed on how much he borrowed from her. Had he paid anything back? Then Allen laid out the theory, the reason they were persisting: "How do you feel about losing your job and being in that situation at your age?"

"Tough. I'm gonna be thirty-eight tomorrow, so kind of like starting—"

"How do you feel about losing your job, owing a certain woman thousands of dollars and finding out she'd been having an affair and going to bed with this guy? If I was in your shoes right now—"

"Um-hmm."

"I lost my job. I owe this woman I was with for a year and thought I cared a lot about five thousand dollars—"

"I do care about her."

"And now I find out she's been sleeping with some guy, and I had suspicions since January and—and . . .

you know. And now I'm back with my wife again. I mean, things aren't real great."

"Not really back with my wife."

"Well, things aren't real great, right? I mean it's a sad story here that I'm hearing."

It *was* a sad story, but not one that ended as the partners speculated. Bob viewed himself as a fighter, the kind of guy who didn't stay down long. Allen said he was a salesman once, which was actually true, and suggested the instinct of a salesman is to remove obstacles. Bob said he was losing interest anyway. Allen implied bar patrons told him about Bob's jealousy. He asked about Bob and Paula's sex life. How Bob got along with Paula's son. About Paula's guns. How Bob got home. About the two different guys Bob told Paula and his wife he lived with. Those guys' vehicles. How his wife contacted him during the separation.

At 3:45 P.M., Taber and Allen quit the interview abruptly, done for now.

The press was also on the wrong track. A reporter had learned about the second shot. SECOND SHOT CLUE IN MURDER. The report quoted Dr. Joe Davis, recently retired Miami-Dade County district medical examiner, a Florida legend credited with pioneering the state's death investigation system, considered by many forensic pathologists to be the nation's best because of its independence and professionalism. "When you're trying to equate motive to the wound pattern, it's fraught with a lot of guesswork and speculation," Davis said. "Anytime you draw a conclusion, it means you're assuming certain things. I usually don't try to read anything into it until it's all over." Was Mark's killer a bad shot who intended the second shell to strike elsewhere? Did he trip as he fired? Was he nervous or using a weapon with a hair trigger that accidentally fired as he turned to leave? After appropriate caution, the great man speculated: "That'd connote a sexual motivation. It'd tend to suggest some sort of sexual revenge/triangle–type motive, if you make certain assumptions." It was *so* tempting. In a way, it was right. *Faggot motherfucker. You like it up the ass?* The second shot *was* rooted in a sexual motive. But it said more about killer than victim. And where police and press were looking was wrong.

At RHS, Pete and Chris were looking forward to Hardee's and trying to recruit another boy. Meanwhile, Derek stayed home. He had an English project to finish, and his family was moving. Derek didn't do much of anything on either project. He spent most of the day sleeping fitfully in the back of his stepdad's pickup.

At 3:00 P.M., Pete popped into Judy Putnam's office at Hardee's to confirm he had the night off. Chris was usually with Pete when he stopped by to pick up his pay or check the schedule. Their old differences long forgotten, Chris would joke with her. Today, when he stuck his head into his former boss's office, he held back. *Distant. Strange.*

Brad's mother stopped by the apartment to see why he missed work. Said he was sick to his stomach. Brad wanted to tell her *so* bad. *If he's gonna shoot the guy just for stopping them from doing something, what's he gonna do if I tell? What's Kevin gonna do to my mother?* They were still talking when Craig stopped by.

Craig felt like unburdening, too. He went over to Julie's. He didn't know why he was about to do what he was about to do. It was stupid. He wanted to see if she cared. It was a test.

* * *

Taber pursued the love triangle, interviewing Bob's sixteen-year-old daughter, who swore her dad was home at the time of the murder.

Then Taber interviewed Bob's wife, Myra. Her husband came home at 9:50 P.M. while she and her children were watching a movie. He'd been working. Sometimes his sales calls ran over a couple of hours. He changed into shorts. Fixed himself a plate with the remains of the sloppy joes and joined them watching the movie. "What's it about?" he asked. His daughter filled him in. The movie bored Myra. Mother and children got ready for bed. Bob stayed up and watched *M*A*S*H*. Came to bed after Myra was asleep.

Taber didn't tell Myra what her husband was doing. He wasn't certain himself. He learned about the family routine and frustrations . . . about the daughter riding the bus an hour every day to high school. The late-night call the daughter got, at perhaps 11:20 P.M. "Who the hell's calling?" Bob said. The separation just ended with Myra's return from New Jersey because the daughter didn't like the large, tough high school up there, so Myra was giving it another try in a region where she hadn't been happy, out in the boonies of Southwest Cape Coral—nowheresville—unemployed, nothing to do, stank, kids hated it. About the gun Bob owned many years ago. Hung over the mantel. Meant for hunting, but he never used it. She didn't want it around—her son was only four or five. Bob took it to his mother's, then sold it.

So it was with a homicide investigation. In a way, it was appalling, the blasé intrusion into intimate details of strangers' lives. . . . Dancing around the obvious extramarital affair, not telling the wife . . . who maybe would want to know and maybe wouldn't . . . maybe knew in her own way and maybe didn't, knowing and not knowing not being such simple things. Appalling, all these words. Words full of the mundane. Part of what was so terrible was the mundane evil of mediocre lives: the lies . . . shattered dreams . . . isolation even in families . . . watching TV in separate rooms . . . coming to bed after she was asleep and getting up after she was gone . . . . "Who the hell's calling?" . . . the $300 car phone bill because the husband had no other phone . . . the separated wife calling collect to a cell phone . . . sometimes his beeper . . . sometimes work . . . living in an efficiency, then with some guy named Jon, somebody she wouldn't know if she fell over him, but not staying because it didn't feel right and there was drinking. . . . Nineteen years of marriage it'd be, come September. Sometimes Bob popped home at noon if it was slow. And there'd be nights he'd be home at 6:00 P.M. but he was rarely home at dinnertime, and if he was he went back out again . . . and nights he worked later, eight, nine or ten o'clock. Sometimes he went to Naples . . . Port Charlotte . . . Marco Island. Strange hours. He wasn't communicative, but she thought he felt bad about the kids. . . . "Who the hell's calling?" . . . Some boy, some boy too interested. "He's been down here without me and the kids for a year. I've no clue what he does when he's out, who his friends are. I've no clue, 'cause I haven't been here. And he's not real talkative."

"Right."

"We're like night and day."

All more than a detective should know about a stranger's life and all unremarkable to Taber, something he'd been exposed to so frequently he was immune. The people Taber dealt with were mostly varying degrees of scum, so much furniture, little colonies in the pestilence of humanity, people whose lives of quiet desperation only became noteworthy with the brief eruption of evil from the mundane . . . a gunshot . . . squeal of brakes . . . fist hitting a face . . . child whimpering, "Daddy touched me there." . . . Self-inflicted gunshots and homicidal gunshots . . . crack pipes . . . Baggies of pot . . . children who weren't virgins and parents who were children. . . . Taber faced a parade of human driftwood, and perhaps that was why he dressed so well, like he just walked off the cover of *GQ*, seams always straight, shirts always pressed, ties always perfect, a man who'd reach down and pluck a small piece of lint from his jacket, as if to say, "See, I'm not one of them. I clean up after them and I put them away, but I'm not, never was and never will be one of them."

Derek would go up to Kevin, tell him he was through. He was getting out of this. Today. He went to Chris's; the two went to Lorraine Drive. Pete, Burnett and Tom were there. Derek looked at Kevin. He couldn't do it. Burnett came up and tried to shake his hand. "You did a good job." Derek backed away. Didn't want to talk about it.

Tom wouldn't be in on the Hardee's robbery. "You're not gonna go with us," Kevin said, concerned about Tom talking—and about his loyalty, since Tom disapproved of the killing.

Like Derek, both Tom and Burnett were starting to feel trapped, and they discussed their predicament. "Man, maybe we shouldn't hang around with Kevin no more, now that we know what we know." It seemed a catch-22: "What would happen if we *didn't* hang around Kevin?" Maybe they should leave town.

Kevin told the boys about his uncle Gary again, how this wasn't the first time he killed somebody with a shotgun.

He wanted a 4Runner for the Hardee's hit. They headed downtown. Now a murder conspirator, Pete still worried about making curfew. It'd be the last time all the boys set out on a mission. They looked for the right vehicle in downtown Fort Myers and south of the city. Later models frustrated Kevin—more sophisticated ignition-locking mechanisms. Older 4Runners were easy pickings. It always impressed Pete, seemed Kevin was done in thirty seconds. They found one on Fowler Street.

A Fort Myers police car crawled by. The boys left the car lot and strolled over to a bench. Kevin lit a Marlboro Red. The officer stopped. Chatted. Left. They failed to steal because police were patrolling.

The sun went down as Kevin and the LOC attempted in vain to steal the 4Runner . . . and Craig walked the familiar route along Chattanooga Drive to the Schuchard home. He chatted with Julie and her parents. "Have you heard about the teacher at Riverdale that had his head blown off?"

"Oh, yeah," Julie's mother said, jumping in, "you *didn't* hear about that, did you?"

"Somebody went up to the door," Craig said, telling the story as though it was something he heard, a rumor around town. The detail was remarkable.

Craig stared into Julie's eyes. He gestured out the door to the garage. "Can I talk to you for a second?"

They went outside. *The last couple of weeks, he's been acting really weird.*

"I'm gonna *have* to tell you this, 'cause you're my friend, and I know I can trust you. You gotta swear to God you won't tell nobody."

"Well, you go ahead." *No big deal, whatever it is.*

"You know that teacher at Riverdale? . . . It was us."

Julie was silent. *He's never been into anything like* this *before. He gets hooked up with the wrong people. He's not a leader, he's a follower.* "Us?" . . . "'Us' who? What's going on, Craig?"

"We were gonna go to Riverdale and blow it up with a homemade bomb."

They walked to the end of a fishing pier in the nearby riverside park.

After more than three hours, what came out was something like a game of telephone. What Kevin told Craig wasn't exactly what happened; what Craig thought he heard wasn't exactly what Kevin had said; what Craig relayed to Julie was part what Kevin said and part Craig's embellishments and part what seemed convenient to fill inevitable gaps, many of which only came to light through Julie's questions. What Julie heard was something else again.

Julie—at times so scared that for once in her life she was nearly speechless—got the impression the teacher was driving around RHS in a golf cart and caught them. . . . He was going to turn them in to the cops. . . . He took two or three peach cans off the others and a pair of gloves off Craig . . . Chris knew the teacher and didn't like him. . . . They went to Brad's and planned the murder. . . . They planned to knock on the teacher's door, shoot him with a shotgun.

They're in Chris's—dark blue? dark green?—car . . . no muffler, a real loud car . . . a Maverick? . . . not a Maverick, but an older car. . . . When he drives it, it's real loud. . . . Three of them were in the car . . . they went to Brad's apartment. . . . They'd been meeting there. . . . Chris, Kevin and Craig were there for sure when the teacher died. . . . Craig had known the other boys three weeks. . . . At Brad's, they decided Craig would knock on the door. . . . Kevin didn't like Mr. Schwebes—thought he's a faggot. . . . Brad's with them when they plan it, but he wasn't with them when they killed. . . . Kevin shot the teacher. . . . Craig's the one who went up to the door . . . 12:30 A.M.? 1 A.M.? . . . Craig put his hat down over his face . . . knocked . . . figured they're just bull-shitting, they ain't gonna do nothing. . . . Didn't know they had a gun . . . the teacher answered. . . . Craig turned and ran without a word. . . . Kevin put on a black ski mask . . . Kevin had a big rifle . . . Kevin's gun . . . Kevin shot . . . Craig looked back . . . the teacher's head exploded. . . . The teacher went to the

ground. . . . Kevin walked up to him, shot him again
. . . . Craig got back in on the right side of the car. . . .
"In his head. Took half his head off. And then he
shot him in his butt."

Julie wondered if Craig wore his Adidas hat or his
Florida Marlins hat, the white one with the little symbol.

Kevin found $300 in the teacher's wallet. "Did you
take any of the money?"

"They were gonna give me some of the money. But
I didn't take it."

Perhaps Craig felt $300 a more credible motive for
murder than the possibility of facing questions from
a school resource officer about some canned fruit
and a pair of gloves. Perhaps it just seemed a credible
detail. Perhaps refusing the money cast him in a more
positive light, the *troubled* co-conspirator, the teen
killer *with a conscience*. "I feel bad. I didn't know they
planned on killing him. I'm just, like, going over and
over in my mind."

Julie, who knew nothing about bombs, wondered
if they were going to mix a whole bunch of stuff together and put it in a fruit can. From what she understood, a Chris and a Kevin . . . *Or was it Robert?* . . . were
at RHS with Craig. She didn't know their last names.
She had no idea how old they were. Just they helped
Craig out. "Did Brad go with you?"

"No."

"There are only four of you guys?"

"There's more."

If Craig would get out, she'd move in with him.

That wouldn't be right, he said, playing the corny
twisted soap opera to the hilt. They had to be together because they both wanted to, not because she
felt she had to. Craig had set himself a trap: if Julie
came to him this way, it wouldn't work.

Julie's impression: *the teacher said he was gonna turn
them in; Chris knew the teacher and didn't like him; they*

made bombs; the gang sold pot; Craig's smoking pot. "Why did you guys *do* this?"

"Well, it's a shame this guy got—It's all *his* fault—If he never came around and stopped us, he'd still have his life."

"Craig, no, it's not the teacher's fault. The cause of it was you guys went to the school to bomb it. Because of him catching you guys, then you guys killed him."

"Two of our friends work at Hardee's," Craig said. Julie figured that might be the Kevin and the Chris. "We're planning on going in and we're gonna hold one of them hostage. It's a ten-thousand-dollar job." The robbery would be his initiation. He'd watch the door. After that, there'd be no turning back.

Julie begged him not to go. She'd go out with him Friday. Craig declined. He needed the money from the robbery—but it sure was nice to hear her say it.

Craig had proven he'd do absolutely anything to impress her.

It struck Julie it'd been hard to get Craig's story straight. Each time it was a little different. He didn't know exactly what they were going to do; they planned it. They were going to shoot the teacher; he didn't know they had a gun. Kevin was hanging out the car window; Kevin was standing. There also were gaps. Craig didn't say where Mr. Schwebes lived. Didn't say who was driving. Wasn't clear what color or kind of car. Still, for a game of telephone played by a couple of high-school dropouts, the story had come out remarkably close to the truth.

"I haven't told anybody else."

"Are you in this—What is it?"

"Call us a gang. Call us whatever you want to."

"If you don't get out, I'm gonna tell," she said, more like an elementary-school kid threatening to rat out a peer to a teacher than the mother of a ten-month-old threatening to turn a murder accomplice over to the cops.

"You might as well put a gun straight to my head."
In Craig's mind, Julie passed the test: she did care; she
wanted him out.

When they got back, Brad was at Julie's house. He
and Craig threw water on each other and wrestled, still
teens in spite of the weight they carried.

Julie lay awake. *I feel bad. I'm scared. I hate to tell, 'cause
Craig's my friend, and I've known him so long.* She thought
about Mark's parents wondering who killed their son.
About Katie. *If it was my daughter, I'd have to know. . . .
I knew Mr. Schwebes. He was real cute. If I was in his mother
and dad's position, I'd want to know who killed my child. . . .
Out of respect for them, that'd be the best thing for me to do.* Julie
tossed and turned. What if someone found out she
knew? What if she told and someone killed her? She felt
sick. She wanted to dig a hole and bury herself. But
Mark Schwebes was dead, and she could alleviate his
family's pain. The decision was all hers.

CHAPTER 23

Snitch

Friday, May 3, 1996

Kevin worked his normal hours Thursday and Friday, and even in retrospect, his coworkers noticed nothing different. "Second shot clue in murder . . . Investigators focus on teacher's relationships," he read in the *News-Press*. "Was Schwebes' death a crime of passion?" Kevin was delighted. Everyone was on the wrong track. The story talked about a doorstep confrontation between the teacher and another man; neighbors described a light-colored early-1980s Ford Tempo; almost the only accurate detail was the loud muffler. "Focusing too much on one theory could distract investigators from the real motive and the right suspects," the story cautioned. Exactly what Kevin hoped.

RHS band students wore garnet T-shirts in tribute to their slain director. Wearing his, Derek went to school with a new resolve: he'd go along with this Hardee's robbery, then get the heck away from the

LOC. He pulled out some paper and envelopes. He'd write notes to his mother and the police and leave them in his car. If anything happened to him, the car would be searched, if not by the police, then at least by his mother. She'd searched Fred's. The letters would explain. If he died in the robbery, police would solve his teacher's murder. And there wouldn't be lingering questions, like those surrounding Fred's death. Somehow, the notes never got written. He'd come to wish they had.

Julie hadn't slept well, and now she paced. "What's wrong?" her mother said. It took thirty minutes to get an answer.

"What if you knew about somebody that got hurt? What would you do?"

"What do you mean, they 'got hurt'?"

"Like buried six feet underneath the ground."

"What do you know?" Near tears.

"I can't tell you." A Mormon, Julie wanted to talk to her bishop. That'd have to wait, her mother said, telling her to call deputies.

At the daily 8:00 A.M. briefing, the Schwebes homicide investigation abruptly changed course: A young lady and her mother wanted to meet Gill Allen at a fishing pier in east Fort Myers. Her name was Schuchard. Julie Schuchard. She had information about who did the murder.

When Jesse Mitchell saw Chris, he had an intuition. With the band director dead, the bizarre boasts and the offer to retaliate for perceived wrongs, Jesse wondered. He remembered other incidents. Some rednecks had accused Chris of homosexuality. "Those boys are dead,"

Chris had said. . . . Chris was walking in from the track with a girl after PE. Some Hispanic boys teased him about his teeth. Chris turned to the girl: "Don't be surprised if you look in the newspaper and there's some dead Mexicans." In hindsight, Jesse found the threats troubling. "Did you kill Mr. Schwebes?" he asked Chris.

"Why would you think that? No. We didn't do nothin' like that."

"Okay," Jesse said, neither hassling his buddy nor believing him. He saw Chris, Pete and Derek together and just knew they were all in on it, from the way they acted, the cryptic speech and knowing glances.

"You have to keep your mouth shut," Derek said. "You're part of this—you can't tell anybody."

At the park where she had talked with Craig, Julie met Allen, Taber and Randy Collmer. She told the detectives what Craig told her and took them on a guided tour that included his house and Brad's apartment. At 10:40 A.M., she gave a videotaped statement at the Lee County Sheriff's Office, nicknamed Six Mile Cypress for the parkway it fronted. She rambled, sharing her life with the detectives. She mentioned she had a new pickup. "Currently my ex-boyfriend has it. He stoled it from me a few days ago."

"Not having a lot of luck with boyfriends, huh?" Allen said.

"No. I'm gonna steal it back, though. Play a game for a while."

She gave the detectives an eyewitness—they thought. "So, he saw him do the shooting?" Allen said.

"Yeah, he seen Kevin do it."

She told them about the planned Hardee's robbery; that they were going to take one of their friends hostage; that they'd be there around 5:00 P.M. for the night shift. Allen probed for tips on how to deal with Craig and Brad. She wanted to be kept out of it. He assured her she would.

"Craig might talk to you. He might. I know he's really scared."

Craig had described the murder so accurately— down to the corner of the house he ran around after he knocked on the door—one had to believe he was there. Julie told them where he worked, and they arranged to bring him in. At 11:21 A.M., they ended the interview so they could call a friend of Julie's and find out Brad's last name.

A freshman trumpet player was handing out garnet-and-gold ribbons to kids wearing band shirts. She had the idea for the band to march around the school and play in tribute to their slain director. "Does everyone have a ribbon?" walking past Derek.

"Can I have a ribbon?" he said.

She had in mind it'd just be marching-band students, no one else. And it was, except a boy from the jazz band marched with them—Derek.

An agent requested a list of past and present Alva Country Diner employees, suggesting Emory Lewis highlight anyone who left under adverse circumstances. Lewis hadn't had much experience with employees leaving on bad terms and offered only one possibility—Derek. Lewis doubted this would lead to the culprits.

It should've been a good day for Craig. Today he'd make the last truck payment to Julie's father. He'd move out of his mother's house now the truck was paid for, but it got complicated. He was picked up at 1:13 P.M.

Allen and Taber successfully confused Craig about

their source. When Craig mentioned Julie Schuchard, Allen acted nonchalant, as though he'd never heard of her, and asked him to spell his life-love's last name. He couldn't.

The interview was a classic. Allen was the bad cop. Bullying, lying, intimidating, mean. Taber was the good cop, playing dumb to boot: *Aw, shucks, don't mind my partner, just tell me the truth. No, I didn't get it, explain it to me again, I didn't understand.*

Allen had a good hand—always did—and he played every card. The Miranda rights. Starting out being a buddy, turning into an asshole. Asking Craig to recount the last week, since Friday night. Closing inexorably on what Craig knew about the dreaded Tuesday. Giving Craig plenty of time to retell Friday through Monday. Plenty of time to think about it, to see it coming. To wonder how much they knew. How much he should say. How much he could risk keeping to himself. Telling Craig they had fingerprints, because it was okay to lie. Throwing around words: blood, DNA. Things a guy couldn't be certain about. What *could* they do with fingerprints? What could blood be made to say? What could DNA tests show? Hadn't the cops just done something to O. J. Simpson, made it look like it was his DNA? Telling Craig someone—or was it some people? . . . it was hard to pin it down—already was talking. Reminding him how well he was known around town, being born and raised here. Implying he'd been seen certain places. On top of this, the cops had the advantage of surprise. This was the last place Craig expected to be. No time to think. And he did, after all, know things, didn't he? Yet, now here it was all twisted around, now he was being accused. Instead of going to them with what he knew, they'd come to him, and they'd gotten a story so twisted it was worthy of his own fabrications. Now that he most needed the truth to be understood, it seemed everyone was determined to believe the lie. Here they were talking truth, and the truth they wanted seemed to be a lie. They wouldn't take his truth, they wanted him to tell them what he told Julie, they wanted that to be true, and now he needed badly for it not to be. Asking questions about blood on his shoes. Making him go over things again and again. And the nice cop, even the nice cop didn't seem to get it, it didn't seem to sink in, he didn't seem so bright, just kept asking over and over: "Tell me again, Craig." Hell, couldn't even keep his name straight. Called him "Kevin" at one point. Fuck, *Kevin*. The irony. And just when he thought he'd said all he needed to say, just when he thought he'd let out the least he could, turned out they knew more, knew about other crimes and plans for other crimes, like they were possessed of some sort of cop psychic ability or maybe, just maybe, really had one of the other guys right now, a guy who clearly was giving them Craig on a silver platter, truth be damned, to save his own ass. Craig just might end up being unable to convince people he wasn't there . . . after all the convincing to Julie that he was. Asking over and over, "Where's the gun?" Pointing out conflicts in his story. Tripping him. Making it so he shook, making it so he was so scared he shivered. And then, right then, demanding unwavering eye contact. Giving lengthy accounts of the charges he could face. Cops couldn't lay a finger on you, but that didn't matter. Turned out they could beat a guy without touching him, make him wince without so much as making a fist. It was a nightmare. It was one of the worst hours in Craig's life.

"You know, there are things about crime I want to tell you before we go any further," Allen said. "People find themselves in all kinds of situations. Most times, a lot of situations are out of their control. Do you know what I'm saying? When people find themselves in that situation they can't control, when things go different than what they thought they were gonna go—"

"I've been in those situations."

"Do you mind if I take your hat off? . . . Thank you," Allen said. "'Cause I keep trying to get down underneath you and see."

When Allen first touched on the subject of the band teacher, Craig said he heard it on the news. Allen interrupted his account of what he claimed to have seen on TV. "So, you've got people that know you all over town, right?"

"Um-hmm."

"Sure. Keep that in mind for me, too, okay? Keep two things in mind for me: one's that we have your fingerprints from before, and the other's that people know you all over town."

It got worse. Allen saw blood on Craig's shoes. "You know, I noticed on your shoes you got some drops down there. Did you cut yourself?"

"Yeah, right here," showing a finger.

"How did you do that?" Taber asked. He was mostly quiet, let Allen do the talking, watched, remained someone Craig could confide in, Allen more the antagonist with each minute.

"That's pretty big drops down there for cutting yourself on that finger," Allen said. Glaring at Craig's hand: "That looks like it's probably a week or so old." Staring at the shoe: "That looks pretty fresh to me."

Craig told about punching the Styrofoam.

The girl has information no one should have; it came from the boy; he has blood on his shoes, Allen thought. "You know, Craig, you look real nervous. And rightfully you should be. 'Cause you're not the first person we've talked to. There are people that can get caught up in things that aren't really their fault. Things happen. And when things happen, people can do one or two things. They can be totally involved in it before or after or during. They can be a witness of it during, and you need to think about that while we're talking. You know where I'm coming from, don't you? So you and I need to be real up front with each other.

'Cause you know we know things. And you need to tell me what happened. Just tell me why it happened. And get it over with, okay? So let's quit beating around the bush. And let's talk about it, okay? All right, go ahead."

"I know the other boy's name is Kevin," Craig said. "I know, okay? He's crazy. He's just nuts." There. It was out. There'd be years of formalities, but in a way it all ended right there, when Craig said, "Kevin."

Now Craig told about Brad's worried call and the boasting in front of the TV. "One of them was Slim— a chubby kid, rotten teeth. Uh . . . Tom."

"What's Tom's last name?" Allen said.

"I don't know Tom's last name." Craig gave the officers the names Kevin, Burnett, Slim, Tom. Knew no last names. He gave the whole story as he'd heard it.

"Craig, you've done real good so far," Allen said. And got straight to the point. "Who was the guy with the hat?"

"I don't know."

"Your heart's jumping out of your chest, son. I know who the guy with the hat was."

"*I* don't."

"You do, too."

"*No,* I don't."

"It was you with the hat."

"It was *not* me with the hat," Craig said. "No, it was *not.*" Craig gave that it was a gang of seven.

Allen wasn't yet convinced by Craig's protestations he wasn't there. His story was too good. "What's gonna happen when I talk to these guys and they tell me—"

"They're gonna shoot me, is what they're gonna do. For fucking running my mouth. That's what they're gonna do."

"Let me tell you something—"

"They're not playing around, and that's obvious," Craig said, not hearing Allen now. "They're gonna fucking shoot me."

"As long as you're being truthful," Allen said, "I can say, 'Okay, this poor boy got into something he didn't think was gonna go the way it went.' Even though, you know, peer pressure's a really strong thing. It's really strong. It's almost to the point where you could understand why some young man would get caught up in something—especially the peer pressure you're talking about. But you know we're gonna prove all of this. You know that, don't you?"

"Yeah."

"You know we're gonna have every one of these boys?"

"Yeah."

"And we're gonna find out the exact facts. Because everybody's gonna be in a room by themselves. And everybody's gonna talk. We're gonna put it all together, and we're gonna know."

Allen switched back to the topic of the blood on Craig's Nike sneakers and quickly had Craig practically begging him to take them. "You can take a sample right now if you want."

"I will."

"Let's do it right now. *Please* do it. If that's what it's gonna take to convince you, *please* do it."

"Believe me, I will."

"Take my shoe."

"I'm going to."

"Do it now."

"Tell me where the gun is."

"I'm telling you the God's honest truth. What gun?"

"I want to measure your shoe," Allen said, keeping Craig off balance. "Stick it up here. Give me your other shoe. Where's the gun?"

Allen reminded Craig about fingerprints, people knowing him around town, telling the truth. Craig implicated Brad, telling the detectives he helped by giving Kevin the phone book.

"You're leaving out some very important stuff," Allen

said. "You talk to this agent a minute. I'm gonna take your shoes out here, and I'll be back in a moment."

Allen left Taber to be good cop, which he was, calmly leading Craig through the story again. The whole shoe thing was, at least for the time being, a bluff. The officers never did request a blood sample.

Taber was done. "Put out your hand like that."

"Yeah, I'm shaking. I'm nervous, yeah."

"If you didn't do nothing, then why are you nervous?"

Allen reappeared. "Listen, son, I want to tell you something. And I want to be perfectly honest with you. Look at me. Don't give me that glare looking at me like you hate me. Because I'm the best friend you've got right now. Did anybody explain to you about what murder is? And about the different degrees of murder?" Allen laid out Florida law, which wasn't well understood by the public and which was going to prove crucial to the futures of the members of the LOC involved in Mark Schwebes's death. "Okay, look at me. In the state of Florida, there's all kinds of different types of murder. Or homicide, if you want to call it that, okay? It starts off with the least and goes to the most severe. Okay? And in between, there's a lot of different things that can affect what happens to an individual that's involved in any one of the stages of this. Okay? Someone who knows about something before— *look* at me—or after and doesn't talk to the police, or hides some information, or keeps it from someone, gets themselves involved. Gets charged just like the guy that pulled the trigger. Okay?"

It was a terribly serious moment—Craig faced real charges, the possibility of years in prison if he didn't cooperate. So did Brad and Burnett and Tom and everyone else who heard about the murder before it happened or after it was done.

"Now you've got first-degree premeditated murder all the way down to justifiable homicide. Justifiable homicide's when a cop shoots someone in the line of duty." Allen looked at Craig. It was working. "You're shaking all over. I want you to take deep breaths."

"I'm cold."

"Why don't you take a deep breath? Justifiable homicide is a cop—somebody comes in your house trying to rape your sister and you have to shoot them, okay?

"First-degree murder's when you sit around, a band teacher takes some stuff from you; you go to an apartment; you plan; you look his address up in the phone book; you find a shotgun; you drive to his house; you knock on his door. He comes to the door and you blow his head off. That's first-degree, premeditated murder. That's the biggest and the worst it can be. And it doesn't matter who pulled the trigger."

Every word was true. It was going to ruin Derek's life and Chris's life and Pete's life, Pete who'd sat there and done nothing. It was going to mar Burnett's life and Tom's life, but they'd recover; Pete, Chris and Derek never would. They'd lose just as surely as if Kevin shot them for refusing to help kill the teacher and almost as completely. In a way, their loss would be worse. They'd live captive lives of humiliation and deprivation, never allowed to forget what they allowed to happen. Even if they never felt an iota of remorse for Mark, they still would face what they did to themselves, the ruination of their lives, the genius Pete would never use, the bike Chris would never ride, the science Derek would never study. And almost no one would feel sorrow for them, because how could anyone feel sorry for boys who killed? People would forget they existed. The boys would sit aging in concrete warehouses until they died in a fight or died from complications of AIDS or died anonymous and broken in old age, never part of the world outside, forced to sit and contemplate what might've been. They'd experience a terrible judgment, and even as they brought it upon themselves, so Kevin brought it upon them—killed their spirit as surely as he killed Mark. The boys now had a protracted agony of publicity and justice and punishment to endure—though they were as yet unaware of their fate.

Craig still had his hand out.

"Put your arm down," Allen said. He played a trump card—Hardee's.

"That was supposed to be my initiation," said Craig, who now had to believe the detectives had *someone.* "I was gonna stand at the door or something. And not let anybody in or out. Something like that." Craig said the boys expected a $4,000 take.

"Why did he say he shot him in the ass?" Allen said.

"'Cause he was a faggot, they said."

"How did they know that?"

"That's what everybody thinks at Riverdale."

Allen, by now, pretty much knew Craig had nothing to do with the murder. He'd suspected it most of the interview. Years of experience told him that. But he kept the pressure on Craig. "You know what accessory is?" He again raised the prospect of witnesses and fingerprints. It got results. "What else have they done?" he demanded, switching gears again.

"The Coke building."

Now the case was huge. Detectives were heading in the wrong direction before Julie called them, but Allen's mind now started churning overtime. He knew about the fires out east, out in Buckingham. *Did they do those? What about the New Life Fitness World fire?* Allen didn't have to be told, he just knew from experience, from years around criminals, from the part of himself that understood where these people were coming from—the part that made him so good at what he did, that where there was a murder and a bombing, there was a spree. A dozen cases would be closed with these arrests. Likely, there'd be even more they'd never know about, petty and not so petty cases that'd stay open. But that was okay, because when they were caught, it'd stop, and many more cases, including, for sure, more murders, would be stopped. That was just how it was. These boys mightn't even consciously know it about themselves, might vow the opposite, but that was how it was, especially with Kevin. Right now, it was vital the detectives get to the boys as soon as they could. Before they could go to Hardee's, where, despite Craig's protestations, the killing of Mark Schwebes suggested more might die. Before they went *anywhere*.

Just to make sure, Allen pushed Craig one final time. "You know what I think? I don't think your initiation was tonight. I think your initiation was the other night. I think they tried to see how brave you were. I think they said, 'We'll get ol' Craig to go up there, knock on the door. We'll use him for a patsy, and that'll be part of his initiation. And when he opens the door, we'll give Craig a real big surprise when we blow the guy's head off.' You had direct knowledge about a murder, about an arson, about a robbery that's supposed to go down tonight at ten o'clock."

"*What?*" Craig said. "You don't think teenagers brag? You think they'd do this shit and not brag? What the *fuck?* I mean, *shit*, we were all sitting there. 'You know this? We did that.' Sure, I fucking heard it."

"I know you did."

"It's a pretty big deal. They set the Coke building on fire. You listen up, you hear shit."

The way Craig's interview ended was one of the most bizarre moments in the investigation and could've got him arrested and charged with first-degree murder. They'd turned off the tape recorder, done, and Craig said something churlish, a trapped, scared, angry teen, and Allen flipped the machine back on. "We're back on tape. It's now twelve after three. Tell me about it."

"About *what?*"

"What you just said."

"I said, '*Yeah*, I was on the doorstep, fucking *right*, yeah.'"

"Who else was there?"

"*Where?*"

"When you were at the doorstep."

"I *wasn't* at the doorstep. I don't *know*."

"I thought you just said you were. Are you trying to play games with me? 'Cause you're gonna lose."

Across town, a sheriff's technician unsealed the door to Mark's duplex and let a couple inside. They searched Mark's things, retrieving a black suit, shirt and trumpet before the technician resealed the door. They were Mark's sister, Pat Schwebes Dunbar, and her husband, and they'd come for clothes to bury him in.

CHAPTER 24

Going Down

Craig wasn't arrested. No one took a blood sample. His tennis shoes vanished into the accumulating piles of evidence. He found himself in a holding cell, until officers could determine if his story held up. He sat all afternoon, then all evening, then into the night.

Taber wasn't sure Craig hadn't been there Tuesday night. The boasts to Julie, detailed knowledge of the murder, blood on his shoes, evasiveness, request for a lawyer—Craig was a suspect. He also was the key— they wouldn't know about these other kids without him. They wouldn't be set to thwart an armed robbery. They'd still be following a false lead.

Deputies still didn't have last names. Luck—in the form of mindless bragging—gave them their break. Now old-fashioned policing took over. Bruce Busbee ran the sheriff's intelligence/pawnshops and felony warrants division. His phone rang. "You know anyone that owns a pawnshop with a son named Kevin?"

"Right off the bat I can't think of any, but let me hang up and think about it, see if I can come up with something." About ten minutes later, it came to him: a man who owned a business they never had problems with. Riverdale Gold, Gun & Pawn Shop. One day the man's son was in there. The man called him "Kevin." Busbee remembered that detail exactly the way cops were meant to remember such details: "This is my son, Kevin."

Command staff joined Allen and Taber for a briefing in the major-crimes unit. The usually taciturn Taber did most of the talking. Officers were assigned to surveillance teams. Narcotics officers were pulled in, most of the robbery/auto-theft unit and some twenty uniforms, district detectives, major-crimes agents—everyone they could get. Pictures of a couple of kids were passed around. Vehicles described. Something was said about illegal firearms. The goal was to detain the boys, secure their cooperation, get them to come of their own volition to Six Mile Cypress for questioning, but not arrest them. No arrests; no Miranda; no lawyers. A radio channel was dedicated for the surveillance team. The channel was unlikely to be compromised either by an LOC member with a scanner or by media.

Deputies threw manpower at the operation. The initial stakeout target was a gray Isuzu with a whip antenna. Agents watched Hardee's. Agents watched Craig's house. Half-a-dozen agents in two cars watched the apartment above the Palm Beach Depot. An agent sat in the parking lot of a church and watched Palm Beach Boulevard. Agents sat at Morse Shores Plaza. An agent sat down the street from Kevin's. A helicopter stood by.

A deputy sat in a marked car in a vacant lot, watching the Palm Beach Depot across the street, looking for an Isuzu P'up. If he spotted it, he was to pull it over, regardless of whether its driver made any traffic infraction, walk to the door, ask for registration, insurance, driver's license—buy time. An unmarked car would arrive and take over. If the vehicle failed to stop, he'd radio his supervisor, who'd decide whether to pursue. He sat for three hours. By 4:45 P.M., the end of his shift, he'd seen neither the truck nor anyone coming or going from the apartment above the dealership.

Brad and Burnett got off work. "Are you gonna do Hardee's?" Burnett said.

"No." Brad expected Burnett to turn left, toward Palm Beach Boulevard; he went right, toward Lorraine Drive. "Where are you going?"

"I want to go to Kevin's anyway, see what's going on."

Pete was drawing arrows on the Hardee's map. He also was second-guessing whether the robbery was such a good idea, having driven by and seen how many customers were there. Maybe he'd wait in the car with Chris again. The current plan—Kevin's—was more elaborate than Pete's original. It wouldn't be a simple drive-through robbery anymore. Kevin wanted to go in, get all the money, even customers' wallets: Chris drives, drops Pete, Kevin and Burnett in face paint, ski masks, gloves, camouflage, boots. At 9:30 P.M., Derek opens the back door, takes the trash to the Dumpster. The boys approach, yelling. Kevin takes Derek hostage, walking him in with the Combat Commander to his head. They get the managers away from the panic buttons. Kevin and Burnett get customers and employees on the floor. Burnett guards them with the Mossberg. Kevin goes through the office for the money bag. Pete secures the front counter. He opens the cash registers, takes the drawers, dumps the cash in a sack. They get the manager's keys and toss them to Chris. Once Chris is sure the robbery's going as planned, he leaves. Kevin and Pete drive the manager's car to a meeting spot somewhere in Tice. Derek stays behind with the other employees, thereby avoiding implication and leaving someone to glean intelligence about the progress of the ensuing investigation. They'd meet at Brad's to get ready for the robbery and again afterward to count money. "If anybody gives you any trouble, just shoot them," Kevin said.

"These are friends of mine," Pete said. "We don't got to get violent. We can do it very calmly. I'll be the victim. That way, nobody gets hurt."

If somebody tries to go for the alarm, if somebody tries to be a hero and take my gun, if someone tries me, I'm gonna pop him, Kevin thought. He showed the boys how to assemble and disassemble the Beretta and the Combat Commander. They dry-fired them and ejected the magazines. Kevin held the guns to Burnett's head, pressing so hard they made indentations. The boys joked about taking a picture.

Kevin wouldn't have an alarm problem at Hardee's if Brad could disable it.

"I don't know jack about alarm systems," Brad said. "There's no way you can get around alarm wires."

"All right," Kevin said. "I need you to run in with me and Burnett, with a gun. Get all the people up front and on the ground. Keep them there while me and Pete get the money." Kevin handed Brad the Beretta. "This is the one you're gonna use."

Holding the weapon, Brad realized he couldn't do it. He'd have to tell Kevin. Try to get him alone and explain. The cold gun frightened him. Its weight. The smell on his fingers. He held the weapon awkwardly in his clammy palms, away from his body, wary, like it might bite.

Of all the boys, Burnett seemed most eager. The others' enthusiasm was tempered by the weight of murder. "I want to hold the gun that killed Schwebes," Burnett said, leering. "I want to use the gun that killed the teacher."

Kevin threw the loaded shotgun in Burnett's hands. "Don't this make you feel like you got balls?" Then he pulled out the rifle with the homemade silencer. "It's very well insulated." As outlandish as all that Disney talk had been, it was becoming believable to Burnett.

Kevin felt it wise none of the others' weapons was loaded tonight. He didn't trust them. Some seemed itching to pull the trigger. Others seemed scarily unreliable. Only he'd have a loaded gun. Even as he planned, he was unsure about the whole idea. Had a bad vibe.

Leaving work at Hardee's, Judy Putnam rounded a corner and stumbled on an incident that struck her as strange. Denny, a mentally challenged deaf-mute, sometimes made fists and poked at other employees, a habit management had been trying to break. Now he poked at Derek, who pulled back and gave him a look Putnam had never seen before. "Are you okay?" she said, startled. Derek hadn't said a word, but that look was troubling. She didn't expect that reaction from a good, conscientious worker, well liked by coworkers and managers.

As Putnam left Hardee's, the phone rang again at Lorraine Drive. "Kevin, are you doin' that today?" Tom said, a moth fluttering around a flame, calling to make sure he was *not* going.

"No," Kevin said.

They're doin' it. He doesn't want me to go. I'm glad. I don't want to go. Tom didn't want to go, even though they were talking about a $2,000 take. He hadn't wanted to go when he heard Kevin talk about that pregnant woman who might try to press the alarm, and if she got in the way, she died. He'd had enough LOC adventures. But he was worried: Kevin had stopped calling. Hadn't included him tonight. They had plans to go to Mike Greenwell's Bat-a-Ball, but Kevin didn't show. Tom felt like a marked man. *Kevin doesn't want me around.* It was like a Mafia soldier falling out of favor with a crime boss, left twisting in the wind before the inevitable hit.

A sheriff's deputy came into Hardee's. Walked back to the office, talked with the manager. *Something's up,* Derek thought. He kept right on working. His fear had peaked. He now believed Kevin knew he wanted out of the LOC. He had reason to worry: The green-uniformed deputy wasn't the only one who'd been to Hardee's. A plainclothes detective also popped in and spoke with the manager. "Is Derek Shields working?"

Not him, the detective thought when the manager pointed Derek out. He looked too clean-cut, too all-American, too much anybody's kid to be a murderer.

Ruby went out to dinner with Kelly and Brian Burns, to Perkins, across the street from Hardee's, parking in the same lot where officers in surveillance cars lay in wait for her son.

Derek took his dinner break. Though conflicted, still he came to Lorraine Drive to tell Kevin how many people were at Hardee's. As he walked in, Kevin stepped from behind the door and grabbed him, left arm around his neck, right hand holding a gun to his head. Derek grabbed Kevin's left arm and twisted it until he let go. "Is that loaded?"

Kevin laughed, uncocking the handgun. "It's always loaded. You better be that scared tonight."

An unmarked sheriff's cruiser rolled down Lorraine Drive. Boys standing around outside. The Isuzu

P'up. The cruiser made a lazy circle at the dead end of the drive and headed up to Orange River Boulevard to wait.

Waiting outside, Brad wanted to get Kevin by himself. He paced, summoning resolve. *He's gonna come down hard if he gets caught. I don't want to get caught up in this.* That included the planned trip to Orlando. *No. Kevin's crazy.*

Kevin started telling Brad about the Cherokees, gesturing at the souvenir bumper leaning against the garage, still boasting.

"Hey, I can't do this. Kevin, I've been thinking about this since you told me, and I'm not gonna do this. I don't mess with guns. I hunt animals; I don't hunt people. I've never held anybody up."

"That's okay," said Kevin, who was coming to believe the only animals worth hunting were humans. "You don't got to. You're new. We really need another person, but you don't have to, if you don't want to."

"I'm just gonna stay home," Brad said. "If something goes down, I guess you guys can still come to my house."

"Pete, you use it." Kevin handed over the Beretta. *It won't have any bullets,* Pete thought. Stuck it in his waistband, just like God carried the Combat Commander. It was the first time he'd ever carried a gun. He also had his new switchblade.

"Kevin's gonna ride with me," Burnett told Brad. "You go ahead. Pete will take you home. We'll follow you guys and take off from there."

Something nagged Kevin. He had a bad feeling, a vibe he couldn't place. He knew one thing, though: if he was going to be arrested, he wanted to be taken down at Lorraine Drive. That's where the guns were. *Suicide by cop. Let them just try it.*

Kevin's worries had substance: Dean Taber and a partner were sitting in an unmarked car about a half-block away, watching, eager to avoid exactly the scenario Kevin had in mind. An unmarked car in another driveway. And two other officers in an unmarked car with the lights off east of where Lorraine Drive met Orange River Boulevard, in case the gray pickup with the distinctive CB antenna took a right instead of the expected left. Deputies made few mistakes in the case, but they made a glaring one at the house—no one covered the back. If Kevin had listened to his vibe and run, he could've slipped unobserved into the darkness, into the wilds of Lehigh Acres, his teen stomping grounds.

Kevin took the Mossberg from under his mattress and threw it to Burnett. "Put it in Pete's trunk. Don't let the neighbors see you." Kevin grabbed his ski mask, headed out the front door, Combat Commander stuffed in his jeans.

Pete, Chris and Brad headed to the apartment. The Mossberg loaded with seven rounds was in the trunk. *We'll organize everything at Brad's,* Pete thought. *But first we'll settle* whether *we're doing this.* Pete didn't like Kevin's more complicated, though potentially more fruitful, plan. *It's a pain in the ass. Too much trouble. Burnett doesn't seem too happy about it, either. I'm gonna try to call it off.* He didn't want Kevin shooting people without provocation and still believed him smarter than that. If they did the robbery, he figured they'd use the money to get Grad Nite supplies. *We didn't get nothing at Dillard's.* Pete headed west on Palm Beach Boulevard. The Nissan had become just like the Yota—a pack rat's nest and a mobile crime scene. Criminal mementos littered the car and trunk. Latex gloves stolen from RHS more than a year ago; Sheraton, Toys "R" Us and pay phone signs from the scavenger hunt six months ago; one of the metal clipboards and business cards from vandalizing the county vehicles on the first

Terror Night; a pair of gloves bought after the meeting in the church parking lot; newspaper coverage of Tuesday's murder; a ski mask and Taser that might be useful tonight. Almost incongruous among all this evidence of the fruition of Pete's fantasies: the black JanSport backpack graffitied with Wite-Out that he lugged to school every day. Evidence he once was a kid—now overwhelmed by evidence he was so no longer.

Brad's smart not to go, Burnett thought as he drove. *Maybe I'll be smart, too, drop Kevin off, head home, go talk to Tom. Maybe I'll stay at Brad's, help count money.* Not that he and Brad would *get* any of the money if they didn't do the robbery. The more he thought about it, the more he wanted out. Could he warn somebody? It wouldn't do for Kevin to get the idea he might rat on him. "You shouldn't tell anybody," Chris had said. "I wouldn't tell, because Kevin would kill *anybody.*" But here was Kevin next to him with a black ski mask, tubes of camo cream and his favorite gun in his pants.

The dedicated radio channel crackled. "We have movement. The truck's leaving the house."

The pair in the pickup with the big antenna passed Taber. "Pickup matching the description leaving."

At 8:34 P.M., "Follow pickup."

At 8:35 P.M., "In the Lorraine Drive area . . . may be the vehicle . . . possibly our suspects. . . . We're behind the truck . . . is the vehicle . . . coming toward you . . . two suspects inside."

Cindi saw Kevin and Burnett drive by. *I never see Kevin alone.* She honked. Still wary of their rivalry over her, she hauled ass. Didn't want them to come over and hang out. It was the last time she ever saw Kevin on the streets.

"Let's stop at the store," Kevin was saying to Burnett. "I need cigarettes." They pulled into the Circle K they frequented so often. "You follow in behind me at Hardee's," Kevin was saying. "And don't let's pick up Tom."

Larry Montgomery—the school resource officer Mark Schwebes told Chris and Tom they might see Wednesday—sat alone in a marked car behind the Cracker Barrel, where the band director ate his last meal. A K-9 unit was parked with him, a specialist with a dog named Caster. The deputies listened to the surveillance radio transmissions.

At 8:41 P.M., "At the Circle K."

Montgomery was pulled into the surveillance because he knew most RHS students at least by sight; and his car was partitioned; and unlike the officers in unmarked cars, he could make traffic stops.

At 8:43 P.M., "Suspects' vehicle approaching Palm Beach Boulevard." Montgomery saw the pickup with the whip antenna pass. The unmarked cars following along Orange River Boulevard slowed to allow him to pull in behind it. The light at Palm Beach Boulevard was red. "Wait for the light change."

At 8:44 P.M., "When the light changes, do it." . . . Green. The pickup made a left turn, west toward Fort Myers.

At 8:45 P.M., "Do it now. Do it now."

Just east of I-75, on the artery along which so many of the LOC's exploits happened, Montgomery threw the switches for his lights and siren.

* * *

Kevin shoved the Combat Commander under his seat.

"Kevin, what do you want me to do?"

"Pull over, I reckon."

"All right." Burnett pulled over three lanes and stopped. "All right. Do we get out?"

"See you in hell."

Burnett looked out his window and saw the guns.

An officer went to the driver's side of the Isuzu, Montgomery to the passenger side. Caster stood ready in case a boy ran. The K-9 officer stood by Burnett's tailgate with his gun pulled.

As Montgomery approached the passenger door, he recognized Kevin, the boy who withdrew his sophomore year after shooting himself in the stomach.

More unmarked cars arrived. Allen and Collmer flew past, made a wide U-turn across the Boulevard and pulled in behind the truck. Soon half-a-dozen cars were there. There was no way for the Isuzu to pull away; it was hemmed in.

"Keep your hands clear," Montgomery told Kevin. "Exit the vehicle."

Kevin stood under the I-75 overpass south of the Caloosahatchee bridge, where he used to get his first glimpse of home seeing the FPL smokestack. He wished he'd listened to his intuition while there was still time to go out the back door, head across the Flint farm and disappear into the woods. He could've even taken the Yota back there. Traffic rumbled overhead. The freedom of road trips, the wandering wildness, the possibility of escape into the woods or on the interstate evaporated.

"Hello," Allen said to Kevin, who was silent. Allen walked on by to Burnett. Taber arrived.

"We're investigating a murder and the possibility of

an armed robbery that's about to take place," Collmer
said. "We're going down to Six Mile Cypress to talk."

Burnett told the officers, who hadn't recognized
Pete's car, that the other boys were in front of them.
Allen and Collmer read him his rights and made
small talk as they drove him to Six Mile Cypress.

Montgomery patted Kevin down. "I'm detaining you
for questioning." He opened a rear door, not offering the option to ride shotgun. Kevin got in behind
the partition.

At 8:46 P.M., "I have Kevin Foster in custody."

"What's going on?" Kevin said.

"I don't know. That'll be explained once we arrive
at headquarters. Don't talk to me."

"Why am I being detained? What's going on?"

"I don't have answers. I'm gonna have to transport you to the Lee County Sheriff's Office at Six Mile
Cypress, where you'll meet with an agent and the
agent will explain exactly what's transpiring."

It was neither intentional irony by deputies nor a
preinterrogation mind game, but as it turned out
Deputy Larry Montgomery—the very person Mark
Schwebes threatened Chris and Tom with—got Kevin
Foster anyway: murder couldn't stop it.

Agents had been watching the apartment above the
auto dealership from behind a tree across the street
for almost ten hours. A car pulled up west of the
building. Three boys got out and walked toward the
rear, where outside stairs led up to the apartment.

At 8:47 P.M., "Three suspects at apartment."

Hidden among some bushes across the boulevard,
an agent had emptied and lined up six Coke cans. It

was dark when he saw the car pull up, the driver get out, the boys start up the steps. "There they are!" he yelled into the radio. By the time he got out of the bushes and crossed the gulf of the seven-lane boulevard, it was all over.

At Brad's, Chris got out of the car, opened the trunk and got his bag. The boys started up the steps intending to listen to some CDs while they waited for Kevin and Burnett. Brad saw flashlights.

Seven officers ran across the street, guns drawn. "Stop! Go to the wall! Put your hands on the wall!" . . . "Lee County Sheriff's Office, up against the wall!" . . . "Freeze!"

The three boys went straight to the wall, leaned with their hands against the building. "Who's Slim?"

"I am," Chris said.

Brad felt handcuffs, saw guns. "I got the big guy."

"Before you check, I have a gun in my waistband," Pete said. "I got a gun."

"Gun!" someone yelled. An agent patted Pete down, finding the handgun and knife. He didn't have a permit to carry concealed weapons—he was too young.

Officers put the boys in separate vehicles, giving them no chance to agree on stories. "Are you willing to come back to our office to answer some questions concerning an investigation we're conducting?" each was asked.

"Yes." Like Kevin, they weren't under arrest and weren't read their rights. They were detained for questioning.

In Pete's car, the two agents were silent. "I guess we're in trouble now," Pete said.

"We'll just go down and talk."

The car Chris was in had no partition. An agent sat in back with him.

As Brad rode to the sheriff's office, he heard officers talking about Chris on the radio: they were making fun of his teeth.

Hardee's was right across the street from Morse Shores Plaza, where Ruby was eating dinner right now, and where the boys only days earlier broke into the trailer and were disappointed by sacks of flour and cornmeal. It seemed so much longer.

Alone among the Lords of Chaos, Derek was working that night, waiting to be robbed. He was running a risk allowing Kevin to hold him at gunpoint. He was the most reluctant participant in the murder and also the boy who knocked on the door. With him gone, Kevin would have one less worry. It didn't entirely surprise him when the others didn't show.

Hardee's employees hadn't known it, but deputies watched over them the better part of the day, through a shift change, into the night. Unnoticed by Mom, agents sat across the street at Perkins, exercising an abundance of caution. They heard from radio traffic that some boys had been detained, but no one was certain if they'd gotten them all. They'd make sure there was no robbery. Perhaps deputies couldn't say it as often as they'd like, but they could say it tonight: they were saving lives.

A couple of RHS boys came into Hardee's about 9:15 P.M. "Aren't you guys supposed to rob this place tonight?"

"You talk to Tom a little too much," Derek said. The boys got something to eat. Derek thought about it, decided to warn them. "You might want to be careful. They're supposed to be coming any time now to hold the place up." Unconcerned about the planned crime, the boys sat down and ate.

Five minutes later, two sheriff's officers came in.

One bought a Coke and asked for the manager. "Is Derek present?"

"Yes," pointing at the kitchen door.

Seeing the door opening, the officers went in. "You're under arrest." Handcuffs snapped.

Derek offered no resistance. Escorting him outside, the officers were a little rough, running him into the door and a car. It was eighteen days since he saw Kevin at the senior picnic. He told himself he'd stop after the diner. After the murder. After Hardee's.

Too late.

Ruby was still at Perkins.

"Kevin's going over to Brad's to help with some homework, and then they plan on going to the beach, and they'll be home around midnight," Kelly told Mom.

Midnight came and went.

CONSEQUENCES

CHAPTER 25

Friday Night

9:14 P.M.

Kevin trusted the boys to keep their mouths shut, through loyalty or reluctance to incriminate themselves. At Six Mile Cypress, Burnett spilled all to Allen, Taber and Collmer. He *thought* Chris's last name was Black; didn't know Pete's, Derek's or Brad's; thought his close friend Tom's was "Troyan," and couldn't guess the spelling, but knew enough to thrill investigators.

Collmer: "Whose idea was it to kill the teacher?"

"It was Chris's, but he was talking just words and Kevin took it more serious and brought the rush on for Chris to go through with it." Burnett feared Kevin: "If I told anybody, I was gonna die."

Taber: "Who told you this?"

"Everybody said Kevin'll kill me if I tell. That's why I'm suffering here. I mean, I've got everything. I've got to tell you guys this."

Burnett at first failed to include himself at the bombing, but he listed others' crimes and alerted investigators Kevin was their man for the Cherokee thefts. His nonchalance was striking. "How much longer am I gonna be here?" he said. "My mom's gonna kill me."

"We'll let you call your mom in a little bit," Taber said. "Hopefully not much longer. But you understand this murder—it's a serious crime."

"Now I have it off my chest, I feel so much better."

"I'm sure you do."

"The only thing I'm worried about is getting killed."

"That's not gonna happen, 'cause we're gonna put them away for a long time."

So many boys, officers and crimes. Mug shots, fingerprints, search warrants, affidavits. Proofreading documents. Calling parents. Kevin was an adult; deputies didn't call Mom.

9:39 P.M.

Three investigators grilled Brad, the first of four interviews lasting until 4:30 A.M. He saw no clocks and lost track of time. The detectives let him tell the story without interruption—to gauge his truthfulness and see if he had new information. Brad provided key details.

"When you say 'they,' who're we talking about? I want everybody's names."

"I don't know none of their last names," Brad said. "I just met these guys. Kevin's the one I'm scared of."

"You all sat and talked about this, correct?" The planned Hardee's robbery.

"They talked about it. I told them I wasn't gonna do it."

"Why didn't you call us?"

"They had a rule—friends don't rat on friends. But I just didn't want to go with it and—"

"You figured if you weren't involved, you didn't have nothing to do with it."

9:42 p.m.

As Brad was interviewed, Allen and Collmer went on tape with Pete. Allen thought Pete remorseless. *Matter-of-fact, no concern, no tears.* All the boys took it lightly.

Collmer: "Off the record, I'm curious why somebody your age would want to see somebody killed."

"I've always wondered what it's like to see a man shot."

Scary, Collmer thought. "How *did* it feel?"

"It kind of made me sick to my stomach."

"What's going on?" Chris repeated at his first interview after the Miranda rights formality. "I don't know what you're talking about. I want an attorney."

They shut the recorder off and walked Chris across the hallway to a holding cell.

"You realize you've invoked?" a captain said. "We now can make no further contact with you. If you want to contact us for anything at all, you'll have to let us know you want to talk."

"Yes, sir. Thank you." No one got Chris an attorney, or even a phone. No one called his parents. No need: he'd turned eighteen just sixteen days ago.

A knock on the door. "Your buddies are being interviewed, and they're implicating you."

After twenty minutes, Chris banged on the door. Taber opened it, scowling. "What do you want?"

"I want to talk."

Chris later said detectives told him he couldn't use the bathroom or have water until he talked.

10:00 p.m.

Taber again read Chris his Miranda rights. "Do you understand all that 'threats, coercion and inducement' means?" A ritual question.

"Yes," Chris said. "It means, you talk or I'll beat the hell out of you."

"Are we doing that?"

"No." Chris didn't volunteer anything. "I can't remember what I did," he said about the day of the murder. "Today's Friday."

The boys hadn't discussed what to do if arrested. In separate rooms, none knew what others were saying. Chris at first feigned ignorance about anything unusual happening—but the other boys' statements belied that. Some felt the game was up, and others were glad to unburden.

Investigators still worked from Craig's story. "You went to Craig's house?" Taber said.

"I have *no* idea who Craig is."

When asked about Mark Schwebes, Chris repeated what he said he read in a newspaper. Then he caved, blaming longtime friend Derek more than newfound hero Kevin: Derek suggested talking to Mr. Schwebes; Derek recognized the teacher's car and pointed out the house; Chris didn't know who had the gun. Taber decided to jolt him. "Let me explain something. This is murder. First-degree murder."

After Taber explained possible charges, Chris yielded more.

"Do you know who Craig is?"

"No, and I don't know why everybody keeps asking."

"The next day y'all got together and talked about it. What happened?"

"Wednesday. . . . Wednesday. . . . Yeah. We talked like every day since Tuesday. Making jokes."

"What kind of jokes? You think it's *funny*?"

"Yeah. Sort of. I'm kind of a sick individual myself."

Tall and beefy, Taber loomed over him. "Why do you think it's funny? You killed somebody . . . *huh?* You think it's *funny* to go out and kill somebody?"

"Perhaps."

"*Why?* Why 'perhaps'?"

"I don't know."

"*Huh?*"

"Should it not be?"

"You think it's *funny* to go out and kill somebody? How would you like somebody to come and kill *you?*"

"Right now, it'd be pretty great."

"You think it's funny to go out and shoot somebody and kill them."

"No . . . it's not. It's serious, I know."

"But you're joking about it?"

"Yeah."

"That means you think it's funny."

"Hmm . . . a little."

Chris denied the group was a gang and wouldn't divulge the name until Taber said it, asking why Chris called Kevin "God."

"I believe he is sometimes. He just impresses me."

"How does he impress you?"

"It's an ambiance some people have. I believe in him more than I believe in religion."

At 10:42 P.M., Chris was again read his Miranda rights and interviewed about the Alva Country Diner. He still believed Kevin and Pete got only $121. "He's trying to blame this on us and collect insurance, and he's telling y'all a flat-out lie, 'cause we didn't get his money. So don't believe that."

At 11:47 P.M., Chris went into yet another interview, this time about the planned Hardee's robbery. He continued to lie when he thought he could, saying there were no written plans.

"Was anybody supposed to be shot tonight?"

"I only think one weapon was gonna be loaded. There was no means or no plans to kill anyone. Absolutely none."

But how could Chris be certain? What if a manager intervened? Mightn't they have shot him?

"They may have. I don't know. I can't vouch for their

emotions and how they were gonna react to a stressful situation. I was in the car."

An agent walked into Kevin's room. "I need to perform this kit on you. Put your hand out." Kevin understood they were testing for gunpowder residue and knew his buddies were talking. Knew the damage wasn't limited to one of the earlier incidents or the Hardee's plan. It was over. On a weeklong adrenaline high, he hadn't slept properly in days. As Kevin rested his head, he hoped the others would come to their senses. *Surely*, they saw the cops had nothing without their words. *Surely*, they understood they'd go free if they kept their mouths shut. It wouldn't be pleasant, but they'd walk. Fuck, they'd laugh.

10:18 P.M.

When Allen came to interview him, Kevin was asleep. A detective's axiom: Only the guilty sleep. The innocent pace. Smoke. Fret about proving innocence. Demand to talk *now*.

"Today's May the 3rd, 1996; it's approximately ten-eighteen P.M. We're at the Lee County Sheriff's Office on Six Mile Cypress. Present in the room will be Kevin . . . Last name Foster?"

"Yeah. *F-O-S-T-E-R.*"

"*F-O-S-T-E-R.* Do you have a middle name, Kevin?"

"Don."

"Don. I remember that." Allen got Kevin's date of birth, address, employer and phone numbers. "I told you about this thing. Before we get started, I'm gonna read it to you." Allen read the Miranda rights, pausing after each sentence to confirm Kevin understood. He had Kevin read and sign that he understood his rights, didn't want an attorney and hadn't been induced or threatened to talk. Kevin swore to tell the truth. "Okay," Allen said. "Kevin, we met in 1994."

"'92."

"I don't know. . . . You had an accident, anyway. Right?"

"Yuh!"

"What happened?" Allen asked.

"I shot myself."

"That's right. I remember that. We got along pretty good back then. I met your mom and dad and your sister. They still in the pawn business?"

"Yeah."

"Okay. You know what we're here to talk about?"

"No, I don't."

"I'll try and help you. We got . . . oh, jeez, a bunch of guys here that you were with tonight . . . ah . . . Derek, Brad . . . ah . . . a couple of Chrises . . . Kevin . . . Pete . . . a whole bunch. Okay? I know you and I can talk man-to-man, right?"

"True."

"I know you're a big enough man to admit when something's gone wrong and take your licks. You have licks coming, right?"

"True."

"I also know these guys looked up to you, right?"

"Not really."

"Well, they tell me."

"Some of them," Kevin replied.

"Which one do you think looks up to you most?"

"Pete."

"How about Chris?"

"Yes. So?"

"How about Derek?" Allen prompted.

"I don't know."

"You don't know about Derek."

"No."

"I've talked to a lot of people. You know me. I got all kinds of stories. I know what it's like to be your age and frustrated. Okay? The guys have been telling me a lot of things that have been going down. Okay? And I'm not so much concerned with those things, 'cause that just led up to things that happened the other night. Okay? Some of the guys are telling me about being out at Riverdale last Tuesday. You know what I'm talking about?"

"Yeah, I know what they're talking about," Kevin answered.

"You were gonna do some trashing out there at the school."

"Trashing?"

"Yeah, that."

"Nuh-uh," Kevin said.

"No?"

"No."

"You don't remember that?" Allen asked.

"We didn't do no trashing."

"Did something stop you?"

"No. We weren't gonna do anything."

"Y'all were out there last Tuesday?" Allen asked.

"Yes."

"Who all was out there?"

"I don't remember," Kevin said.

"How many guys?"

"Three or four."

"Which ones do you think were out there? Was Chris out there?"

"I think so," Kevin replied.

"How about Pete?"

"No. I don't think so."

"No? How about Derek?"

"Mmmmmm . . . no."

"Who all was in which cars?" Allen asked.

"We were all in different cars."

"Who was in the car you was in?"

"Um . . . it was me and . . . I think it was Chris."

"Okay. And I know there was a door left open out there. You guys went and got stuff out?"

"I wasn't out there." Kevin saw he wasn't going to talk his way out of this easily.

"Yeah. Out at the school."

"What are you talking about?"

"Out at the school. Some of the guys were telling me there was a door left open. I don't know if you were one of the ones that went there and got some stuff out," Allen said.

"No. I don't know."

"You don't know. I thought we was gonna be up front with each other and be a man about this."

"I am. I have to figure out what I'm doing here. I'm in handcuffs. I've been sitting here."

"You're not handcuffed now, though. We're up front with each other, right?"

"Yeah," Kevin answered.

"Then I'm gonna be up front with you, and we're gonna talk man-to-man. I know what happened out there the other night. I've been talking all day long. I know who all was there, and they've all told me the story. So, this is your opportunity to tell me the story from your perspective, okay? While we're talking, I'll tell you things to prove I know things. And if I'm honest with you like that, I want you to be honest with me, okay? All right, I know there was a door left open and several things were taken out to go to the auditorium. Now you tell me something."

"Like what?"

"Like who was over at the auditorium and what stopped them," Allen said.

"I don't know what you're talking about. I *don't*."

"Kevin, you know what I'm talking about, son. You're over there with these guys. You're gonna go out there and do some trashing. And somebody stops you. I've got not one, not two, not three, but four or five guys— all the guys was out there—telling me what took place and who was there. And they tell me this guy comes back and gets in you guys' face and takes some stuff—

I know *that*, okay? I also have those items that man took. Okay?"

"Okay."

"And the gloves weren't worn all the time, so there's fingerprints, okay?" Allen sounded like he was confiding in Kevin, a good way to lie. Detectives were allowed to lie to suspects, and Allen did so when it suited.

"Okay." Kevin could be certain for himself, unsure for Chris and Tom.

"So. Now you tell me some stuff."

"No, I don't think I will."

"Why?"

"'Cause this is fucked up. Y'all are trying to do something," Kevin said.

"I'm trying to get your side of the story."

"I ain't giving my side of the story."

"You're gonna let these guys say the whole thing? You need to give your side, Kirk."

"I ain't—"

"I'm sorry: Kevin."

"I know I did something—this is not right."

"What's not right about it?" Allen said.

"This don't—fucking . . . no."

"Have I told you a lie yet?"

"No. . . . I don't know."

"Well, I haven't. I was up front and honest."

"Y'all are trying to pin shit on me," Kevin said.

"I'm not trying to pin nothing on anybody. I'm just telling you up front and honest what I know. I'm asking everybody their side, okay? It's as simple as that. This is your chance to tell me your side of the story."

"I don't have a story. I want a lawyer. This is *bull . . . shit!*"

"Okay. This is gonna end this statement. It's now ten-thirty," Allen wrapped up.

Kevin put himself at the school. Didn't dispute something was interrupted and unnamed things confiscated by a man. It seemed to Allen a door opening—

but it slammed shut. Kevin was the only member of the Lords of Chaos who conceded virtually nothing.

10:20 p.m.

While Kevin was interviewed, Burnett called his mother. "I was witness to a crime."

A deputy got on the phone. "With your permission, we want a statement."

The Burnetts went to Six Mile Cypress. His mother wanted to call their next-door neighbor, a locally prominent lawyer.

His father hoped for the best. "He's only a witness."

Burnett's mother returned home at 2:30 A.M., knowing little, except her son had been arrested. She called her neighbor, who came right over.

Judy Putnam was at Six Mile Cypress, too, learning her most trusted employee, another she considered a good worker and an employee she'd been sorry to lose had planned to rob her. When she saw Kevin's picture, her eyes widened: they'd never talked, but he was familiar—a regular.

When Ruby got home from dinner at Perkins, she found Lorraine Drive encircled by crime scene tape, sheriff's cruisers parked at odd angles up and down the street, cops in dark suits walking in and out of her front door, deputies wearing disposable gloves carrying family possessions to a van, neighbors staring from across the street. "What's happening?" Ruby said. "What's going on?" Officers wouldn't tell her. Ruby became distraught. "Is somebody hurt?"

"I can't tell you anything," a deputy said. "I'm just here to keep anyone from crossing the tape."

Ruby became more emotional.

"We're holding the house for a homicide investigation," another officer said.

Ruby neared hysteria. "Oh, no. One of the kids has been hurt."

"No, no, no. It's a murder investigation from early this week. Calm down about the boys; it wasn't one of them."

Where's Kevin? . . . Kevin's still out with the boys. Kevin's going to come home. . . . Ruby waited. And waited. And waited. Kevin never came home again.

Six Mile Cypress bustled. Some of the boys glimpsed each other. Detectives dropped names. "And everyone has given me a statement, okay?" Allen said. Though Kevin's statement wasn't much, what did the others know? Knowing their buddies were talking, each wanted to get his version out. Previous Friday nights, the boys created chaos; this Friday night, chaos engulfed them.

Most officers disliked the boys and their families—though some felt empathy for Derek or sympathy for Burnett. Major Bonsall stood behind one-way glass, watching and listening to the interrogations. *Sick to their stomachs at being caught, but the word "remorse" isn't in their vocabulary,* he thought. *Matter-of-fact. Empty. Some capable of doing it on their own, and others capable of doing* anything *in a group.* Even for a twenty-four-year veteran, from road patrol to senior officer, this was a bizarre crime. *Marginal people enthralled by a devilish central figure. You have to be marginal to follow someone down that path.* His disgust rose. *It's their fantasy world in which they're important.*

In addition to his full-time job at Six Mile Cypress, Bonsall taught criminal justice at the University of South Florida. The night Mark Schwebes was murdered, Bonsall's students worked late finishing term papers, among them Kelly Foster, who wrote while her brother left, killed and returned. Long after he masturbated and fell asleep, Kelly studied in her room.

10:28 P.M.

Pete confessed to the diner robbery. "Whenever we want to do something, we write down all our information, get maps and shit. So . . . ah . . . we had detailed maps, times of people in and out . . . uhm . . . description of employees. We had the description of vehicles and . . . we had the works." He described the Hardee's plan.

"You'd almost have to shoot somebody, wouldn't you?"

"No. We didn't want to shoot anybody."

"But you had already shot somebody."

"We didn't want to do that again. Two in one week is—"

"You didn't want to do that again?"

"Not me personally. I don't know about Kevin."

"Had you mapped it like at the other diner? Where's the map book to that?"

"It should be at Kevin's. . . . I did that," Pete said, a point of pride. "I made the map."

10:30 P.M.

Burnett wouldn't go home soon. Agents interviewed him twice about the diner. At 12:11 A.M., about crimes in city jurisdiction. At 1:07 A.M., about grand-theft auto and arson. Burnett was cooperative once he understood what detectives knew. Despite LOC rules, the others boasted about Alva. In their retelling, they'd become black-clad comic-book characters. *Biff, pow, splat* . . . and even if Lewis was shot, he'd get up afterward and everyone would go home happy.

"All black," a sheriff's investigator echoed. "So they

went out to Alva on unknown date. They came to you and bragged?"

"They get off on that."

Done, the investigator started to leave.

"Am I in a lot of trouble?" Burnett said.

10:50 P.M.

Interviewed by Allen, Derek sketched the basics of the murder.

"Okay," Allen said. "And when Mr. Schwebes took that, what happened?"

"We all got mad, and we just went to the store."

Allen and Derek briefly discussed the boys' other crimes. Derek said they tried to rob the diner.

"What do you mean 'tried to'?"

"Well, he wasn't carrying no money or anything."

"What did they do to him?"

"Left him alone and took his car," Derek answered,

Allen asked about the interrupted Hardee's robbery. "Who were they gonna kill?"

"No one."

"You planned on killing somebody?"

"I was hoping not."

"You guys got a club or—"

"Just a little group thing."

"What do you call it?"

"LOC," Derek replied.

"What's LOC?"

"Kevin came up with it: Lords of Chaos."

"What do you call Kevin in this group?"

"Kevin. . . . Oh—you mean nicknames? They call him God."

"Lords of Chaos. . . . Kevin's *God*?"

"Yeah."

"Why is Kevin God?"

"'Cause he's the one that planned and did everything," Derek explained.

"Did you see Kevin with the shotgun?"

"Yeah."

"Did you see him point it at Mr. Schwebes?"

"No, because I was running," Derek answered.

"Was he pointing the shotgun when you knocked?"

"Yeah."

"Was he waiting to ambush Mr. Schwebes?"

"Yes."

"Did he shoot Mr. Schwebes?" Alllen asked.

"Yes."

"And you were there?"

"Yes."

"Anything else you want to tell me?"

"Can I have protection from Kevin?"

"I can't guarantee you anything. Not at this point." Off tape, Allen told Derek, "You're on your own." *Derek will get his protection from Kevin,* Allen thought. *Only the boy doesn't seem to understand in what form.* Derek's protection would be a Lee County Jail cell.

11:09 P.M.

Brad outlined what he knew about the diner. "I guess the guy was coming outside. He pulled a gun on him."

"Who? Who's 'he'?"

"Kevin."

"Kevin Foster's saying all this?"

"Foster," Brad repeated. "*That's* his last name. All these guys, every single one of them, I met a week ago. They keep asking me questions about last names. I don't know any of them except Chris Black."

Brad feared Kevin.

"You're not worried about that now?"

"They told me I don't have to be. But . . . I don't know."

"He'll probably never draw another free breath."

The conversation shifted to Hardee's. "So this robbery was imminent?"

"Oh, yeah. There was nothing—besides you guys—that was gonna stop Kevin," Brad said. "Nothing."

11:32 P.M.

An agent walked into Pete's room. "You have information concerning Hardee's?"

"Yes. I just want to get it out."

The agent turned on the recorder. *No tears. No remorse. But Pete's the most cooperative.* "What guns did you have?"

"I had a . . . uhm . . . unloaded nine-millimeter," Pete said, as though "unloaded" made a difference; he would've been charged even if it had been a toy gun.

"Was there plans to hurt anybody?"

"No."

"Are you sure? 'Cause we're speaking to everybody. Nobody was to be shot?"

"No. I work here, and I care about these people. We just wanted the money. We had no intentions to do any harm to anyone, except if someone really . . . ah . . . became a hero."

"What would happen if somebody became a hero?"

"Kevin probably would've had to warn 'em first, maybe."

"Do you think Kevin woulda shot them?"

"Probably."

"Do you think Kevin woulda shot people regardless?"

"No . . . no. He's smarter than that."

Midnight

Allen called Mark Schwebes's sister, Pat Schwebes

Dunbar, in spite of his exhaustion. "We've got the people who killed Mark."

Meanwhile, Derek was giving a statement about the planned Hardee's robbery.

"Tom who?"

"I don't know his last name," Derek said. He explained other kids sometimes called him Mob.

"You know what Mafia stands for, right? 'Mothers And Fathers of Italian Americans.'"

"Yeah? That's what it stands for?"

"It's a *joke*, man."

"Oh. Sorry." Derek wouldn't laugh for months.

Later, on tape about Alva, Derek was less sure how much money was taken. He also clarified motives for destroying Lewis's truck.

"This is mostly because you're mad at Lewis, right?"

"That's why *I* did it. *They* did it for fun."

12:11 A.M.

The LOC's crimes crossed jurisdictions. Twentieth Judicial Circuit law enforcement agencies were focused on working together. Sheriff's officers notified the Fort Myers Police Department. Caring only about crimes within police jurisdiction, a Fort Myers police officer interviewed Burnett about the bombing. "Were you there?"

"I wasn't." Burnett didn't have a lawyer—hadn't asked for one. He was scared, no idea what to say.

At the same time, police detectives interviewed first Pete, then Chris, about crimes in Fort Myers. Pete listed participants in the bombing, concluding, "And, um . . . Tom. I'm unfamiliar with his last name."

Likewise, Chris included, "Um . . . Tom. I don't know his last name."

They murdered a man because he might've turned

Tom in. Their leader threatened to kill Tom for his loose mouth. They didn't know his last name.

In addition to closing the Coke case, police were on a fishing expedition. "What we're wanting to do, Pete, is get everything cleared up now, so we don't have to come back on ya later."

"All right." Pete gave a succinct account of the LOC's progression. "I'll just start at the beginning. We did the . . . um . . . the four, five fires and construction site. . . . The Hut, that was one night. . . . And then, the next Friday, we did the Coca-Cola building, and the Friday after that, we carjacked the guy at the Alva Country Diner and then . . . we . . . ah . . . killed Mr. Schwebes."

"Were you involved in that?"

"I was there. I was in the car. I didn't really . . . There was no . . . deal like, if we don't—"

"Okay." The murder was outside city jurisdiction. "You recall stealing any vehicles? Any 4Runners?"

"We tried to take a couple of cars," Pete said. "I wasn't there, 'cause I have a curfew. I had to get home; then I'd sneak out." Much later, he'd laugh at this. "Master criminal with a curfew," he told *Dateline NBC*.

One of the first things Chris mentioned was a newspaper story incorrectly reporting eight propane tanks in the Coke building: there were ten, he insisted. He thought his role—waiting in Kevin's truck—less incriminating than those of the others.

"Were you involved in the fire at the Coca-Cola plant?"

"You mean personally or just accessory?"

"The answer would be the same, wouldn't it?"

"I suppose. But the charges could be different."

A police detective summed up Florida law: "The charges aren't going to be any different. If you participated, you participated." By the same logic, he'd be charged with first-degree murder—even though he sat in the car and neither shot Mark nor saw him shot.

"Well, then, if you put it that way, I was involved." Chris

said the boys hadn't discussed the bombing ahead of time. "It was just right as we did it. It just appeared."

Chris tried to distance himself, claiming someone lit the fire with a cigarette lighter, then admitting he saw Kevin's "flash bomb." . . . "I thought nothing of it, 'cause he always has that type of thing in his truck."

Chris told detectives "propane's fun." He ruled out a grudge against the owners, the company or the product. "I know it sounds bad to you-all, but that's the way we think. You may not be aware of that, but that's what most people think. Destruction's fun."

"Did you enjoy it?"

"Somewhat," Chris said. "It's fun to do things. I mean, regardless of the consequences."

"Well, when you're young, you just got to do things to have fun sometimes."

"Sounds cliché," Chris said, missing the sarcasm. He gave the group's acronym and name.

"That sounds like a gang."

"Yes, but we don't think of ourselves as a gang. 'Militia' is probably the closest word."

"Do you know what a militia is?"

"It's an organized group of militant people, usually hired to do things. But we weren't hired, so it's not totally correct."

"Were you attempting to accomplish anything?"

"Not really. Just a lot of self-awareness and, like, self-esteem."

Even within Chris's circle of friends—misfits rejected by the more popular crowd—self-esteem was hard to achieve. Chris was intelligent, but Derek had the college scholarship. Chris was mean, but Kevin was sadistic. Chris had a vivid imagination, but Kevin made fantasies real. Chris was creative, but Pete was smarter, more articulate, a better artist. Even in his brotherhood of outcasts, Chris was second-best.

4:00 A.M.

Ruby sat outside her house much of the night. It was 4:00 A.M. before she got word. "The boys are arrested," Burnett's mother said. "They're charged with killing the teacher." Angry and frightened, she couldn't believe either her son or Kevin could've done it.

With Kelly in tow, Ruby headed to the Lee County Jail, where she saw a deputy who sometimes patronized the pawnshop. *Good. Maybe I'll find out what's going on.* "Can I see Kevin?"

"He's not checked in."

Some thirty minutes later, the deputy came out again. "Your son killed the teacher. He's gonna fry."

"Does my son have a lawyer?" Kelly collapsed on the floor. Ruby raised her voice. "*Does* my son have a lawyer?"

"No."

"Then my son hasn't confessed to anything."

"He's the only one."

"Fine. I want you to get a lawyer for my son. And I want to speak to my son."

The deputy disappeared for about thirty seconds. "Your son doesn't want to see you."

Ruby spent the night with a friend in Lehigh Acres. From the beginning, she maintained Kevin's innocence.

In the justice system's machinations, the charges would change—some that could've been brought wouldn't be filed, and some that later turned out to be false weren't pursued. The boys weren't even all arrested yet; some never would be; detectives still sought Tom LNU—last name unknown. Not charged in the murder, Christopher Thomas Burnett, seventeen, faced at least six charges related to crimes with Kevin or the LOC. Initial charges against Kevin Don Foster, eighteen,

Peter Edward Magnotti, seventeen, Christopher Paul Black, eighteen, and Derek Shields, eighteen, included premeditated first-degree murder, RICO (being in a racketeer-influenced and corrupt organization), RICO conspiracy, multiple counts of arson, criminal mischief and petty theft, cruelty to animals, armed robbery, and armed carjacking and attempted armed robbery.

Collectively, they'd racked up seventy-eight counts. With twenty-two, Pete managed to beat Kevin by one. There'd be no thought of bond. It was serious all right.

CHAPTER 26

The Gun Show

Saturday, May 4, 1996

A search of the Lorraine Drive home continued as evidence technicians displayed mug shots and confiscated weaponry at a Six Mile Cypress press conference—weaponry suggesting an armed militia more than a gun dealer's private collection. Some smilingly called it "the gun show."

"Amidst widespread media speculation," the press release said, "the actual investigation was following a different path which would lead to a local, self-styled criminal gang—the Lords of Chaos." The reality: until Julie's Friday-morning phone call, deputies pursued their own speculations—as Bob and Paula could attest.

Among the two dozen guns, ski mask and crime scene photos, a seized snapshot from Lorraine Drive was displayed: Naked above tight white jeans, Kevin straddled the arm of a couch, hairless torso leaning against off-white wall, mouth set in exaggerated grin revealing clenched, perfectly white teeth, square jaw set forward, cheeks dimpled, eyes wide, eyebrows arched. His right hand supported the barrel of an AR-15 semiautomatic; his left index finger lay loosely on the trigger. An eight-inch surgical scar started at the top of his abdomen, ran around the dimple of his belly button, disappearing into the waist of his jeans.

Scrutinizing the mug shots, Jeremy Arnold realized he could identify the boys. No doubt about that roly-poly face. "Chris was the short, fat kid at the phone booth." Looking at the photo of Kevin: "That kid ran in front of the car." He couldn't find the taller boy: Tom hadn't been identified, so his picture wasn't there. Arnold also recognized Derek. *Wasn't at the auditorium; in middle-school band with my son.* He'd expected a more mundane story behind Mark's death; the guns and the gang appalled him.

Notified by Gill Allen, Pat Schwebes Dunbar also attended the press conference. By 6:00 A.M., Allen had been up twenty-four hours, but he took time to phone. Years later, she'd praise deputies for how they treated her family.

Because they were under eighteen, Pete and Burnett were initially held at the Southwest Florida Juvenile Detention Center.

Joe Magnotti sought a lawyer. He felt as though he was watching himself moving in slow motion through a suffocating fog. The charges his son faced were staggering, and he struggled to understand: "My boy worshiped the guy. Kevin seemed a likable guy." But Joe had known something was wrong. "He can really fool you. He's got two natures." It was the worst day of the wounded combat veteran's life: In his heart, Joe knew the charges true. It was as though someone took a running kick to his stomach.

Pete told his father he couldn't understand why he was charged in the murder. When the others plotted the shooting, he was driving Vicki home; when he came back, Kevin told him, "Get in the car, we're going somewhere." "We didn't dare ever say no to him. I feared for my life," Pete said.

Deputies descended on Lorraine Drive at 10:00 A.M. They'd stay more than eight hours, seeking firearms, ammunition and gang writings and paraphernalia.

"My former wife will sue for anything broken or missing," John Foster warned.

Deputies seized twenty-one firearms—pistols, revolvers, rifles, shotguns and automatic weapons (including some without serial numbers).

Investigators wondered about the relationship between Ruby and Kevin, the mom and son who left messages for each other on pages torn from pornographic magazines. Was there something Oedipal? Intimate? Or just a twisted psychology?

Deputies didn't search three derelict cars parked in the yard, a break for Kevin. The diner plans were stashed in a broken-down black Duster. Investigators would never find them. Ruby made sure of it. *Somebody's trying to frame my son. One of the boys who wasn't arrested put these here.* Deputies also hadn't found other detailed writings. Ruby cleaned out Kevin's room before agents could return. *I'll put it in a storage unit until he's out.* "My son's innocent," she told a friend who helped.

Ruby knew she had to get Kevin a lawyer. Perhaps the one they saw about the driver's license?

Cindi was driving home when her pager beeped. "Kevin's the one that killed the band teacher."

"You're crazy. You don't know what you're talking about." She almost wrecked. Drove to Lorraine Drive. Crime scene tape. *No way.* From her answering machine, which logged the time of calls, she knew Kevin called at 11:00 P.M. She *talked* with him before midnight. He was accused of *killing* someone in the intervening hour?

Born in Patchogue, New York, Mark Schwebes had four siblings. The family moved to Florida when Mark was three, and he took trumpet lessons in Cape Coral as a young boy. He played six days a week, sometimes practicing scales for two hours, happy to play alone, so single-minded that his family, in spite of their love of music, sometimes asked him to practice in the yard.

Mark's talent and dedication paid off. The U.S. Marine Corps recruited him from Cypress Lake High School for the marine band. After a four-year enlistment, Mark studied music education at Florida State University, then started teaching, moving schools regularly as he pursued his goal to return to Lee County as a high-school band director, preferably at Cypress Lake.

A close friend got that job, but Mark was delighted with Riverdale, where band was taken seriously and he wasn't asked to teach shop or otherwise distracted from his first loves—playing and teaching music.

He was proud of the band program's influence on kids. His role in life was passing music to another generation. One Christmas, his niece and nephews got fifteen classical CDs from Uncle Mark, and he encouraged their musical ambitions.

Mark favored music you could feel—jazz, blues, bebop. His idol was Miles Davis, his favorite Davis album *Sketches of Spain,* and his college nickname of "S'miles" combined his own surname and his jazz hero's. Pachelbel's Canon was Mark's classical favorite, and he loved the passion of gospel music.

Memorial service eulogies: "To give music to the soul of a child is a special gift, and Mark had that gift." . . . "We were willing to work hard for him. He made a difference in our lives." . . . "He sure was fired up about music." . . . "This is a loss for kids as well as all the friends." . . . "He made us play like never before."

That's what Mark always wanted to do. Tightly clutching a tissue, Pat Schwebes Dunbar was embraced after the service by a band booster and surrounded by students, parents, Mark's neighbors and community members. The crowds emphasized the irony: a teacher who was a favorite of students, who dedicated his life to students, was killed by students.

Tracked to his Chattanooga Drive home by a reporter, Craig detailed his LOC membership and encounters with the others. "What it boils down to is this man was shot for nothing. He's got to have family, people who give a fuck. Kevin took his life over some food and gloves. It was ignorant, asinine and stupid. Kevin's fucked up. He's crazy. The shit he'd want to do was scary. He wanted to be chased, to see if he could outrun the cops and how many cars he could get to follow him. If he doesn't do something wrong in a day, if he doesn't steal a car or something, it's a wasted day."

Told it wasn't a gang when invited to join, Craig agreed the LOC was different and tried to explain: "Gang violence is a pretty big deal, and it was going around a lot, and we didn't want to be part of that. They're a bunch of pussies. They can't fight on their own. They've got to form a gang just to jump one person."

He dropped a bombshell: Disney World. In the feverish activity at Six Mile Cypress, no one asked about future schemes, and the boys didn't volunteer.

Students climbed into buses for the four-hour drive to Orlando and Grad Nite festivities at Disney World.

Four didn't show: Chris, Pete, Derek and, according to the chaperone's list, another boy—whose ticket Kevin bought.

On the way back, a teacher on Jesse Mitchell's bus held up the newspaper: TEENS KILLED TEACHER. The impact was nothing like the shock awaiting Jesse when he heard about the Disney plan. Chris hadn't said a word.

Sunday, May 5, 1996

The LOC's fantasy world came to life in newsprint and breathless broadcasts. Passing a corrections officer's desk in jail on Sunday, Derek saw the headline stripped across the front page: TEENS KILLED TEACHER/RACIST GANG ALSO ADMITS TO TORCHING COKE PLANT. His heart sank. The boys were "heavily armed . . . led by a gun fanatic . . . racist . . . homophobic." They were remorseless, vacant-souled, militia wanna-bes. Possibly, Satan worshipers. The real local militia leader said, "They ought to get the electric chair."

They put me down as the core four? Derek thought. *I never really considered myself a member. The LOC was a bunch of stupid kids acting up. I thank God it stopped. I didn't realize what was really going on until after that murder.*

When the Blacks picked up the paper, the bottom fell out of their world. Chris's mother went to her son's room and lay on his bed, her face in his pillow, his fading smell all she had left. *Is there another Chris I don't know about? One he never showed us? I thought I knew him so well.*

So that's *who Kevin was,* Julie Schuchard thought— the Kevin she knew at Lee Middle, the dork she used to be mean to. It was *such* a small town. Kevin, Derek and Burnett were middle-school acquaintances who attended a different high school courtesy of forced busing. She'd shared a band class with Pete, copied his papers; this cute, quiet little guy, straight A's, played clarinet like her, the only boy who did. She'd live in fear for days after the arrests. But she knew she'd done right. She might've saved lives. *Kevin should have a public execution.* She fantasized telling the band director's family about thinking of them so often, about the maternal instinct that guided her to turn the boys in.

It'd be better for everybody to bond than be driven apart by all the drama, her mother said. So Julie went to Craig's. "If *I* didn't tell, I was gonna tell you because I knew *you'd* tell," he said. When Julie had briefly believed his story, she wanted to help. Craig had been fired, and she even contemplated leaving town with him. When she saw he'd lied, it drove her away. She moved into a sagging, poorly furnished trailer with her latest boyfriend—an unemployed sometime-tiler-drywaller-landscaper whose hard living far exceeded his sixteen years.

Julie discovered notoriety had mixed results. Publicity cost her two jobs. On the other hand, she got $200 for a proposed movie that promised more, but didn't materialize. Her dad brought the arson reward sign home from the Coke building. "You need to call. You deserve it." Nothing came of it.

Not everyone supported Julie. One of Kevin's long-time friends dropped by the trailer several times a week, rode with them to Timber Trails, suggested she not give a deposition. "Back out of it. It was a cop that killed Schwebes. I don't think it was Kevin. I've known Kevin all my life."

Craig's mother blamed her: "It's all your fault Craig's in this mess because you told."

"I like you and stuff, no offense," Brad said, "but I wish you hadn't done that. I already lost two or three apartments and three or four jobs."

Julie was in the Circle K when a boy she didn't know came up. "Thanks for saving my life."

"What are you talking about?"

He ignored the question, paid the clerk, then paused at the door. "Thanks again."

"Do you know who that was?" Julie's new boyfriend said. "That's Thomas Torrone."

"No way," Julie said, awed as if brushed by a celebrity.

The boys were allowed to use a phone after their first appearance in front of a judge. "Ma, I guess you seen the paper," Derek said in the New York accent he'd kept in spite of a decade in Florida. The weight was crushing him. He'd disappointed his mother and stepfather, but they'd stick by him and visit frequently.

Chris's mother did most of the talking; his father listened. "When can we see you? . . . What's up with a lawyer? . . . Did you do it? . . . Why? . . . What the hell? . . . Whose fault is it? . . . What kind of time are you looking at? . . . We thought we raised you better." The Blacks made a decision: he was their son; they'd stand behind him. They'd support him through twenty-seven months in jail, through a plea bargain, into prison.

Kevin didn't call home. He slept, only awakened to eat, hear new charges and be fingerprinted each time, following bureaucratic procedure.

Bam! Bam! Bam! "Foster! Foster! Foster!"

Kevin rubbed sleep from his eyes. "What the fuck, man!"

Keys in his door. "Get up! You got another charge."

"Ah, shit." Kevin estimated he was fingerprinted thirteen times. Still, he didn't call Mom. Later he'd say, "I wasn't given the opportunity; I tried and couldn't get through." But he also remembered her words after the driver's license arrest: *If you're ever arrested again, there's no point writing or calling.* It would take ten days to gather the courage.

* * *

A deputy interviewed Craig again after reading the newspaper story about Disney. "Okay, and shoot . . . what was that? Shoot every—"

"—every nigger they saw."

"Was there any talk about if kids get hurt? There's a *ton* of kids at Disney World."

"No, it's just Kevin's twisted mind, you know?"

"Is there any other thing that we don't know about?"

"That's about it. I mean, that just hit me yesterday when the reporter was talking about the gun with the silencer. That's the gun they were gonna take."

"There's no way he could've, now that I think back on it," Chris would say of Kevin's Disney plan. "The only thing we were vaguely serious about was trying to sneak in alcohol, which would probably have been impossible. But we were gonna try. We wanted to be all drunk and happy on Grad Nite. But no, there was absolutely no planning of any forceful takeover/hostile terrorist action in Disney World regarding the costumes and the assassination of African Americans. No. That's absolutely false. There's no way you're ever gonna sneak a firearm or anything into Disney World."

It suited Pete, Chris and Derek—outnumbered by blacks at the Lee County Jail—to deny the Disney plan. Three years before the April 1999 massacre at Columbine High School, some were skeptical. Others absolutely believed. "I wouldn't put anything past them," Lee County Sheriff John J. McDougall said. "I've no doubt whatsoever they would've carried it through. Every other plan they had, they executed. It was like a vortex of blood lust and arson. It was consuming them. They couldn't get enough. They wreaked havoc on a community in a very short period of time."

A state attorney's investigator later asked Burnett, "Was he serious?"

"He was very much serious."

"If you all hadn't been caught, what do you think would've happened?"

"He would've went to Disney World and followed through with the plan."

"And this was kind of a culminating event in the short history of the Lords of Chaos?"

"Yes, it was."

"And the four key members of the Lords of Chaos were all going to be involved?"

"Yes, sir."

"Would you've considered that a Lords of Chaos mission?"

"Um . . . yes, I would. Yes, sir."

Investigators and prosecutors mostly agreed with Burnett. Kevin would at least have *tried*. Once, people wouldn't have believed he'd lead the Coke bombing, diner robbery or murder. Once, a community newspaper dismissed the Lords of Chaos as juvenile. They'd set out to be taken seriously. They'd drafted—though failed to mail—a document announcing their intentions. "It's gonna show people they aren't messing with a dumb person," Kevin had said, "that I'm really serious. I'm gonna cause destruction and mayhem." In custody, they'd regret their success.

CHAPTER 27

Rumors

Monday, May 6, 1996

At 2:00 P.M., as the boys spent their third day in the Lee County Jail, Mark Schwebes was buried with his trumpet. *When he played that trumpet, it was like setting his soul free*, Pat Schwebes Dunbar thought. *When Mark wanted to cry, you could hear it in his trumpet; when he wanted to laugh, you could hear it in his trumpet.* In lieu of flowers, the family asked for donations to a scholarship fund for the RHS band boosters.

The first day back at RHS, rumors flew. The cash that tabloid TV offered students to go on camera fueled the fire. Extra deputies roamed the school. Wanna-bes scrawled LOC graffiti, more than a little scary to teachers reeling from the blows of a colleague's death and their students' arrests. Students discussed gangs. "Stupid." . . . "A waste of time." . . . "Nothing but trouble." Speculation swirled about who was in the LOC. There was enough talk *before* the shooting that some asked why it didn't surface faster. "A lot of teachers probably knew about this," one boy said. "A lot of students knew there was a group of kids, but I don't think anybody knew they were supposedly committing crimes. If the teachers knew these kids might have problems, they could've maybe said, 'Hey, you need help,' you know, 'You need someone to talk to,' or something."

Not yet arrested or even identified, Tom attempted damage control. "I wasn't involved," he told a friend. "I was in the gang, but I didn't go with them to the Coca-Cola plant or the Alva Diner."

Pete's prom date, Vicki, also found the connection a liability. "You were supposed to go to the prom with a murderer." She tried to ignore it. *Pete didn't do anything. He's easily manipulated.*

Gill Allen and Randy Collmer worked their way through hangers-on, acquaintances and kids who'd heard rumors. Students were interviewed in a windowless, closet-size room to give reluctant interviewees a sense of privacy. The detectives heard there were 210 members . . . they were going to finish what they started . . . they were going to do stuff to band members. "I didn't think they'd do anything like that, 'cause I grew up with them," one boy who considered joining said. "I was in Boy Scouts with Chris." The detectives closed in on the elusive Tom. One student knew Tom was a sophomore and described the boy's redneck buzz cut with the bangs up front and tail in back. Armed with a yearbook, the agents asked another to point Tom out.

"I wasn't part of their gang or whatever it was," Jesse Mitchell said. "Sooner or later, I guess, they were gonna get caught, so I just let that happen. I wasn't gonna be a tattletale. It wasn't hurting me any. There's pretty much nothing I could've done."

Jesse was on investigators' list of associates and a target of other students ("You hang around Chris, don't you?"). He was hassled by kids who said they loved Mr. Schwebes and bugged by the media, these reporters who told him they were trying to get something positive out of what happened, cajoled him into staying on the phone and lured him into making statements he didn't know if he even meant—confused as he was after his friend's arrest. He meant to speak for the good, but when he later saw what he'd said, somehow it didn't come out as he imagined, and he felt tricked. To top it off, there was his mother. "My mom's real religious, and it seems anything that's wrong, you know, is signs of Satan. Seemed they're doing something that was taking over their body and not themselves."

Carrying notes from Mom and Kelly, the criminal defense attorney that Kevin had seen the morning after the murder visited him. Afterward, Richard Fuller told Ruby the case would burden a sole practitioner. "You'll never be able to afford the defense this is gonna take. This is gonna be Fort Myers' O. J. trial. Get the family together, review diaries and calendars. Write everything you remember. Determine where Kevin was." She should contact Bob Jacobs at the public defender's office.

Some who worked alongside the assistant public defender thought him Nixonian. He had the aura of a man from humble roots made good, a slightly worn air, a hint of paranoia—looking around the courtroom as though concerned he'd be attacked. Jacobs also had a tremor that worsened at key times, such as during closing arguments. To a casual observer or jury member, the trembling suggested nervousness.

Jacobs knew almost all his clients were guilty—of something—and he knew most lost. He seemed used to losing, though he'd made a successful life and would become the elected head of his circuit's office. The public defender faced a huge workload. It was never possible to prepare like a private attorney. But Jacobs, who believed in redemption and opposed the death penalty, would make extraordinary efforts in Kevin's defense.

To avoid conflicts of interest, the public defender's office could represent only one of the boys. The others got court-appointed attorneys from a pool of private lawyers.

While the boys sat in the cocoon of jail, investigators debated whether the figures peering into the Starvin Marvin on the hazy video were Kevin and Chris; recovered the Toyota remains behind Burnett's barn; delivered Kevin's Mossberg, unfired shells and spent casings from the murder scene to a firearms examiner; searched the boys' homes; seized and searched the boys' cars; sifted through the remains of the Coke building for the ignition device; searched the pawnshop and storage unit Ruby squirreled her son's possessions in; determined the origins of engines seized at the pawnshop; processed dozens of items for fingerprints and submitted evidence for DNA tests.

Brian Kelley, a state attorney's investigator, brought racketeering expertise. Assigned to the organized-crime unit, he'd done gang and conspiracy investigations. A former army ranger, he was familiar with explosives. His first involvement was a daylong meeting at Six Mile Cypress with cooperating agencies, including investigators from Orlando interested in the Disney angle. He was a guy even a Lord of Chaos could like: treated a guy decently, and if you cooperated, he might do a small favor. This style paid dividends—he got more out of the boys than others. Kelley tracked down the school district employee who kept fire extinguisher records and linked the one from the Bronco to RHS through the serial number; got class schedules; reviewed Pete's computer disks; tracked down Kevin's longtime friends. If Kelley hadn't insisted on repeat searches of the Fosters' property, there would've been no "Declaration of War," no Hardee's plans, no computer short stories.

Tuesday, May 7, 1996

Tom's mother accompanied her son to Six Mile Cypress, where he turned himself in, telling Allen he was involved in the bombing, then invoking his Miranda rights. The last to be charged, he faced only one second-degree arson count, had no prior record, and arson wasn't considered violent, so he'd likely get far less than the maximum fifteen year sentence. Others who knew about the murder before or after it happened walked away scot-free. Brad Young and Craig Lesh, among others, weren't charged with any wrongdoing.

Tom joined Pete and Burnett at the juvenile detention facility, segregated from others because of the racial aspects of the case and its notoriety.

Pastor Wayne Beeler, of the First Baptist Church of Buckingham, on Orange River Boulevard—in whose parking lot the Lords of Chaos formed—ministered to the three, giving them Bibles and pointing them to John 3:3: "Verily, verily I say unto thee, except a man be born again, he cannot see the kingdom of God."

Meanwhile, still working through RHS, Allen and Collmer interviewed Abe Ellsworth. "You don't erase part of the tape and just splice in a little piece or something?" a paranoid Ellsworth said.

"No, no, no, we're not that good," Allen said. "Yet." *Some of the boys are clamming up,* he thought. Friends were arrested; the media besieged homes and RHS; some boys feared arrest if they admitted even peripheral involvement. And then some interviews were simply bizarre.

Pursuing rumors Kevin might've killed others, Allen and Collmer interviewed a sophomore. "You been telling people you've been down to the Everglades with Kevin?" Allen said.

"I might've stretched the truth a little bit about that, yes, sir."

"Why don't you enlighten me?"

"I added myself into one of the rumors to make it sound better."

"What's the rumor?"

"That he's killed a . . . He picked up a guy down on Martin Luther King, took him out into the Everglades and shot him."

That was what detectives had heard: Kevin picked up a black hitchhiker, shot him and dumped him in the swamp. The boy explained he was trying to attract attention and impress a cute freshman. "Actually, I heard rumors about him killing his aunt or something like that. You know . . . ah . . . that's probably just another one of those stupid rumors."

"Where was that supposed to happen at?"

"Out in Texas."

"An aunt?"

"Yes. There are so many rumors going around, sir."

Of course, it was an uncle, and dead Uncle Gary was very much alive.

"I'd seen so damned much death that death don't bother me," Uncle Gary said. A veteran, three years in 'Nam. "I didn't make friends, because they shifted them back over to the States in body bags." Survived. "I wonder how, but I did. Hell, I've been trying to figure out how I survived the rest of it." Married Ruby's sister. "All of them married, I guess you could say, Vietnam veterans. Her parents were real good people, and they were raised up as Catholics. The upbringing those kids had was a good, wholesome upbringing. You couldn't ask for better people in the world. There was eight of them kids. There's no telling how the kids are going to turn out, or how the grandkids are going to turn out. The '60s were the rebellious times, and they were right in the middle of it. Ruby was the worst one of the bunch. That whole goddamned bunch. I can't blame it on the parents. The whole bunch went crazy. Some of the things my son has done, it kind of makes me wonder if insanity runs in that family and they're afraid to admit it."

Mary had difficult times. "She had a complete, absolute nervous breakdown. No expression, like a damn zombie. Hell, it was damn near a year before she even talked to me. Empty-nest syndrome. No more babies to take care of."

The day before Valentine's Day 1993, in the twenty-second year of their marriage, was good. "We had one of the most marvelous days in the world. I heard the pistol slide out of the holster." A .38 special. Hollow-point bullets. "Don't leave too much for a damn autopsy." Mary was forty-six. "I ain't heard [nothing] out of none of the in-law bunch since it happened. I was prime suspect for murder one. They thought I did it."

Uncle Gary wasn't included in the obituary. "They wouldn't even let me have a say in the headstone. Ruby Catherine is the one that bought the damn thing. I was left out of that deal completely. Nobody wants to admit a member of their family will commit suicide. That whole bunch still thinks I did it, even though I sent them the death certificate and the autopsy report. I'm still sleeping in the same bedroom where she killed herself, so that should tell anybody in the world ain't no damn way I did it. I'm *sleeping,* too."

Uncle Gary wasn't shaken that he was supposed to be dead, shot by his nephew: "This day and time, nothing surprises me. Ruby Catherine was, I guess you could say, the wild child. She kind of got blackballed from the family years ago. Ruby was the worst of the bunch.

"They come down to visit us one time. She was still married to Ronnie." (That was Ron Newberry, husband number one.) Uncle Gary remembered the visit well, on account of the see-through negligee he said Ruby wore.

"Kevin was set up by his friends," Ruby told business associates, creditors, a jeweler, but never the cops. "Kevin was home; he didn't kill anyone. He didn't do it. I was home with him. He was asleep."

She'd never again live on Lorraine Drive. The strain on her finances, the intrusive media, the need to protect Kelly, a growing dislike of the neighborhood, the connection to bad events all contributed to her decision. How could *anyone* know how to handle it? What to tell relatives reading about it in an Albuquerque newspaper, hearing about it in a barbershop halfway across the country, seeing it on *Good Morning America*? For three weeks, Ruby didn't go to the pawnshop. Within a month of Kevin's arrest, her partner withdrew, and Ruby later sold it and took time off to focus on her son's case.

A grand jury of eighteen citizens asked to review evidence in first-degree murder cases neared the end of its six-month term. Proceedings were shrouded in confidentiality, and jurors' identities weren't made public, although they were picked from voter registration records twice a year, a sort of especially demanding jury duty rewarded only with a sense of civic responsibility and a $15 per diem.

Witnesses represented each phase of the investigation. Two Pine Manor residents heard gunshots and glimpsed people fleeing; Allen and Taber investigated and made the arrests—and then there was Craig and Julie. The pair sat in the grand jury's witness room awaiting Craig's turn. "Kevin was a really nice guy," Craig said. "He did this and that for me. Kevin was there if I needed to talk. He's a cool guy I had fun with."

"He killed somebody," Julie said. "You think he's *cool*?"

He'd do anything for you, no matter the risk, Craig thought, remembering Kevin's offer to help with his Toyota. But he testified.

It took four hours to indict Kevin, Pete, Chris and Derek. Tougher sentences were possible because the jury found that the boys were members of the Lords of Chaos, meeting Florida's definition of a criminal street gang. Death or life in prison with no chance of parole were the only possible trial outcomes. Meanwhile, prosecutors reviewed myriad other charges.

The grand jury's indictment meant Pete would be prosecuted as an adult. "What do you think's gonna happen to me?" he asked the deputy who transferred him to the adult Lee County Jail. Also charged as adults, Burnett and Tom were transferred to the jail.

Burnett called Cindi. "Will you marry me?"

"We'll talk about it when you get out," she said. *You can't really hurt someone's feelings in jail. They ain't got nothin' to live for.* For a while, she lay low. Eventually she ended up visiting Ruby.

Ruby broke down crying. "It isn't true," she said. "Kevin isn't supposed to be in jail. Kevin and Peter were laughing and talking on the Yota's tailgate when I got home. Peter went home. Kevin was on the phone late."

"He called me around eleven."

"That's what he said," Ruby said, perking up. "I woke up. The phone was on Kevin's chest. I put it back on the receiver. Was that you on the phone?"

"No," Cindi said. "He didn't fall asleep talking with me. He called me, and I blew him off. I don't know who he was talking to."

"The phone was off, like he fell asleep talking to *somebody.*"

Cindi and Ruby studied newspaper pictures of Kevin's codefendants. "Who's that?" Cindi said. *I*

*don't know where these kids come from. Bunch of kids that
don't hang out with him accusing him of murder.*

"That's Peter Magnotti."

"Who's he?"

"Who's these other kids?" Ruby said. The other
boys pinned it on Kevin. "Pete's the one that done it,"
she said, contradicting the story about Kevin and
Pete talking on the Yota tailgate.

Whoever did it, Cindi didn't believe Kevin was involved. It freaked her out. *I hung out with him for a year.
We were all real tight.* Over time, Cindi came to believe
Kevin might've been framed. It bothered her she
knew only Kevin, Burnett and Tom. She hung out with
them so much—how come she hadn't known these
other boys?

By the time Cindi understood the significance of
Kevin's 11:00 P.M. answering machine message, it was
too late. "I might have it still," she told Ruby. She raced
home and retrieved two tapes from a dresser. *Maybe
he'll be on one of them.* But she cleared her busy answering machine frequently, and the message was gone.
*If I had any idea he had anything to do with it at all, I
would've kept it.*

Ruby invited Cindi to lunch. "Do you believe it?"
Ruby kept asking. "Do you think he did it?" She went
over dates and times, talking ninety to nothing. "He
was somewhere else this date . . . He didn't have the
Yota this date. . . . I got home at this time. . . . Kelly
was doing a term paper." Cindi found it hard to
follow. Ruby scrawled notes and repeated questions
Cindi had already answered. "Around what time did
you talk to him? Are you *sure*?"

Afterward, Cindi avoided Ruby and Kelly. "There
might be retaliation," her mother warned her. "Stay
out of it."

CHAPTER 28

"Kevin Put Me Here"

For two weeks after their arrests, Derek and Chris shared a cell. Derek learned about the Disney World scheme, dragging details from Chris: "We were gonna steal Goofy costumes and use those to rob *banks*."

Derek asked if—as police told his mother—he would've been shot at Hardee's. Chris was initially evasive, then reassuring. The pair slept twenty hours a day. Chris lost twenty-seven pounds and read seven books his first month in custody.

Pete disliked jail the most—the throwing of feces and urine, drumming on walls and toilets, incessant mindless screaming, banging on doors, the incoherent babbling he dubbed quasi-Spanish, the endless litany of questions at his bars. "Why'd you do that stuff?" Or his least favorite, "You called that guy *God*?"

Some inmates admired the boys—graffitied LOC on cell walls, got LOC tattoos, sought autographs. Others hassled: "Chaos. Hey, Lords of Chaos." Derek gave a smile, a provocative wave, blew a kiss. He grew his hair to avoid recognition. A trustee ran up to Kevin's cell.

"Who are you?" he demanded. Kevin told him. "I found God!" the trustee said, dancing.

Pete gave his lawyer character witnesses, then discovered they wanted nothing to do with him or, worse, said what they now thought. He responded to classmates' betrayal with fury: "I'd like to convey a general 'fuck you' to anyone out there in this land of tiny-brained, inbred, ass-fucking, pigeon-molesting, cornhusking, trailer-occupying, mouth-breathing, shit-eating, fuck-head assholefaggotnazibastard cockroaches!! (whew) They can be real fucking friendly when you're in class, but get accused of killing a teacher and watch the bastards get personal!" He told Chris, "I looked at the newspaper and this wave of cold, black despair enveloped me like a smothering blanket of death. Kevin put me here." His mother cried when he said he wanted to kill himself.

Their cells had two bunks, a metal toilet/sink unit, a slab of metal for a table. Some had a polished metal mirror. Inmates could have two sheets, a blanket, a pillowcase and four books. Because they weren't allowed to keep Styrofoam cups, they made a game of stockpiling them; Derek once accumulated fifty-seven.

It especially hurt Derek he wouldn't graduate. The school rescinded credits for his absence the last month. Though he wasn't on suicide watch, Derek's mental state was precarious, and he neither ate nor exercised. Vividly detailed dreams about the murder came nightly, Derek knowing that the murder was real, even as he dreamed. He also dreamed about Mr. Schwebes, who showed up in unfamiliar places. At the store. At the park. In other dreams, a faceless assailant shot Derek in the chest or made him kneel and shot him in the head.

Isolated and locked down except for a half-hour shower, Kevin handled jail best. At first, three guards escorted him whenever he left his cell because of his reported racism. Once a week, they took him to the roof for an hour of sunlight and fresh air. Once a week, family and friends visited behind glass for two hours. He'd screwed up and knew it, each front-page headline (YOUTHS PLOTTED WAR ON LEE) another reminder. Fuck, now the media accompanied stories with beautifully executed takes on the LOC logo.

He was too impulsive, executing goals in the wrong order. Because he misjudged others' propensity, to talk, he was denied a chance at bigger schemes. If they could garner this kind of attention—much for what they *hadn't* accomplished, the Disney plot—how much more could they have achieved?

Sitting in their cells, tedium broken by meals, showers, attorney conferences and family visits, Pete, Chris and Derek started a correspondence, letters reflecting Pete's and Chris's immaturity, Derek's more adult but less imaginative interior life.

Chris proposed they cash in with a book, *The Chaos Chronicles,* recounting the story from their point of view. He listed who could play major characters in a movie. Pete suggested merchandising the symbol and name with action figures, school supplies and books.

At first, Pete expressed regret over their plight, but none for Mark. A lot of people on the outside support us, he said. They'd get out soon. They should take their parents out to dinner. He'd move to California with his cat and be anonymous. He'd repeat senior year.

If he did get out, Chris wrote Pete, he'd be "the most law-abiding fucker on this planet!" In optimistic moments, he anticipated light punishment—perhaps time served. Failing that, Tennessee was the best state for inmates; perhaps he could be transferred there.

Derek also wrote about getting out. He'd party with a case of beer. "I'm going to buy a brand-new car," he said. "No more of these secondhand pieces of shit that break down or get me in trouble."

One of the showers Derek used was across from Kevin's cell. Kevin threw him candy and tried to be friendly, an effort to persuade him not to turn state.

"You're the one we're all worried about." Kevin said Mom would provide his alibi. Derek should join them. Sometimes Kevin threatened, "Don't say anything to them anymore." A gang colonel was a friend. He'd get anyone who snitched.

By now, Derek felt he'd never liked Kevin. Took to calling him "fuckboy" or "fuckface." Asked his attorney to pass Kevin's threats and criminal boasts on to prosecutors. *He's done enough damage.*

Derek's mother, Virginia, was contacted by Chris's mother, who said Ruby wanted to meet about an alibi. Virginia didn't know Ruby beyond passing her in jail. She wanted no part of it.

Pete also talked with Kevin and heard threats against Burnett, Tom, Brad and Craig. "Are you testifying?" Kevin asked. "No," Pete said, sincerely. He rejected a forty-five year plea offer. *That's a whole hell of a lot of years.* The state wouldn't have a strong case, Kevin said. Could Pete's attorney suppress his statements? He could join the airtight alibi Mom would provide. *Good idea,* Pete thought.

Using a simple number code, Chris wrote Pete, "Don't let Kevin drag you with him. He can't get out of this. If you go with K, you'll go all the way down."

But pragmatism required keeping relations with their former leader cordial, as Pete told Chris. "I'm waiting to get some lil' nugget of info that could be used against him."

The resulting agreements weren't made public, and the other boys were unaware they'd been betrayed, but within two months Burnett and Tom conceded enough to investigators that they might get reduced bonds. Pastor Beeler persuaded sixty-five First Baptist members to sign a petition urging the boys' release. Some of Tom's black friends were among thirty-five supporters in court. Lee Circuit

Judge William Nelson lowered Burnett's bond from $150,000 to $10,000 and Tom's from $100,000 to $5,000, and the two were released. Tom let forth a yelp of delight and wrapped his arms around his mother. Burnett alternated between smiles and tears as he left with his parents.

That night, Beeler told congregants that Burnett and Tom were Christians who'd turned from Kevin "God" Foster to the New Testament God. "We can have these boys back in the community. I'm not afraid of them. There's nothing evil about them—if there was, it's gone. Anybody who sits down with them privately is going to see they're not evil devil worshipers." Mentioning public reaction to the boys' jail-booking mug shots, he preached, "It's not what's in their eyes, it's what's in their hearts."

PASTOR: LORDS OF CHAOS HAVE FOUND LORD OF LORDS, the next morning's newspaper trumpeted. Readers lacked faith in the Chaos teens. "It sure is convenient how people 'find' God when they get caught," one wrote.

Pete was apoplectic. "To my dismay I found a flock of letters today denouncing Burnett and Tom's religious devotion—fuck you, Fort Myers! I was there, that wasn't fake, I feel as strongly as they do, now these scumbags are trying to say the whole thing was to save our ass! (Maybe it was, but fuck 'em.)"

Later, Pete urged Chris to pursue religion only if sincere. "I know I wasn't, and now I've got my parents and everyone thinking I'm all into it, and I can't tell them the truth."

Chris said he hadn't found God, but was researching the Bible. "Jeez I'm lonely, this sucketh a great deal," he wrote.

Kevin's rare, brief letters contained no facts about his case. "Don't worry," he wrote a cousin. "I'm fine and I'm innocent, so I'll be out soon." In another letter, he said, "I'll have to come visit y'all after I get the hell out of here." He sent Christmas cards. He invited Cindi to visit. She didn't reply.

John's natural children had seldom seen their adoptive brother; he never visited; they hadn't corresponded, and he never called. Their jail visit followed a familiar pattern. "I didn't do it," Kevin would say from behind glass. "I was at home." Ruby was usually the one who brought up the murder, trotting out her latest theories: Pete was in charge. Pete drew the Hardee's robbery plan (which Ruby neglected to mention had her son's fingerprints on it). Kevin wasn't involved.

Kevin started a dance with Mom over the facts that'd continue for years. "What's going on with the guns?" she said, realizing the boys had three with them the night of their arrests.

"I didn't take loaded guns with me anywhere. I wouldn't do that."

"*Why* were the guns with you?"

"Pete wanted me to show him how to take them apart and put them together."

Made sense to Ruby: *That's why they weren't loaded,* she thought.

Outwardly, Kevin stuck to his innocence. But nagging doubts about prosecutors' evidence prevented stating as effective a denial as he would've liked and weakened his ability to come up with a plausible alternative explanation. Evidence dripped out through the court discovery process. From Pete, he heard blood covered the shotgun. Even *that* wouldn't be fatal: it didn't mean *he* fired it. He scrutinized discovery materials, seizing on erroneous details, circling "wooden" in a fingerprint report because the Mossberg had a synthetic stock. He scrutinized property receipts. On the list of seized weapons, he scrawled, "Missing a nickel .22 pump-action rifle. Was in safe." He filed motions demanding the return of property. The state attorney's office returned home videos and adult movies deemed of no evidentiary value. Son and Mom celebrated these concessions as triumphs.

Kelley and Taber drew blood from Kevin and his co-defendants. "It won't be my blood you found," a co-operative Kevin said.

When they took Chris's blood, he had to lie down. Afterward, he passed out in the jail elevator. He told corrections officers he hated blood, and they laughed. "If you don't like blood, why'd you blow that guy's brains out and jerk off afterward?" one said, confusing him with Kevin.

Derek's attorney advised him not to keep his copy of the voluminous discovery in jail. Officers might pass it around. Inmates might read it, then offer to testify. Kevin loaned him six hundred pages. Reading Chris's statements, Derek felt sick. How much his friend changed in the LOC, how far he got into it, how excited he was. Pete had been into it, too, and his flat statement bothered Derek, but Chris was scary. Derek quit reading, his diner suspicions confirmed—he and Chris *had* been shafted. *If it'd gone bad, Kevin would've killed Lewis.* Derek wrote a letter of apology to Pat Schwebes Dunbar, publicly expressed regret and embarked on a self-improvement campaign.

Chris read the first 2,947 pages of discovery that eventually ballooned to six-thousand. From the court papers, he, too, learned about being cheated. But he couldn't bring himself to hate Kevin, casting him as a hero in his comic book's fantasy world, sometimes a badass spooky bandit gang leader named Kazin, writing Pete: "I started my own story about two months ago, and it has the four of us personified therein. Derek's some blind fighting monk, I'm some big dude with two swords (light and dark), Kev's a mage with really cool pyrotechnic hands, and you play this dude who has a bad fuckin' crossbow and ends up getting turned into some funky Jackal-human creature."

He sent pages of elaborate ideas, hoping Pete

would draw a comic book. Chris would get his mother to take it to Kinko's, make color copies, bind it. The boys would have something resembling an actual comic book. Pete drew characters he'd created in middle school or earlier—Good Bro, Psycho Bro and Cygnus, as real as a small child's imaginary friends.

Two months after their arrests, prosecutors filed a notice of intent to seek the death penalty for Kevin, Pete, Chris and Derek.

Chris had his mother send his Marvel comics trading cards so he could copy the pictures. His parents brought a portable TV to visitation. He missed TV when, through jail routine, guards' capriciousness or other inmates' viewing preferences, he couldn't see his favorites. When he could watch, the ads for video games he couldn't buy or play made him want to cry.

Chris's general knowledge reflected tens of thousands of hours of TV. "It scares the hell out of me seeing how you know so many lyrics from 'Sesame Street,'" Pete wrote. "That kind of shit just ain't healthy for an 18-year-old." Their senses of humor stuck in middle school, Chris and Pete traded questions, mostly trivia about TV shows, fantasy books, cartoons, comic books, movies, computer games and themselves. ("Beavis and Butt-Head are: A. Doing well in school. B. Running for president. C. Lords of Chaos in training." Or, in another letter, "How come we never noticed that if you add an 'O' to our name you get 'LOCO'? Why does that make so much sense?" Or, in still another, "When does Dick Clark jump up and say, 'It's all a joke—you're on 'TV's Bloopers 'n Practical Jokes'? [I'm starting to get worried.]") Chris created acronyms from the letters LOC: Loud Obnoxious Children or Lost Our Cars. Pete decorated his envelopes to Chris with slogans and cartoons; much of

his humor played on butts, body fluids and gays. After
joking about a stock they should've bought, Chris wrote,
"We'd be rich by now and could buy our way out of
here like O. J."

Even in jail, Rebecca Magnotti nourished her son's
fantasy world, bringing a magazine to visitation so he
could see through the glass the computer games he
was missing. Pete wrote Chris about them in detail,
drooling the way others drooled over girls.

The pair spent a good deal of time and correspondence scheming—to have Pete's lawyer disbarred for
an alleged breach of attorney-client privilege, to get
out, to move closer so they could communicate more
easily through letters passed by others or coded messages tapped out on the plumbing.

Derek was first to understand the risk that the jail
correspondence might be read. The boys kept writing in spite of their lawyers' requests to stop. Pete
baited detectives: "If you guys do read (if you can) our
mail—I did call you <u>swine</u>; I'd also like to add a whop-
ping <u>fuck you!</u>"

Eventually Pete was deposed by Kevin's attorney,
armed with Pete's letters and itching to get hold of the
ones he'd received from Chris and Derek.

"You're the author of the documents?" Bob Jacobs
said, then forced Pete to concede one comment after
another. "You threatened to kill Tom? . . . You ever talk
about straightening 'different faggoty people's asses'
out? . . . At one point you said Brad was off the kill list.
Do you recall making that statement?"

"That was a joke." But it was clear it could be made
to seem otherwise.

"Who was *on* the kill list? . . . You have several drawings referring to a 'King Butt.' Is there a person who's
associated with King Butt? . . . You indicated 'if Brad
gets out of line he'll be dealt with.' In what way? . . .
You talk about 'who's the real Smurf?' . . . What's *that*
all about?"

"That's a little comedic drawing I drew to Chris. It had a police-lineup kind of deal with four characters, three who obviously weren't Smurfs and one who was."

"You talk about 'nailing Burnett's punk ass to the wall.' What did you mean? You recall ever making the statement that you'd 'twist around the truth to make me look good'? . . . You ever recall talking about rationing your canteen for murder, contraband and blow jobs? . . . You talked about 'those damn masons.' What are your feelings toward Masons?"

"I was talking about the masons who laid the bricks in the wall."

"Like the Pink Floyd song?"

"No, the wall. Like, surrounding us."

"Brick masons?"

"Yeah." Pete saw the confusion. "Not the Freemasons."

"On one envelope, you indicated the paper was recycled from your favorite pets? . . . Would you like to shake hands with a proctologist? . . . You indicated you were still waiting to get a little nugget of information on Kevin that could be used against him."

The stream of letters became a trickle, reserved for when Pete had something important to communicate.

Derek was treated to a two-hour drive to Tampa where, in handcuffs and leg irons, he was interviewed by a forensic psychiatrist. Retained by Derek's attorney, defense expert Dr. Daniel Sprehe (*Spray*) listened as Derek told him Chris and Pete drew him into the Lords of Chaos and introduced him to Kevin, a coercive leader with an arsenal of guns. Kevin held a loaded handgun to Derek's head. Derek didn't understand why the Coke plant was bombed; Kevin pressured him into it. Kevin had diabolical control and insisted on the killing.

Sprehe found Derek unusually sincere, unevasive and verbal. Less than 10 percent of such patients were as cooperative. Derek's dreams indicated post-traumatic stress disorder. The boy was traumatized, nervous and frightened of Kevin. "He began to promote Kevin to almost superhuman abilities, with the ability to hunt him down and kill him, no matter what, and he more and more felt under Kevin's control," Sprehe later said.

When Sprehe asked why he didn't avoid Kevin, Derek couldn't answer. Why didn't he tell his parents? Why didn't he leave town? Why didn't he stay with a relative? Derek said he didn't want to get his other buddies in trouble. Grasping for an explanation, he offered peer pressure.

Derek took 2½ hours of psychological tests. Reviewing them, Sprehe said he wasn't depressed. He was paranoid—not unusual for someone jailed on serious charges. He also exhibited higher than usual "overcontrolled hostility." That meant he had hostilities but was unwilling to reveal them to a normal degree. In deposition, Sprehe explained what might prompt a person to release overcontrolled hostility: "Gang reinforcement, sharing with him that they have hostilities; then he's allowed, as a kind of peer group acceptable behavior, to show his."

After the session, Sprehe wrote: "This young man doesn't have any major mental illness but has a personality disorder of a 'passive-dependent personality.' The type of person who'd be easily influenced, easily led and easily stampeded into being fearful for his life."

Later, Sprehe conceded Derek was evasive about the diner robbery, saying only he hadn't been there and failing to mention revenge was his idea. Sprehe also explained how it was possible Derek could be so afraid of Kevin when other boys were allowed to leave. "In all of these clubs or gangs, there's an inner circle of ardent devotees and then a fringe group who like to think of themselves as members, too, but aren't really in the inner circle and don't come to every meeting and aren't in on the planning sessions. I can understand there could've been some fringe characters who would be allowed to go on their way and not be in on this activity."

Sprehe thought the LOC's devotion to chaos and mischief was a statement of anger at the world, a philosophy Derek later rejected. "As he was rejecting it, he was saying, 'God, the whole thing was crazy,' but at the time, he thought it was quite noble."

Fred Shields Jr. would've been twenty-three. The fourth anniversary of the day he went into a coma passed. Then the fourth anniversary of his death. Derek felt sorry for himself. People wanted him dead. He hated seeing his sister using a walker after a car crash that could've killed her. He was moved when he heard Pete's mother sent a get-well card. He got so frustrated sometimes he punched his cell wall or threw a book at the door or tried to destroy the shower.

Another vivid dream, a dream that felt so real: Fred comes to Derek in jail, as he does frequently now. "What are you doing here?" Fred says. "You're not supposed to be here." Derek has no answer. Fred holds him. "It's gonna be all right."

Derek completed his GED. What got him through his jail depression was his family, a dream where Mr. Schwebes forgave him, reading the Bible—and Christianity. In the last six months, he faced an especially difficult period. Worried about a sister hospitalized with a mystery illness, frustrated by his inability to talk reliably with his family—whose phone was disconnected— he found himself on his knees, praying. "Without God, you ain't gonna get far. If he wants, he'll knock you down until you start seeing him. All he wants is for you to have a relationship with him." When his sister recovered, he took it as a sign. He'd come full circle from dismissing

God after Fred's death. With his renewed faith, his search for a father was over.

Derek's dream: He's in Mr. Schwebes's jazz class at the auditorium. He loses control—can't face the teacher. He leaves the class. The bell sounds. He heads back to retrieve his books, hoping Mr. Schwebes is gone. A kid says, "Mr. Schwebes is looking for you." He sneaks in to get his books. Mr. Schwebes appears. Derek falls to his knees, crying. "I'm sorry. I wanted to stop it. I was too much of a coward." Mr. Schwebes hugs him: "Don't worry about it. I forgive you. It's over."

It's the last dream Derek has about the murder. Sometimes he still sees Mark Schwebes, but they're always good dreams.

CHAPTER 29

Turning State

His parents standing behind him, holding hands, Burnett again faced Judge Nelson and agreed to a deal. At his side was the Reverend Israel Suarez, Nation's Association leader named one of George H.W. Bush's "Thousand Points of Light" for years of work with the community's poorest. Burnett had support from the Baptist church and a Catholic church whose members petitioned the court. "He's going to do good," Suarez said. "He's trying to give back to the community."

Prosecutors dropped some charges. Evidence showed Burnett was trying to leave the group. He had no prior criminal record, he'd paid some restitution, he was only seventeen and he'd worked since he was released.

If Burnett stuck to his deal, he'd get something vastly better than the worst-case scenario of a life sentence—two years in the county jail on weekends and ten years' probation, one hundred hours' community service, a share of investigative and prosecution costs and restitution. He must cooperate, testify, pass a polygraph, accept a guilty verdict and waive some rights (including to appeal). If he failed to follow through or committed another crime, prosecutors could void the agreement and request a sentence up to fifty years.

Pat Schwebes Dunbar felt the punishment lenient. Prosecutor Bob Lee, whose fluorescent WWJD ("What Would Jesus Do?") bracelet was incongruous under the traditional dark suit he wore in court, said, "It adequately punishes him. I tend to judge by actions more than words. The actions he's taken are consistent with some rehabilitation. He's cooperated completely."

Nelson said Burnett could start serving his sentence immediately on weekends. "You need to make arrangements with the jail to get in," the judge told him. "It's just as hard to get in as to get out."

The newspaper was distributed throughout the jail, and the day after Burnett's court appearance, a front-page story proclaimed he'd testify. It got worse inside (TEEN DETAILS PLANS FOR DISNEY SLAUGHTER) with Burnett's account of what the boys had done and might've done. Pete wrote Chris, "What's of paramount importance is—NAILING BURNETT'S SORRY PUNK-ASS TO THE FUCKING WALL! THAT SCHEMING, LYING FUCKBALL IS GOING TO SERIOUSLY FUCK US UP IF WE DON'T DO SOMETHING ABOUT IT."

When defense lawyers later deposed him, Burnett had done none of his community service but paid some restitution. He no longer remembered Pastor Beeler's name. He admitted he didn't tell the whole truth. He *had* sat in on the planning for the diner and for Hardee's. He *had* glimpsed Pete's written plans.

"Now, at this point in time, did you consider yourself part of the group?" Pete's attorney asked.

"No."

"Why would you be at Kevin Foster's house discussing plans for a robbery if you didn't consider yourself a part of this group?"

"I didn't discuss anything of the robbery," Burnett answered.

"I'm not saying you discussed anything. I'm asking why would you choose to associate yourself with these people if you didn't feel you were a part of them?"

"Because Kevin made me be a part of them," Burnett replied.

"We're back to the notion you're there only because you're afraid Kevin will do something to you if you don't show up?"

Why hadn't he told anyone? "I didn't know how long he was gonna be in jail. I was afraid if he got out what would happen. Still afraid. I've thought about it, and if he gets out, I'm gone."

"Did Chris change after he met Kevin?" Chris's attorney asked.

"I met him pretty close to the time he started hanging out with Kevin, and he was quiet, and when it started getting toward the end, he was getting crazier."

"Was there sort of a buildup since he met Kevin?"

"A buildup?" Burnett said.

"He went from quiet—"

"Yes."

"Quiet to talkative?"

"Talkative to crazy."

"Crazy being?"

"He wanted to do crimes," Burnett said.

"Went from passive to active? Went from peaceful to violent?"

"Yes, sir."

"What do you think the cause of that change was?"

"Kevin," Burnett said.

"Is there some sort of control Kevin has? Is there something Kevin does?"

"I really don't know what it is about him. I haven't been able to figure it out."

"But with you, it was fear."

Derek's attorney took a turn. "I see you saying Kevin's a man who had access to many weapons, without a heart, crazy. You related comments he made which showed little regard for human life. Do you recall where you indicated there was some remorse stated about Mr. Schwebes's death and what was his comment at that time?"

"He said he hated everyone equally."

"He was a man who put a gun to your head on twenty separate occasions; is that correct?"

"Yes, sir," Burnett said.

"He threatened your family?"

"Yes, grandparents and everything."

"Grandparents included. He was a man who coerced you into being a part of this group? He was a man who said, 'Everyone's going to participate in this crime or I'm going to kill you'?"

"Yes, sir."

"He was a man you personally—you *personally*—considered killing?"

"Oh, yes."

"He was a man that made you contemplate suicide?"

"Yes, sir."

Tom, who'd been working and going to church, went before Judge Nelson and pleaded no contest to arson. In exchange for testifying, prosecutors agreed he'd be sentenced to a year in the Lee County Stockade, ten years' probation, one hundred hours' community service and restitution. Prosecutor Lee said, "He'll be very important. He was on the edge of this group early on. He tried several times to get out." Tom also could start serving time immediately on weekends. He cried at his sentencing.

Kevin was right about Tom. Given the opportunity, he leaked everything he knew. "It's more, yeah, like a clique. Everybody hung out, and then we just gave it a name," he told Kelley.

"Anyone who didn't participate, Kevin threatened with death?" Kelley said.

"Yes," Tom said. "'Cause, um . . . 'cause it's like, you know, he figured if you didn't do it physically, like he did? You wouldn't have a problem telling on him. But if you did it *with* him, you wouldn't tell on yourself. And now that I think about it, instead of wastin' my time talkin' with Burnett on the phone I coulda been talkin' to a Fort Myers police officer, but that never happened that way."

Pete received a photocopy of a newspaper clipping—SWIFT JUSTICE NOT LIKELY FOR LORDS OF CHAOS—with a handwritten note: "Peter, show this to your lawyer because this should drop that concealed weapons charge on you. Also, tell him where you were Tuesday night, April 30, 1996. You were not anywhere near Pine Manor. Just have your lawyer call. Signed, Mom."

Pete showed Rebecca Magnotti the note—the one she hadn't signed—turned the clipping over to his attorney and asked his mother to call Ruby, his self-appointed second mother. Rebecca talked to the Blacks; she talked to the Shieldses; why not talk to the Fosters?

"I can't believe Peter and the other guys are telling all these lies," Ruby told Rebecca. "All these things I read in the discovery aren't true. We hired somebody to help me go over everything and prove these things didn't happen. Kelly and I and some other friends will testify Peter and Kevin were home. They slept, and they were lying on the roof, and then they were looking at the stars. Peter was in our house with Kevin the night of April thirtieth."

"That's not true," Rebecca said, remembering how she waited for Pete.

"Could you contact the other mothers?" Ruby said. "We could meet. In our house, maybe. I'd like five minutes to explain these things didn't happen. Just give me fifteen minutes, and I can prove it to you."

Rebecca would love things to be that simple, to get in her car and go to a house and sit, graciously listening, as Kevin Foster's mother explained how there'd been a silly mistake, how none of this had happened and her son didn't lead Rebecca's only child and these other boys to murder. Such a session would end politely, perhaps even with an apology from Mrs. Foster for how her high-spirited son triggered this misunderstanding: "But you mustn't mind him. He's a good boy. He didn't mean any of it." They'd all shake hands and go to their homes and everything would be right again, Peter playing computer games in his room, listening to CDs, pestering her to buy him a book, grudgingly helping his dad with lawn mower engines. "Did you send a letter to Peter?"

"Yes."

A couple of days later, Ruby called back. "I just want to talk some more about the discovery and how these things can't be true," she said.

I don't want to listen, Rebecca thought. "Did Kevin tell you anything?"

"Kevin didn't confess to anything."

"Don't be talking to her anymore," Joe said. "Next time she calls, just tell her you don't want anything to do with her."

The phone rang again. Rebecca talked with Ruby briefly and gave the phone to her husband.

"The earlier calls upset my wife," he said. "Please don't call here anymore." He hung up.

Rebecca discussed with Pete this alibi Ruby was willing to give. "I wish it was true," he said.

The details seemed so specific. Did Pete spend the night lying on the roof at the Foster house, watching the stars? He thought back, back to before Kevin shot himself, back to a night at Lorraine Drive before Shawn died, before Kevin left school, before it all got so complicated. "Yes, we did that," he said, "but a long time ago."

Teetering on the edge of betrayal in February 1997, Pete signed a proffer to explore the possibility of a plea bargain provided the state wouldn't use his statements if they couldn't agree. Hearing rumors, Kevin said, "I'm gonna have *his* family killed, too." He told Derek, "Once he gets up in court and testifies, he better hope he kissed his parents one last time."

In March, the state sweetened its offer to thirty-two years. Pete's attorney persuaded him they'd do no better. Pat Schwebes Dunbar told prosecutors the family could accept no less than one year for every year of Mark's life. While it was possible to get gain time, Florida inmates were required to serve at least 85 percent, which meant twenty-seven of the thirty-two years. Joe Magnotti opposed it. Couldn't Pete go to a home for wayward boys and straighten up? Pete pleaded guilty, but he wasn't happy with the deal. "What are you unhappy about?" Chris's attorney later asked.

"The length of time I have to do. I mean, I'm going through a lot for you people."

"*Excuse* me?"

"Not getting much in return."

"Did you have a sentence in mind that you believe was fair?"

"Probably something less than this."

"Like?"

"I don't know. Something reasonable. Maybe like fifteen years, twenty years."

John Foster was found dead in April 1997. He'd been dead so long the date couldn't be determined. "Melted into the mattress," Ruby told people. He was cremated. Kevin would've predicted he'd feel nothing—especially after the bad years. The good times surely had been obliterated. But when they told him, Kevin cried alone in his cell. Tears washed over him and flowed for hours. Tears for John or for himself? Tears for his lost father or for the man he'd never be?

Less than two weeks before his scheduled trial, Derek was still holding out for something better than life. He met with his attorney, who showed him blown-up pictures. The first: Mr. Schwebes sitting on a stool. The second: Mr. Schwebes's face after Kevin shot him. The third: Mr. Schwebes's body. "These ones aren't that bad," reaching for another. "These other ones are worse."

"That's it," Derek said, breaking down. "I don't want no more. It's over."

Back in jail, he again broke down, in the elevator. Placed on suicide watch, he was observed every fifteen minutes for two weeks. Then he was hustled into court to accept a life sentence. He felt cheated by a Machiavellian bargain between the state and his attorney. A life sentence was the worst possible outcome. No death sentence would've been upheld: he didn't pull the trigger.

When it was Kevin's turn to see the pictures, he came back laughing. "It just looks like he got beat up," he said, leaning against Derek's bars. Derek felt like reaching through and strangling him.

When Kevin found out about the plea bargain, Derek could hear him screaming down the hall. "Derek! Derek! Derek!" Corrections officers relayed death threats. On the way to medical, Derek passed Kevin's cell. Derek blew a kiss. "I love you," he said. It was one of the last times they spoke.

Derek went before Judge Isaac Anderson Jr. knowing he'd never be eligible for parole. It was true that laws could be changed, but the trend was toward greater severity, not leniency. Florida had resolved a prison overcrowding crisis. Tourist murders had made crime a hot issue. Rehabilitation had been abandoned. Law enforcement endorsed a statewide campaign, STOP—Stop Turning Out Prisoners. Within a few years, crime reports declined. Some credited tougher sentences. Derek would be in prison the rest of his life. He was nineteen.

Derek's dream: The guy's chasing him again. He doesn't see his face. He's going to be shot in the chest again. He's going to be made to kneel and shot in the head again. He finally sees the guy's face: Kevin.

Chris finally made the proffer for his plea bargain in October 1997. He didn't want to put his family through a trial. They'd stood by him, and he wouldn't see them exposed to still more attention.

Pete, at least, saw what prosecutors were trying to pull. "Don't, I repeat, don't plead out to life!!!!" he wrote. "It's fuckin' stupid. You might as well go to trial, because life's what you'll get anyway (and you lose your appeals)."

Chris ignored his best friend's advice.

Kevin had watched his cohorts fall like dominoes. After twenty-one months in jail, he faced trial alone.

CHAPTER 30

To Speak the Truth

Craving neither courtroom spectacle nor Old Testament revenge, Mark's family approved a deal prosecutors offered Kevin on the eve of trial. "Life without the possibility of parole," prosecutor Randy McGruther said. "That offer's still open." McGruther was red-cheeked and chunky, a beardless Santa Claus with short, sandy hair and an infectious grin. His jovial manner hid shrewd intelligence.

"I told him I wanted him to sleep on it," said Bob Jacobs, public defender. "It's my understanding he's turning down the offer." Turning to his client: "Is that correct?"

"Yes, sir." Kevin wore a dark blue suit, blue shirt, red tie, black shoes with gold buckles and tortoiseshell glasses. Five armed bailiffs stood within easy reach.

"If you accept, the case will be over today," Jacobs said. "The state would waive the death penalty."

Neither Kevin nor Mom would countenance a deal. For Kevin, it would've been an anticlimax. To him, life in prison was harsher and less glamorous than "Old Sparky."

The offer bolstered Ruby's confidence. Kevin would go free.

McGruther thought Ruby was calling the shots. Starting with the premise, "Let's see why he couldn't have done it," she convinced herself he didn't. She posed the questions Kevin's attorneys voiced.

Jury selection started the day after the Fort Myers City Council unanimously imposed a teen curfew. March 3, 1998, was a rare morning in Southwest Florida. Mist rose from retention ponds. Spectators saw their breath as they hustled to the Lee County Justice Center. Court officials anticipated a circus. Newspaper reporters and columnists sat in the courtroom. Still photographers and TV crews crammed into a room behind the courtroom, straining to hear a tinny loudspeaker, cameras pressed against the window. Clerks issued hundreds of jury summonses, fearing an unbiased jury would be hard to find.

Jurors would meet Kevin's attorneys, Jacobs and Marquin Rinard; prosecutors Marshall King Hall, Bob Lee and McGruther and Judge Isaac Anderson, who ran his courtroom strictly, though not without humor. He didn't wear his heart on his sleeve, declined media interviews and dodged the limelight. He told Jacobs to end a digression, told Hall to sit down, posed jurors his own questions, told an attorney he was invading witnesses' space by standing too close to the witness-box, told a repetitive prosecutor to move on.

Opposing camps sat on opposite sides up front, supporters behind them. Ruby, wearing a tight denim miniskirt, a 1960s relic that would've looked good on her in her teens, sat with daughter Kelly, husband number two, Joe Bates, husband number three, Brian Burns, and others of the Foster clan behind the defense. They looked hard, weathered and unkempt. *Like something out of* Deliverance, a prosecutor thought. *Something wrong with the gene pool.* "I ain't got nothing to say to nobody," Bates said. He was heavyset. He scrutinized the jury and took notes. The trial would shock Lee County, he predicted.

Pat Schwebes Dunbar, her parents, other relatives and friends sat with a victim advocate behind prosecutors. The trial started slowly, stretches of dead time between the questioning of potential jurors. Mark's parents circulated photos of grandchildren. Mark's father worried. "A jury's emotional," he said. "They make the wrong decisions."

"Jury selection's like a job application," Rinard told potential jurors. "Not necessarily a job anybody wants, but we're interviewing you for a job."

The process is called voir dire. "A fancy word which means 'to speak the truth,'" prosecutor Bob Lee said.

Court language was formal and stilted, but jury selection was conversational and relaxed. Jurors got a civics lesson in the rights of the accused and his accusers and the workings of a criminal jury trial. Both sides educated jurors about *this* trial—the likely testimony of codefendants, the paucity of physical evidence, the concept of peer pressure, the anticipated alibi defense.

"You know of anything stronger than a mother's love?" McGruther asked, without elaborating. McGruther had awakened in the middle of the night. The physical evidence was weak: shells that couldn't be proved to have been fired from a shotgun; these shells found not in Kevin's possession, but in Pete's trunk. No DNA. No other physical evidence. The defense could question whether Kevin had time to kill Mark. A codefendant might negate his plea bargain on the stand, turning uncooperative. *What'll Chris do?*

The day of Ruby's deposition, prosecutor Lee stormed into a room in the state attorney's office. "We're fucked," he'd said. Memorable, because the language was so out of character, the concern so apparent.

McGruther wanted death, a penalty he believed should be reserved for the worst. Kevin led a pack of kids like dogs. Seeking adventure, they thought themselves bulletproof. Kevin was the engine, but they used him, too: Kevin this badass telling stories; now they're badass, too, by association. *You dragged so many in with you. You murdered Mark, but you took away the lives of the others.*

Jurors got their first exposure to Kevin—at the defense table in a suit that rendered him more collegiate than criminal, head bowed to hear an attorney's whispered confidence, meticulously printing on a yellow legal pad, looking less thug than public defender intern. Always pale, his freckled Irish skin turned pallid in jail. Deprived of exercise, he seemed slight. Whether potential jurors said they favored or opposed the death penalty, had or hadn't heard of the Lords of Chaos, had or hadn't formed an opinion, Kevin sat inscrutable and mirthless. The suit changed daily . . . blue, gray, pinstripe; the expression never did.

"We have something called presumption of innocence," Rinard said.

"It's like a cloak of innocence," Jacobs said, his tremor—a slight shaking of his head—making him appear nervous. He gestured to the prosecutors. "The only people who can take that away are these folks."

To Kevin's supporters, the process felt like "*guilty* until proven guilty." Here was Kevin in jail, in the orange jumpsuit, no bond, not convicted, only accused and still not allowed to attend John's funeral. Nothing felt fair: The release of all this evidence the media devoured and regurgitated in some twisted form that made Kevin's guilt certain. The bias in Lee County, where everyone assumed everything reported and repeated about these boys was true. How could they pick a fair jury? Everyone had heard of the case.

Kevin's defense had filed eighteen motions seeking a change of venue. But Judge Anderson would consider moving the trial only if they failed to seat a jury. And Anderson was *black*. The process was a charade. *O. J. Simpson notwithstanding, how many accused of first-degree murder walk free?*

"Kevin's been charged with first-degree *premeditated* murder," Rinard said. The assistant public defender was pale, slight, quiet and scrappy. Easily underestimated, he was a keenly intelligent, quick-witted, irreverent and pragmatic man who assumed most of his clients guilty. "The state's alleging this is an act he had enough time to reflect upon and decided to proceed with anyway."

Jacobs put his hands on Kevin's shoulders: "Do you think everybody charged with first-degree murder is guilty? There are situations such as the Richard Jewell case, where he was completely exonerated, got an apology from the FBI, got settlements from the media, and he was never shown to be this horrific criminal the press made him out to be." Jewell was wrongly accused in the 1996 Summer Olympics bombing in Atlanta.

"What's the phrase? 'Where there's smoke there's fire,'" Rinard said. "Let's go through the smoke: Kevin got arrested. We all agree law enforcement agencies don't pull people off the streets and arrest them without good reason, right? That's the problem with saying, 'presumption of innocence.'"

"What if the court instructed you the defense doesn't have to prove anything?" Jacobs said. "The state has the burden."

"In every criminal proceeding, a defendant has the absolute right to remain silent," Judge Anderson explained. "At no time is it the duty of a defendant to prove his innocence. From the exercise of a defendant's right to remain silent, a jury isn't permitted to draw any inference."

"Does everyone understand what the judge just said?" Rinard said. "Kevin Foster can do nothing. He can put his head down on the table and sleep. We don't have to present witnesses. Although his life's on the line we don't have to do anything. You can't go back there in your deliberation and say, 'But he didn't get up and say he didn't do it, he slept. He obviously doesn't care, he must've done it.'"

"Let me explain how the death penalty is handled in Florida," prosecutor McGruther said. "The trial's really done in two parts. The first part's the guilt phase, and the jury determines whether the defendant's guilty. You don't have to make any decisions regarding the death penalty—in fact, you should keep that out of your mind."

The guilt phase required a unanimous verdict. "If he's guilty, then it goes to the penalty phase," McGruther said. Jurors would then advise the judge on Kevin's penalty. For this, only a majority was necessary.

"There are two penalties—either death or life in prison," prosecutor Lee said. "The decision's ultimately the judge's." Lee was a lay preacher who came across as a Boy Scout. He had a practiced calm. At times, he was slightly imperious. He didn't acknowledge Kevin's presence until the second day of jury selection, when he pointed to him for emphasis.

The judge was required to give the jurors' recommendation great weight, but Anderson had proved his independence, twice ignoring death recommendations.

"What the judge will do if there's a guilty verdict is he'll tell you about aggravating factors for the death penalty and mitigating factors against," McGruther said. "You weigh those."

Jurors were quizzed about their exposure to media coverage and their feelings about the death penalty. Could they be impartial? Did they believe everything they read or heard? Could TV news convey all the facts? Could jurors set aside media reports and rumors? Would they be tempted to find Kevin not guilty or guilty of a lesser offense such as second-degree murder or manslaughter to avoid confronting the death penalty? Could they follow instructions regardless of their emotions?

"It concerns us some jurors might vote for guilt because they really want to apply the penalty," Lee said, "or they might vote for innocence so they never have to."

If the aggravating circumstances outweighed the mitigating circumstances, could jurors vote for death? Could they individually announce in open court they'd done so? Could they sign the verdict form?

Some potential jurors emphasized their unsuitability. Others were dismissed by prosecutors, defenders or the judge. Rejected jurors: "An eye for an eye and a tooth for a tooth, and that equals the death penalty." . . . "A person's time to die would be left up to God in whom I believe. However that comes, it comes, but I don't think I'd be part of that decision." . . . "I knew the band teacher." . . . "I live in the area where things happened, and I'm close to some of the people affected. Our church holds services at RHS, and we had meetings to praise God for our building still being there."

After individual voir dire, jurors were questioned in groups of twenty-five about broader topics in a process called generalized voir dire.

"One of the first things we ask is whether any of our potential jurors know the witnesses," Lee said. He listed seventy-nine. "One of the concerns the state and defense have is whether it might play on your mind, like, 'Oh, my gosh, someday I have to see this man and answer for my verdict.'"

Had any potential juror been a crime victim? A witness? Strongly opposed the jury system? Participated in civil disobedience? Known anyone in the justice system? Could jurors ignore any dislike they might develop for one of the lawyers? Would cameras and reporters intimidate them?

"There's no right or wrong answers," Lee said.

Both sides were concerned about the influence of television. "I'm sure all of you realize this isn't Hollywood, this is Fort Myers," Lee said. "Will everyone assure both sides you'll not apply things you've seen on TV or in movies to this case?"

"We're not Hollywood actors," Rinard said. "I can guarantee you John Grisham you're not going to get."

Prosecutors wanted to know if any juror harbored malice against the justice system. Would jurors listen to codefendants who got sweetheart deals? ("Have you ever heard the saying 'If you cast a character for hell, you don't get angels for stars'?" McGruther said.) Could each juror deal with sitting down with eleven strangers to discuss guilt, knowing a unanimous verdict was required?

"At the conclusion, the judge will give you instructions," Lee said. "You may not like that law. Will everyone here assure both the state and the defendant that, even if you don't like the law, you'll nonetheless follow it, because that's your duty?"

The public defenders wanted to know if anyone harbored malice against accused criminals. "The jury doesn't sit there and judge the person," Rinard said. "They judge the facts."

Were jurors prejudiced by crimes for which Kevin wasn't on trial? "Do you think things you've heard about the fires or other things involving Kevin—or that the media said involved him—would bleed over?" Jacobs said.

Could jurors avoid deciding the case before the defense was even presented? "Anybody ever heard of something called the 'Heidi Bowl'?" Rinard said.

November 17, 1968. Oakland Raiders against the

New York Jets. With 1:05 on the clock, the Jets lead 32 to 29. With the game running late, NBC cuts to commercials, then to a made-for-TV movie, *Heidi*. In the last forty-two seconds, the Raiders score 14 points, winning 43 to 32.

"A national TV audience missed one of history's greatest endings to a football game because they were watching *Heidi*," Rinard said. "What does that have to do with this?" His eyes scanned the jurors. "I have Ms. Barnes confused. She has no idea. You don't know what the final score is until you watch the whole game."

"It's like a prizefight," Jacobs said. "The state goes first. And the first couple of rounds—because we haven't put on our case—we're getting beat up. Will you all promise to wait until the fifteenth round? I guarantee you we're not going to throw in the towel."

Jurors should be attentive and discerning. "One of your responsibilities is to evaluate the witnesses," Rinard said. Jurors could ask themselves whether one witness was consistent with others. Were witnesses straightforward? Honest? Could witnesses have seen what they said they saw or heard what they said they heard?

Jurors weren't to discuss the case, conduct their own investigation or read or listen to news.

"I'd like all the jurors to look at the defendant," Lee said. "Are each of you emotionally capable—if the evidence convinces you beyond a reasonable doubt—of coming back into this courtroom and rendering a verdict of guilty?"

"Can you look at Kevin and presume him to be innocent?" Jacobs countered.

Not all the potential jurors could, and more were rejected: "I believe the kid's guilty, I got to be honest." . . . "If the evidence was overwhelming he's innocent, of course I'd change my views, but at this point in time I don't feel he is." . . . "You can't pretend you never heard anything." . . . "I do know people that knew Kevin as a young child, and I've heard stories. I can't disregard what they've told me."

On the third day of jury selection, Kevin wore a brown jacket that softened him and tan slacks. Trish watched as he looked from the unfamiliar coat to his family and flashed a sheepish half-smile.

"Do you feel you'd be affected by the media?" Jacobs had asked one potential juror.

"Definitely. I see an individual now they bring in the courtroom dressed up in glasses and like he wouldn't hurt a fly, and I've seen pictures of him the other way."

It took three days to select twelve and two alternates from seventy-five candidates. "We're not accepting the panel," Jacobs said to Anderson, laying foundation for appeal. "There's been far too pervasive publicity." But the jury was sworn. Jacobs renewed his motion for a change of venue. Denied. The defense repeatedly asked for the jury to be sequestered. Denied.

The jurors were mostly not from Florida. One was single, two widows, the rest married. Collectively, they had twenty-six children, and some were grandparents. Four were retired. Two opposed the death penalty, another was reluctant to impose it and two vacillated. For three, this wasn't their first trial. Three said they'd never heard of the LOC.

Juror number one was working and missed the publicity, though his wife was addicted to Court TV. A 1980 transplant to Florida for college, he was a residential real-estate appraiser, sole provider for his wife and three children under five.

"Let's talk about your feelings on the death penalty," Lee had said.

"That's a very touchy subject. If you have morals and you're religious . . . Sometimes I think, 'Maybe this isn't right and we shouldn't be doing this.' Other times, well, 'Look at this horrendous act this individual committed. Maybe it *is* allowable in the eyes of God.'"

Number two, Rose Marie Martie, a widowed nurse who read Harlequin romances and played with her two schnauzers, made the jury in spite of misgivings about the death penalty. She also was skeptical about codefendants testifying: "They'd be a little bit more biased." Not that she was impressed with Kevin. *Sitting there nonchalant, like you haven't done anything.*

Number three was a city administrator and NASCAR fan. During voir dire, he said he hoped to hear from Kevin.

Juror number four was a widowed real-estate agent. She did church work, read religious material and warned the court she had bad coughing spells. She was well aware of the LOC and not a death penalty fan.

"If someone's sentenced to life in prison, do you believe that person's ever going to get out?" Rinard said. "In Florida, under the law, it's not possible: life in prison without the possibility of parole means that person will stay in prison." *Perhaps if jurors know of Florida's life-means-life toughness, they'll give Kevin life.*

Number five was another death penalty opponent spending his retirement fishing and boating.

"I heard you say your wife was retired, but I didn't hear what she retired from," Rinard said.

"She's been retired all her life."

Number six worked in a school cafeteria and as a cocktail waitress.

Number seven had heard of the LOC in 1996, but not since. A computer support technician, she cooked, played tennis and bicycled.

Number eight was new to Florida and hadn't heard of the LOC. A housewife from Michigan, she played golf, biked, boated and traveled with her banker husband. She, too, was skeptical about codefendant testimony. "It'd be difficult to sit and listen, because you don't know if they're out to save their own hides.

I'm hoping the state wouldn't say, 'If you say this and this, we'll give you a lighter sentence.'"

Number nine was a nurse and soccer grandma.

Number ten, Brad Weatherly, had lived in Lee County only fifteen months and hadn't heard of the case. Married with three children, he managed a tile store and volunteered at church. He was going through a crisis of conscience about the death penalty that wouldn't be eased by Kevin's case. "If you asked me six months ago, I was very pro." A lifetime Florida resident, he'd accepted the death penalty without question. *We killed Bundy—we've always been in favor.* "The Karla Faye Tucker case has made me reevaluate. And I'm not saying I'm now opposed, but it's not as black-and-white. It has to be examined individually." On death row for murder, Tucker had become a Christian. The Bible said any person in Christ was a new creation. *She should've been spared.* Weatherly was determined to view Kevin as innocent. He looked forward to a strong defense: the state would have to prove Kevin guilty.

Juror number eleven, John Quelet, said he could put newspaper articles out of his mind and hadn't formed fixed opinions. A retired building contractor, he was a death penalty proponent who built furniture, fished and golfed. Quelet realized he was looking at Kevin, the guy he'd judge. *Calm. Quiet. Unemotional.*

Number twelve, a retired schoolteacher who quilted, sailed and gardened on Sanibel Island, didn't take the newspaper, only occasionally watched TV and didn't know a teacher was killed.

These people would decide Kevin's fate.

CHAPTER 31

Prosecution

He's going to look like an inmate, juror Brad Weatherly thought. *He's going to look guilty.* But that man at the defense table wasn't an attorney—he was Kevin. *All dressed up. No earrings. No ponytails. No tattoos. Doesn't look like a gang leader.*

Behind the mask—hair longer and curlier than the close crop familiar to newspaper readers, wearing glasses, dapper in a gray jacket, cream shirt and red tie on day four—Kevin was enjoying himself. The eyes fixed on him as he walked into court after each break made him feel like the middle-school math contests. *The trial could be won, though likely not by Jacobs,* he thought. Still, it was fun.

Marshall King Hall gave the state's opening argument. He was patriarchal, calm, gentlemanly. Called women "ma'am" and Judge Anderson "His Honor." Weatherly found Hall intimidating, commanding. "Mark Schwebes made a fatal mistake. He stopped to help two kids. But they weren't just any young people: They were members of the Lords of Chaos. . . . The defendant, when told by Chris, 'He's got to die,' thought about it and said words to the effect, 'Yeah, we can do that.'" Hall strolled in front of the jury box, studying the floor, left hand thrust in pocket, deep in thought and troubled. Gave jurors a sidelong glance. Paused to let the statement sink in. Repeated it, dragging it out: "'Yeah, we can do that.' And four members of the Lords of Chaos then commenced to plan the murder." Hall summarized the killing, pacing his speech deliberately, every gesture premeditated.

"These four young men then left, went to a gas station, put a little gas in the car, got a Coke, urinated on the side of the building and went on back to Kevin's. They had what you'll hear described as 'a group hug for a job well done.' Ladies and gentlemen, you won't be hearing from angels."

Hall raised an issue best revealed by the state. "The evidence you'll *not* hear is any physical evidence placing the defendant at the scene. Additionally, the evidence you'll *not* hear is any physical evidence placing Pete, Chris and Derek at the scene. But what you *will* hear is sworn testimony that all four were there, and Kevin—a young man whose code name was God, leader of the Lords of Chaos—shot, killed and murdered Mark Schwebes."

Gill Allen and Dean Taber sat behind Mark's family. Taber contemplated Kevin and his plans. Blowing up the hospital propane tank. Ramming an ambulance packed with explosives into the jail. Maybe not Disney. But someone would've been shot at Hardee's. *You'd have escalated. If not with others, then alone.*

In the defense's opening statement, Bob Jacobs undermined Kevin's codefendants. "Some will testify truthfully. Others who have cut deals have motives, and they'll testify falsely. Kevin wasn't at the scene of this crime."

Jacobs was sincere, genial and gentle, but seemed vaguely uncomfortable. When he stood, his tremor was more obvious. A bright man eager to win over jurors, he could seem ingratiating and patronizing. Every day, he entered the latest newspaper, Internet and TV accounts into the record and asked for a mistrial, which Anderson daily denied. Every day, Anderson asked jurors if they'd followed his instructions to avoid media coverage; they always said they had.

Prosecutors invoked a rule that bars witnesses from the courtroom to forestall testimony modeled on others' statements. Ruby and Kelly were ejected. Though she heard daily accounts from note-taking family and media, Ruby didn't hear the evidence firsthand. Did she maintain Kevin's innocence because she wasn't directly exposed to evidence to the contrary? From a mother's love? Or as a cynical lie?

Brian Kelley, the state attorney's investigator, was among skeptics. She was _too_ good, he reasoned. She could only have an answer for every question, an explanation for every inconvenient fact, a solution for every enigma, if she knew the truth. You'd have to know what happened to be able to argue away from it.

The prosecution told jurors a story, narrated by witnesses. Deputy John Glowacki told of finding the dead teacher. Mark Schwebes's neighbors described gunshots and a loud muffler and gave the time, about 11:30 P.M. Paramedic Cory Younger told of working on Mark. The last call of his seventeen-year EMS career stuck in his mind. "The brain stem's responsible for your heartbeat, your respirations," he said. "When someone's recently deceased, sometimes the brain stem continues to function in a rudimentary form for several minutes after the heart has stopped. There still may be attempts for the body to breathe. He had a few movements, but this was brain stem activity. He was moving no air."

Crime scene technician Rick Joslin verbally walked jurors through the crime scene. He recounted the autopsy and removal of shotgun pellets from Mark's body. The state used Joslin to introduce photographs of Mark, photographs Kevin and Ruby said looked like Mark had been beaten. Jacobs argued some were too inflammatory to show jurors. Jurors passed the pictures quickly. *More than what was in the paper,* juror Rose Marie Martie thought. Glimpses of the bloodstained house and Mark's body. *Gruesome.*

"Is that unusual that you can't find fingerprint evidence?" McGruther said.

"No," Joslin said.

"Of all the items sent to FDLE, did any reveal evidence tying Kevin, Pete, Chris or Derek—or any other named individual or lead in this investigation—to that crime scene?"

"Not that I'm aware of."

Jacobs emphasized this. "There's no physical evidence that connected my client with the crime scene."

Only Kevin's mouth.

Pete walked in, hands clasped behind his back, though he wore no handcuffs, a long-sleeved white shirt under his red jail-issued jumpsuit. "I met him in middle school. He was my best friend."

Pete summarized his deal, best of the so-called core four, the prospect of freedom in middle age. He named the LOC members. "We wanted to go around Fort Myers destroying whatever we could." He told of the code names, of Kevin's invention of the name Lords of Chaos, of his own invention of the symbol.

"Could you draw us that now on the board?" Lee said.

Juror Weatherly liked Lee's style. Easy to follow.

Pete drew the symbol.

Martie was impressed by Pete's invention of the symbol. *A waste. You could've done something great. So artistic, so talented. How did you get involved?*

Allen looked at Pete's symbol. *The name, the symbol, the Declaration of War were mostly you. You were a planner. Little general. The cool head of the group. Physically incapable of bullying, but mentally capable. Mentally manipulating Kevin. Kevin would've become a liability. Would've outgrown his usefulness.*

"Judge, is there a need to let that remain on the board?" Jacobs said. "I'd ask it be erased." It was.

Kevin watched Pete, eyes unwavering, expression blank. *I should've wasted their whole fuckin' ass that night. I should've aced everybody in the car.*

Lee wanted to know *who* decided to go to RHS.

"The group. We wanted to break the windows."

"Whose idea was that?"

"Probably Kevin's."

"You say 'probably.' You were part of the group. As best as you recall, whose idea was it?"

"It was a group decision."

You're the mastermind, juror John Quelet thought. *A serious instigator. You got off easy.*

Pete told of taking stuff at the school and of the boys waiting outside the auditorium. Mark pulling up and Kevin hiding, then running. Chris's anger, and Kevin rejecting the suggestion to follow the teacher.

Weatherly stared at Kevin. Purposely tried for eye contact. *Nothing. No expression.*

An exception to courts' usual ban on hearsay allows statements of co-conspirators, so Pete testified what Chris said. "Chris was very angry. They wanted to kill him."

"Who wanted to kill him?" Lee said.

"Chris."

"What did he say?"

"'He's got to die.'"

"Was there a reaction from the defendant?"

"He got excited. He felt we could pull that off."

Chris paged Pete from Lorraine Drive with Kevin's number and the familiar 666. . . . "That symbol, six-six-six, do you know whether that has any significance?" Lee said.

"It's the sign of the Devil."

You gave us more than anybody, Taber thought. Pete mightn't have been remorseful the Friday night at Six Mile Cypress, but he was upset. *With you, the school should've picked up on something. A little loner. That's why you were hanging around them. All loners. All without friends. Kevin befriended you all.*

Pete told of his own reservations. "Just going up there and shooting him on the doorstep would draw authorities very quickly and would get us caught very quickly. Kevin wouldn't listen. He thought his plan would work. I told him there's no reason I'd go, because I'd have no purpose, but he told me I had to."

"Why didn't you try to stop it?"

"There's nothing I could do to stop Kevin."

"Why didn't you call the police?"

"I didn't want to. There's a host of other things we'd done."

Jacobs—who often unsuccessfully objected—objected once more: Kevin was on trial for the murder and nothing else. Anderson sustained the objection before any of the LOC's other exploits could come out.

"Why was it the four of you and not some of the other members?" Lee said.

"We were the four most intelligent and capable."

But your intelligence level and Kevin's intelligence level worked against you, Allen thought.

Pete described the drive to Pine Manor. "Kevin was brooding. He was psyching himself up for the kill.

Acting really sullen. Angry. Me and Chris were talking. He told us to shut up. And then he started singing. It was a variation of the 'Santa Claus Is Coming to Town' song. 'He knows when you're sleeping, he knows when you're awake.' Something about 'showing up on your front door.'"

Kevin and Derek got out. "I saw the two of them walk around the front of the house. At that point I couldn't see them. But I heard two shots. I saw Derek come running toward us, and Kevin followed after him."

"How did Derek react?"

"He was shaking. Nervous. Appeared sick."

"How did Kevin react?"

"He seemed excited. I asked him what happened, and he didn't want to upset Derek, so he said it very quietly, raised his hand in the middle of his face and off to the side and said, 'Gone.'"

The boys returned to Lorraine Drive. "Chris was supposed to receive credit for this, because it was to make sure he wouldn't get in trouble."

It was Kevin's ambition for a long time, Allen thought. *He fulfilled that. Boosted his standing. Boosted his recruitment. Got over that hurdle. Now murder would go on just to be a part of the overall plan.*

"Why was Mark Schwebes killed?" Lee said.

"He'd caught our friends. And we didn't want them turned in."

"After the killing, what did the defendant tell you he did?"

"He told me as he was laying in bed thinking about the murder, he was masturbating."

"What did he actually say?"

"He was jerking off."

"Did he ever say to you why he'd chosen the shotgun?"

"It'd leave no ballistics traces. There's no rifling in the barrel. It wouldn't score the bullets, and they wouldn't be identified back to that gun."

The only remorse you had was talking to us, Allen thought. *You felt you were secretly leading, using Kevin's brawn.*

Lee asked about Burnett and Tom's plea agreements. "Did you have a conversation with the defendant once he learned they were going to cooperate?"

"Yes, sir. Approximately six months after I was arrested. In jail."

"What did the defendant say he was going to do?"

"He didn't want Burnett or Tom to testify. He didn't say anything out loud, but he'd give me this gesture." Pete drew his finger across his throat.

"What did you understand that to mean?"

"He was going to have someone kill them."

"At some point, did he approach you or anyone on your behalf about the possibility of working together for an alibi?"

"He said due to lack of hard evidence the state wouldn't have a strong case, and he wanted me to have my lawyer see if he could suppress my statement, and by doing that, I could join him in his story. I thought it was a good idea at the time. I received an anonymous letter from Kevin's mother with a newspaper clipping, and she was asking me to tell my lawyer to get in contact and tell her where I really was on the night of the thirtieth. I had my mother call Kevin's mother."

"How do you feel about the defendant, Kevin, who was your best friend?"

"I don't bear any ill will."

On cross-examination, Jacobs poked at Pete's story, asking a rapid series of unrelated questions aimed at highlighting any small thing that might help the defense, trying to leave the impression Kevin's attorneys were hard at work, and if jurors didn't see the point, they should listen more closely, because there was more here than met the eye, a conspiracy, if only they could see it. "I believe you said Chris, Derek and Kevin and yourself were at Kevin's around eleven-thirty. Isn't it true you believed Kevin's mom and sister were there? . . . And was Chris making jokes on the way over to Mr. Schwebes's? . . . What time are you usually asked to be in the house on school nights?. . . You said your mother was angry because you were out until midnight. Did you tell her what you'd done?"

"No, sir."

"Did you tell anyone at school the next day what you had done?"

"Yes, sir."

"Were you laughing and bragging?"

"Mildly."

Jacobs brought up the jail letters. "Did you ever threaten to kill Tom?"

"Jokingly."

"Did you ever indicate that Peter Franceschina of the *News-Press* is an asshole and he's going to die?"

"Yes, sir."

Juror Weatherly found Jacobs's tremor off-putting.

On redirect, Lee cleared the smoke. "Who was the man who left the car with the shotgun? Who was the man that returned immediately after you heard those shots with the shotgun?"

"Kevin."

Jeremy Arnold testified next. At dinner, "Mark didn't really tell me he was going to do something. He just made the comment to the two boys, 'Don't be surprised if Montgomery calls you to the office tomorrow morning.'"

"Do you see the individual you saw running in front of your car?" prosecutor McGruther said.

Arnold had seen Kevin for a couple of seconds with no glasses and cropped hair, but it was enough.

"Yes, I do. He has a suit and tie and glasses on. The young fellow over there."

Hair bleached blond, Brad was now working as a painter.

"You could've prevented—" Jacobs said.

"Yes, sir."

"Craig could've prevented it?"

"Yes, sir, he could."

"Knowing what you knew, you never called the police?"

"Right."

If you know somebody's going to do something, you should speak up, juror Martie thought. *But it's hard. It's a good thing the girlfriend told. More innocent people would've been killed.*

Burnett still was an electrician's helper.

You wanted to be a member, wanted to join, Taber thought. *But you mightn't have gone as far as the others.*

"Who was the individual that brought you into the group?" Lee said.

"Kevin."

Kevin and Pete were the leaders; these others were just followers, Martie thought.

At Winn-Dixie: "We stayed around in the parking lot for a couple minutes, and Tom got paged and had to go home, and I faked that my pager went off, so I took Tom home. So I could say my mom was calling and get away."

At least you left, Martie thought.

Burnett and Tom got off lightly, Allen thought. *But Burnett was the most remorseful. If Kevin had his way, each and every one of them would've ended up killing somebody. He wasn't gonna be the only one.*

* * *

After a weekend break, the trial's fifth day started with Tom, now eighteen and finishing senior year. Tom had short hair, wore an ill-fitting gray double-breasted suit with a gold tiepin and sat wide-eyed, answering questions monosyllabically, using as few words as possible. Prosecutors made him tell the whole story, as they had Pete, and as they would every boy who testified.

A hillbilly, gullible, impressionable, Taber thought. *But you would've gone further.*

As Tom described his encounter with Mark, he spoke softly. "Chris started doing a temper tantrum, saying Mr. Schwebes had to die. Kevin said, 'Yeah.'" But Tom left with Burnett. "When they were talking about killing the teacher, me and him just left."

Kevin called at 12:32 A.M. "He told me it was done. For a second, I didn't know what he was talking about. Then I got an idea. I was like, 'Whatever,' and I hung up."

Kevin wanted to share his enthusiasm, Allen thought. *It was everything to him from ego to sex. To recruit and stay in power, he had to prove he was willing to do these things.*

The next day, "Derek was in the lunchroom crying because he was mourning the death of his band director," Tom said. Chris showed no remorse.

Juror Quelet glanced at Kevin, again seeking reaction—and again seeing none. *Like a bump on a log. Maybe if I saw some emotion. . . .*

Tom seemed shaken by Jacobs, who got him to concede he told Cindi that Kevin was framed.

"Isn't it true you made a great deal with the government?" Jacobs said.

"Yes, sir."

"You were ready to tell them anything they wanted in order to get the deal?"

"Anything."

* * *

The courtroom was packed for Chris's testimony. Now nineteen, Chris seemed angry. *Does the boy have a soul?* Pat Schwebes Dunbar wondered. Martie felt sorry for the Schwebes family. *Mark was in the wrong place at the wrong time.*

Kevin sat at the defense table in dark gray slacks and a dark blue coat, head down as Chris testified. *You didn't think this would happen to you,* Taber thought.

Even when he walked by him, Chris wouldn't look at Kevin. He blinked. Looked down. Slim was still fat. Chris called Derek "Mr. Shields," Mark "Mr. Schwebes," Kevin "Mr. Foster."

Chris knew Mark. "Myself and Mr. Shields, who consisted of the entire keyboard class, were placed under his care on two or three separate occasions." Outside the auditorium, Chris had been evasive. "I was just being, I guess you could say, a smart-ass. He thought he recognized me. I told him, 'I don't think so.' He asked us who the guy was that ran away. I told him I didn't know." Chris said he'd felt fear and anger. "More anger. I felt Mr. Schwebes had to die." No one argued against the idea. "Burnett was enthusiastic." Derek said nothing.

At Lorraine Drive, Kevin disarmed the burglar alarm. "Derek looked through a street map to try to locate the address of Mr. Schwebes." Kevin ran around the house looking for things. Chris stayed in the living room. He saw Kevin carrying the shotgun.

In Pine Manor, Derek left the car empty-handed. But Chris didn't see the shotgun in Kevin's hands, either. Nor did he see the gun after the murder. "Kevin immediately entered the vehicle. I heard something hit the back floorboard. That was all."

Chris looked everywhere except at Kevin. The more he incriminated his hero, the more uncomfortable he grew. "Those look like the shells Kevin had inside the car," he said. He blinked. Looked down.

At Brad's apartment the next evening, Kevin bragged. "Mr. Foster was saying he was laughing when he came back." A long silence in the courtroom.

You were the only one of the core four who wouldn't have broken away, Taber thought. He remembered the interview the night of the arrests. *You laughed. You'd do it again.* It gave Taber chills. *Coldhearted, smart-ass little kid. No regard for human life. Thought you were the toughest thing in the world and nothing was gonna happen to you.*

Hall asked why Mark was killed.

"He was in our way."

Juror Weatherly thought Chris combative; the other boys seemed humbled. He watched Rinard, about to cross-examine. *Where did you buy that suit? K mart?*

Though a month from the end of senior year, Chris had applied to no colleges, won no scholarships and had no postgraduation plans, Rinard said. He asked Chris to describe trial preparation, three hours in the state attorney's office the day before, reviewing his statement. He made Chris go through the story all over again.

"I'd never tendered a plan to kill Mr. Schwebes." Chris suggested a robbery. "I said nothing about him being killed."

Asked the significance of the 666, Chris said, "I don't know. Look in the Bible."

Billy Hornsby was an FDLE crime lab analyst specializing in ballistics. He testified to what could and couldn't be said about the shotgun. "Most shotguns are smooth-bored," he said. "They have no rifling." He couldn't say the shotshells were *fired* from Kevin's weapon. "These two shotshells have been chambered in and ejected from the shotgun. I was able to replicate the extractor, the ejector and the shell-stop marks. The two shotshells were cycled through *that shotgun* to the exclusion of all others."

Done deal, Weatherly thought. The juror had never hunted and didn't shoot. He viewed the ballistics tests as crucial. Other witnesses put Kevin at the crime scene, but nobody witnessed him kill Mark. When Hornsby showed two photographs illustrating the match between shotshells and shotgun, Weatherly sensed a turning point. *That seals it: this is the guy who committed the murder.*

Other jurors also were paying close attention. Martie didn't know much about guns and found the explanation helpful. And Hornsby's testimony was a key moment for Quelet, who found the match between the ejector mechanism and the nick in the shell incriminating.

Jail pale like the others, Derek spoke softly, breathless. "He was my jazz band teacher. ... It had to do with the exposure of the LOC." Derek came back after he went home because, he said, "If they're gonna go through with this, maybe I could talk them out of it." Besides, Kevin told him, "You need to come back."

Derek didn't recall looking at the map at Kevin's house. He twice refused to knock on the door. "You're all gonna do as I say," Kevin said. "Or else you're gonna die."

"I knocked on the door. Mr. Schwebes didn't come right away. I saw Kevin standing there with the gun raised, and that's when I heard the locks being opened. I didn't look into his face. I froze. Mr. Schwebes said, 'Yes, may I help you?' and I ran." Derek heard one more word: "Who?"

In the car, Pete asked if Mark was dead. "Kevin gave a little chuckle, and then he said, 'He sure the hell ain't alive.' I was curled up into a ball."

Derek didn't like Kevin; he was never a friend.

Rinard cross-examined. "You chose to go back to the Winn-Dixie. You chose to walk out of that car and knock on the door. And you knocked knowing if he opened that door he was going to get shot?"

"Yes."

"And you knocked anyway?"

"Yes. Because I was planning to try to push him out of the way."

"But you didn't?"

"No. I got scared."

"You turned around, and he got shot?"

"Yes."

"Because you knocked on the door?"

"Yes."

Because the defense—exploring one of Ruby's pet theories—suggested Derek made up his account, the state sought Anderson's permission to play part of Derek's tape-recorded police statement. "He's being attacked by implying he's fabricated and recently come up with this," McGruther said. "We can produce a prior consistent statement."

"Judge, we're objecting," Jacobs said. "They could do that on every witness. You don't seem concerned, but I think it's highly improper."

"Tell it to the Supreme Court. You'll get an opportunity, I believe," Anderson said, a comment that gave Kevin grounds for appeal. Judges weren't allowed to make up their minds before all the evidence was presented.

"I certainly hope the court's not prejudging our case," Rinard said.

Anderson backpedaled. "Not for me to make that decision, it's for them," he said, gesturing to the jury box. "Guilt or innocence."

"It may not be going to the Supreme Court, Judge," Rinard said, baiting, a hint of a smile.

"Whatever," Anderson said.

The statement was played. Taber remembered Derek's tears. The genuine remorse. The only one.

McGruther made further efforts at rehabilitation. "Mr. Rinard asked you about some unflattering comments you made about Kevin in letters you'd written while you were in jail, saying things like 'I hope they get him.' Could you tell us how you feel about Kevin?"

"Back then, I hated him pretty bad. Because if it wasn't for him, I wouldn't have been in any of this stuff. As of now, no, I don't hate him like I did, because I remember my mom told me never to hate anyone. I don't like him, but I don't hate him."

Even the prosecutor felt for Derek. *We could've let you out of jail right after you were arrested,* McGruther thought. If you looked simply at the act—the way Derek used his familiarity with Mark to set him up—that was one thing. But when you looked at the *kid,* you didn't think the guy would ever do anything wrong. "You talked about making money on a movie deal," McGruther said. "Would you trade that for making the night of April 30, 1996, go away?"

"Yes."

"Trade it for your freedom?"

"Yes."

"Trade it to have Mr. Schwebes's life back?"

"Yes."

Rinard took another turn.

"You can't bring Mr. Schwebes back, can you?"

"No."

"You can save your own self, though, can't you?"

"Yes."

"That's what you did by entering into this plea agreement, right?"

"Yes."

People don't do anything they don't want to, Allen thought. He glowered at Derek. *Smart. No personality.*

"You were sitting in your driveway, and you chose to go back to the Winn-Dixie, correct?" Pinard said.

"Correct."

"You chose to get out of that car and walk up to the door and knock on the door?"

"Correct."

"So you're responsible for yourself being here in this predicament?"

"Yes."

CHAPTER 32

Alibi

The defense's first move when the prosecution rested after just two days was to ask Judge Anderson to acquit Kevin, a motion almost always entered, almost always denied. "The state hasn't proven a *prima facie* of guilt," Bob Jacobs said. "As they indicated in their opening statement, no physical evidence fixes our client with the scene. The only evidence that does are indicted co-conspirators." Even if Anderson wouldn't hand down a not guilty verdict and send Kevin home, maybe he'd reduce the charge. "We'd ask the court not to find him not guilty, but to reduce it to second-degree murder."

"The motion's denied," Anderson said. "There's sufficient evidence to go to the jury."

Such a good case, juror Brad Weatherly thought. *Definitely, absolutely hoping for a good defense.*

For months the buzz around the justice center was Kevin's defense would be a spectacle: the boy whose mom promised an alibi. When the defense came, it was lackluster, flat and passionless, in the author's opinion—as though Jacobs was going through the motions, presenting a case he didn't believe in.

Ruby thought the only member of Kevin's team who believed in her son and worked for him was a paralegal, Jamie Wooten. Possessed of nervous energy rivaling that of a man on speed, Wooten fussed with the computer at the defense table and hustled in and out of the courtroom. "Boots," Kevin nicknamed him after his characteristic footwear.

So many issues could've been raised to invoke reasonable doubt: the initial love triangle. Craig's confession. The blood on Craig's shoes—and where *were* those shoes? The similarity between Craig and Kevin in height and complexion. Conflicting eyewitness accounts. Jacobs raised some of these issues in deposition, a concession to lists of questions from Ruby, who combed early discovery materials, highlighting and marking with Post-it notes, drawn to discrepancies, until the sheer volume overwhelmed her. Almost all the 174 witnesses interviewed before trial were either wrong or conspiring to convict an innocent man, she said. Her son was on trial for a crime he didn't commit to protect the gay sons of the local KKK from exposure. She was sorry, she didn't mean anything by it, but Mark Schwebes was a victim of his lifestyle. Why had he moved so quickly from school to school? The boys killed him because he gave them drugs for sex and it got out of hand. The boys killed him because one was jealous of another's relationship with him. He was killed by the jealous boyfriend of the woman he dated. He was killed by a sheriff's deputy's jealous ex-wife who wanted to date him. *Isn't it strange how all these people on this one night were in a position to kill him? Perhaps they all got together and did it.*

First to testify for the defense was Shawn's father, Bud Jeffries, who said they were working the day of the murder and that—*if* he gave Kevin a ride that day—he *might* have dropped him off as late as 4:30 P.M.

"You were a close personal friend of Ruby. In fact, you visited with Ruby shortly after Kevin was arrested, didn't you?" Randy McGruther said. "You visited with her several times since then, haven't you?"

All Jacobs could do was get Bud to say Kevin never threatened anyone and was a good worker and then follow Bud with another coworker, testifying Kevin was an excellent worker, a peaceful kid who did what he was told.

An employee of the public defender's office, Roberta Harsh, drove the route Kevin was alleged to have driven the night of the murder. Now she traced the route with a Magic Marker, pushing in colored pins at key locations. "At ten thirty-six P.M., the trip odometer in my car was set at zero, and I left Lorraine Drive," she said, inserting a pin. She made the stops Kevin was alleged to have made and feigned the actions Kevin was alleged to have carried out. She stopped at the Circle K and made a phone call, leaving a message on Jacobs's answering machine. Drove to Cypress Drive, then to the gas station to check the map. "I stopped at the gas station at eleven oh-five; I departed at eleven-twelve." Drove to Mark's duplex—another pin—then to the furniture store. "I got out, opened the trunk, simulated removing my tag and placing another tag on the vehicle." Then back to the duplex to simulate the murder. At the Bell Tower Shops—pin—Harsh simulated discarding the stolen tag. At the RaceTrac, she paused six minutes to simulate buying gas and sodas and urinating on the side of the building. "I began at ten thirty-six P.M. and returned to Lorraine Drive at eleven fifty-nine P.M.— thirty-three-point-four miles."

Weatherly scrutinized the timeline. *Proves nothing.*

"You drove the speed limit?" McGruther said.

"Except on the interstate. The speed limit's now seventy; I drove sixty."

"So, you actually drove *under* the speed limit, and you were still back at Kevin's before midnight?"

"One minute before midnight, yes."

A pager jolted spectators who were intently focused on Harsh. "Next one that goes off belongs to the court," Anderson said.

Full control of the courtroom, Weatherly thought. *When his eyes meet your eyes, something happens in your spine. A look every parent should have.*

"The bottom line, it takes twenty-four minutes, even driving as you did, to go from Kevin's to Mark's house?" McGruther said.

"When you know exactly where it is, yes."

"And, leaving at ten thirty-six, you were actually— even after traveling around in Pine Manor a little bit and stopping to look at the map—you were back . . . Let's see"—McGruther scrutinized the stops, mileages and times elaborately charted by the defense and set up on easels across the front of the courtroom—"the final time back at Cypress and eighth—and this is after you drove around Pine Manor, found the place, looked at this map, went around the block and then parked next to that lot—you were at Mr. Schwebes's house at eleven twenty-two."

Plenty of time to do it, juror Rose Marie Martie thought. Juror John Quelet thought the timeline backfired.

"I don't have any further questions."

A month earlier, in deposition, a friend of Ruby's swore she saw Kevin at the pawnshop the evening of the murder. Now, in court, she said she didn't. "I made a mistake," she said. "I thought—because Ruby had his truck—Kevin was there. And he wasn't."

The woman did see Kevin and two friends when she went to Lorraine Drive. The boys loaded up a four-wheeler, which Ruby then drove to the woman's house.

The importance of this testimony was that at one time Ruby hoped Pete would say he was one of the boys who helped load the ATV. But his testimony demolished that hope. Now the woman's words had the feeling of a bridge leading nowhere.

"These ATVs, was there ultimately a problem with them?" Lee said.

"Yes, sir. My husband went to sell them and found out they'd been stolen." Kevin didn't commit murder—he couldn't have: he was helping Mom fence stolen property.

The next witness contradicted Ruby's friend. A girl testified she did see Kevin at the pawnshop between 4:30 and 5:00 P.M. the day of the murder. Again the alibi took on the feeling of an unfinished, unsatisfactory work. The witnesses didn't agree; the story was unpolished.

The girl said she talked to Kevin at about 5:30 or 6:00 P.M., then went fishing with her aunt at Matlacha Pass Bridge. She talked with Kevin again from 11:30 P.M. until midnight.

"Did Kevin put you on hold?" Jacobs said. "Was there an indication why?"

"He was calling Cindi to tell her happy birthday."

The girl's memory of an ordinary evening two years earlier was impeccable: after she hung up with Kevin, she did her cousin's nails, smoked a cigarette with her aunt and went to bed.

Lying, Weatherly thought. *Insulting my intelligence.* He stopped listening. Resumed scrutinizing Kevin, who remained impenetrable. *Give me* something. . . . *Nothing.*

"And yet you never told the police anything about

seeing the defendant that day or talking to him on the phone the night of the murder, did you?" Lee asked.

Pregnant silence. "I don't guess I told them."

A diary, which the girl said she had, was lost; a notebook she produced contained only a few notes about April 30 and almost nothing else.

Not much to work with in the way of witnesses, Allen thought.

Criminal defense lawyer Richard Fuller recalled seeing Kevin about the suspended driver's license the morning after the murder. "It's pretty vague, because two years lapsed by the time I was called and asked to recall the situation, but he came in with, I think it was his mother, and we talked," Fuller said. His new client showed no sign of strain. "His attitude was very calm, cool, no problem. Just a typical fellow with a traffic problem. It knocked me to the ground when I read the newspaper."

After Kevin's arrest, Ruby had called. "Ms. Foster told me she'd spoken to her son: he was innocent," Fuller said. "If that's the case, obviously Kevin was somewhere else, and, therefore, it'd be my advice to get the family together, see if there were any diaries. Oftentimes you have a calendar in the kitchen. Maybe you have a doctor or dentist appointment. Go back and try to determine what actually went on, so you can establish exactly where Kevin was." Fuller visited Kevin in jail, but the complexity of the case was daunting and the solo practitioner declined it, punting to the public defender.

Ruby gave her alibi—with details about when she looked at her watch, what trivial comments were made and when she fixed herself food—including the part about the friend buying the ATV and Kevin loading the trailer.

Martie thought Ruby was lying from the get-go. *I don't even know what time I get home from work; you're so definite.* There was an air of unreality about it all.

Ruby testified she was in control of Kevin in the days before the murder. McGruther showed that in deposition she said she wasn't. "Is it still your testimony you stayed on top of him during this time?"

"I'm going to say I didn't say yes. . . . No. . . . Maybe not."

You really weren't paying attention, Martie thought. *You were more in tune with setting up your new business.*

Ruby said Kevin *wasn't* at the pawnshop after all; she talked with him on the phone at 4:30 P.M., as was their habit, and assumed he was home—though she couldn't be certain where he was before 9:00 P.M.

You don't know what *he did that night,* Weatherly thought. *Maybe you never asked.*

"Now, the police in that first search warrant—to your knowledge—they didn't take a stainless-steel shotgun?" McGruther said. "Because the stainless-steel shotgun wasn't in your house. In fact, you hadn't seen that stainless-steel shotgun since April twentieth."

"That's right."

"You're very close to Kevin?"

"I'm very close to all of my children."

"You love him very much. In fact, he and Kelly are kind of your anchors?"

"All of my children are."

There was something between you and Kevin, Taber thought. *You were jealous. You know he wasn't home. A mother's intuition, if nothing else. You don't care whether he killed. You'd do anything to get your son out of this. Conniving. A liar. You were his biggest problem.*

"In fact, you gave Kevin the stainless-steel shotgun as a present for Christmas," McGruther said. "That was the one you took out of the pawnshop, correct? He'd been admiring it before that, and you pulled it out of inventory."

"My son shoots skeet. My husband shot trap. And that gun was bought for him to use at the skeet range."

"You certainly didn't intend him to use it for anything else, did you?"

Kevin must've got some of that bad blood from you, Martie thought.

At the jail the night of Kevin's arrest, Ruby ran into a deputy and sometime pawnshop client. She didn't say Kevin couldn't have committed the crime because he was home. "He didn't give me the chance."

"Did you tell *any* law enforcement officer that weekend he couldn't have done this because he was home?"

"No, sir. I didn't."

If it was my son, I would've started hollering right off the bat, Martie thought. *You waited too long and concocted this story.*

Kevin was arrested Friday night; deputies served the search warrant at Lorraine Drive on Saturday. "I believe you said a few minutes ago you cooperated very much," McGruther said.

"I sure did."

"Okay. Good." McGruther paced the courtroom. "Did you tell them at that time that Kevin couldn't have done this thing he was arrested for because he was at home?"

"No, sir, I didn't. After my home was seized, I couldn't explain to them what was going on. I sat nine hours in the street trying to find out what was going on. They didn't tell me."

"You didn't—"

"I didn't tell *anybody*."

"But you knew he was arrested for the murder of Mark Schwebes?"

"No, sir, not until the next morning."

"The next morning, then, did you tell law enforcement, 'Wait a minute, that happened last Tuesday night. He was home all night'?"

"No, sir. I waited until I got some advice from an attorney."

Understandable, Quelet thought, staring at Ruby. *Not even unbelievable. But it just doesn't go together.*

Ruby had dealt with state attorney's investigator Brian Kelley during the pretrial investigation. "Did you ever tell Kelley, 'Wait a minute, my son's sitting down there in that jail charged with a murder he didn't commit because he was home'?" McGruther said.

"No, sir."

"Have you visited your son in jail?"

"Every week."

"Pretty nasty place, isn't it? But since May 3, 1996, until just recently, you never told anybody he was home that night, did you?"

"I told my attorney. I told Mr. Fuller on Sunday after my son was arrested. I told friends."

But it wasn't enough: Kevin did too much, too fast, too soon—and his defense was too little, too slow, too late.

A father, Weatherly sympathized with Ruby. *Anything to save his life. "Not my son. No way. Must've been instigated." I don't fault you for that. What any normal mother would do who loves her son.*

"Did you ever tell anybody Kevin fell asleep talking on the phone that night?"

"No, sir."

"Pardon me?" McGruther said, to be sure jurors remembered the answer.

"No, sir."

"Did you ever tell anybody Pete was there that night?"

Ruby avoided a direct answer. "The boys were there earlier in the evening. I didn't see them. My daughter heard them."

"You didn't see any of the boys, did you?"

"I saw silhouettes."

You're trying to save your son, Martie thought. Ruby's testimony was Martie's turning point. Kevin was guilty. Martie had sympathy for the parents of the other boys—but not for Ruby or her remorseless son.

Jacobs tried to rehabilitate Ruby. "You're sure of the times you told the jury you saw your son?"

"I'm very sure."

"And between eleven and the time you left for Mr. Fuller's office the next day, was Kevin in your home?"

"Kevin was in my house the entire time. He never left."

A black widow, Allen thought. The detective was suspicious of the pawn business. *That type of business is notorious for being shady. Your whole life's a pawn. You knew from day one. It's a mother's right—a natural instinct— to protect your children, but there comes a point at which that instinct or that right has got to be controlled. You can't accept the fact you don't have control of him, that we now have control of him.*

After Ruby was done, McGruther addressed the judge out of the presence of the jury. "Yesterday after court adjourned, we received a letter from the stockade. The letter basically said, 'I'm in jail. I've been housed here near Kevin. I've heard him talking on the phone. I'm hearing a one-sided thing where he's telling people to lie, set up an alibi so he can walk.' We did have two investigators go there. They've prepared an activity report. I just received it. I've given a copy to the defense. Quite frankly, at this time, we're not sure if we want to call this guy. If we make a determination after the close of the defense alibi witnesses to do it, then I guess we'll address it at that point."

A shot across the bow of the defense. McGruther hoped it'd keep Kevin off the witness stand. *He could sway people. All it takes is one juror.* What the witness claimed to have heard was Kevin trying to keep people in line. "Damn it, I told you just stick with that version," Kevin had said. "The only person who could say differently is dead." Mark? Or John?

Cindi took the stand. "A little bit after eleven, he called on the answering machine. 'Cindi, pick up.' Whatever. 'Calling to say happy birthday.' He called again around twelve—a little bit after twelve—and then I talked to him."

Kevin left a message; Kevin talked with her. But the times weren't incompatible with an intervening murder, and Cindi wouldn't say otherwise.

"Did you ever speak with Tom at Marina 31?" Jacobs said. "Did he ever tell you he thought Kevin was framed?"

"Yes, he did."

"Did he tell you Kevin did this crime?"

"He said he didn't think he done it."

On cross-examination, Cindi told Lee she went to her birthday party the night of the murder.

"Where was the party?" Lee said, polite and controlled.

"Moore Haven." More than an hour's drive from Fort Myers.

"Who was there?"

"A lot of people," Cindi said. One of them: the girl who earlier testified she was fishing at Matlacha.

"So, she wasn't fishing at Matlacha?"

"She was with me in my truck." Now Cindi had helped Lee impeach one of Kevin's witnesses.

"Now, you have, since the defendant's arrest, talked to Ruby, haven't you? And isn't it true she's told you she went to bed and woke later to find him on the couch asleep with the phone on his chest?"

"Correct." Cindi couldn't know Ruby dropped this story.

Someone got to Cindi, Ruby later would bitterly complain. The girl disappeared for a year, couldn't be found anywhere, and when under subpoena, she caught a last-minute flight through a storm from Atlanta and reappeared in court, Cindi was no longer on the Foster team.

Kelly was working at an arts-and-crafts store. "I'm waiting for a final appointment from the Collier County Sheriff's Office as a correctional officer."

Jacobs walked her through April 30. "Do you recall having class? And what was that class?"

"Research methods in criminology."

"At nine-thirty, did you see Kevin?"

"He was out in the yard. At ten o'clock, a set of boys arrived—I couldn't tell you who—and my brother was outside talking with them. I know my brother was outside because I recognized his voice, and I heard just familiar voices. One set of them left at ten-thirty. They left a few minutes before my mother arrived around eleven."

"Did you ever see him leave the house?"

"No."

No more credible than Ruby, Weatherly thought.

Lee cross-examined. "Are you absolutely certain the events you've talked about occurred on April 30, 1996?"

"Yes, I am."

"Positive?"

"Yes."

"Isn't it true, ma'am, that during those nights when you were studying for your finals, you had your door closed and you didn't want to be bothered by anyone—especially your brother?"

"No, it's not. There are always boys at my house. You get used to it."

"Isn't it true you never went to your professor,

Major Bonsall, of the Lee County Sheriff's Office, and ever told him about this alibi?"

"I never discussed anything with Major Bonsall. It wasn't his place. He was my professor; that's school; that's not this case. I don't discuss my private family issues at school. I was concentrating on finishing my degree. He did request my term paper back. Due to the fact we have moved since then, I've lost the term paper."

"*I* asked for that term paper," Lee said. "We asked because we just wanted to look at the date."

"I don't have it. I've moved three times in the last two years, roughly."

The jurors don't like Ruby and Kelly's efforts to play them, Allen thought. The detective was right. Martie was skeptical about the lost term paper. *How come it got lost?*

"You want very much for it to be the night of April 30, 1996, don't you?" Lee said.

"Excuse me?"

"You want it very much to be that night."

"It *was* that night."

"It was that night. Okay. . . . Your mom has helped you with these dates and times, hasn't she?"

"Not specifically."

"You say you kept notes. Where did you keep them?"

"I kept them in my daily planner."

"And yet despite the obvious importance—and you'd understand that because you have a degree in criminology—you don't have the original notes?" Lee said.

"Because I copied things, over the course of looking at them, and water spilled on them. They got worn and not too legible. So I recopied them."

"So—despite the degree in criminology—you threw away the original notes?"

"Yes."

"And—despite their importance—you let them get

water damaged, and I think at one point you told me Coca-Cola damaged, too, and that's why you threw them away?"

"I had a soda when my planner was opened, and they'd gotten wet."

"So, we have no way of knowing now from any tangible evidence what those original notes looked like? . . . Isn't it true, Ms. Foster, that you never came forward to tell the police about this alibi?"

"I didn't tell anyone because I was never asked. Our attorney told us to remain quiet until we were asked."

"Isn't this your brother's life we're talking about? This is your brother here, Kevin, here on trial for his life, correct?"

"Yes."

"You love him very much?"

"Yes."

"You'd do anything to try to save his life?"

"I wouldn't lie. I was taught to tell the truth, and that's what I've done."

Kevin later regretted not testifying. In his gut, he was itching to mount the witness stand and match wits with prosecutors. After two years' near-complete silence, it'd be the first time in all the thousands of words said and written that any came from him. Plus, he'd be the star, the total focus of attention, the most eagerly watched kid at the math contest. But Kevin took his attorney's advice.

Get up there and set the record straight, Weatherly thought. *Say, "This is who I am. This is where I was."* But the juror would've been shocked if Kevin had testified. *That's fantasy world. That doesn't happen. You can't help yourself.*

The defense had lasted less than a day.

That's the defense? Weatherly thought. *Here's a guy's*

life on the line. That's *all they had?* That *was the best they could do?*

Prosecutors were back in action.

"I helped Ruby pack up everything in Kevin's room," a friend testified. Ruby asked her to come over the night after Kevin's arrest. "Some of it was taken to one of our storage units, and some was put in the trash. Ruby wanted everything out of the room before the police would come back."

Jacobs elicited that Ruby said Kevin was innocent.

"She didn't tell you that he was home the previous Tuesday, did she?" McGruther said.

"I don't recall her saying that, no, sir."

Because she hadn't thought of it yet. "Nothing further."

Sharon Magaskil testified she traveled to Fort Myers from Albuquerque a few weeks after Kevin's arrest to lend support to her aunt Ruby. At dinner, McGaskil took notes on a calendar.

"Were they trying to think of where he was on various nights, or did they seem to know?" McGruther said.

"They were trying to relay what they remembered." McGaskil explained that, in fact, they were relaying what Kevin had told them.

"Was it your opinion this was the first time they'd done this?"

"Yes."

Spectators felt an urge to hug Rebecca Magnotti, a small, gentle woman. Despite her years in the United States, her accented English remained imperfect.

Lee handed Magnotti a piece of paper. "What's that?" he said.

"This is a letter Peter got in the county jail. Somebody mailed to him, and he showed it to me, and then he said it was signed, 'Mom.' I said, 'Who is this "Mom"?'"

"Are you the 'Mom' that wrote that?" Lee said.

"No. I did not write." Much later she called Ruby. "I asked for Ruby Foster, and they said she was not home. I said, 'This is Rebecca Magnotti, Peter's mother.'" Ruby came on the phone; Kelly also was on the phone. "The first thing Mrs. Foster told me was she couldn't believe Peter and the other guys were talking all this lies about Kevin. And then she said all the things that happened are not true, it did not happen. And then she told me she and Kelly and some other friends, they would testify Peter was home in their house with Kevin at the night of April thirtieth and Peter spent the night over there and lie down on the roof or somewhere else to watch the stars."

"Did you agree with that?"

"No, sir."

"Do you know Peter wasn't spending the night?"

"He did not spend the night, because he came home. I was waiting."

"Did you tell Mrs. Foster that wasn't true?"

"I told her that was not true. Peter came home. Yes, sir." That terrible night when she waited up alone, concerned for her only child and unable to reach or even read him at this age, immersed in this foreign culture; loving him but knowing she sounded only angry as she chided him for violating his curfew; fear in her stomach about what he did these days, what he'd been pulled into, who he'd become. Waiting for him that night and waiting for his return from teenage exile; worried for her son and yearning for her lost child. And then—when she found out three days later—only a vast desolate emptiness, an incomprehensible wasteland of grief from which she'd never recover.

"You refused to cooperate with this attempt, then, to put together a false alibi?" McGruther said.

"I just drop it. I did not pursue it because I know it was not true."

You *should've got a Purple Heart,* Martie thought. *Your son did wrong, and you weren't going to lie.*

Thought Quelet, *Beautiful. Everything you said, I can take that to the bank.*

Jacobs tried to distract attention. "The night Mr. Schwebes was shot, you were waiting up for your son, weren't you? Did he call you that night at some time and say he was at the Bell Tower movie?"

"Yes, sir. He told me Derek had car problem and they are going to drive him home."

But it was futile: Rebecca Magnotti's heart—the kind of heart Kevin couldn't understand—had moved everyone in the room. Her testimony was what those who were there would remember of the trial years later, long after she died, too young and too sad.

CHAPTER 33

Verdict

The next day, both sides made closing arguments in the crowded courtroom. Gill Allen and Dean Taber sat up front with the Schwebes family. The Foster clan took their usual seats behind the defense. Prosecutor Bob Lee went first. The case came down to a simple question: "Did Kevin Foster coldly and deliberately murder Mark Schwebes to protect the Lords of Chaos, or was he quietly at home with his mother and sister?"

Much of the disputed evidence was irrelevant. "The issue is, after he got home, did in fact the various members of the Lords of Chaos begin to flock around their leader? And did that path start first to the mall, to the high school and ultimately to the doorstep of Mr. Mark Schwebes? The public defender's own investigator, by her precise retracing of the routes, established there was sufficient time."

Lee discussed defense witnesses. He dismissed Ruby's friend as not credible. He dismissed the girl who went fishing. "You have a hopeless conflict: She said she recalls the day because she went fishing out at the Matlacha bridge in Pine Island. And yet Cindi—

a friend of hers—said she was actually at the opposite end of the state, over by Lake Okeechobee, at a party at Moore Haven. But most telling was, when the police talked to her just after the murder, she was asked what she knew, and her response—after the police even said is there anything else they should know—was 'No, I don't know anything else.'"

Lee had no problem with Cindi's testimony that Kevin called around 11:00 P.M. and around midnight. "All the Lords of Chaos made it back to Kevin's right before midnight; that's what they said." And he used Cindi to raise a question: "She said Ruby kept asking if she thought Kevin did it. Now, why would Mrs. Foster keep asking if Cindi thought he did it if Mrs. Foster knew full well he *hadn't* done it because he was home? Ruby kept asking about the time of the call Cindi said she received, and she kept writing down notes. If Mrs. Foster knows the time—because she was standing right there, like she testified—why, in August of 1996, is she quizzing Cindi? I submit it's because she did *not* know. Cindi testified that, several months after Kevin's arrest, Ruby didn't know the defendant even talked to Cindi on the phone that night. *Did not even know.* This isn't what Mrs. Foster claimed.

"Then there's Kelly, the defendant's sister. Kelly very much wanted you to believe what apparently *she* now believes, that her brother was home and couldn't have done it. She wants you to believe that, and she probably believes it now, too. This is one of those puzzles you really don't have to figure out: is she mistaken or is she intentionally misrepresenting the facts? All you have to decide is if you believe she's wrong."

Kelly testified she threw away her original notes. "Does that make sense?" Lee said. "It might make sense for someone who's not had an education in criminology. But the original notes are the best evidence that she made them, like she said. Instead, she's got copies." Kelly said her mom didn't look at the notes. "You saw Ruby. Can you imagine anyone—especially her daughter—stopping Mrs. Foster from looking at those notes? And most telling again is that—despite the class in criminology and a degree and a course Kelly's taking from Major Bonsall—she never approached Major Bonsall and said, 'Hey, you've got the wrong guy. It wasn't my brother. He was home. Please help us to right this wrong.' Does her silence make sense?

"Now, Ruby's testimony. Really, I'm not going to say much about that. When we consider this is the defendant's mom who's desperately defending— I mean, her testimony was almost like a lioness defending her cubs. She's going to defend her son at all costs.

"But the final desperate chapter in this saga about the alibi really was given to you by a grieving Rebecca Magnotti. Ruby tried to get Mrs. Magnotti to go along with what must've been Plan A of the alibi. We're seeing Plan B here in court, apparently. The first plan was Kevin and Pete were to stick together and Ruby and Mrs. Magnotti were to stick together and say the two boys were at the Foster home. And Mrs. Foster and Mrs. Magnotti would swear to that. But—as much as Mrs. Magnotti no doubt wanted her son out of jail—she had too much integrity to go along. And she said no, because it wasn't true. I'd submit that's the end of this alibi situation.

"You might've been puzzled that when the shotgun was retrieved, it had red shells in it, and you saw the red shells versus these green the defendant used in the murder. This isn't something that's immediately obvious. Those two green shells deliberately rammed into that shotgun were specifically chosen by Kevin, I'd submit, because they were killing loads. That number one buck had a large pellet; the red shells had what was called birdshot. The defendant specifically chose those green killing loads, and I'd submit that's strong evidence of premeditation. He went to kill, and that's what he put in the gun to make sure.

"The defendant's palm print was on the shotgun. We also introduced a newspaper. You may've been puzzled. That newspaper was found with the shotgun, and that newspaper had in it an account of the killing. And on the newspaper was the defendant's fingerprints. There he is, not only in front of the TV re-creating it, but he's keeping a newspaper article memorializing what he's done.

"When we presented Pete, Chris and Derek, they came in their prison red jumpsuits. We didn't attempt any makeover. There are serious problems in terms of the character of these young men, these Lords of Chaos. But remember who chose them, remember whose friends they were, whose associates. The defendant chose the witnesses, not the state. These young men, by the defendant's choice, became witnesses because he chose them as co-conspirators. So remember, people tend to associate with people they have things in common with. As the defense attacks the character of these other Lords of Chaos, it's like sharply honing a sword that someone's going to fall upon: the sharper you hone it, the deeper it actually goes into yourself.

"Now, last night, I kept thinking about this case, and I kept thinking about the mask." Lee held up the ski mask. "I kept thinking about this alibi claim. Ladies and gentlemen, the mask used by the defendant was used by him to conceal his identity as the cold-blooded killer of an innocent, unarmed schoolteacher. And the alibi's just as if he turned it around, and now he wants to pull the wool over your eyes. Please don't let him do that."

Bob Jacobs gave the defense's closing argument. The state hadn't proved the case. The system was biased, the publicity overwhelming. Though it didn't have to, the defense *had* presented a case.

"The state made a lot of defense witnesses not going forward to police," Jacobs said. "What good would that have done? Ruby and Kelly testified their house was searched several times, that they were shut out of their home while the police rummaged through, took what they wanted." The family didn't talk because Richard Fuller—the first attorney they consulted—told them not to. "Kevin was already tried and convicted in the press. The sheriff's department said they had their man. The police took the words of what one called 'punk scumbags.' The police chose to believe all these boys who were framing Kevin to make their sweet deals." Sure, Kelly didn't go to Major Bonsall. "But just think about it. Her house had been searched several times, her life had been disrupted—*that*, and her brother had been arrested for first-degree murder." And Kelly couldn't find her term paper because deputies took her computer disks.

What about witnesses the state hadn't presented, including neighbors with differing accounts of the night of the murder? One neighbor said the car pulled out of Mark's driveway, not the road. "It's interesting—Pete, Chris and Derek say they were on the street," Jacobs said. "What else are those boys lying about?" What about missing witnesses? "Brad talked a lot about Craig. But did he testify? No. Why not?" What about missing evidence? Where was the red gas can Kevin was supposed to have had at the auditorium? Why wasn't every piece of evidence analyzed at the lab? And what of the firearms examiner's testimony about evidence that *was* analyzed—the weapon. "He couldn't testify those casings you saw were fired from that shotgun. No matter how much the state wants him to, he can't. He can't even say the shot found at the Schwebes house came from either the casings *or* that shotgun."

And what about discrepancies in testimony? How could Kevin have gone to Edison Mall after the boys got out of school at 2:10 P.M. and also gotten home from work at 4:30 P.M.? Who sat in which seat in the car the night of the murder? When was Craig present?

Jeremy Arnold initially couldn't identify the boy who ran in front of his car near the auditorium. "It wasn't until later, when he saw photographs in the newspaper and at a press conference, 'Oh, yeah, it must be him.'" Arnold's identification was flawed: He couldn't see Kevin properly at the auditorium. And he didn't see Kevin carrying a red gas can, he saw a Wal-Mart bag—yet Mark had already confiscated that and put it in the Bronco.

What about the actions of the other boys? Chris said the teacher had to die. Chris called 411 to find Mark's number and address. Chris paged Pete. "Chris was in the same cellblock with Derek, where they plotted and planned to frame Kevin. He went to the state attorney's office last Sunday for several hours in preparation for his testimony, as did all the other ones who testified. Derek could've gotten an Academy Award.

"Pete got up on the witness stand, raised his hand and said, 'I swear before God to tell the truth.' But what else did he say? He said he didn't believe in God. So, how could he swear to tell the truth if he has such a belief? And he's dealing with these satanic symbols. How can we believe him?"

Pete—not Kevin—designed the LOC symbol Pete drew on the board in court. Pete didn't leave when he could have, before the murder. Pete didn't see who fired the shots. Pete laughed and bragged. The shotgun was in Pete's trunk. In their jail letters, the three friends—Jacobs stumbled, incorrectly identifying them as "he, Derek and Burnett, the unholy troika who did this murder"—wrote in secret code, and

Pete threatened to kill Tom, Brad and a reporter. He threatened Burnett. He wrote of movie deals and "getting stuff" on Kevin. "This is Pete, now. The one who wrote the manifesto, the Declaration of War. The true leader of the Lords of Chaos. He talked about a little pawn who'd be used as a bargaining chip. Keep in mind he says Kevin was a leader, he was God, he formed the group—yet Pete wrote the manifesto, designed the symbol, had the shotgun in his car, had a ski mask and a box of gloves in his trunk."

Anything to raise reasonable doubt. Kevin's code-fendants saw evidence passed along by their attorneys. Burnett, Tom and Brad smoked pot. Tom got a generous deal from the state. Pete and Derek believed Ruby and Kelly were home when they supposedly went to Lorraine Drive the night of the murder. "And, how hypocritical: Derek said he went to school, he bought a Riverdale ribbon, he went to the eulogy for the teacher, he cried. But he was the one who chose to knock on the door, and we submit he was the one who fired the fatal shot. Burnett said he didn't go to Pine Manor, but we submit he did. He was the fourth person who was there. Kevin was not."

Jacobs went through the timeline again, mostly succeeding in showing that no one agreed on the time of anything. "What does this timeline show us? It shows us Kevin didn't commit this murder. Kevin's a law-abiding citizen. Schwebes was killed at eleven-thirty P.M. on the thirtieth. Ruby and Kelly testified Kevin was home. Are they unworthy of belief because they're his mother and sister? Of course not. If anyone were accused of the commission of a crime at eleven-thirty P.M. on a Tuesday, who'd testify for us, if not family?

"Kevin was a working man, a carpenter by trade. One would assume—unless you worked at night—working people who keep a regular reliable job would be home, especially at eleven o'clock, where in this case he had an appointment with his lawyer the next day at eight o'clock.

"The state argued the murder was to protect Tom and Burnett," Jacobs said, though he meant Tom and Chris. (He'd also confuse Mr. Magnotti with Mr. Schwebes in an argument that, in the author's opinion, rambled, stumbled, lacked focus and sounded remarkably like Ruby.) "What difference would it make to Kevin if he was reported to the school resource officer? Why would he kill somebody to protect those two? They were the only ones that were students; he wasn't. Does that make any sense? Of course not.

"We submit Pete and the others chose the wrong path and then, when they were caught, they plotted to put the blame on Kevin. Who shot Mark Schwebes? We submit it was Derek. He told Chris and Tom he kept them from getting arrested, from being reported to the school resource officer. Why else would he go to this eulogy service? Why would he wear a garnet-and-gold ribbon? Why would he cry? He did it, and he couldn't face up to his responsibility.

"We'd submit Pete was there. Chris was there; we'd submit he was the one who knocked. There was a fourth person, and that was Burnett. Derek told you he knew this teacher; he was in jazz band. Of course, Derek would stand back from the door before he fired the shots—he didn't want to be recognized.

"If Kevin's guilty, would he be calling someone to wish them a happy birthday at about the time the shooting was committed? Is it reasonable that if you committed murder, you'd be worried about a suspended driver license the next day? The state said there's no physical evidence to connect Kevin to this crime. And that's true. There's none. These other boys testified against Kevin to get their deals—for their own self-interest—and to frame Kevin."

* * *

The evidence is overwhelming, even if circumstantial, juror John Quelet thought. *I don't see how you could've done a better job.*

Jacobs did everything he could for that guy, Randy McGruther thought. *I don't know what he could've done differently.* McGruther stood to give the state's rebuttal. "The timeline that was up here, ladies and gentlemen, is relevant only if you believe the alibi witnesses.

"Pete and Derek both told you they had conversations with Kevin in the Lee County Jail. And both of them told you Kevin told them his mother was going to give him an alibi. Just going to give it to him. A gift. Like she did the shotgun for Christmas—the shotgun that killed Mark Schwebes.

"What did Ruby tell Rebecca Magnotti? That she and Kelly and some friends would testify Pete was at their house with Kevin all night. Now, I submit to you, Rebecca Magnotti would like nothing better than for that to be the truth. It must've been awfully tempting for her to say, 'Yeah, okay, I'll get on that bandwagon.' She didn't. And she told you why she didn't: because it wasn't true.

"It's like so many other things in the alibi: *was* there a time Pete spent the night at Kevin's? Probably. *Did* they spend time, at some point, lying on the roof looking at the stars? Probably. Did they do it on April 30, 1996? No. I'm not going to stand here and tell you everything you heard from the alibi witnesses never happened. Because I submit to you most of it did—but not on April 30, 1996.

"Just like Rebecca Magnotti, Ruby and Kelly wished the alibi was true, wished he was home, wished Ruby's friend had come and picked up the ATVs—and they may've talked themselves into it by this time. If you keep telling yourself something over and over and over, you begin to believe it. But it doesn't make it true. I don't necessarily castigate Ruby for wanting to believe her son was home: she's a mother. I'd submit to you there are any number of people you'd never hear the truth from again if they felt it could bring Mark Schwebes back to life. But that can't happen, either."

McGruther touched on some of the witnesses, starting with Roberta Harsh's drive. "Use your common sense about that, folks. What you take out of her testimony is just that it's a twenty-four-minute trip. Yes, they made stops. But it's a twenty-four-minute trip, driven very conservatively. I don't have a problem with that—that fits the evidence you heard from the state.

"Richard Fuller, the attorney, came in and said, 'Yeah, I saw him on May first.' Fine. Mark Schwebes was undergoing an autopsy at that time. That doesn't mean Kevin couldn't have pulled the trigger. Fuller said Kevin was calm, said he was natural. I'd submit we could add the word 'cold' to that, ladies and gentlemen of the jury.

"Then there was Kelly. I submit to you there's a number of you who want to believe Kelly; I submit to you Kelly wants to believe Kelly. Again, what did Rebecca Magnotti say? That Ruby and Kelly and some of their friends will testify Pete was home with Kevin.

"One thing should strike you as funny—and I kind of wish the timeline was still up here—because you had Ruby saying that at eleven oh-four that night she came in and saw Kevin smoking. It was at eleven oh-four on April 30, 1996. Now, what reason, what motivation, did Ruby have on April 30, 1996—on that particular day—to remember precisely what time she came in her house and what Kevin was doing? None whatsoever. This is another day in the very hectic and very busy life of a woman trying to start a new business, working long hours, and really the one thing on her mind is getting this business going. So much so that—as she finally told you yesterday from the witness stand—she couldn't really keep track of what Kevin was doing. So where's the motivation on April 30,

1996, to remember things so precisely as 'at eleven oh-four'? Not 'around,' even, or 'somewhere around eleven.' Where does that motivation come from on April thirtieth? I submit to you it doesn't. When does it arise? After he's arrested and she's going to give him an alibi.

"In about every case I've done over the past nineteen years, there's always somebody you can say is a hero. I was beginning to think we weren't going to have our hero. But we did yesterday—Sharon Magaskil." The reluctant witness loved the woman she helped impeach. "She came to Florida two to three weeks after Kevin was arrested to lend support to Ruby. Not the weekend after he was arrested, but two to three weeks later. And what happened? Ruby and Kelly are upset about Kevin's arrest, they go out to eat. It's like, 'Let's figure out what happened, let's figure out where he was.' And then—for the first time—Magaskil starts making notes. Not Ruby, not Kelly, but Magaskil starts making notes on a calendar about where Ruby and Kelly are saying Kevin was. Did she ever say he was home? Did she ever say anything about ATVs? No. Did you hear that she was simply recording what Ruby and Kelly were relaying from Kevin? Yes, you did."

Sitting with Kevin's supporters, Magaskil cried.

Did the other boys frame Kevin? "There's no suggestion anywhere in the evidence there was motivation to frame somebody they all said they were friends with." And the prosecution played the tape of Derek's statement to show his story was unchanged. "The truth hasn't changed," McGruther said, "unless he talked to Ruby in the interim." And what about those sweetheart deals? "Thirty-two years in prison for Mr. Magnotti. He's eighteeeen. . . . And natural life without the possibility of parole—in other words, 'You die in prison, Chris. . . . And Derek, you die in prison, too.' Those are the '*sweetheart' deals* they got."

McGruther picked up a newspaper. "Item forty-seven in evidence. Fort Myers *News-Press*. Thursday, May 2, 1996." He paced slowly, reading headlines. "'BEST FRIENDS SEARCH FOR A MOTIVE.' . . . 'RIVERDALE HIGH ENDURES SECOND TRAGEDY.' . . . 'FRIENDS MOURN LOSS.' The article about Mark Schwebes's death. And whose fingerprints are on here? Kevin's." McGruther approached the defense table. "One of the reasons for the Lords of Chaos was to make headlines," he said, throwing the newspaper on the table in front of Kevin. "You made 'em."

McGruther sat down. *If Kevin had picked up the shot-shells, he might've got away with it. If he tossed the shotshells and shotgun. If no one made statements. If there'd been no boasting. But then, the boasting went with keeping the gun and newspaper clipping. Overconfidence.* There was something unsettling, sick and creepy about this case and about Kevin. Weirdness. Unresolved questions. Intimations of incest. Strange snippets of fact in an otherwise unclear picture. McGruther looked at Kevin. During one of the search warrants, police found a jar of what looked like semen in his bedroom. McGruther shuddered. The sooner this was done with, the better.

The judge gave the jury a lengthy series of instructions and reminders about charges Kevin could be convicted of, the difference between justifiable and unjustifiable homicide, what a weapon is, elements the state had to prove beyond a reasonable doubt, premeditation, the presumption of innocence and assessing witness credibility. "In just a few moments, you'll be directed to the jury room. The first thing you should do is elect a foreman. The foreman presides over your deliberations. It's the foreman's job to sign and date the verdict form. Your verdict finding the defendant either guilty or not guilty must be unanimous."

At 11:50 A.M., with a promise lunch would be provided, jurors retired.

"We need to pick a foreman first," Brad Weatherly said.

"Go for it," someone said. With that, Weatherly got the job.

The jurors sat around a conference table in a ten-by-twelve-foot room. Enough room to pace, with a rest room off to one side.

Weatherly saw the jury as a unit—there was no "I." *We as a jury reach our decision. We vote. We recommend.* The paper ballots were anonymous. Weatherly knew where he stood. In his scrutiny of the key players, he saw the Schwebeses sobbing. *I want to do what* you *want done.*

After an hour, the jury sent out a note. "It says, 'Derek tape. Ms. Magnotti's testimony. All pictures. Letter from "Mom" to Pete. Cindi's testimony. Derek's testimony.'" Anderson squinted, turning the paper in his hands. "And down in the lower right-hand corner, 'May jurors smoke, please, outside?' I'm answering negative: they may not smoke. What about the rest of it?" Over Jacobs's objections, the judge allowed jurors the pictures and letter from Mom. They'd have to rely on their recollection of everything else.

"That's good!" Ruby said when she heard about the jurors' request. "I'm glad they got the letter, because all I said was to tell the truth."

He was out for no good, juror Rose Martie thought. *Out to kill, and he really seemed to enjoy it. No remorse. Hardhearted. I would've liked to have heard his side.* Certain things stuck in her mind. The stolen tag. The quest to find Mark's address. The group hug. The shot-gun. Shotshells. The prosecutor throwing down the newspaper. Ruby. Martie listened to her colleagues. *None of us, not one, believe a word Ruby said. Same with Kelly. Especially losing that paper she was working on.*

After another twenty-five minutes and another question, Anderson told jurors they couldn't have a list explaining what each picture was. "What's de-picted speaks for itself."

Mothers would do anything for their children, Pat Schwebes Dunbar thought as she waited. *If you gave my mother a choice April 29, my mother would've done any-thing. None of us raised our children to be murderers. For almost two years, I've believed he's guilty. If he's guilty, I hope he's found guilty. I don't take any joy whatsoever if they come back with a guilty verdict, because here's another young man who'll die.* Dunbar reserved her greatest con-tempt for Derek, her brother's student, the Judas.

Inside the jury room, there wasn't much discussion. One juror didn't understand the ballistics testimony and sought explanation from the others. The gun clinched it. Jurors dragged deliberations out because they wanted lunch and felt it ought to look like they were working. In reality, the decision was simple.

Juror John Quelet found the trial exciting, the re-alization of his responsibility daunting. *This guy's life's in my hands.* He listened to each witness, trying to piece together the testimony jigsaw. It became an hour-by-hour ordeal, trying to tie everything together and wor-rying about the decision. But he knew with certainty as he walked into the jury room. *Done deal.*

The vote was easy.

* * *

The news came at 2:06 P.M. "Apparently, the jury's reached a verdict," Anderson said. It'd taken two hours and sixteen minutes. "Mr. Weatherly, are you the foreman? You have the verdict form. Would you give it to the clerk. Madam clerk, would you publish the verdict."

The courtroom was silent. The clerk read, "In the Circuit Court of the Twentieth Judicial Circuit in and for Lee County, Florida. Criminal action. *State of Florida* versus *Kevin Don Foster.* Case Number 96-1362 CF-B. Verdict. We the jury find as follows as to the charge: The defendant is guilty of first-degree premeditated murder. So say we all, this 11th day of March, 1998. W.B. Weatherly, foreman."

Kevin showed no reaction. Ruby stared straight ahead.

We've lost several generations, Allen thought. *It's a failure of our whole system. We failed the children.* Gone was the certainty of severe and immediate punishment he grew up with. He never thought of talking back to police. Yet it happened frequently now. *I don't think it's the kids so much as us. We don't take them to task for what they do. Nothing happens. We're allowing them to get away with it. And our entertainment has taken the reality out of violence.*

It's the parents' fault, Mark's mother thought. The family also blamed the school for not recognizing troubled kids and considered filing a civil action against the school district.

The judge polled each juror, "Is this your verdict?" They were thanked and told to be back in a month to recommend a penalty.

"Mr. Foster, the jury having found you guilty of first-degree premeditated murder, the court hereby adjudicates you guilty and remands you to the custody of the Lee County Sheriff's Office," Anderson said.

Someone would've died within a couple of weeks even if Mark hadn't, Allen thought. *Maybe the pregnant Hardee's clerk.* He watched the bailiffs close around Kevin as the defendant stood. Kevin's needy eyes sought a bailiff's. He seemed to be asking what to do, like a child waiting to be told, sheepish and vulnerable. As a bailiff gestured, he headed for the clerk's table, crossing forever from the world of the woman seated behind him to the world of prison. *Your boasting showed you believed there'd be no consequences,* Allen thought. *Nobody would dare cross you. You were God. You're conniving right now. You're a Charles Manson. Long-range plans. Power. Greed. Vast imagination, but your imagination wasn't productive; it was destructive. The only limitations you had were your age and your finances. If you'd used your lack of morals to try to make a profit, you could've made a lot of money.*

The bailiffs escorted Kevin to the clerk's table, where he was again fingerprinted. They handcuffed him and hustled him out a rear door, down private stairs, back to jail.

Ruby fled the courtroom by a side door, still surrounded by the clan, given the courtesy of a back exit to avoid the media. She had nothing to say now, needed time to collect herself. The Fosters hadn't beaten the system. But this was round one, not the final bell. They'd try something else. She'd rescue Kevin yet.

Pat Schwebes Dunbar cried.

CHAPTER 34

Penalty

The 3:00 A.M. hang-up calls to juror Brad Weatherly's house started a couple of days after the verdict. Weatherly worried for his wife and children. Though he couldn't know, he suspected the source. Being a juror was dangerous: still, what good would it do to report a suspicion?

As the Burnetts pulled into their driveway, a red laser dot danced over them. *A laser pointer? Or a weapon with a sighting device?* Like Weatherly, they thought they knew who was trying to intimidate them.

Prosecutors let it go. Ruby Foster was the emotional mother of a young man on trial for his life. She could be forgiven—just—for losing touch with reality. But Ruby wouldn't let go—she'd nurse her grudges.

Court reconvened to decide Kevin's penalty April 9.

Bob Durham, RHS principal, was the prosecution's only witness: "Band director's a job that's one of the most demanding because their day's never done. The fall's full of the football season. After that they go into the concert season, and when that's over, it's the summer band camps. They're one of the best-known faculty members, because they're involved in so much.

"We had lost the student band boosters, and parents had lost interest and drifted away. Mark got the parents and band boosters involved again. He added twelve members. He built a flag corps. He was working with middle-school band directors who fed to our program.

"If I was to say 'devastating,' that'd be an understatement. We had ten to twelve additional counselors for the next couple of weeks, and through the end of the year, we were on call with counselors available at any time—and we used them. To have one of your teachers taken away in this fashion was a shock to the school and community and parents. People started questioning, 'Do I want to be at school at night?' There was a drop-off in many activities.

"It's not something you just walk away from. I don't think it'll ever leave me."

Kevin's team paraded twenty-five witnesses through the courtroom.

No remorse, juror Rose Marie Martie thought. *I hope you repent while you're in for what you did. You would've done more damage if you hadn't started bragging and got caught. You were going to go to Disney World and kill all the blacks.*

First to testify was a black former neighbor who said Kevin helped start her car and offered to loan a riding lawn mower: "I had a long conversation with him, and he was very helpful. I was alone, and he said if I need anything done around the house, all I had to do was ask."

Kevin was reliable and a friend of Shawn's, said Bud Jeffries. . . . "Kevin was like his big brother," Shawn's mother said. "Kevin's always been there for me. He was kind to my son, he was kind to me, and I just can't take that away from him." Other witnesses also highlighted Kevin's compassion for Shawn. "He was just very attentive, and Shawn went through a lot of rough times, and he was one of the kids that went out of their way. He was gentle, very polite and well-mannered." . . . "I don't believe he did it. I don't think Kevin has it in him."

Roy and Ellen Johnson, guardians of their paraplegic grandson, Brendan, testified that Kevin had befriended Brendan on a Big Red Boat Cruise arranged by the Make-A-Wish Foundation. They never forgot Kevin's kindness to Brendan when most wouldn't have bothered. They hadn't seen or heard from Kevin in years, but Ellen stayed in touch with Ruby and sent a mass card to the jail.

Kevin was well-mannered and cut a retired law enforcement officer neighbor's lawn. "I've known him since he was a little tyke."

Ruby's husband number one, Ron Newberry—Kelly's father—said Kevin was a real fine person, not that he saw him much since he was young. Newberry mailed a letter of encouragement to the jail; Kevin didn't reply.

None of these people had any association with Kevin after about age fourteen, Weatherly thought.

Paul Gilbert testified from his wheelchair: "He's like a son, because he was always there for me. The whole family's always been there for me."

Maybe he's got a good heart, Quelet thought.

Onetime best friend Drew—now a twenty-year-old student injured playing college basketball—limped in with a cane. Drew never saw Kevin threaten anybody—not that he saw him much at all after February 1996.

Drew's mother described Kevin, as "a very loving young man that cared about his friends. I feel very sorry for people that don't know Kevin the way we do."

"In your experience as a schoolteacher, isn't it true

sometimes young people show one face to teachers and a very different face to peers?" Lee said.

"We all have a tendency to do that."

"My opinion, he's innocent," said Brian Burns, Ruby's husband number three. "He's always been a good boy. I've never seen him lose his temper." And yes, Ruby and Kelly had been living with Brian since Kevin's arrest.

Trish's father said Kevin seemed up front and honest when he came to take Trish out.

"He's an all-American any mother would be proud to have," a friend's mother said. "I have two sons. If I couldn't get them to do something, I'd call Kevin, and he'd stop by and do what I asked. If he couldn't do it then, he said, 'I'll be back later this evening or tomorrow.'"

"Do you love him as a son?" Bob Jacobs said.

"Yes."

"Have you ever been convicted of a felony involving dishonesty or false statement?" Lee said.

"Yes."

Said Kevin's stepsister, "He's my stepbrother. I love him, and I don't believe he's capable of this."

"You don't feel you know him very well?" Mc-Gruther said.

"No."

Kevin's stepbrother-in-law saw him four or five times. "So, at family gatherings and such, he minded his manners," prosecutor Randy McGruther said. "But that's all you know."

All from when he was younger, Martie thought. *Nobody recent.*

Jacobs read an affidavit from Kevin's stepbrother serving in the navy. "This is to certify that I do know Kevin D. Foster, a relationship is that he's my brother, and he's an outstanding citizen, a model student and a hard worker, having a job in construction."

The character witnesses struggled to help Ruby's

boy without stretching the truth. Testimony was lackluster, reflecting the oddly cold quality of their friend at the defense table.

Weatherly scrutinized Kevin, still hoped for something, yet saw nothing. *You never let us in. You just sit there emotionless.*

Kelly Foster's turn: "My brother and I have been very close our entire lives. We're as close as any brother and sister could be. Ever since my brother was born, I've always been taking care of him. I protect him. I love him. He's everything to me. He's a very excellent draftsman, and he helped his old high-school teacher with the senior classes as a sophomore and freshman. I don't want you to take my brother's life. He's a valuable human being, even if you don't see that. He's a caring and compassionate human being, and I want my brother to live."

"You'd do anything to try to save his life?" Lee said.

"Yes, I would," Kelly said. "But I wouldn't lie. You—yourself—and the media have branded me a liar, and I don't appreciate it."

"Ma'am, I never called you a liar."

"Yes. But the implications have branded me in the media among this town and people, and I don't appreciate it."

Kevin again had nothing to say. He wouldn't demean himself pleading for life in front of a bunch of strangers who'd already convicted him. He wondered what might've made a difference. Dressing as he liked to dress instead of in this fucking jacket and tie? Eye contact with the jury? Varying his facial expression? Taking the stand? The verdict was Jacobs's fault for an insipid defense, Anderson's fault for bias, Lee County's fault for stacking the deck. The trial was rigged; it should've been moved. The jurors had made up their minds. The other boys had betrayed him. *The only reason they got me on that crap was because*

of the number of times and the number of people they got up
there to say I told them about the shit.

Lee County expected a prolonged and difficult
jury selection, weeks of testimony, twists and turns and
a valiant defense. It was surprising, even disappointing, that the showy part in open court was over so fast.
Most were unaware of the exhaustive investigation that
preceded the trial. Where other jurisdictions could be
criticized for their handling of death penalty cases—
drunken defense attorneys, defenses so wanting that
college students could show defendants were wrong-
fully convicted—it was nearly inconceivable an unsub-
stantiated charge against one of the LOC boys
would've survived to imprison him. If Lee County had
shortcomings, lack of thoroughness preparing for a
high-profile trial wasn't one of them. The process
was so thorough, even deputies who played minor
roles, such as guarding a recovered stolen vehicle or
interviewing a car dealer, were deposed. The state
even subpoenaed the telephone records of the owner
of the tag the boys stole at the mall.

Over a period of more than twenty-one months, six
defense attorneys—assisted by even more attorneys,
paralegals, investigators and other staff—and two
primary prosecutors—supplemented with additional
prosecutors and their own investigators—logged
hundreds of hours investigating the case, mostly out
of the public eye, interviewed 174 people, sometimes at length, occasionally repeatedly and gener-
ated more than six thousand pages of records so
others could see the process had been fair and thorough. The sworn statements and other evidence
convicted Kevin Foster. Pat Schwebes Dunbar likened
the experience of reading the court record to her kids
denying with a purple tongue that they had eaten
purple ice cream.

* * *

Ruby's turn. One last chance to say what she wanted. One last chance to show the world this paragon who was her son. One last chance to convince by replaying his enviable life in a fifty-six-slide show.

Ruby retold the saga of Kevin and Shawn. "My son spent six months every single weekend at the hospital with this child. When he was at his worst, Kevin was there to pick him up, take him out of his bed, cheer him up. Kevin's a good kid. He appreciates his friends and loves them to death and was like a brother. It tore him up. When Shawn died, it was the week Kevin was shot. They talked on the phone until Shawn was unconscious enough and couldn't talk.

"My son did not do this," Ruby said. "I don't want my son to die for something he did not do."

Very much of a schemer, McGruther thought. *He gets it from you. A family trait. The apple doesn't fall far from the tree, but he's worse.*

Hall cross-examined. "Your son has had a rather idyllic growing up, has he not, with many advantages? The advantages of going to Europe. The advantage of having kittens. The advantage of having dogs."

"If you call that an advantage, yeah."

"The advantage of being extremely loved by a loving and protective mother?"

"Loving mother, parents, friends, family, everything."

"You do love him, do you not?"

"Yes, I do."

"You'd do anything for him?"

"I'd do anything but lie for my son."

You went on all these great trips, but there wasn't that kind of love you needed, Martie thought. *I didn't come from a rich family, but I was loved.*

He probably was everything you said, Weatherly thought. *Unfortunately, he's also this. At what point are parents accountable? How many hundreds of thousands of eight- and nine-year-old kids are at home playing Doom? It's against the law to walk into a movie theater and yell "Fire!" And if that's a crime, it's certainly a crime what we allow our kids to watch and play with. Parents should assume responsibility. What are my kids doing? Who're they hanging out with? Where are they? Who're their friends' parents?*

Juror John Quelet was also pondering responsibility. Ruby hadn't discouraged Kevin's wildness; he had access to guns and the pawnshop. *She's at the store, he's loose. The biggest thing we had was respect for parents and respect for families.* But since then, a decline in morality. The stimulation of entertainment. New technology. *You want to know about guns? Just go put in* G-U-N-S. *Click. You're going to know everything you ever wanted to know and some things you didn't.*

Lee presented the state's closing argument. Two aggravating factors: the murder was to avoid arrest and it was cold, calculated and premeditated, without pretense of moral or legal justification. Jurors must weigh these against mitigators. "The majority of the witnesses in mitigation really didn't know the defendant or see him in the critical months before the murder," Lee said. "There was a character on the TV show *Leave It To Beaver*, Eddie Haskell. He was a bright young man, and when the parents of the Beaver were present, Eddie Haskell was always the epitome of politeness. 'Yes, Mrs. Cleaver. No, Mrs. Cleaver. You look very nice today.' But when the parents weren't there, he was always sticking it to the Beaver and had a very nasty personality. We're dealing with an individual who shows one face here and another face there. Now, which is the one you're to assess? Are you to assess this mitigation based upon when he was a baby, when he was a young child standing in front of the Eiffel Tower? People change, and we have to assess them as they are, not as perhaps they once were. Does being a cute little boy mitigate or excuse the murderous acts of an individual when they grow up?

"If you think about it, all of the evidence you heard really proves Kevin has absolutely no excuse. He had every advantage. He had no history of abuse. No history of drugs. No alcohol abuse. No fits of uncontrolled anger. Everybody said he was a mild-mannered young man. He wasn't deprived. No evidence of mental problems. This was a choice made by a young man who had every advantage, and yet in cold, calculated and premeditated fashion, unencumbered by any problems—"

Jacobs objected: "He's trying to turn mitigating evidence into aggravators."

"Overruled."

"This evidence is the farthest thing from mitigation," Lee said. "The defendant's claim to mitigating factors is simply another attempt to escape accountability—something he shouldn't be permitted to do—and he shows a consistent pattern of that attempt, just as he desperately ran from Mark's door to escape accountability. So, now you've seen a desperate attempt to play on our sympathies and divert you from following the law.

"How dare they? How dare they?

"I don't believe you'll stand for that. I don't believe today there's going to be a group hug. Today's the day Kevin must be held accountable with the punishment that fits the crime. Not the police, not the prosecution, not the judge, not you, not anyone but the defendant is responsible for his presence here. He can honestly blame no one but himself for facing the death penalty he rightfully faces. There must be consequences to terrible actions, actions he chose, and today's that day when he must face those consequences.

"The defendant was spotted by Mark Schwebes, and this killing was done to protect himself. Mark

knew there was a third person." Jeremy Arnold also saw
Kevin. "Almost like a deer in headlights, the defendant
turned and looked and kept running. Mr. Arnold saw
him face-on. The defendant's fears of arrest were justified." Kevin was protecting Chris, Tom and himself.
"If those two are caught, the third will be identified very
shortly. That's why this murder had to occur that
night—because the evidence was there, and they had
to stop Mark from reporting it.

"The defendant was concerned with more than
just exposure of himself, Chris and Tom. This group
was his power source. He was the god—with a little *g*.
He wouldn't be a big man anymore if this group was
exposed."

Lee reminded jurors of the LOC's code of silence.
"This killing was an extension of that rule, because
Mark was about to talk, and as a result had to die.

"There's one motivating plan throughout, from
beginning to end of everything Kevin seems to do in
this case, and that's to avoid the consequences. Everything he's doing is designed to avoid arrest." The
stolen license tag. Wiping the tag clean. Moving the
cars from the auditorium. Wearing gloves. Wiping the
fire extinguisher. Choosing the shotgun. Wearing a
mask. "And the defendant ran off at the first sign of
trouble. As Mr. Schwebes pulled up, Kevin immediately ran off, leaving his lost, wary Lords of Chaos literally holding the bag, the blue Wal-Mart bag, which
you've seen. No effort was made to retrieve the fire
extinguisher or cans: if Mark's dead and everything's
been wiped clean, that stuff means nothing.

"After the murder, the defendant gave credit to
Chris and then later told Tom, 'You don't have to
worry anymore.' It was as if he was telling them, 'This
was your doing, not mine,' and yet he still managed
to keep the macho image that he did it for them.

"How about even after his arrest? After learning the
first of his core group had agreed to testify, he said he

hoped Pete kissed his parents 'bye. He already threatened to eliminate Burnett and Tom. He's trying to intimidate them so they won't testify.

"If the killing of an unarmed schoolteacher didn't pose a problem, if presenting a false alibi didn't pose a problem, then presenting a false image to you certainly is no problem."

The murder was premeditated: Kevin resisted following Mark. Consulted the phone book. Called 411 for Mark's number. Called again for Mark's address. Called Mark's machine. Retrieved the stolen license tag. Planned at his home on Lorraine Drive. Rejected alternate plans. Read the map. Schemed to avoid ballistics. "He isn't planning how to kill, but how to escape. Even before the act is done, he's already figuring out how he's going to escape accountability." Kevin called Mark again from Circle K. Psyched himself up for the kill. Checked the map. Checked the neighborhood. Wore the mask and gloves. Used green shells with heavy killing loads. Parked out of sight. Lay in wait, hiding behind Derek. Took aim. Racked the shotgun for the second shot. "This was no spontaneous thing, 'Yeah, let's go do it.' This was a cold, calculated decision.

"He passed the shotgun out the window. That's interesting, isn't it? He didn't just walk right out of the house. Why? We don't know for sure, although we can be pretty sure Kelly and Ruby were home. But think of the planning: If he passes the shotgun out the window, he never has to answer a question if he happens to be spotted in the house. If he walks through the living room and Ruby comes out, he'll have to explain, and his Mom would stop him. Planning is what this is, not a spontaneous urge to kill."

Kevin cooled from his initial anger. "He had to use his thought processes, very carefully going through the details of how to carry this out. There was a lot of time between the point where Mark interrupted the

Lords of Chaos and his death. You have a couple of hours for tempers to cool." The drive alone was twenty-four minutes. "That's plenty of time to cool, to reflect and think about what you're doing, and yet here's one of the really chilling things about this case: on the way there, the defendant sat psyching himself up. He'd *chosen* to pump adrenaline back into his system because he'd cooled.

"That shotgun has a trigger pull of seven pounds. It's not a hair trigger. It took seven pounds of pull. Twice. It took a deliberate decision, a deliberate act— twice—to kill.

"That red cloud was the blood and tissue of his victim exploding from the impact of that shotgun shell, and yet he took time for a second shot. That second shot, as a helpless Mark Schwebes laid up in a fetal position, was an executioner's act so there'd be no doubt his victim would never get up again."

Jamie Wooten, the paralegal, snoozed at the defense table. *They keep the courtroom too cold to get tired*, Weatherly thought.

"There was no panic in Kevin. He was laughing as he ran back to the car." Kevin took time to change the tag and wipe it clean. "He congratulates his Lords of Chaos. Could anything be more bizarre? Because just opposite town at that same moment you have paramedics and law enforcement standing around a fallen Mark Schwebes, and at Kevin's, they're having a group hug for a job well done."

Later, Kevin would masturbate. "I can't think of anything colder," Lee said. The next morning, Kevin sees Fuller. By afternoon he'd be bragging. "He's gloating. He's reenacting it in front of the television. This killing had no shred of moral or legal pretense. Everything points to its complete senselessness."

There was no feud between Mark and Kevin. No harsh words at the door. "The victim's last words were almost like summing up his whole life: 'Yes, may I help you?'"

Kevin's support group was absent now. Trish Edwards's father was the only one in court.

"I suspect in a few moments when I sit down, you'll hear a plea for mercy," Lee said. "You heard it from his mother, from his sister. The word 'mercy' derives from a Latin term, *merces*, M-E-R-C-E-S. What that Latin word means is 'to pay' or 'to reward.' What reward does the defendant deserve? What payment has he brought upon himself? People must be held accountable by punishment which fits the crime; that's what justice is."

Trish's father left. Kevin was among strangers now, facing death alone.

Bob Jacobs rose and faced the jury. "Kevin will die in prison," he said. "That's a fact. You decided that when you found him guilty of first-degree premeditated murder. You cannot be easy on him. You couldn't give him a break, even if you wanted. You'll determine when he becomes physically dead. Will he die in prison when God says? Or will he die when the governor signs his death warrant, as he's done four times in the past week?

"You exercise a godlike power. Picture Kevin as a small bird, and you have him in your hands. You have the power to crush him or put him in a cage. The process is a qualitative one in which you weigh the proprieties of letting a boy—Kevin—live his life in prison without any possibility of parole versus the propriety of putting him to death."

Jacobs had known there was little chance of avoiding conviction, but he heartily believed in redemption, hated the death penalty and hoped for a life sentence. He made a stab at deflating prosecution arguments. "Two hours isn't a lot of time to cool down." Then, "If an arrest was going to take place, Mr. Schwebes would've called the police. Did he? No. He said, 'I'm going to tell the school resource officer tomorrow.' There was no arrest. There was no possibility of arrest. And even if he did report Chris and Tom, what would that mean? A two-, or three-day suspension? Kevin wasn't even a student. Why wasn't Jeremy Arnold killed? Why was he alive to testify? It doesn't make sense, folks. And why weren't Chris and Derek killed, if they could turn in the group?

"Mark's life had value. As does Kevin. No more, no less. We are, after all, talking about the state wanting to take a human life. What happened was a tragedy for the Schwebes family. We don't deny that. But it's a tragedy for the family of Kevin also. Don't make it worse by sentencing this boy to death.

"Why is age a mitigating factor? Because of the nature of youth. Youth's a time of the ever-present now. Erma Bombeck once said, 'I've learned our kids need love most when they deserve it least.' Kevin was eighteen. Do rational human beings execute children?"

Jacobs encouraged jurors to look at Kevin's positive character traits and family background. "He was a good person," Jacobs said, as though Kevin was already dead. "He was a caring person. He cared for people who had disabilities. He went to the hospital every weekend for his friend Shawn. You heard of his compassion. You heard how he treated Mr. Gilbert. Does *that* person deserve to die?

"You heard of his going to Lee Vo-Tech. Getting a certificate in drafting. You heard he took courses and got his GED. You heard he went to college. You heard what a good work record he had. There's potential here for rehabilitation, although it'll be in prison for the rest of his life. Life satisfies the state's demand for punishment. Proportionality doesn't allow this to be a death penalty case.

"Let's talk a little bit about life without parole.

Think about having to spend the rest of your life in a small room with a toilet and a sink and a bed. It's like spending the remaining days of your life in a regular-size bathroom. That's punishment enough. Someone tells you when to get up. Someone tells you when and what you can eat. Someone tells you when to go to bed. Someone tells you what to read. What you can't read. No drives in the country. No walks in the woods. No quiet walks on the beach. Kevin's life's over. All life is sacred. The commandment not to kill lives within all of us as long as—"

"Objection," Lee said. "That's a misstatement of the law: it's 'Thou should not commit murder.'"

"Sustained."

"As long as there's life, there's hope," Jacobs said. "We're taught to love and forgive, not hate and seek revenge, and I ask you not to do that today. Remember what events took place this week two thousand years ago. We'd submit to you the quality of mercy is twice blessed. Mr. Lee would scoff at that, but we submit it's twice blessed. It's blessed by the person who gives it and the person who receives it. Somewhere, someday, you'll have to come to grips with the decision you make today.

"In your deliberation, you'll see chaos turns to clarity. I plead with you, please consider this young man, please show him mercy and choose life. What other mercy do we have but forgiveness, redemption and salvation? Every person is a miracle of life, and every person is God's child. Thank you."

The jury room was silent. Weatherly read the judge's instructions. He hoped his colleagues had—as he had—prayerfully sought the right thing. He viewed the decision as very personal. He called for an immediate vote, not wanting to hear what everybody else thought. The first vote was eight to four for death. If the vote had been tied, the jurors would've walked out then and there and recommended life.

The jurors went over everything again. One kept repeating if the others got life, Kevin should get more. Another said, "If you were to pull the switch, could you do it to find out later he was innocent?" But no one thought Kevin innocent.

Weatherly called for a second vote, which swung further against Kevin, nine to three.

The process would haunt Weatherly. *When they do execute him, what makes me any less responsible than he was?* Weatherly had played a role in Kevin's death; Kevin's blood was on his hands as Mark's was on Kevin's.

Martie voted against death. *It's not right. Life imprisonment's enough. God's the only one who decides when your time's up.*

Though a death penalty proponent in jury selection, Quelet also voted against. Kevin was eighteen when he shot Mark; he was influenced by Pete; he was influenced by Mom; he was given access to weapons. The case was circumstantial. No one saw Kevin pull the trigger. There was little physical evidence. Kevin had a legitimate other side. *Is this an eye for an eye, a tooth for a tooth? Why take a life when there are so many questions about guilt and innocence?*

When the jury came back, the courtroom was again crowded. Kevin's family and friends were back.

"A majority of the jury—by a vote of nine to three—advise and recommend to the court that it impose the death penalty," the clerk read.

Ruby put a hand to her head. Anderson polled jurors. Trish cried. Ruby lowered her head.

Before Kevin Foster is put to death, if he will agree to see me, I will have a one-on-one conversation with him, Pat Schwebes Dunbar thought. *It's not that I'll be forgiving, it's not that I'll ever understand him, but I need to see him as a person.*

I'd like Kevin to make a decision for Christ before he dies, Weatherly thought. *I'd hope that someone—if not me— would be able to present to him the truth.*

At home, Martie completed a scrapbook about the trial, including newspaper clippings her father saved, and worried about Ruby. *She lives too close. She could come after us. She don't know who voted for life.*

At a May 28 hearing, both sides presented more evidence. Appearing in a blue suit, Kevin had cropped the hair he grew out for trial. Over Jacobs's objections, Pat Schwebes Dunbar read a family statement.

"My mind keeps screaming, 'Not Mark, oh my God, not Mark,'" Dunbar read, voice breaking. "This whole process—being notified by a law enforcement officer; trying to make funeral arrangements but not being able to see his body to mentally verify it's truly Mark that's been killed, finding ourselves in the middle of a media feeding frenzy while we try to grieve.

"Mark hasn't been forgotten, and we're still in very different states of grief. Mark was beginning to realize dreams he worked so hard for through his years in school, the Marine Corps, college and his teaching career. He was using his love of music to teach another generation." Dunbar wiped a tear. "He was building his first home. I'd been down over the spring break prior to his death and went with my husband and children and Mark to pick out carpeting and cabinets. Mark showed us the lot his house was being built on and the model. He showed us the room he'd set aside for my parents and the room for my boys when they spent the night with their Uncle Mark. He also showed us where he'd put the piano he hoped to purchase and explained to us how he'd use assorted musical instruments to decorate. He was so excited.

"If a child wanted to quit his program because their family didn't have the money to pay rent on an instrument, Mark would pay, sometimes going without grocery money, because he knew he could count on his family, his parents. And he knew he was making an investment.

"He had fantastic plans for his band students. He had several kids that had difficulties in their families and wouldn't be able to attend band camp, so he wanted to establish a scholarship. Mark was also hoping to take his band to Paris, France, in 1998 to represent Florida and the United States.

"He also told me about friends he was making. He could go out with friends for an evening of shooting pool. He joined a billiard team. He was planning a trip to the annual Florida Bandmasters conference in Ocala with his friend from college who's another area high school band director. We mourn the loss of Mark's dreams.

"My youngest sister shared conversations with Mark during difficult times in her marriage and while trying to become a parent. Today she and her husband are happy and the parents of the three-month old baby that'll never know the love and support of his Uncle Mark." Dunbar was sobbing now. "Neither will Mark be able to see the happiness and fulfillment of my sister and her family. She's questioned her religious beliefs, has faced fear and uncertainty of becoming a victim within her own home, and now to learn about death in a horrible violent way. My brother's suffered the loss of his only brother. His pain cannot be shared with the sisters, simply because we're sisters.

"It's very hard to watch our parents try to cope. We've watched the energy, enthusiasm and joy leave them, seeing their eyes fill with loss, bewilderment. And we know we're powerless to bring the joy back.

We all grow up expecting our children to bury us, not for us to bury them. When that does happen, your life loses focus, and you don't know how to find your way. Mark's murder has been especially hard because of the sense of betrayal my parents felt. The very kids he dedicated his life to helping took his life. My parents raised us to reach out and help others. Mark did this all his life until the minute he died.

"I hate what happened to Mark. I hate that he was murdered. I hate the way he was killed. That he died on his own doorstep without one of the many people that loved him beside him. I hate that my parents and I will live with the last memory of Mark's home as a place of blood and violence. But most of all I hate that there was a choice for everyone involved and they chose to make the wrong choice.

"I'm so sorry and so angry our lives and the reality of our lives as we knew them ended that day, and we cannot ever go back to who we were before Mark died. I want my normal life back. I want to enjoy life again. But I'm angry I've been forced to become the person I am today. I don't want to hate. That's a part of me I don't recognize and I don't want to become familiar with.

"Every time I'm in a classroom, every time I'm on a field trip and every time I meet one of my children's friends, I wonder if one of those children is capable of murder and would they hurt me or someone in my family. Mark was the victim of murder, but so is everyone in our family. No penalty can ever begin to relieve the pain of death and loss or fill the ache in our hearts."

McGruther introduced the twenty-seven-count companion case involving the LOC's other crimes, Kevin named in all but one. "If they were caught in this action they were involved in on April 30, 1996, they'd then in fact tell the school resource officer of other events."

Jacobs tried again. The state hadn't proved there was going to be an arrest. Mark didn't call police, he went to dinner. Jacobs also argued proportionality and bias: The day of Kevin's penalty phase, a man was sentenced in Lee County to life—not death—on murder, kidnapping and other charges. And, "Had a change of venue been granted, a different result would've surely occurred."

Again Kevin declined to testify, submitting an affidavit proclaiming his innocence and rehashing the alibi.

Kevin appeared at sentencing June 17 in jail red.

"We'd appreciate if the court would allow him to dress for this proceeding," Jacobs had said.

"Why?" Judge Anderson said. "This case is over as far as that's concerned, so there'll be no effect on the trier of fact in this case. The trier of fact has concluded whatever it is they have to do."

Mark saw Kevin, Anderson said. Mark took incriminating evidence from Chris and Tom. "From that point, the defendant was inexorably connected to an imminent investigation of the Lords of Chaos. The potential for arrest and exposure was very real and quite worrisome. Each member knew that in the two months preceding, the group engaged in numerous criminal acts, and each would be facing significant charges beyond those which might be presented by the exposure of their criminal conduct at Riverdale High School. The possibility of arrest and prosecution for all of the criminal actions which had been engaged in by the Lords of Chaos was a cold reality to the defendant, especially if members were questioned and disclosed to law enforcement what the Lords of Chaos had done."

The judge found the murder was committed to avoid arrest, and he gave this great weight. Anderson found six LOC members participated in the conspiracy, including Burnett and Tom. The murder was the maturation of the LOC and, though Burnett and Tom didn't go along for the ride, they knew about it before and immediately after. The judge found the murder premeditated, and he gave this great weight.

Anderson considered mitigating factors. "It's uncontroverted the defendant was eighteen," he said. "Counsel cites no case where the court is compelled to find age of the defendant should be a mitigating factor where the defendant was neither a minor nor possessed of a young mental or emotional age. To the contrary, based upon the evidence presented, it's plain the defendant was anything but young mentally or emotionally or even chronologically. Indeed, the defendant hadn't attended school for some two years, had traveled overseas and had completed his GED and taken other courses in preparation for life as an adult. Parenthetically, the court observes that when an eighteen-year-old becomes the ostensible leader of a group of criminals known as the Lords of Chaos, then meticulously plans and carries out the shotgun slaying of a man whose misfortune was to be at the wrong place at the wrong time, that young man loses the right to have age taken into consideration."

Anderson didn't see it as his place to judge the proportionality of giving Kevin a death sentence. That was the Florida Supreme Court's territory. The sentence wasn't disproportionate to those given other LOC core members. "Counsel's assertion the defendant is not any more culpable than any of the other three is patently ludicrous," the judge said. "Kevin Foster was the most culpable."

Anderson had considered the testimony of Kevin's character witnesses. "Nearly all of them stated it'd been quite some time since they had any contact. One witness, a former Riverdale High School teacher, described the defendant as a very loving young man. She concluded by stating, 'I feel sorry for people who don't know Kevin.' Of course, Mark didn't know Kevin. But that didn't keep Kevin from shooting him in the face with a shotgun.'"

Anderson said the defense listed twenty-three possibly mitigating factors. "The court has considered each and every one and provides each one of them with very little weight individually and very little weight collectively. They've run the gamut from the sublime to the ridiculous. For example: the defendant was a premature baby; he was abandoned by his natural father; he'll adjust well to prison.

"In essence, the defendant presented two personalities to the world. One personality would allow the defendant to look after a man confined to a wheelchair. The other would allow him to meticulously plan and carry out a cold, calculated and premeditated murder. None of the witnesses who testified in favor of the former were even remotely aware of the latter. It's that personality the defendant exhibited on the evening of April 30, 1996, when he brutally executed Mark Schwebes."

Kevin in an affidavit continued to insist on his innocence, and it was likely his family would also. "Lingering or residual doubt isn't a mitigating factor," Anderson said. "Lest anyone misconstrue this statement by inferring this court has such a doubt, let me make it clear I do not. The jury had no reasonable doubt about the defendant's guilt. This court has no doubt the right person—Kevin Don Foster—has been tried, convicted, and is soon to be sentenced for this murderous act. The fact the defendant still protests his innocence is irrelevant.

"The aggravating circumstances far outweigh the mitigating circumstances. Each one of the aggravating factors, standing alone, would be sufficient to outweigh the paucity of mitigation found in Kevin Foster's now twenty years of existence on this earth. The recommendation of death by the jury is clearly supported by the evidence. This court agrees with the jury that in weighing the aggravating circumstances against the mitigating circumstances, the scales of life and death tilt unquestionably to the side of death.

"Kevin Don Foster, you have not only forfeited your right to live among us, but under the laws of the state of Florida, you have forfeited your right to live at all. Accordingly, it is hereby ordered and adjudged that the defendant will be transported to the Department of Corrections to be securely held on death row until his sentence can be carried out as provided by law. May God have mercy on your soul."

Jacobs said he'd appeal. "Of course," Anderson said. "You have thirty days to appeal, and the court expects you to. That concludes the Foster matter."

The judge was wrong.

CHAPTER 35

Prison

Sumter Correctional Institution

Pete's mother immigrated, a mail-order bride marrying an older man. Rebecca Magnotti was, by all accounts, a solicitous, polite, somewhat shy woman slightly out of place in her adopted home. She didn't know how to reach her only child as he slipped into this strange American adolescent never-never land with his computer and his games and his music and his movies and his clothes and his dark imaginings and these friends. Helpless, she watched him self-destruct and knew Joe—ill at ease with the modern world and with his so much younger son—was helpless, too. Rebecca endured the media and the questions and the sneers and the averted eyes, and then she saw Joe collapse under the strain, devastated, repeatedly hospitalized, suddenly old. In spite of her pain and her shyness and her humiliation, she took the stand in front of TV cameras and hostile eyes in a packed court to refute Ruby's alibi. Perhaps she expected to watch Joe die, but even then life couldn't be cruel enough, because—diagnosed with lung cancer that spread to her brain—she died in a hospice, only fifty-six, her son in prison and her husband now quite alone . . . to die nine months later, at eighty-three. Her son, for all his faults, all his confused adolescent rebellion—exacerbated by alienated genius—and all his terrible lack of common sense and alleged remorselessness, still was a boy and still must endure prison, with its humiliations, and the distant loss of his mother and father and, piled upon these losses, the knowledge of his own wasted genius, of what he threw away.

"I'm sorry this all had to happen," he said, ending the statement that secured his plea bargain. It was hardly remorse.

When a representative for the Magnotti estate asked a bank teller to explain $69,000 missing from Joe's account, she said Pete—released for his father's funeral—came in with an expired driver's license and prison ID card. "That's impossible. Peter Magnotti's in state prison, and they don't let them out for nothing." The teller was charged with grand theft.

Now alone among 1,315 men at Sumter Correctional Institution, a thirty-year-old rural prison two miles off I-75, midway between Fort Myers and death row, Pete missed both funerals. He didn't bother to appeal his sentence. And he was the luckiest—Joe left a trust providing $100 each month in his canteen account, and he *would* get out some day, perhaps in 2026 if he could survive prison. By which time he'd be forty-six and institutionalized and would do . . . exactly what?

Okaloosa Correctional Institution

Chris was among 613 men in Okaloosa Correctional Institution, outside Crestview in the Florida Panhandle, near the Alabama border, colder and more classically Southern than Fort Myers. Okaloosa was a great improvement over the Lee County Jail, where he waited twenty-seven months. He did a drug education program, took a wellness course, started running and weight lifting, got his weight down to 160 pounds. Even if he sometimes regained a few pounds, it was a delightful achievement overcoming something that caused him so much grief. But Okaloosa lacked intellectual stimulation: it wasn't that he should *enjoy* prison, but this was downright boring.

Chris mopped floors on weekends, but there was no full-time work. He'd be happy to learn a trade, but Okaloosa didn't offer vocational programs. He longed to move someplace with more to occupy the mind.

Looking back, he felt so green at the time of his arrest—falling for being told his buddies were implicating him, believing he didn't face severe consequences because all he did was drive, minimizing that he suggested and planned murder.

He regretted he and his "brother," Pete, couldn't be together. He worried Pete would kill himself after his mother, then father died—but they weren't even in the same time zone and, under Florida rules, would never be in the same prison.

Chris's parents moved to Tennessee, and he got few visits. Chris regretted what he put his parents through, regretted prison—but when asked would he do it all again if he could be certain he wouldn't be caught, he didn't hesitate: "Yes." He knew Kevin wanted to kill. "He was always planning on doing somebody." To him, it was fun, and he remained enamored of Kevin, recalling the Disney World scheme almost fondly in spite of the difficulties it sometimes created behind bars: "Kevin talkin' about goin' down in the tunnels they got below there, like blowin' up shit with dynamite and acting like he was diggin' for gold and all that stuff." He chortled. "Crazy bastard."

Remorse wasn't part of his emotional repertoire.

New River West Correctional Institution

"I was responsible," Derek said. "I could've stopped it—I could've, and I should've."

New River West was close enough to Florida State Prison that when Kevin was out on the yard for recreation, Derek could see his familiar lanky form milling with other inmates in the distance—though too far away to exchange words. The two prisons were part of a cluster on flat farmland north of Gainesville: New River West, Florida State, Union, New River East.

People ran their mouths, inmates fought, guards hassled, but prison wasn't as the public imagined. "All you've got to do is walk up here and be a man and you won't have no problems." Derek had meals to eat, weights to lift, a yard to jog in, chapel services and a Bible study to attend, TV to watch, radio to listen to, 802 men to mingle with, work to go to—a forty-hour week as a "seamstress," starting at twenty cents an hour and earning raises to thirty-five cents, $56 each month to pad his canteen account. He could take computer classes and contemplated college correspondence courses. With cataracts obscuring his implant lens, he was moved to North Florida Reception Center, near Lake Butler, for surgery, temporarily improving the vision in his left eye from 20/100 to 20/35. It was like a vacation. Besides, it was late August in north central Florida, and Lake Butler had more windows and fans than New River West.

Derek almost grew to *like* New River West. Still, prison was bad in ways other than the supposed violence, rape and degradation, bad in more mundane ways. The penitentiary was an exercise in humiliation—few choices, no privacy, highly controlling corrections officers. It was insipidly depressing when you let it get to you: the guards' pettiness, other inmates' pathos, the blandly painted, sparsely furnished, cavernous institution, monotony. "We're not here for them to rehabilitate us in any way. We're here for them to punish us." Prison punished by denying Derek's dream to see every corner of the country, forbidding him children, suffocating outside friendships, trapping him in a sort of perpetual round-the-clock high school without the stimulant of classes. He'd never live free in the adult world.

He was frustrated he couldn't work outside, do something to help, maybe build homes. Lifers used to be assigned to work relief—work outside prison under controlled circumstances—but too many escaped, spoiling it for the others; so now, only prisoners who had two years or less left to serve were in community work squads, a category Derek might never fit, though he kept hoping, doggedly pursuing appeals.

Derek wanted to reconcile with the Schwebes family. He had to release his resentments, just as he hoped they would: He forgave his natural father and started phone conversations and correspondence. He said he knew who killed Fred, but became less concerned his brother's murderer be caught. Whether the perpetrator knew it, Fred's murder was destroying him. He'd pay even if he was never charged. Retribution wasn't right. Derek wouldn't seek revenge against Emory Lewis now, if he had it to do over. He even tried to relinquish hating Kevin. "I've no more hard feelings against him anymore. You gotta confess your sins one day. Kevin's just tearing himself up." He became uncertain he'd testify again, were Kevin granted a new trial. Kevin should be punished—especially because he wouldn't own up—though not with death. Death was retribution. But Derek was past caring. What did he have to gain by testifying? What could they do to him now? His sentence was unconstitutional because it was indefinite. Life was death: "It's the same sentence. You stay in here until you die." His plea agreement was Draconian and illegal. "They manipulated a nineteen-year-old kid. I was in no state of mind to make a decision."

Not that the LOC was the worst thing that ever happened. Even with life in prison stretching before him, Derek didn't hesitate: It was Fred's death, the ruling event in his life. "That hit worse than the shotgun blast."

Derek's parents were burdened by illness and couldn't afford the trip, and he saw them rarely. He was grateful they supported him. "I think it brought them closer together. We've been through a lot." Then he was moved to De Soto Correctional Institution Annex, close enough to home to hear familiar radio and see local TV. It didn't offer full-time work, but his mother, fighting cancer, could visit.

Time in the Lee County Jail around Latin Kings and Folk Nation members helped him see the Lords of Chaos as a gang, regardless of Kevin's semantics. "It was no militia. It was a group of stupid kids, but you can call it a little gang. It was no cult, like everyone keeps saying."

Derek set a goal to help kids avoid his mistakes. Professionals couldn't fix the problem. Adults couldn't. Only people who'd been there could get kids to listen, open up, get real. He found ways to get his message out, recording a public-service video and agreeing to a newspaper interview because he believed his story might show kids the undesirable consequences. "Be careful. Watch who you're with." Confronted with something like the LOC, "go straight to someone and tell them." If he could relive April 16 through May 3, 1996—the eighteen days from renewing his acquaintance with Kevin to an act that earned him life behind bars—Derek would've tried to detach quicker. At the least, after the Coke bombing. He mightn't have gone to police, but he would've stayed away.

* * *

Derek had been interviewed about the Hardee's plan. "So, you were willing to let Mr. Foster point a gun to your head for the fourth time?"

"Yeah."

"No problems?"

"What do you mean?"

"You had no problems with that?"

"I guess not. I just did whatever he said." Derek was beginning to understand it wasn't an adequate answer. He still had no explanation. Kevin said he'd kill at Hardee's if he encountered a problem. Derek thus knew the gun was loaded, yet he was willing to let Kevin take him hostage. If it dawned Kevin might really use that gun—to kill another innocent person or to kill him—he did nothing about it. He disliked Kevin from the start, but hung out with him; was intimidated by his temper, but came back repeatedly; objected to the murder, but knocked on the door; was repulsed by the killing, but told no one.

"If I wouldn't have ran into him, I wouldn't have gotten into this stuff. Chris is the one that introduced me to Kevin. I can't blame him for introducing me. I should've got out of it myself."

But he didn't.

Union Correctional Institution

On February 5, 1999, Kevin Foster returned to Lee County one last time, driven the six hours down from Florida's death row to enter a plea in the remaining charges against him. In exchange for his plea of no contest, prosecutors dropped some charges, a deal Ruby bitterly opposed, saying her son was tricked into it while she was on vacation. Spurning the publicity he once sought, Kevin asked prosecutors not to notify the media.

Again silent in court, Kevin offered an affidavit: "I did not commit these crimes, but unfortunately in the situation I now find myself, my only reasonable course of action is to accept this plea agreement. I was never part of the Lords of Chaos, nor did I commit any of these alleged charges. However, in the interest of ending this case, I accept this plea."

He got another four years tacked on to his death sentence and was driven back to Union Correctional Institution, where he awaits the execution of his sentence. Kevin has followed the appeals path typically taken by death row inmates and been disappointed at every turn, including before the Supreme Court of Florida.

Until she herself pleaded guilty to a charge of conspiracy to commit murder and served her own prison sentence, Ruby visited her son almost every weekend, commuting from Fort Myers, sometimes with Kelly (who never did get hired as a correctional officer), sometimes with Trish, sometimes with others.

Kevin passes his time on death row reading, watching television, listening to the radio, writing letters and using the recreation yard. On one inmate Internet site, Kevin welcomes correspondence from "anyone who is willing to brighten my lonely days."

"My opinion is most people don't know the true face of evil because they don't know themselves," Kevin once wrote the author. "They don't ever turn out the lights and look deep into the place they call their souls to see what they really are."

Kevin looked—and it fascinated him.

Author's Note

Like jury foreman Brad Weatherly, I approached Kevin Foster determined to view him innocent until proven guilty. Despite his conviction, Kevin and his mother insisted on his innocence. For eighteen months, Kevin and I exchanged dozens of letters and spent more than one hundred hours conversing on death row.

After confessing to the murder, Kevin asked me a favor—to murder three witnesses: Burnett, Tom and Brad. I went to Randy McGruther, who arranged for Brian Kelley and other state attorney's investigators to use me as a cooperating witness.

During covert surveillance, Ruby Foster gave me a shotgun, suggested I cover the bodies with lime to prevent animals from digging them up and urged Craig also be killed. On death row, Kevin repeated his scheme while I wore a concealed wire. Mother and son reached plea agreements on new charges of conspiracy to commit first-degree murder. Ruby was released from prison in 2004.

The full story of what happened between Kevin and me would fill another book.

The Schwebes family established a scholarship to benefit students pursuing degrees in music education. To make a contribution, write Mark C. Schwebes Memorial Scholarship, Administrator, 523 East Cherokee Court, Woodstock, GA 30188.

I began reporting this story on May 1, 1996, for the *News-Press* in Fort Myers, Florida, standing outside Mark Schwebes's duplex, wondering for just a second if his death might be related to his school and—three years before Columbine—quickly dismissing the idea.

Much of the narrative of *Someone Has to Die Tonight* is reconstructed from about ten thousand pages of court records. The sworn statements and depositions of more than 180 witnesses, including all the boys, and the full trial transcript were primary sources.

For narrative reasons or out of respect for the privacy of individuals not charged in the LOC case, or both, I have omitted some who were present during events described here. In a few cases, I combined similar scenes into one event. Many law enforcement officers played a role in the capture and conviction of the LOC; only a handful are acknowledged.

Thanks to all at the Twentieth Judicial Circuit of Florida, Florida Department of Law Enforcement, Florida Department of Corrections, Lee County Sheriff's Office, Fort Myers Police Department, District 21 Medical Examiner's Office and other agencies who helped during the research for this book.

The story took me to Alabama, Florida, Louisiana, Mississippi, Missouri and Texas. Thanks to all who assisted in those visits.

Thanks to those who talked with me about the people, places and events described here, either during the reporting for this book or when I was covering the story for the *News-Press* or both.

Thanks to all former colleagues at the *News-Press* in Fort Myers, Florida, especially Sam Cook, David Dorsey, Peter Franceschina and Bob Norman.

Thanks to Nolen-Martina Reporting Services, especially Connie DeMarsh, Gail Johns and Lisa M. Windhorst.

Thanks to the staff of the Twentieth Judicial Circuit of Florida's State Attorney's Office for your guidance, professionalism, steady demeanor and skills through the cooperating witness process.

I owe a particular debt to Brad Windsor, a former colleague at the *News-Press,* now at *USA TODAY,* for a meticulous style edit. Any remaining errors are mine. Thanks to all who read part or all of the manuscript in progress.

Thanks to Shachar Bar-On, Liz Brown, Keith Morrison and all at *Dateline NBC.* And to Karen Cooper of the Southern Association of Forensic Scientists.

Thanks to those who provided technical advice and public records assistance.

Thanks to those who helped me navigate professional questions and ethical issues or assisted me in the quest for an agent and publisher. Some of the best lessons come not in acceptance but rejection.

Thanks to my literary attorney, Bob Pimm, and to Gary Carr at Rising Moon Public Relations. Thanks to my editor at Kensington Publishing, B. Tweed, to copy editor Stephanie Finnegan and to Editor-in-chief Michaela Hamilton.

Life's a journey, and space won't allow me to list all who helped me to this station along the ride. We are an accumulation of experience—even my darkest has been valuable. My deepest gratitude to fellow travelers at Dulwich College, the University of North Carolina at Chapel Hill, newspapers and in the U.S. Army.

To those I owe amends, apologies; to those who helped me recover, gratitude. In memory, Sean Patrick Wetmore, 1969–2005.

My deepest thanks is reserved for my wife, Carol, without whom none of this would've been possible. I knew I married a forensic pathologist—but it turned out I also married the best editor I've ever had.

Jim Greenhill
North Fort Myers, Florida,
and Durango, Colorado
September 2005

MORE MUST-READ TRUE CRIME
FROM
M. William Phelps

MORE MUST-READ TRUE CRIME
FROM PINNACLE